T0335386

LECTURES IN GAME THEORY FOR COMPUTER SCIENTISTS

Games provide mathematical models for interaction. Numerous tasks in computer science can be formulated in game-theoretic terms. This fresh and intuitive way of thinking about complex issues reveals underlying algorithmic questions and clarifies the relationships between different domains.

This collection of lectures, by specialists in the field, provides an excellent introduction to various aspects of game theory relevant for applications in computer science that concern program design, synthesis, verification, testing and design of multi-agent or distributed systems. Originally devised for a Spring School organised by the ESF Networking Programme on Games for Design and Verification (GAMES) in 2009, these lectures have since been revised and expanded, and range from tutorials concerning fundamental notions and methods to more advanced presentations of current research topics.

This volume is a valuable guide to current research on game-based methods in computer science for undergraduate and graduate students. It will also interest researchers working in mathematical logic, computer science and game theory.

KRZYSZTOF R. APT is Professor at the University of Amsterdam and a Fellow at Centrum Wiskunde en Informatica (CWI), Amsterdam.

ERICH GRÄDEL is Professor for Mathematical Foundations of Computer Science at RWTH Aachen University, Germany.

LECTURES IN GAME THEORY FOR COMPUTER SCIENTISTS

Edited by

KRZYSZTOF R. APT

Centrum Wiskunde en Informatica (CWI), Amsterdam

ERICH GRÄDEL

RWTH Aachen University

CAMBRIDGE
UNIVERSITY PRESS

University Printing House, Cambridge CB2 8BS, United Kingdom

One Liberty Plaza, 20th Floor, New York, NY 10006, USA

477 Williamstown Road, Port Melbourne, VIC 3207, Australia

314-321, 3rd Floor, Plot 3, Splendor Forum, Jasola District Centre, New Delhi - 110025, India

103 Penang Road, #05-06/07, Visioncrest Commercial, Singapore 238467

Cambridge University Press is part of the University of Cambridge.

It furthers the University's mission by disseminating knowledge in the pursuit of education, learning and research at the highest international levels of excellence.

www.cambridge.org
Information on this title: www.cambridge.org/9780521198660

© Cambridge University Press 2011

First published 2011

A catalogue record for this publication is available from the British Library

ISBN 978-0-521-19866-0 Hardback

Contents

Contributors

Krzysztof R. Apt
CWI & University of Amsterdam

Christof Löding
RWTH Aachen University

Marcin Jurdziński
University of Warwick

Erich Grädel
RWTH Aachen University

Antonín Kučera
Masaryk University

Laurent Doyen
CNRS & ENS Cachan

Jean-François Raskin
Université Libre de Bruxelles

Stephan Kreutzer
University of Oxford

Joseph Y. Halpern
Cornell University, Ithaca, NY

Preface

Game playing is a powerful metaphor that fits many situations where interaction between autonomous agents plays a central role. Numerous tasks in computer science, such as design, synthesis, verification, testing, query evaluation, planning, etc. can be formulated in game-theoretic terms. Viewing them abstractly as games reveals the underlying algorithmic questions, and helps to clarify relationships between problem domains. As an organisational principle, games offer a fresh and intuitive way of thinking through complex issues.

As a result mathematical models of games play an increasingly important role in a number of scientific disciplines and, in particular, in many branches of computer science. One of the scientific communities studying and applying games in computer science has formed around the European Network 'Games for Design and Verification' (GAMES), which proposes a research and training programme for the design and verification of computing systems, using a methodology that is based on the interplay of finite and infinite games, mathematical logic and automata theory.

This network had initially been set up as a Marie Curie Research Training Network, funded by the European Union between 2002 and 2006. In its four years of existence this network built a strong European research community that did not exist before. Its flagship activity – the annual series of GAMES workshops – saw an ever-increasing number of participants from both within and outside Europe. The ESF Research Networking Programme GAMES, funded by the European Science Foundation ESF from 2008 to 2013, builds on the momentum of this first GAMES network, but it is scientifically broader and more ambitious, and it covers more countries and more research groups.

This book grew out of the lectures given at a Spring School organised by the GAMES Networking Programme in Bertinoro, Italy, from May 31 to June 6, 2009, with almost eighty participants, most of them students or postdoctoral young researchers from all over Europe.

For eight out of the nine courses presented at this school, the lecture notes have now been revised and expanded, and are presented to a wider audience as a collection of

Lectures in Game Theory for Computer Scientists,

covering various aspects of finite and infinite games. It is of course not possible to cover in a Spring School or in a collection of lectures all facets of 'games for computer science', not even for those games that are used for the synthesis and verification of reactive systems. The lecture notes we have assembled range from tutorials concerning fundamental notions and methods to more advanced presentations of specialized topics of current research.

Krzysztof R. Apt presents *A Primer on Strategic Games*, focusing on fundamental notions of strategic games such as best response, Nash equilibrium, Pareto efficient outcomes, strict and weak dominance, mixed strategies, and discusses the relation between these notions in the context of iterated elimination of strategies. He also introduces the basics of mechanism design and of the underlying class of games, called pre-Bayesian games.

Christof Löding gives an introduction to *Infinite Games and Automata Theory*. He illustrates how the theory of automata on infinite words can be used to solve games of infinite duration with complex winning conditions, for example specified by logical formulae, and why infinite games are a useful tool to solve problems about automata on infinite trees such as complementation and the emptiness test.

Marcin Jurdziński provides a selective survey of *Algorithms for Solving Parity Games*. Parity games are a class of ω-regular games, i.e., games on graphs whose payoff function is computable by a finite automaton on infinite words. First, a divide-and-conquer algorithm is discussed for solving games with two important special cases of the parity payoff function: repeated reachability (Büchi) and eventual safety (co-Büchi) games. Then, a number of state-of-the-art algorithms for solving parity games are presented. Algorithmic techniques applied include divide-and-conquer and value iteration for computing parity progress measures, as well as non-trivial combinations of the two.

In his lecture, **Erich Grädel** goes *Back and Forth Between Logic and Games*, focusing on first-order and fixed-point logic, and on reachability and parity games. He discusses the general notion of model-checking games.

While it is easily seen that the meaning of first-order logic is captured by reachability games, more effort is required to see that parity games are the appropriate games for evaluating formulae from least fixed-point logic and the modal μ-calculus. The algorithmic consequences of this result are discussed. Then the reverse relationship between games and logic is explored, namely the question of how winning regions in games are definable in logic. Finally, the relationship between logic and games is discussed for more complicated scenarios provided by inflationary fixed-point logic and the quantitative μ-calculus.

Antonín Kučera presents a survey on *Turn-Based Stochastic Games*, with a taxonomy of winning objectives in such games, a discussion of their basic properties, and an overview of the existing results about existence and construction of optimal strategies. He devotes special attention to games with infinitely many vertices.

Laurent Doyen and **Jean-François Raskin** present an introduction to *Games with Imperfect Information: Theory and Algorithms.* They study observation-based strategies that rely on imperfect information about the history of a play. Such games occur in the synthesis of a controller that does not see the private state of the controlled system. For a different kind of objective, they exhibit algorithms for computing the set of states from which a player can win with a deterministic or randomised observation-based strategy.

Stephan Kreutzer introduces *Graph Searching Games* explaining the use of games for distinguishing between simple and complicated graphs. The unifying idea of graph searching games is that a number of searchers want to find a fugitive on an arena defined by a graph or hypergraph. Depending on the precise definition of moves allowed for the searchers and the fugitive and the type of graph the game is played on, this gives a number of variants of graph-searching games, which lead to different complexity measures of graphs.

Finally, in his lecture *Beyond Nash Equilibrium: Solution Concepts for the 21st Century*, **Joseph Y. Halpern** addresses shortcomings of Nash equilibrium, the central solution concept of classical game theory, from a computer science perspective. For example, Nash equilibria are not robust in the sense that they do not tolerate faulty or unexpected behaviour, they do not deal with coalitions, they do not take computation costs into account, and they do not deal with cases where players are not aware of all aspects of the game. Halpern discusses alternative solution concepts that try to address these shortcomings.

We hope that this collection of lectures will be helpful as an introduction and guide to current research on game-based methods in computer science, and will attract new researchers to this field. We wish to thank the European Science Foundation ESF for financing the GAMES Networking Programme. We acknowledge in particular their generous support for the GAMES Spring School in Bertinoro and for the preparation of this collection of lectures. Finally, we thank Joel Uckelman for his help in preparation of this volume.

Krzysztof R. Apt and Erich Grädel   Amsterdam and Aachen

PS. A comment about the cover: the expression 'to outfox somebody' suggests that foxes are experts in game theory.

1

A Primer on Strategic Games

Krzysztof R. Apt

CWI and University of Amsterdam

Abstract

This is a short introduction to the subject of strategic games. We focus on the concepts of best response, Nash equilibrium, strict and weak dominance, and mixed strategies, and study the relation between these concepts in the context of the iterated elimination of strategies. Also, we discuss some variants of the original definition of a strategic game. Finally, we introduce the basics of mechanism design and use pre-Bayesian games to explain it.

1.1 Introduction

Mathematical game theory, as launched by Von Neumann and Morgenstern in their seminal book, von Neumann and Morgenstern [1944], followed by Nash's contributions Nash [1950, 1951], has become a standard tool in economics for the study and description of various economic processes, including competition, cooperation, collusion, strategic behaviour and bargaining. Since then it has also been successfully used in biology, political sciences, psychology and sociology. With the advent of the Internet game theory became increasingly relevant in computer science.

One of the main areas in game theory are ***strategic games*** (sometimes also called ***non-cooperative games***), which form a simple model of interaction between profit maximising players. In strategic games each player has a payoff function that he aims to maximise and the value of this function depends on the decisions taken *simultaneously* by all players. Such a simple description is still amenable to various interpretations, depending on the assumptions about the existence of *private information*. The purpose of this primer is to provide a simple introduction to the most common concepts used in strategic games: best response, Nash equilibrium, dominated strategies and mixed strategies and to clarify the relation between these concepts.

In the first part we consider the case of games with *complete information*. In the second part we discuss strategic games with *incomplete information*, by introducing first the basics of the theory of *mechanism design* that deals with ways of preventing *strategic behaviour*, i.e., manipulations aiming at maximising one's profit. We focus on the concepts, examples and results, and leave simple proofs as exercises.

1.2 Basic concepts

Assume a set $\{1, \ldots, n\}$ of players, where $n > 1$. A ***strategic game*** (or ***non-cooperative game***) for n players, written as $(S_1, \ldots, S_n, p_1, \ldots, p_n)$, consists of

- a non-empty (possibly infinite) set S_i of ***strategies***,
- a ***payoff function*** $p_i : S_1 \times \ldots \times S_n \to \mathbb{R}$,

for each player i.

We study strategic games under the following basic assumptions:

- players choose their strategies *simultaneously*; subsequently each player receives a payoff from the resulting joint strategy,
- each player is ***rational***, which means that his objective is to maximise his payoff,
- players have ***common knowledge*** of the game and of each others' rationality.[1]

Here are three classic examples of strategic two-player games to which we shall return in a moment. We represent such games in the form of a bimatrix, the entries of which are the corresponding payoffs to the row and column players.

Prisoner's Dilemma

	C	D
C	2, 2	0, 3
D	3, 0	1, 1

---

[1] Intuitively, common knowledge of some fact means that everybody knows it, everybody knows that everybody knows it, etc.

Battle of the Sexes

	F	B
F	2, 1	0, 0
B	0, 0	1, 2

Matching Pennies

	H	T
H	1, −1	−1, 1
T	−1, 1	1, −1

We introduce now some basic notions that will allow us to discuss and analyse strategic games in a meaningful way. Fix a strategic game

$$(S_1, \ldots, S_n, p_1, \ldots, p_n).$$

We denote $S_1 \times \ldots \times S_n$ by S, call each element $s \in S$ a **joint strategy**, or a **strategy profile**, denote the ith element of s by s_i, and abbreviate the sequence $(s_j)_{j \neq i}$ to s_{-i}. Occasionally we write (s_i, s_{-i}) instead of s. Finally, we abbreviate $\times_{j \neq i} S_j$ to S_{-i} and use the '$_{-i}$' notation for other sequences and Cartesian products.

We call a strategy s_i of player i a **best response** to a joint strategy s_{-i} of his opponents if

$$\forall s_i' \in S_i \ p_i(s_i, s_{-i}) \geq p_i(s_i', s_{-i}).$$

Next, we call a joint strategy s a **Nash equilibrium** if each s_i is a best response to s_{-i}, that is, if

$$\forall i \in \{1, \ldots, n\} \ \forall s_i' \in S_i \ p_i(s_i, s_{-i}) \geq p_i(s_i', s_{-i}).$$

So a joint strategy is a Nash equilibrium if no player can achieve a higher payoff by *unilaterally* switching to another strategy.

Finally, we call a joint strategy s **Pareto efficient** if for no joint strategy s'

$$\forall i \in \{1, \ldots, n\} \ p_i(s') \geq p_i(s) \text{ and } \exists i \in \{1, \ldots, n\} \ p_i(s') > p_i(s).$$

That is, a joint strategy is Pareto efficient if no joint strategy is both a weakly better outcome for all players and a strictly better outcome for some player.

Some games, like the Prisoner's Dilemma, have a unique Nash equilibrium, namely (D, D), while some other ones, like the Matching Pennies, have no Nash equilibrium. Yet other games, like the Battle of the Sexes, have multiple Nash equilibria, namely (F, F) and (B, B). One of the peculiarities of the Prisoner's Dilemma game is that its Nash equilibrium is the only outcome that is not Pareto efficient.

Let us return now to our analysis of an arbitrary strategic game $(S_1, \ldots, S_n, p_1, \ldots, p_n)$. Let s_i, s'_i be strategies of player i. We say that s_i **strictly dominates** s'_i (or equivalently, that s'_i is **strictly dominated by** s_i) if

$$\forall s_{-i} \in S_{-i} \; p_i(s_i, s_{-i}) > p_i(s'_i, s_{-i}),$$

that s_i **weakly dominates** s'_i (or equivalently, that s'_i is **weakly dominated by** s_i) if

$$\forall s_{-i} \in S_{-i} \; p_i(s_i, s_{-i}) \geq p_i(s'_i, s_{-i}) \text{ and } \exists s_{-i} \in S_{-i} \; p_i(s_i, s_{-i}) > p_i(s'_i, s_{-i}),$$

and that s_i **dominates** s'_i (or equivalently, that s'_i is **dominated by** s_i) if

$$\forall s_{-i} \in S_{-i} \; p_i(s_i, s_{-i}) \geq p_i(s'_i, s_{-i}).$$

Further, we say that s_i is **strictly dominant** if it strictly dominates all other strategies of player i and define analogously a **weakly dominant** and a **dominant** strategy.

Clearly, a rational player will not choose a strictly dominated strategy. As an illustration let us return to the Prisoner's Dilemma. In this game for each player, C (cooperate) is a strictly dominated strategy. So the assumption of players' rationality implies that each player will choose strategy D (defect). That is, we can predict that rational players will end up choosing the joint strategy (D, D) in spite of the fact that the Pareto efficient outcome (C, C) yields for each of them a strictly higher payoff.

The Prisoner's Dilemma game can be easily generalised to n players as follows. Assume that each player has two strategies, C and D. Denote by C^n the joint strategy in which each strategy equals C and similarly with D^n. Further, given a joint strategy s_{-i} of the opponents of player i denote by $|s_{-i}(C)|$ the number of C strategies in s_{-i}.

Assume now that k_i and l_i, where $i \in \{1, \ldots, n\}$, are real numbers such that for all $i \in \{1, \ldots, n\}$ we have $k_i(n-1) > l_i > 0$. We put

$$p_i(s) := \begin{cases} k_i|s_{-i}(C)| + l_i & \text{if } s_i = D \\ k_i|s_{-i}(C)| & \text{if } s_i = C. \end{cases}$$

Note that for $n = 2, k_i = 2$ and $l_i = 1$ we get the original Prisoner's Dilemma game.

Then for all players i we have $p_i(C^n) = k_i(n-1) > l_i = p_i(D^n)$, so for all players the strategy profile C^n yields a strictly higher payoff than D^n. Yet for all players i strategy C is strictly dominated by strategy D, since for all $s_{-i} \in S_{-i}$ we have $p_i(D, s_{-i}) - p_i(C, s_{-i}) = l_i > 0$.

Whether a rational player will never choose a weakly dominated strategy is a more subtle issue that we shall not pursue here.

By definition, no player achieves a higher payoff by switching from a dominant strategy to another strategy. This explains the following obvious observation.

Note 1.1 (Dominant Strategy) *Consider a strategic game G. Suppose that s is a joint strategy such that each s_i is a dominant strategy. Then it is a Nash equilibrium of G.*

In particular, the conclusion of the lemma holds if each s_i is a strictly or a weakly dominant strategy. In the former case, when the game is finite, we can additionally assert (see the IESDS Theorem 1.3 below) that s is a unique Nash equilibrium of G. This stronger claim does not hold if each s_i is a weakly dominant strategy. Indeed, consider the game

	L	R
T	1, 1	1, 1
B	1, 1	0, 0

Here T is a weakly dominant strategy for the player 1, L is a weakly dominant strategy for player 2 and, as prescribed by the above Note, (T, L), is a Nash equilibrium. However, this game has two other Nash equilibria, (T, R) and (B, L).

The converse of the above Note of course is not true. Indeed, there are games in which no strategy is dominant, and yet they have a Nash equilibrium. An example is the Battle of the Sexes game that has two Nash equilibria, but no dominant strategy.

So to find a Nash equilibrium (or Nash equilibria) of a game it does not suffice to check whether a dominant strategy exists. In what follows we investigate whether iterated elimination of strategies can be of help.

1.3 Iterated elimination of strategies I

1.3.1 Elimination of strictly dominated strategies

We assumed that each player is rational. So when searching for an outcome that is optimal for all players we can safely remove strategies that are strictly dominated by some other strategy. This can be done in a number of ways. For example, we could remove all or some strictly dominated strategies simultaneously, or start removing them in a round robin fashion starting with, say, player 1. To discuss this matter more rigorously we introduce the notion of a restriction of a game.

Given a game $G := (S_1, \ldots, S_n, p_1, \ldots, p_n)$ and (possibly empty) sets of strategies $R_1, \ldots, R_n$ such that $R_i \subseteq S_i$ for $i \in \{1, \ldots, n\}$ we say that $R := (R_1, \ldots, R_n, p_1, \ldots, p_n)$ is a **restriction** of G. Here of course we view each p_i as a function on the subset $R_1 \times \ldots \times R_n$ of $S_1 \times \ldots \times S_n$. In what follows, given a restriction R we denote by R_i the set of strategies of player i in R.

We now introduce the following notion of reduction between the restrictions R and R' of G:

$$R \rightarrow_S R'$$

when $R \neq R'$, $\forall i \in \{1, \ldots, n\}$ $R'_i \subseteq R_i$ and

$$\forall i \in \{1, \ldots, n\} \ \forall s_i \in R_i \setminus R'_i \ \exists s'_i \in R_i \ s_i \text{ is strictly dominated in } R \text{ by } s'_i.$$

That is, $R \rightarrow_S R'$ when R' results from R by removing from it some strictly dominated strategies.

In general an elimination of strictly dominated strategies is not a one step process; it is an iterative procedure. Its use is justified by the assumption of common knowledge of rationality.

Example 1.2   Consider the following game:

	L	M	R
T	3, 0	2, 1	1, 0
C	2, 1	1, 1	1, 0
B	0, 1	0, 1	0, 0

Note that B is strictly dominated by T and R is strictly dominated by M. By eliminating these two strategies we get:

	L	M
T	3, 0	2, 1
C	2, 1	1, 1

Now C is strictly dominated by T, so we get:

	L	M
T	3, 0	2, 1

In this game L is strictly dominated by M, so we finally get:

	M
T	2, 1

□

This brings us to the following notion, where given a binary relation $\rightarrow$ we denote by $\rightarrow^*$ its transitive reflexive closure. Consider a strategic game G. Suppose that $G \rightarrow_S^* R$, i.e., R is obtained by an iterated elimination of strictly dominated strategies, in short **IESDS**, starting with G.

- If for no restriction R' of G, $R \rightarrow_S R'$ holds, we say that R is **an outcome of IESDS from** G.
- If each player is left in R with exactly one strategy, we say that G **is solved by IESDS**.

The following simple result clarifies the relation between the IESDS and Nash equilibrium.

Theorem 1.3 (IESDS) *Suppose that G' is an outcome of IESDS from a strategic game G.*

  (i) *If s is a Nash equilibrium of G, then it is a Nash equilibrium of G'.*
  (ii) *If G is finite and s is a Nash equilibrium of G', then it is a Nash equilibrium of G.*
  (iii) *If G is finite and solved by IESDS, then the resulting joint strategy is a unique Nash equilibrium.*

Exercise 1.1   Provide the proof.   □

Example 1.4   A nice example of a game that is solved by IESDS is the *location game* due to Hotelling [1929]. Assume that that the players are two vendors who simultaneously choose a location. Then the customers choose the closest vendor. The profit for each vendor equals the number of customers it attracted.

To be more specific we assume that the vendors choose a location from the set $\{1, \ldots, n\}$ of natural numbers, viewed as points on a real line, and that at each location there is exactly one customer. For example, for $n = 11$ we have 11 locations:

and when the players choose respectively the locations 3 and 8:

we have $p_1(3,8) = 5$ and $p_2(3,8) = 6$. When the vendors 'share' a customer, they end up with a fractional payoff.

In general, we have the following game:

- each set of strategies consists of the set $\{1, \ldots, n\}$,
- each payoff function p_i is defined by:

$$
p_i(s_i, s_{3-i}) := \begin{cases} \dfrac{s_i + s_{3-i} - 1}{2} & \text{if } s_i < s_{3-i} \\[2mm] n - \dfrac{s_i + s_{3-i} - 1}{2} & \text{if } s_i > s_{3-i} \\[2mm] \dfrac{n}{2} & \text{if } s_i = s_{3-i}. \end{cases}
$$

It is easy to see that for $n = 2k + 1$ this game is solved by k rounds of IESDS, and that each player is left with the 'middle' strategy k. In each round both 'outer' strategies are eliminated, so first 1 and n, and so on. □

There is one more natural question that we left so far unanswered. Is the outcome of an iterated elimination of strictly dominated strategies unique, or in game theory parlance: is strict dominance **order independent**? The answer is positive. The following result was established independently by Gilboa et al. [1990] and Stegeman [1990].

Theorem 1.5 (Order Independence I) *Given a finite strategic game all iterated eliminations of strictly dominated strategies yield the same outcome.*

As noted by Dufwenberg and Stegeman [2002] the above result does not hold for infinite strategic games.

Example 1.6 Consider a game in which the set of strategies for each player is the set of natural numbers. The payoff to each player is the number (strategy) he selected.

Note that in this game every strategy is strictly dominated. Consider now three ways of using IESDS:

- by removing in one step all strategies that are strictly dominated,
- by removing in one step all strategies different from 0 that are strictly dominated,
- by removing in each step exactly one strategy.

In the first case we obtain the restriction with the empty strategy sets, in the second one we end up with the restriction in which each player has just one strategy, 0, and in the third case we obtain an infinite sequence of reductions. □

The above example shows that in the limit of an infinite sequence of reductions different outcomes can be reached. So for infinite games the definition of the order independence has to be modified. An interested reader is referred to Dufwenberg and Stegeman [2002] and Apt [2007] where two different options are proposed and some limited order independence results are established.

The above example also shows that in the IESDS Theorem 1.3(*ii*) and (*iii*) we cannot drop the assumption that the game is finite. Indeed, the above infinite game has no Nash equilibria, while the game in which each player has exactly one strategy has a Nash equilibrium.

1.3.2 Elimination of weakly dominated strategies

Analogous considerations can be carried out for the elimination of weakly dominated strategies, by considering the appropriate reduction relation $\rightarrow_W$ defined in the expected way. Below we abbreviate iterated elimination of weakly dominated strategies to **IEWDS**.

However, in the case of IEWDS some complications arise. To illustrate them consider the following game that results from equipping each player in the Matching Pennies game with a third strategy E (for Edge):

	H	T	E
H	1, −1	−1, 1	−1, −1
T	−1, 1	1, −1	−1, −1
E	−1, −1	−1, −1	−1, −1

Note that

- (E, E) is its only Nash equilibrium,
- for each player, E is the only strategy that is weakly dominated.

Any form of elimination of these two E strategies, simultaneous or iterated, yields the same outcome, namely the Matching Pennies game, that, as we have already noticed, has no Nash equilibrium. So during this eliminating process we 'lost' the only Nash equilibrium. In other words, part (*i*) of the IESDS Theorem 1.3 does not hold when reformulated for weak dominance.

On the other hand, some partial results are still valid here.

Theorem 1.7 (IEWDS) *Suppose that G is a finite strategic game.*

(i) *If G' is an outcome of IEWDS from G and s is a Nash equilibrium of G', then s is a Nash equilibrium of G.*

(ii) *If G is solved by IEWDS, then the resulting joint strategy is a Nash equilibrium of G.*

Exercise 1.2 Provide the proof.   □

Example 1.8 A nice example of a game that is solved by IEWDS is the **Beauty Contest game** due to Moulin [1986]. In this game there are $n > 2$ players, each with the set of strategies equal $\{1, \ldots, 100\}$. Each player submits a number and the payoff to each player is obtained by splitting 1 equally between the players whose submitted number is closest to $\frac{2}{3}$ of the average. For example, if the submissions are $29, 32, 29$, then the payoffs are respectively $\frac{1}{2}, 0, \frac{1}{2}$.

One can check that this game is solved by IEWDS and results in the joint strategy $(1, \ldots, 1)$. Hence, by the IEWDS Theorem 1.7 this joint strategy is a (not necessarily unique; we shall return to this question in Section 1.5) Nash equilibrium.   □

Exercise 1.3 Show that the Beauty Contest game is indeed solved by IEWDS.   □

Note that in contrast to the IESDS Theorem 1.3 we do not claim in part (ii) of the IEWDS Theorem 1.7 that the resulting joint strategy is a *unique* Nash equilibrium. In fact, such a stronger claim does not hold. Further, in contrast to strict dominance, an iterated elimination of weakly dominated strategies can yield several outcomes.

The following example reveals even more peculiarities of this procedure.

Example 1.9 Consider the following game:

	L	M	R
T	0, 1	1, 0	0, 0
B	0, 0	0, 0	1, 0

It has three Nash equilibria, (T, L), (B, L) and (B, R). This game can be solved by IEWDS but only if in the first round we do not eliminate all weakly dominated strategies, which are M and R. If we eliminate only R, then we reach the game

	L	M
T	0, 1	1, 0
B	0, 0	0, 0

that is solved by IEWDS by eliminating B and M. This yields

	L
T	0, 1

So not only IEWDS is not order independent; in some games it is advantageous *not* to proceed with the deletion of the weakly dominated strategies 'at full speed'. The reader may also check that the second Nash equilibrium, (B, L), can be found using IEWDS, as well, but not the third one, (B, R).

□

To summarise, the iterated elimination of weakly dominated strategies

- can lead to a deletion of Nash equilibria,
- does not need to yield a unique outcome,
- can be too restrictive if we stipulate that in each round all weakly dominated strategies are eliminated.

Finally, note that the above IEWDS Theorem 1.7 does not hold for infinite games. Indeed, Example 1.6 applies here, as well.

1.3.3 Elimination of never best responses

Finally, we consider the process of eliminating strategies that are never best responses to a joint strategy of the opponents. To motivate this procedure consider the following game:

	X	Y
A	2, 1	0, 0
B	0, 1	2, 0
C	1, 1	1, 2

Here no strategy is strictly or weakly dominated. However, C is a **never best response**, that is, it is not a best response to any strategy of the opponent. Indeed, A is a unique best response to X and B is a unique best response to Y. Clearly, the above game is solved by an iterated elimination of never best responses. So this procedure can be stronger than IESDS and IEWDS.

Formally, we introduce the following reduction notion between the restrictions R and R' of a given strategic game G:

$$R \rightarrow_N R'$$

when $R \neq R'$, $\forall i \in \{1, \ldots, n\}$ $R'_i \subseteq R_i$ and

$\forall i \in \{1, \ldots, n\}$ $\forall s_i \in R_i \setminus R'_i$ $\neg \exists s_{-i} \in R_{-i}$ s_i is a best response to s_{-i} in R.

That is, $R \rightarrow_N R'$ when R' results from R by removing from it some strategies that are never best responses.

We then focus on the iterated elimination of never best responses, in short **IENBR**, obtained by using the $\rightarrow_N^*$ relation. The following counterpart of the IESDS Theorem 1.3 then holds.

Theorem 1.10 (IENBR)   *Suppose that G' is an outcome of IENBR from a strategic game G.*

(i) *If s is a Nash equilibrium of G, then it is a Nash equilibrium of G'.*
(ii) *If G is finite and s is a Nash equilibrium of G', then it is a Nash equilibrium of G.*
(iii) *If G is finite and solved by IENBR, then the resulting joint strategy is a unique Nash equilibrium.*

Exercise 1.4   Provide the proof.   □

Further, as shown by Apt [2005], we have the following analogue of the Order Independence I Theorem 1.5.

Theorem 1.11 (Order Independence II)   *Given a finite strategic game all iterated eliminations of never best responses yield the same outcome.*

In the case of infinite games we encounter the same problems as in the case of IESDS as Example 1.6 readily applies to IENBR, as well. In particular, if we solve an infinite game by IENBR we cannot claim that we obtained a Nash equilibrium. Still, IENBR can be useful in such cases.

Example 1.12   Consider the following infinite variant of the location game considered in Example 1.4. We assume that the players choose their strategies from the open interval $(0, 100)$ and that at each real in $(0, 100)$ there resides one customer. We have then the following payoffs that correspond to the intuition that the customers choose the closest vendor:

$$p_i(s_i, s_{3-i}) := \begin{cases} \dfrac{s_i + s_{3-i}}{2} & \text{if } s_i < s_{3-i} \\[2mm] 100 - \dfrac{s_i + s_{3-i}}{2} & \text{if } s_i > s_{3-i} \\[2mm] 50 & \text{if } s_i = s_{3-i}. \end{cases}$$

It is easy to check that in this game no strategy strictly or weakly dominates another one. On the other hand each strategy 50 is a best response to some strategy, namely to 50, and no other strategies are best responses. So this game is solved by IENBR, in one step. We cannot claim automatically that the resulting joint strategy $(50, 50)$ is a Nash equilibrium, but it is straightforward to check that this is the case. Moreover, by the IENBR Theorem 1.10(i) we know that this is a unique Nash equilibrium.   □

1.4 Mixed extension

We now study a special case of infinite strategic games that are obtained in a canonical way from the finite games, by allowing mixed strategies. Below $[0, 1]$ stands for the real interval $\{r \in \mathbb{R} \mid 0 \leq r \leq 1\}$. By a **probability distribution** over a finite non-empty set A we mean a function

$$\pi : A \to [0, 1]$$

such that $\sum_{a \in A} \pi(a) = 1$. We denote the set of probability distributions over A by ΔA.

Consider now a finite strategic game $G := (S_1, \ldots, S_n, p_1, \ldots, p_n)$. By a **mixed strategy** of player i in G we mean a probability distribution over S_i. So ΔS_i is the set of mixed strategies available to player i. In what follows, we denote a mixed strategy of player i by m_i and a joint mixed strategy of the players by m.

Given a mixed strategy m_i of player i we define

$$support(m_i) := \{a \in S_i \mid m_i(a) > 0\}$$

and call this set the **support** of m_i. In specific examples we write a mixed strategy m_i as the sum $\sum_{a \in A} m_i(a) \cdot a$, where A is the support of m_i.

Note that in contrast to S_i the set ΔS_i is infinite. When referring to the mixed strategies, as in the previous sections, we use the '$_{-i}$' notation. So for $m \in \Delta S_1 \times \ldots \times \Delta S_n$ we have $m_{-i} = (m_j)_{j \neq i}$, etc.

We can identify each strategy $s_i \in S_i$ with the mixed strategy that puts 'all the weight' on the strategy s_i. In this context s_i will be called a **pure strategy**. Consequently we can view S_i as a subset of ΔS_i and S_{-i} as a subset of $\times_{j \neq i} \Delta S_j$.

By a **mixed extension** of $(S_1, \ldots, S_n, p_1, \ldots, p_n)$ we mean the strategic game

$$(\Delta S_1, \ldots, \Delta S_n, p_1, \ldots, p_n),$$

where each function p_i is extended in a canonical way from $S := S_1 \times \ldots \times S_n$ to $M := \Delta S_1 \times \ldots \times \Delta S_n$ by first viewing each joint mixed strategy $m = (m_1, \ldots, m_n) \in M$ as a probability distribution over S, by putting for $s \in S$

$$m(s) := m_1(s_1) \cdot \ldots \cdot m_n(s_n),$$

and then by putting

$$p_i(m) := \sum_{s \in S} m(s) \cdot p_i(s).$$

The notion of a Nash equilibrium readily applies to mixed extensions. In this context we talk about a **pure Nash equilibrium**, when each of the constituent strategies is pure, and refer to an arbitrary Nash equilibrium of the mixed extension as a **Nash equilibrium in mixed strategies** of the initial finite game. In what follows, when we use the letter m we implicitly refer to the latter Nash equilibrium.

Lemma 1.13 (Characterisation) *Consider a finite strategic game $(S_1, \ldots, S_n, p_1, \ldots, p_n)$. The following statements are equivalent:*

(i) m is a Nash equilibrium in mixed strategies, i.e.,

$$p_i(m) \geq p_i(m'_i, m_{-i})$$

for all $i \in \{1, \ldots, n\}$ and all $m'_i \in \Delta S_i$,
(ii) for all $i \in \{1, \ldots, n\}$ and all $s_i \in S_i$

$$p_i(m) \geq p_i(s_i, m_{-i}),$$

(iii) for all $i \in \{1, \ldots, n\}$ and all $s_i \in support(m_i)$

$$p_i(m) = p_i(s_i, m_{-i})$$

and for all $i \in \{1, \ldots, n\}$ and all $s_i \notin support(m_i)$

$$p_i(m) \geq p_i(s_i, m_{-i}).$$

Exercise 1.5 Provide the proof.   □

Note that the equivalence between (i) and (ii) implies that each Nash equilibrium of the initial game is a pure Nash equilibrium of the mixed extension. In turn, the equivalence between (i) and (iii) provides us with a straightforward way of testing whether a joint mixed strategy is a Nash equilibrium.

We now illustrate the use of the above theorem by finding in the Battle of the Sexes game a Nash equilibrium in mixed strategies, in addition to the two pure ones exhibited in Section 1.3. Take

$$m_1 := r_1 \cdot F + (1 - r_1) \cdot B,$$
$$m_2 := r_2 \cdot F + (1 - r_2) \cdot B,$$

where $0 < r_1, r_2 < 1$. By definition

$$p_1(m_1, m_2) = 2 \cdot r_1 \cdot r_2 + (1 - r_1) \cdot (1 - r_2),$$
$$p_2(m_1, m_2) = r_1 \cdot r_2 + 2 \cdot (1 - r_1) \cdot (1 - r_2).$$

Suppose now that (m_1, m_2) is a Nash equilibrium in mixed strategies. By the equivalence between (i) and (iii) of the Characterisation Lemma 1.13 $p_1(F, m_2) = p_1(B, m_2)$, i.e., (using $r_1 = 1$ and $r_1 = 0$ in the above formula for $p_1(\cdot)$) $2 \cdot r_2 = 1 - r_2$, and $p_2(m_1, F) = p_2(m_1, B)$, i.e., (using $r_2 = 1$ and $r_2 = 0$ in the above formula for $p_2(\cdot)$) $r_1 = 2 \cdot (1 - r_1)$. So $r_2 = \frac{1}{3}$ and $r_1 = \frac{2}{3}$.

This implies that for these values of r_1 and r_2, (m_1, m_2) is a Nash equilibrium in mixed strategies and we have

$$p_1(m_1, m_2) = p_2(m_1, m_2) = \tfrac{2}{3}.$$

The example of the Matching Pennies game illustrated that some strategic games do not have a Nash equilibrium. In the case of mixed extensions the situation changes and we have the following fundamental result due to Nash [1950].

Theorem 1.14 (Nash) *Every mixed extension of a finite strategic game has a Nash equilibrium.*

In other words, every finite strategic game has a Nash equilibrium in mixed strategies. In the case of the Matching Pennies game it is straightforward to check that $(\frac{1}{2} \cdot H + \frac{1}{2} \cdot T, \frac{1}{2} \cdot H + \frac{1}{2} \cdot T)$ is such a Nash equilibrium. In this equilibrium the payoffs to each player are 0.

Nash's Theorem follows directly from the following result due to Kakutani [1941].[2]

Theorem 1.15 (Kakutani) *Suppose that A is a non-empty compact and convex subset of $\mathcal{R}^n$ and*

$$\Phi : A \to \mathcal{P}(A)$$

such that

- $\Phi(x)$ *is non-empty and convex for all* $x \in A$,
- *the **graph** of* Φ, *so the set* $\{(x, y) \mid y \in \Phi(x)\}$, *is closed.*

Then $x^* \in A$ exists such that $x^* \in \Phi(x^*)$. □

Proof of Nash's Theorem. Fix a finite strategic game $(S_1, \ldots, S_n, p_1, \ldots, p_n)$. Define the function $best_i : \times_{j \neq i} \Delta S_j \to \mathcal{P}(\Delta S_i)$ by

$$best_i(m_{-i}) := \{m_i \in \Delta S_i \mid m_i \text{ is a best response to } m_{-i}\}.$$

Then define the function $best : \Delta S_1 \times \ldots \times \Delta S_n \to \mathcal{P}(\Delta S_1 \times \ldots \times \Delta S_n)$ by

$$best(m) := best_1(m_{-1}) \times \ldots \times best_1(m_{-n}).$$

It is now straightforward to check that m is a Nash equilibrium iff $m \in best(m)$. Moreover, one can easily check that the function $best(\cdot)$ satisfies

---

[2] Recall that a subset A of $\mathbb{R}^n$ is called **compact** if it is closed and bounded, and is called **convex** if for any $\mathbf{x}, \mathbf{y} \in A$ and $\alpha \in [0, 1]$ we have $\alpha \mathbf{x} + (1 - \alpha)\mathbf{y} \in A$.

the conditions of Kakutani's Theorem. The fact that for every joint mixed strategy m, $best(m)$ is non-empty is a direct consequence of the Extreme Value Theorem stating that every real-valued continuous function on a compact subset of $\mathcal{R}^\ell$ attains a maximum.   □

1.5 Iterated elimination of strategies II

The notions of dominance apply in particular to mixed extensions of finite strategic games. But we can also consider dominance of a *pure* strategy by a *mixed* strategy. Given a finite strategic game $G := (S_1, \ldots, S_n, p_1, \ldots, p_n)$, we say that a (pure) strategy s_i of player i is **strictly dominated by** a mixed strategy m_i if

$$\forall s_{-i} \in S_{-i} \ p_i(m_i, s_{-i}) > p_i(s_i, s_{-i}),$$

and that s_i is **weakly dominated by** a mixed strategy m_i if

$$\forall s_{-i} \in S_{-i} \ p_i(m_i, s_{-i}) \geq p_i(s_i, s_{-i}) \text{ and } \exists s_{-i} \in S_{-i} \ p_i(m_i, s_{-i}) > p_i(s_i, s_{-i}).$$

In what follows we discuss for these two forms of dominance the counterparts of the results presented in Section 1.3.

1.5.1 Elimination of strictly dominated strategies

Strict dominance by a mixed strategy leads to a stronger notion of strategy elimination. For example, in the game

	L	R
T	2, 1	0, 1
M	0, 1	2, 1
B	0, 1	0, 1

the strategy B is strictly dominated neither by T nor M but is strictly dominated by $\frac{1}{2} \cdot T + \frac{1}{2} \cdot M$.

We now focus on iterated elimination of pure strategies that are strictly dominated by a mixed strategy. As in Section 1.3 we would like to clarify whether it affects the Nash equilibria, in this case equilibria in mixed strategies.

Instead of the lengthy wording 'the iterated elimination of strategies strictly dominated by a mixed strategy' we write **IESDMS**. We have then the following counterpart of the IESDS Theorem 1.3, where we refer to Nash equilibria in mixed strategies. Given a restriction G' of G and a joint mixed strategy m of G, when we say that m is a Nash equilibrium of G' we implicitly stipulate that each strategy used (with positive probability) in m is a strategy in G'.

Theorem 1.16 (IESDMS) *Suppose that G is a finite strategic game.*

(i) *If G' is an outcome of IESDMS from G, then m is a Nash equilibrium of G iff it is a Nash equilibrium of G'.*

(ii) *If G is solved by IESDMS, then the resulting joint strategy is a unique Nash equilibrium of G (in, possibly, mixed strategies).*

Exercise 1.6 Provide the proof. □

To illustrate the use of this result let us return to the Beauty Contest game discussed in Example 1.8. We explained there why $(1, \ldots, 1)$ is *a* Nash equilibrium. Now we can draw a stronger conclusion.

Example 1.17 One can show that the Beauty Contest game is solved by IESDMS in 99 rounds. In each round the highest strategy of each player is removed and eventually each player is left with the strategy 1. On account of the above theorem we now conclude that $(1, \ldots, 1)$ is a *unique* Nash equilibrium. □

Exercise 1.7 Show that the Beauty Contest game is indeed solved by IESDMS in 99 rounds. □

As in the case of strict dominance by a pure strategy we now address the question of whether the outcome of IESDMS is unique. The answer, as before, is positive. The following result was established by Osborne and Rubinstein [1994].

Theorem 1.18 (Order independence III) *All iterated eliminations of strategies strictly dominated by a mixed strategy yield the same outcome.*

1.5.2 Elimination of weakly dominated strategies

Next, we consider iterated elimination of pure strategies that are weakly dominated by a mixed strategy.

As already noticed in Subsection 1.3.2 an elimination by means of weakly dominated strategies can result in a loss of Nash equilibria. Clearly, the same observation applies here. We also have the following counterpart of the IEWDS Theorem 1.7, where we refer to Nash equilibria in mixed strategies. Instead of 'the iterated elimination of strategies weakly dominated by a mixed strategy' we write ***IEWDMS***.

Theorem 1.19 (IEWDMS)   *Suppose that G is a finite strategic game.*

(i) If G' is an outcome of IEWDMS from G and m is a Nash equilibrium of G', then m is a Nash equilibrium of G.

(ii) If G is solved by IEWDMS, then the resulting joint strategy is a Nash equilibrium of G.

Here is a simple application of this theorem.

Corollary 1.20   *Every mixed extension of a finite strategic game has a Nash equilibrium such that no strategy used in it is weakly dominated by a mixed strategy.*

Proof It suffices to apply Nash's Theorem 1.14 to an outcome of IEWDMS and use item (i) of the above theorem.   □

Finally, observe that the outcome of IEWMDS does not need to be unique. In fact, Example 1.9 applies here, as well.

1.5.3 Rationalizability

Finally, we consider iterated elimination of strategies that are never best responses to a joint mixed strategy of the opponents. Following Bernheim [1984] and Pearce [1984], strategies that survive such an elimination process are called rationalizable strategies.[3]

Formally, we define rationalizable strategies as follows. Consider a restriction R of a finite strategic game G. Let

$$\mathcal{RAT}(R) := (S'_1, \ldots, S'_n),$$

where for all $i \in \{1, \ldots, n\}$

$$S'_i := \{s_i \in R_i \mid \exists m_{-i} \in \times_{j \neq i} \Delta R_j \ s_i \text{ is a best response to } m_{-i} \text{ in } G\}.$$

Note the use of G instead of R in the definition of S'_i. We shall comment on it below.

Consider now the outcome $G_{\mathcal{RAT}}$ of iterating $\mathcal{RAT}$ starting with G. We call then the strategies present in the restriction $G_{\mathcal{RAT}}$ **rationalizable**.

We have the following counterpart of the IESDMS Theorem 1.16, due to Bernheim [1984].

Theorem 1.21   *Assume a finite strategic game G.*

---

[3] More precisely, in each of these papers a different definition is used; see Apt [2007] for an analysis of the conditions for which these definitions coincide.

(i) Then m is a Nash equilibrium of G iff it is a Nash equilibrium of $G_{\mathcal{RAT}}$.

(ii) If each player has in $G_{\mathcal{RAT}}$ exactly one strategy, then the resulting joint strategy is a unique Nash equilibrium of G.

Exercise 1.8 Provide the proof. □

In the context of rationalizability a joint mixed strategy of the opponents is referred to as a **belief**. The definition of rationalizability is generic in the class of beliefs w.r.t. which best responses are collected. For example, we could use here joint pure strategies of the opponents, or probability distributions over the Cartesian product of the opponents' strategy sets, so the elements of the set ΔS_{-i} (extending in an expected way the payoff functions). In the first case we talk about **point beliefs** and in the second case about **correlated beliefs**.

In the case of point beliefs we can apply the elimination procedure entailed by $\mathcal{RAT}$ to arbitrary games. To avoid discussion of the outcomes reached in the case of infinite iterations we focus on a result for a limited case. We refer here to Nash equilibria in pure strategies.

Theorem 1.22 *Assume a strategic game G. Consider the definition of the $\mathcal{RAT}$ operator for the case of point beliefs and suppose that the outcome $G_{\mathcal{RAT}}$ is reached in finitely many steps.*

(i) Then s is a Nash equilibrium of G iff it is a Nash equilibrium of $G_{\mathcal{RAT}}$.

(ii) If each player is left in $G_{\mathcal{RAT}}$ with exactly one strategy, then the resulting joint strategy is a unique Nash equilibrium of G.

Exercise 1.9 Provide the proof. □

A subtle point is that when G is infinite, the restriction $G_{\mathcal{RAT}}$ may have empty strategy sets (and hence no joint strategy).

Example 1.23 *Bertrand competition*, originally proposed by Bertrand [1883], is a game concerned with a simultaneous selection of prices for the same product by two firms. The product is then sold by the firm that chose a lower price. In the case of a tie the product is sold by both firms and the profits are split.

Consider a version in which the range of possible prices is the left-open real interval $(0, 100]$ and the demand equals $100 - p$, where p is the lower price. So in this game G there are two players, each with the set $(0, 100]$ of strategies and the payoff functions are defined by:

$$p_1(s_1, s_2) := \begin{cases} s_1(100 - s_1) & \text{if } s_1 < s_2 \\ \dfrac{s_1(100 - s_1)}{2} & \text{if } s_1 = s_2 \\ 0 & \text{if } s_1 > s_2 \end{cases}$$

$$p_2(s_1, s_2) := \begin{cases} s_2(100 - s_2) & \text{if } s_2 < s_1 \\ \dfrac{s_2(100 - s_2)}{2} & \text{if } s_1 = s_2 \\ 0 & \text{if } s_2 > s_1. \end{cases}$$

Consider now each player's best responses to the strategies of the opponent. Since $s_1 = 50$ maximises the value of $s_1(100 - s_1)$ in the interval $(0, 100]$, the strategy 50 is the unique best response of the first player to any strategy $s_2 > 50$ of the second player. Further, no strategy is a best response to a strategy $s_2 \leq 50$. By symmetry the same holds for the strategies of the second player.

So the elimination of never best responses leaves each player with a single strategy, 50. In the second round we need to consider the best responses to these two strategies in the *original* game G. In G the strategy $s_1 = 49$ is a better response to $s_2 = 50$ than $s_1 = 50$ and symmetrically for the second player. So in the second round of elimination both strategies 50 are eliminated and we reach the restriction with the empty strategy sets. By Theorem 1.22 we conclude that the original game G has no Nash equilibrium.

□

Note that if we defined S_i' in the definition of the operator $\mathcal{RAT}$ using the restriction R instead of the original game G, the iteration would stop in the above example after the first round. Such a modified definition of the $\mathcal{RAT}$ operator is actually an instance of the IENBR (iterated elimination of never best responses) in which at each stage all never best responses are eliminated. So for the above game G we can then conclude by the IENBR Theorem 1.10(i) that it has at most one equilibrium, namely $(50, 50)$, and then check separately that in fact it is not a Nash equilibrium.

1.5.4 A comparison between the introduced notions

We introduced so far the notions of strict dominance, weak dominance, and a best response, and related them to the notion of a Nash equilibrium.

To conclude this section we clarify the connections between the notions of dominance and of best response.

Clearly, if a strategy is strictly dominated, then it is a never best response. However, the converse fails. Further, there is no relation between the notions of weak dominance and never best response. Indeed, in the game considered in Subsection 1.3.3 strategy C is a never best response, yet it is neither strictly nor weakly dominated. Further, in the game given in Example 1.9 strategy M is weakly dominated and is also a best response to B.

The situation changes in the case of mixed extensions of two-player finite games. Below, by a ***totally mixed strategy*** we mean a mixed strategy with full support, i.e., one in which each strategy is used with a strictly positive probability. The following results were established by Pearce [1984].

Theorem 1.24 *Consider a finite two-player strategic game.*

(i) *A pure strategy is strictly dominated by a mixed strategy iff it is not a best response to a mixed strategy.*

(ii) *A pure strategy is weakly dominated by a mixed strategy iff it is not a best response to a totally mixed strategy.*

We only prove here part (i). Pearce [1984] provides a short, but a bit tricky proof based on Nash's Theorem 1.14. The proof we provide, due to Fudenberg and Tirole [1991], is a bit more intuitive.

We shall use the following result, see, e.g., Rockafellar [1996].

Theorem 1.25 (Separating Hyperplane) *Let A and B be disjoint convex subsets of $\mathbb{R}^k$. Then there exists a non-zero $c \in \mathbb{R}^k$ and $d \in \mathbb{R}$ such that*

$$c \cdot x \geq d \text{ for all } x \in A,$$

$$c \cdot y \leq d \text{ for all } y \in B.$$

Proof of Theorem 1.24(i).

Clearly, if a pure strategy is strictly dominated by a mixed strategy, then it is not a best response to a mixed strategy. To prove the converse, fix a two-player strategic game (S_1, S_2, p_1, p_2). Also fix $i \in \{1, 2\}$ and abbreviate $3 - i$ to $-i$.

Suppose that a strategy $s_i \in S_i$ is not strictly dominated by a mixed strategy. Let

$$A := \{x \in \mathbb{R}^{|S_{-i}|} \mid \forall s_{-i} \in S_{-i} \ x_{s_{-i}} > 0\}$$

and

$$B := \{(p_i(m_i, s_{-i}) - p_i(s_i, s_{-i}))_{s_{-i} \in S_{-i}} \mid m_i \in \Delta S_i\}.$$

By the choice of s_i the sets A and B are disjoint. Moreover, both sets are convex subsets of $\mathbb{R}^{|S_{-i}|}$.

By the Separating Hyperplane Theorem 1.25 for some non-zero $c \in \mathbb{R}^{|S_{-i}|}$ and $d \in \mathbb{R}$

$$c \cdot x \geq d \text{ for all } x \in A, \tag{1.1}$$

$$c \cdot y \leq d \text{ for all } y \in B. \tag{1.2}$$

But $\mathbf{0} \in B$, so by (1.2) $d \geq 0$. Hence by (1.1) and the definition of A for all $s_{-i} \in S_{-i}$ we have $c_{s_{-i}} \geq 0$. Again by (1.1) and the definition of A this excludes the contingency that $d > 0$, i.e., $d = 0$. Hence by (1.2)

$$\sum_{s_{-i} \in S_{-i}} c_{s_{-i}} p_i(m_i, s_{-i}) \leq \sum_{s_{-i} \in S_{-i}} c_{s_{-i}} p_i(s_i, s_{-i}) \text{ for all } m_i \in \Delta S_i. \tag{1.3}$$

Let $\bar{c} := \sum_{s_{-i} \in S_{-i}} c_{s_{-i}}$. By the assumption $\bar{c} \neq 0$. Take

$$m_{-i} := \sum_{s_{-i} \in S_{-i}} \frac{c_{s_{-i}}}{\bar{c}} s_{-i}.$$

Then (1.3) can be rewritten as

$$p_i(m_i, m_{-i}) \leq p_i(s_i, m_{-i}) \text{ for all } m_i \in \Delta S_i,$$

i.e., s_i is a best response to m_{-i}.   □

1.6 Variations on the definition of strategic games

The notion of a strategic game is quantitative in the sense that it refers through payoffs to real numbers. A natural question to ask is: do the payoff values matter? The answer depends on which concepts we want to study. We mention here three qualitative variants of the definition of a strategic game in which the payoffs are replaced by preferences. By a **preference relation** on a set A we mean here a linear order on A.

In Osborne and Rubinstein [1994] a strategic game is defined as a sequence

$$(S_1, \ldots, S_n, \succeq_1, \ldots, \succeq_n),$$

where each $\succeq_i$ is player's i **preference relation** defined on the set $S_1 \times \cdots \times S_n$ of joint strategies.

In Apt et al. [2008] another modification of strategic games is considered, called a **strategic game with parametrised preferences**. In this approach each player i has a non-empty set of strategies S_i and a **preference relation** $\succeq_{s_{-i}}$ on S_i parametrised by a joint strategy s_{-i} of his opponents.

In Apt et al. [2008] only strict preferences were considered and so defined finite games with parametrised preferences were compared with the concept of **CP-nets** (Conditional Preference nets), a formalism used for representing conditional and qualitative preferences, see, e.g., Boutilier et al. [2004].

Next, in Roux et al. [2008] *conversion/preference games* are introduced. Such a game for n players consists of a set S of *situations* and for each player i a *preference relation* $\succeq_i$ on S and a *conversion relation* $\rightarrow_i$ on S. The definition is very general and no conditions are placed on the preference and conversion relations. These games are used to formalise gene regulation networks and some aspects of security.

Finally, let us mention another generalisation of strategic games, called *graphical games*, introduced by Kearns et al. [2001]. These games stress the locality in taking a decision. In a graphical game the payoff of each player depends only on the strategies of its neighbours in a given in advance graph structure over the set of players. Formally, such a game for n players with the corresponding strategy sets $S_1, \ldots, S_n$ is defined by assuming a neighbour function N that given a player i yields its set of neighbours $N(i)$. The payoff for player i is then a function p_i from $\times_{j \in N(i) \cup \{i\}} S_j$ to $\mathbb{R}$.

In all mentioned variants it is straightforward to define the notion of a Nash equilibrium. For example, in the conversion/preferences games it is defined as a situation s such that for all players i, if $s \rightarrow_i s'$, then $s' \not\succ_i s$. However, other introduced notions can be defined only for some variants. In particular, Pareto efficiency cannot be defined for strategic games with parametrised preferences since it requires a comparison of two arbitrary joint strategies. In turn, the notions of dominance cannot be defined for the conversion/preferences games, since they require the concept of a strategy for a player.

Various results concerning finite strategic games, for instance the IESDS Theorem 1.3, carry over directly to the strategic games as defined in Osborne and Rubinstein [1994] or in Apt et al. [2008]. On the other hand, in the variants of strategic games that rely on the notion of a preference we cannot consider mixed strategies, since the outcomes of playing different strategies by a player cannot be aggregated.

1.7 Mechanism design

Mechanism design is one of the important areas of economics. The 2007 Nobel Prize in Economics went to three economists who laid its foundations. To quote from *The Economist* [2007], mechanism design deals with the problem of 'how to arrange our economic interactions so that, when everyone behaves in a self-interested manner, the result is something we all like'. So these interactions are supposed to yield desired social decisions when each agent is interested in maximising only his own utility.

In mechanism design one is interested in the ways of inducing the players to submit true information. This subject is closely related to game theory, though it focuses on other issues. In the next section we shall clarify this connection. To discuss mechanism design in more detail we need to introduce some basic concepts.

Assume a set $\{1, \ldots, n\}$ of players with $n > 1$, a non-empty set of **decisions** D, and for each player i

- a non-empty set of **types** Θ_i, and
- an **initial utility function** $v_i : D \times \Theta_i \to \mathbb{R}$.

In this context a type is some private information known only to the player, for example, in the case of an auction, the player's valuation of the items for sale.

When discussing types and sets of types we use then the same abbreviations as in Section 1.2. In particular, we define $\Theta := \Theta_1 \times \cdots \times \Theta_n$ and for $\theta \in \Theta$ we have $(\theta_i, \theta_{-i}) = \theta$.

A **decision rule** is a function $f : \Theta \to D$. We call the tuple

$$(D, \Theta_1, \ldots, \Theta_n, v_1, \ldots, v_n, f)$$

a **decision problem**.

Decision problems are considered in the presence of a **central authority** who takes decisions on the basis of the information provided by the players. Given a decision problem the desired decision is obtained through the following sequence of events, where f is a given, publicly known, decision rule:

- each player i receives (becomes aware of) his type $\theta_i \in \Theta_i$,
- each player i announces to the central authority a type $\theta_i' \in \Theta_i$; this yields a joint type $\theta' := (\theta_1', \ldots, \theta_n')$,
- the central authority then takes the decision $d := f(\theta')$ and communicates it to each player,
- the resulting initial utility for player i is then $v_i(d, \theta_i)$.

The difficulty in taking decisions through the above described sequence of events is that players are assumed to be rational, that is they want to maximise their utility. As a result they may submit false information to manipulate the outcome (decision). To better understand the notion of a decision problem consider the following two natural examples.

Example 1.26 [Sealed-bid Auction]

We consider a **sealed-bid auction** in which there is a single object for sale. Each player (bidder) simultaneously submits to the central authority his type (bid) in a sealed envelope and the object is allocated to the highest bidder.

Given a sequence $a := (a_1, \ldots, a_j)$ of reals denote the least l such that $a_l = \max_{k \in \{1, \ldots, j\}} a_k$ by argsmax a. Then we can model a sealed-bid auction as the following decision problem $(D, \Theta_1, \ldots, \Theta_n, v_1, \ldots, v_n, f)$:

- $D = \{1, \ldots, n\}$,
- for all $i \in \{1, \ldots, n\}$, $\Theta_i = \mathbb{R}_+$; $\theta_i \in \Theta_i$ is player's i valuation of the object,
- for all $i \in \{1, \ldots, n\}$, $v_i(d, \theta_i) := (d = i)\theta$, where $d = i$ is a Boolean expression with the value 0 or 1,
- $f(\theta) := \text{argsmax } \theta$.

Here decision $d \in D$ indicates to which player the object is sold. Further, $f(\theta) = i$, where

$$\theta_i = \max_{j \in \{1, \ldots, n\}} \theta_j \text{ and } \forall j \in \{1, \ldots, i-1\} \ \theta_j < \theta_i.$$

So we assume that in the case of a tie the object is allocated to the highest bidder with the lowest index.

$\square$

Example 1.27 [Public project problem]

This problem deals with the task of taking a joint decision concerning construction of a **public good**,[4] for example a bridge. Each player reports to the central authority his appreciation of the gain from the project when it takes place. If the sum of the appreciations exceeds the cost of the project, the project takes place and each player has to pay the same fraction of the cost. Otherwise the project is cancelled.

This problem corresponds to the following decision problem, where c, with $c > 0$, is the cost of the project:

- $D = \{0, 1\}$ (reflecting whether a project is cancelled or takes place),
- for all $i \in \{1, \ldots, n\}$, $\Theta_i = \mathbb{R}_+$,
- for all $i \in \{1, \ldots, n\}$, $v_i(d, \theta_i) := d(\theta_i - \frac{c}{n})$,

---

[4] In Economics public goods are so-called not excludable and non-rival goods. To quote from Mankiw [2001]: 'People cannot be prevented from using a public good, and one person's enjoyment of a public good does not reduce another person's enjoyment of it.'

- $f(\theta) := \begin{cases} 1 & \text{if } \sum_{i=1}^{n} \theta_i \geq c \\ 0 & \text{otherwise.} \end{cases}$

If the project takes place $(d = 1)$, $\frac{c}{n}$ is the cost share of the project for each player. $\qquad\qquad\qquad\qquad\qquad\qquad\qquad\qquad\qquad\qquad\qquad\qquad\quad\square$

Let us return now to the decision rules. We call a decision rule f **efficient** if for all $\theta \in \Theta$ and $d' \in D$

$$\sum_{i=1}^{n} v_i(f(\theta), \theta_i) \geq \sum_{i=1}^{n} v_i(d', \theta_i).$$

Intuitively, this means that for all $\theta \in \Theta$, $f(\theta)$ is a decision that maximises the **initial social welfare** from a decision d, defined by $\sum_{i=1}^{n} v_i(d, \theta_i)$. It is easy to check that the decision rules used in Examples 1.26 and 1.27 are efficient.

Let us return now to the subject of manipulations. As an example, consider the case of the public project problem. A player whose type (that is, appreciation of the gain from the project) exceeds the cost share $\frac{c}{n}$ should manipulate the outcome and announce the type c. This will guarantee that the project will take place, irrespective of the types announced by the other players. Analogously, a player whose type is lower than $\frac{c}{n}$ should submit the type 0 to minimise the chance that the project will take place.

To prevent such manipulations we use **taxes**, which are transfer payments between the players and central authority. This leads to a modification of the initial decision problem $(D, \Theta_1, \ldots, \Theta_n, v_1, \ldots, v_n, f)$ to the following one:

- the set of decisions is $D \times \mathbb{R}^n$,
- the decision rule is a function $(f, t) : \Theta \to D \times \mathbb{R}^n$, where $t : \Theta \to \mathbb{R}^n$ and $(f, t)(\theta) := (f(\theta), t(\theta))$,
- the **final utility function** of player i is the function $u_i : D \times \mathbb{R}^n \times \Theta_i \to \mathbb{R}$ defined by

$$u_i(d, t_1, \ldots, t_n, \theta_i) := v_i(d, \theta_i) + t_i.$$

We call then $(D \times \mathbb{R}^n, \Theta_1, \ldots, \Theta_n, u_1, \ldots, u_n, (f, t))$ a **direct mechanism** and refer to t as the **tax function**.

So when the received (true) type of player i is θ_i and his announced type is θ'_i, his final utility is

$$u_i((f, t)(\theta'_i, \theta_{-i}), \theta_i) = v_i(f(\theta'_i, \theta_{-i}), \theta_i) + t_i(\theta'_i, \theta_{-i}),$$

where θ_{-i} are the types announced by the other players.

In each direct mechanism, given the vector θ of announced types, $t(\theta) :=$

$(t_1(\theta), \ldots, t_n(\theta))$ is the vector of the resulting payments. If $t_i(\theta) \geq 0$, player i *receives* from the central authority $t_i(\theta)$, and if $t_i(\theta) < 0$, he *pays* to the central authority $|t_i(\theta)|$.

The following definition then captures the idea that taxes prevent manipulations. We say that a direct mechanism with tax function t is **incentive compatible** if for all $\theta \in \Theta$, $i \in \{1, \ldots, n\}$ and $\theta'_i \in \Theta_i$

$$u_i((f, t)(\theta_i, \theta_{-i}), \theta_i) \geq u_i((f, t)(\theta'_i, \theta_{-i}), \theta_i).$$

Intuitively, this means that for each player i announcing one's true type (θ_i) is better than announcing another type (θ'_i). That is, false announcements, i.e., manipulations, do not pay off.

From now on we focus on specific incentive compatible direct mechanisms. Each **Groves mechanism** is a direct mechanism obtained by using a tax function $t(\cdot) := (t_1(\cdot), \ldots, t_n(\cdot))$, where for all $i \in \{1, \ldots, n\}$

- $t_i : \Theta \to \mathbb{R}$ is defined by $t_i(\theta) := g_i(\theta) + h_i(\theta_{-i})$, where
- $g_i(\theta) := \sum_{j \neq i} v_j(f(\theta), \theta_j)$,
- $h_i : \Theta_{-i} \to \mathbb{R}$ is an arbitrary function.

Note that, not accidentally, $v_i(f(\theta), \theta_i) + g_i(\theta)$ is simply the initial social welfare from the decision $f(\theta)$.

The importance of Groves mechanisms is then revealed by the following crucial result due to Groves [1973].

Theorem 1.28 (Groves) *Consider a decision problem* $(D, \Theta_1, \ldots, \Theta_n, v_1, \ldots, v_n, f)$ *with an efficient decision rule* f. *Then each Groves mechanism is incentive compatible.*

Proof The proof is remarkably straightforward. Since f is efficient, for all $\theta \in \Theta$, $i \in \{1, \ldots, n\}$ and $\theta'_i \in \Theta_i$ we have

$$u_i((f, t)(\theta_i, \theta_{-i}), \theta_i) = \sum_{j=1}^{n} v_j(f(\theta_i, \theta_{-i}), \theta_j) + h_i(\theta_{-i})$$

$$\geq \sum_{j=1}^{n} v_j(f(\theta'_i, \theta_{-i}), \theta_j) + h_i(\theta_{-i})$$

$$= u_i((f, t)(\theta'_i, \theta_{-i}), \theta_i).$$

$\square$

When for a given direct mechanism for all $\theta \in \Theta$ we have $\sum_{i=1}^{n} t_i(\theta) \leq 0$, the mechanism is called **feasible**, which means that it can be realised without external financing.

Each Groves mechanism is uniquely determined by the functions $h_1, \ldots, h_n$. A special case, called the **pivotal mechanism**, is obtained by using

$$h_i(\theta_{-i}) := -\max_{d \in D} \sum_{j \neq i} v_j(d, \theta_j).$$

So then

$$t_i(\theta) = \sum_{j \neq i} v_j(f(\theta), \theta_j) - \max_{d \in D} \sum_{j \neq i} v_j(d, \theta_j).$$

Hence for all θ and $i \in \{1, \ldots, n\}$ we have $t_i(\theta) \leq 0$, which means that the pivotal mechanism is feasible and that each player needs to make the payment $|t_i(\theta)|$ to the central authority.

We noted already that the decision rules used in Examples 1.26 and 1.27 are efficient. So in each example Groves' Theorem 1.28 applies and in particular the pivotal mechanism is incentive compatible. Let us see now the details.

Re: Example 1.26 Given a sequence θ of reals we denote by θ^* its reordering from the largest to the smallest element. So for example, for $\theta = (1, 5, 4, 3, 2)$ we have $(\theta_{-2})^*_2 = 3$ since $\theta_{-2} = (1, 4, 3, 2)$.

To compute the taxes in the sealed-bid auction in the case of the pivotal mechanism we use the following observation.

Note 1.29   *In the sealed-bid auction we have for the pivotal mechanism*

$$t_i(\theta) = \begin{cases} -\theta^*_2 & \text{if } i = argsmax\,\theta \\ 0 & \text{otherwise.} \end{cases}$$

Exercise 1.10   Provide the proof.   □

So the highest bidder wins the object and pays for it the amount $\max_{j \neq i} \theta_j$.

The resulting sealed-bid auction was introduced by Vickrey [1961] and is called a **Vickrey auction**. To illustrate it suppose there are three players, A, B, and C whose true types (bids) are respectively 18, 21, and 24. When they bid truthfully the object is allocated to player C whose tax (payment) according to Note 1.29 is 21, so the second price offered. Table 1.1 summarises the situation.

This explains why this auction is alternatively called a **second-price auction**. By Groves' Theorem 1.28 this auction is incentive compatible. In contrast, the **first-price auction**, in which the winner pays the price he

Table 1.1 *The pivotal mechanism for the sealed-bid auction*

player	type	tax	u_i
A	18	0	0
B	21	0	0
C	24	−21	3

offered (so the first, or the highest price), is not incentive compatible. Indeed, reconsider the above example. If player C submits 22 instead of his true type 24, he then wins the object but needs to pay 22 instead of 24. More formally, in the direct mechanism corresponding to the first-price auction we have

$$u_C((f,t)(18,21,22),24) = 24 - 22 = 2 > 0 = u_C((f,t)(18,21,24),24),$$

which contradicts incentive compatibility for the joint type $(18, 21, 24)$. □

Re: Example 1.27 To compute the taxes in the public project problem in the case of the pivotal mechanism we use the following observation.

Note 1.30 *In the public project problem we have for the pivotal mechanism*

$$t_i(\theta) = \begin{cases} 0 & \text{if } \sum_{j \neq i} \theta_j \geq \frac{n-1}{n}c \text{ and } \sum_{j=1}^n \theta_j \geq c \\ \sum_{j \neq i} \theta_j - \frac{n-1}{n}c & \text{if } \sum_{j \neq i} \theta_j < \frac{n-1}{n}c \text{ and } \sum_{j=1}^n \theta_j \geq c \\ 0 & \text{if } \sum_{j \neq i} \theta_j \leq \frac{n-1}{n}c \text{ and } \sum_{j=1}^n \theta_j < c \\ \frac{n-1}{n}c - \sum_{j \neq i} \theta_j & \text{if } \sum_{j \neq i} \theta_j > \frac{n-1}{n}c \text{ and } \sum_{j=1}^n \theta_j < c. \end{cases}$$

Exercise 1.11 Provide the proof. □

To illustrate the pivotal mechanism suppose that $c = 30$ and that there are three players, A, B, and C whose true types are respectively 6, 7, and 25. When these types are announced the project takes place and Table 1.2 summarises the taxes that players need to pay and their final utilities. The taxes were computed using Note 1.30.

Suppose now that the true types of players are respectively 4, 3 and 22 and, as before, $c = 30$. When these types are also the announced types, the project does not take place. Still, some players need to pay a tax, as Table 1.3 illustrates. One can show that this deficiency is shared by all feasible incentive compatible direct mechanisms for the public project, see [Mas-Collel et al., 1995, page 861-862].

Table 1.2 *The pivotal mechanism for the public project problem*

player	type	tax	u_i
A	6	0	−4
B	7	0	−3
C	25	−7	8

Table 1.3 *The pivotal mechanism for the public project problem*

player	type	tax	u_i
A	4	−5	−5
B	3	−6	−6
C	22	0	0

1.8 Pre-Bayesian games

Mechanism design, as introduced in the previous section, can be explained in game-theoretic terms using pre-Bayesian games, introduced by Ashlagi et al. [2006] (see also Hyafil and Boutilier [2004] and Aghassi and Bertsimas [2006]). In strategic games, after each player selected his strategy, each player knows the payoff of *every other player*. This is not the case in pre-Bayesian games in which each player has a private type on which he can condition his strategy. This distinguishing feature of pre-Bayesian games explains why they form a class of games with *incomplete information*. Formally, they are defined as follows.

Assume a set $\{1, \ldots, n\}$ of players, where $n > 1$. A **pre-Bayesian game** for n players consists of

- a non-empty set A_i of **actions**,
- a non-empty set Θ_i of **types**,
- a **payoff function** $p_i : A_1 \times \ldots \times A_n \times \Theta_i \to \mathbb{R}$,

for each player i.

Let $A := A_1 \times \ldots \times A_n$. In a pre-Bayesian game Nature (an external agent) moves first and provides each player i with a type $\theta_i \in \Theta_i$. Each player knows only his type. Subsequently the players simultaneously select their actions. The payoff function of each player now depends on his type, so after all players selected their actions, each player knows his payoff but does not know the payoffs of the other players. Note that given a pre-Bayesian game, every joint type $\theta \in \Theta$ uniquely determines a strategic game, to which we refer below as a θ-game.

A **strategy** for player i in a pre-Bayesian game is a function $s_i : \Theta_i \to A_i$. The previously introduced notions can be naturally adjusted to pre-Bayesian games. In particular, a joint strategy $s(\cdot) := (s_1(\cdot), \ldots, s_n(\cdot))$ is called an **ex-post equilibrium** if

$$\forall \theta \in \Theta \ \forall i \in \{1, \ldots, n\} \ \forall a_i \in A_i \ p_i(s_i(\theta_i), s_{-i}(\theta_{-i}), \theta_i) \geq p_i(a_i, s_{-i}(\theta_{-i}), \theta_i),$$

where $s_{-i}(\theta_{-i})$ is an abbreviation for the sequence of actions $(s_j(\theta_j))_{\neq i}$.

In turn, a strategy $s_i(\cdot)$ for player i is called **dominant** if

$$\forall \theta_i \in \Theta_i \ \forall a \in A \ p_i(s_i(\theta_i), a_{-i}, \theta_i) \geq p_i(a_i, a_{-i}, \theta_i).$$

So $s(\cdot)$ is an ex-post equilibrium iff for every joint type $\theta \in \Theta$ the sequence of actions $(s_1(\theta_1), \ldots, s_n(\theta_n))$ is a Nash equilibrium in the corresponding θ-game. Further, $s_i(\cdot)$ is a dominant strategy of player i iff for every type $\theta_i \in \Theta_i$, $s_i(\theta_i)$ is a dominant strategy of player i in every (θ_i, θ_{-i})-game.

We also have the following immediate counterpart of the Dominant Strategy Note 1.1.

Note 1.31 (Dominant Strategy)   *Consider a pre-Bayesian game G. Suppose that $s(\cdot)$ is a joint strategy such that each $s_i(\cdot)$ is a dominant strategy. Then it is an ex-post equilibrium of G.*

Example 1.32   As an example of a pre-Bayesian game, suppose that

- $\Theta_1 = \{U, D\}$, $\Theta_2 = \{L, R\}$,
- $A_1 = A_2 = \{F, B\}$,

and consider the pre-Bayesian game uniquely determined by the following four θ-games. Here and below we marked the payoffs in Nash equilibria in these θ-games in bold.

		L				R	
		F	B			F	B
U	F	**2, 1**	2, 0	U	F	2, 0	**2, 1**
	B	0, 1	2, 1		B	0, 0	2, 1

		F	B			F	B
D	F	3, 1	2, 0	D	F	3, 0	2, 1
	B	**5, 1**	4, 1		B	**5, 0**	4, 1

This shows that the strategies $s_1(\cdot)$ and $s_2(\cdot)$ such that

$$s_1(U) := F, \; s_1(D) := B, \; s_2(L) = F, \; s_2(R) = B$$

form here an ex-post equilibrium.   □

However, there is a crucial difference between strategic games and pre-Bayesian games.

Example 1.33   Consider the following pre-Bayesian game:

- $\Theta_1 = \{U, B\}$, $\Theta_2 = \{L, R\}$,
- $A_1 = A_2 = \{C, D\}$.

<table>
<tr><td align="center" colspan="3">L</td><td></td><td align="center" colspan="3">R</td></tr>
<tr><td></td><td align="center">C</td><td align="center">D</td><td></td><td></td><td align="center">C</td><td align="center">D</td></tr>
<tr><td>U   C</td><td align="center">2, 2</td><td align="center">0, 0</td><td></td><td>C</td><td align="center">2, 1</td><td align="center">0, 0</td></tr>
<tr><td>D</td><td align="center">3, 0</td><td align="center">1, 1</td><td></td><td>D</td><td align="center">3, 0</td><td align="center">1, 2</td></tr>
</table>

<table>
<tr><td></td><td align="center">C</td><td align="center">D</td><td></td><td></td><td align="center">C</td><td align="center">D</td></tr>
<tr><td>B   C</td><td align="center">1, 2</td><td align="center">3, 0</td><td></td><td>C</td><td align="center">1, 1</td><td align="center">3, 0</td></tr>
<tr><td>D</td><td align="center">0, 0</td><td align="center">2, 1</td><td></td><td>D</td><td align="center">0, 0</td><td align="center">2, 2</td></tr>
</table>

Even though each θ-game has a Nash equilibrium, they are so 'positioned' that the pre-Bayesian game has no ex-post equilibrium. Even more, if we consider a mixed extension of this game, then the situation does not change. The reason is that no new Nash equilibria are then added to the 'constituent' θ-games. (Indeed, each of them is solved by IESDS and hence by the IESDMS Theorem 1.16(ii) has a unique Nash equilibrium.) This shows that a mixed extension of a finite pre-Bayesian game does not need to have an ex-post equilibrium, which contrasts with the existence of Nash equilibria in mixed extensions of finite strategic games.   □

To relate pre-Bayesian games to mechanism design we need one more notion. We say that a pre-Bayesian game is of a ***revelation-type*** if $A_i = \Theta_i$ for all $i \in \{1, \ldots, n\}$. So in a revelation-type pre-Bayesian game the strategies of a player are the functions on his set of types. A strategy for player i is called then ***truth-telling*** if it is the identity function $\pi_i(\cdot)$ on Θ_i.

Now, as explained in Ashlagi et al. [2006] mechanism design can be viewed as an instance of the revelation-type pre-Bayesian games. Indeed, we have the following immediate, yet revealing observation.

Theorem 1.34   *Given a direct mechanism*

$$(D \times \mathbb{R}^n, \Theta_1, \ldots, \Theta_n, u_1, \ldots, u_n, (f, t))$$

associate with it a revelation-type pre-Bayesian game, in which each payoff function p_i is defined by

$$p_i((\theta_i', \theta_{-i}), \theta_i) := u_i((f, t)(\theta_i', \theta_{-i}), \theta_i).$$

Then the mechanism is incentive compatible iff in the associated pre-Bayesian game for each player truth-telling is a dominant strategy.

By Groves's Theorem 1.28 we conclude that in the pre-Bayesian game associated with a Groves mechanism, $(\pi_1(\cdot), \ldots, \pi_n(\cdot))$ is a dominant strategy ex-post equilibrium.

1.9 Conclusions

1.9.1 Bibliographic remarks

Historically, the notion of an equilibrium in a strategic game occurred first in Cournot [1838] in his study of production levels of a homogeneous product in a duopoly competition. The celebrated von Neumann's Minimax Theorem proved by von Neumann [1928] establishes an existence of a Nash equilibrium in mixed strategies in two-player zero-sum games. An alternative proof of Nash's Theorem, given in Nash [1951], uses Brouwer's Fixed Point Theorem.

Ever since Nash established his celebrated theorem, a search has continued to generalise his result to a larger class of games. A motivation for this endeavour has been the existence of natural infinite games that are not mixed extensions of finite games. As an example of such an early result let us mention the following theorem due to Debreu [1952], Fan [1952] and Glicksberg [1952].

Theorem 1.35 *Consider a strategic game such that*

- *each strategy set is a non-empty compact convex subset of a complete metric space,*
- *each payoff function p_i is continuous and quasi-concave in the ith argument.[5]*

Then a Nash equilibrium exists.

More recent work in this area focused on the existence of Nash equilibria in games with non-continuous payoff functions, see in particular Reny [1999] and Bich [2006].

---

[5] Recall that the function $p_i : S \to \mathbb{R}$ is **quasi-concave in the ith argument** if the set $\{s_i' \in S_i \mid p_i(s_i', s_{-i}) \geq p_i(s)\}$ is convex for all $s \in S$.

The issue of complexity of finding a Nash equilibrium has been a long standing open problem, clarified only recently, see Daskalakis et al. [2009] for an account of these developments. Iterated elimination of strictly dominated strategies and of weakly dominated strategies was introduced by Gale [1953] and Luce and Raiffa [1957]. The corresponding results summarised in Theorems 1.3, 1.7, 1.16 and 1.19 are folklore results.

Apt [2004] provides uniform proofs of various order independence results, including the Order Independence Theorems 1.5 and 1.18. The computational complexity of iterated elimination of strategies has been studied starting with Knuth et al. [1988], and with Brandt et al. [2009] as a recent contribution.

There is a lot of work on formal aspects of common knowledge and of its consequences for game theory. see, e.g., Aumann [1999] and Battigalli and Bonanno [1999].

1.9.2 Suggestions for further reading

Strategic games form a large research area and we have barely scratched its surface. There are several other equilibria notions and various other types of games.

Many books provide introductions to various areas of game theory, including strategic games. Most of them are written from the perspective of applications to Economics. In the 1990s the leading textbooks were Myerson [1991], Binmore [1991], Fudenberg and Tirole [1991] and Osborne and Rubinstein [1994].

Moving to the next decade, Osborne [2005] is an excellent, broad in its scope, undergraduate level textbook, while Peters [2008] is probably the best book on the market on the graduate level. Undeservedly less known is the short and lucid Tijs [2003]. An elementary, short introduction, focusing on the concepts, is Shoham and Leyton-Brown [2008]. In turn, Ritzberger [2001] is a comprehensive book on strategic games that also extensively discusses *extensive games*, i.e., games in which the players choose actions in turn. Finally, Binmore [2007] is a thoroughly revised version of Binmore [1991].

Several textbooks on microeconomics include introductory chapters on game theory, including strategic games. Two good examples are Mas-Collel et al. [1995] and Jehle and Reny [2000]. Finally, Nisan et al. [2007] is a recent collection of surveys and introductions to the computational aspects of game theory, with a number of articles concerned with strategic games and mechanism design.

References

M. Aghassi and D. Bertsimas. Robust game theory. *Mathematical Programming*, 107(1-2):231–273, 2006.

K. R. Apt. Uniform proofs of order independence for various strategy elimination procedures. *The B.E. Journal of Theoretical Economics, 4(1)*, 2004. (Contributions), Article 5, 48 pages. Available from `http://xxx.lanl.gov/abs/cs.GT/0403024`.

K. R. Apt. Order independence and rationalizability. In *Proceedings 10th Conference on Theoretical Aspects of Reasoning about Knowledge (TARK '05)*, pages 22–38. The ACM Digital Library, 2005. Available from `http://portal.acm.org`.

K. R. Apt. The many faces of rationalizability. *The B.E. Journal of Theoretical Economics, 7(1)*, 2007. (Topics), Article 18, 39 pages. Available from `http://arxiv.org/abs/cs.GT/0608011`.

K. R. Apt, F. Rossi, and K. B. Venable. Comparing the notions of optimality in CP-nets, strategic games and soft constraints. *Annals of Mathematics and Artificial Intelligence*, 52(1):25–54, 2008.

I. Ashlagi, D. Monderer, and M. Tennenholtz. Resource selection games with unknown number of players. In *AAMAS '06: Proceedings 5th Int. Joint Conf. on Autonomous Agents and Multiagent Systems*, pages 819–825. ACM Press, 2006.

R. Aumann. Interactive epistemology I: Knowledge. *International Journal of Game Theory*, 28(3):263–300, 1999.

P. Battigalli and G. Bonanno. Recent results on belief, knowledge and the epistemic foundations of game theory. *Research in Economics*, 53(2):149–225, June 1999.

B. D. Bernheim. Rationalizable strategic behavior. *Econometrica*, 52(4):1007–1028, 1984.

J. Bertrand. Théorie mathematique de la richesse sociale. *Journal des Savants*, 67: 499–508, 1883.

P. Bich. A constructive and elementary proof of Reny's theorem. Cahiers de la MSE b06001, Maison des Sciences Economiques, Université Paris Panthéon-Sorbonne, Jan. 2006. Available from `http://ideas.repec.org/p/mse/wpsorb/b06001.html`.

K. Binmore. *Playing for Real: A Text on Game Theory*. Oxford University Press, Oxford, 2007.

K. Binmore. *Fun and Games: A Text on Game Theory*. D.C. Heath, 1991.

C. Boutilier, R. I. Brafman, C. Domshlak, H. H. Hoos, and D. Poole. CP-nets: A tool for representing and reasoning with conditional ceteris paribus preference statements. *J. Artif. Intell. Res. (JAIR)*, 21:135–191, 2004.

F. Brandt, M. Brill, F. A. Fischer, and P. Harrenstein. On the complexity of iterated weak dominance in constant-sum games. In *Proceedings of the 2nd Symposium on Algorithmic Game Theory*, pages 287–298, 2009.

A. Cournot. *Recherches sur les Principes Mathématiques de la Théorie des Richesses*. Hachette, 1838. Republished in English as *Researches Into the Mathematical Principles of the Theory of Wealth*.

C. Daskalakis, P. W. Goldberg, and C. H. Papadimitriou. The complexity of computing a Nash equilibrium. *Commun. ACM*, 52(2):89–97, 2009.

G. Debreu. A social equilibrium existence theorem. *Proceedings of the National Academy of Sciences*, 38:886–893, 1952.

M. Dufwenberg and M. Stegeman. Existence and uniqueness of maximal reductions under iterated strict dominance. *Econometrica*, 70(5):2007–2023, 2002.

The Economist. Intelligent design. *The Economist*, 18 October 2007.

K. Fan. Fixed point and minimax theorems in locally convex topological linear spaces. *Proceedings of the National Academy of Sciences*, 38:121–126, 1952.

D. Fudenberg and J. Tirole. *Game Theory*. MIT Press, Cambridge, Massachusetts, 1991.

D. Gale. Theory of n-person games with perfect information. *Proceedings of the National Academy of Sciences of the United States of America*, 39:496–501, 1953.

I. Gilboa, E. Kalai, and E. Zemel. On the order of eliminating dominated strategies. *Operation Research Letters*, 9:85–89, 1990.

I. L. Glicksberg. A further generalization of the Kakutani fixed point theorem, with application to Nash equilibrium points. *Proceedings of the American Mathematical Society*, 3:170–174, 1952.

T. Groves. Incentives in teams. *Econometrica*, 41:617–631, 1973.

H. Hotelling. Stability in competition. *The Economic Journal*, 39:41–57, 1929.

N. Hyafil and C. Boutilier. Regret minimizing equilibria and mechanisms for games with strict type uncertainty. In *Proceedings of the 20th Annual Conference on Uncertainty in Artificial Intelligence (UAI-04)*, pages 268–27, Arlington, Virginia, 2004. AUAI Press.

G. Jehle and P. Reny. *Advanced Microeconomic Theory*. Addison Wesley, Reading, Massachusetts, second edition, 2000.

S. Kakutani. A generalization of Brouwer's fixed point theorem. *Duke Journal of Mathematics*, 8:457–459, 1941.

M. Kearns, M. Littman, and S. Singh. Graphical models for game theory. In *Proceedings of the 17th Conference in Uncertainty in Artificial Intelligence (UAI '01)*, pages 253–260. Morgan Kaufmann, 2001.

D. E. Knuth, C. H. Papadimitriou, and J. N. Tsitsiklis. A note on strategy elimination in bimatrix games. *Operations Research Letters*, 7(3):103–107, 1988.

R. D. Luce and H. Raiffa. *Games and Decisions*. John Wiley and Sons, New York, 1957.

N. G. Mankiw. *Principles of Economics*. Harcourt College Publishers, Orlando, Florida, second edition, 2001.

A. Mas-Collel, M. D. Whinston, and J. R. Green. *Microeconomic Theory*. Oxford University Press, Oxford, 1995.

H. Moulin. *Game Theory for the Social Sciences*. NYU Press, New York, second, revised edition, 1986.

R. B. Myerson. *Game Theory: Analysis of Conflict*. Harvard University Press, Cambridge, Massachusetts, 1991.

J. F. Nash. Equilibrium points in *n*-person games. *Proceedings of the National Academy of Sciences, USA*, 36:48–49, 1950.

J. F. Nash. Non-cooperative games. *Annals of Mathematics*, 54:286–295, 1951.

N. Nisan, T. Roughgarden, E. Tardos, and V. J. Vazirani, editors. *Algorithmic Game Theory*. Cambridge University Press, 2007.

M. J. Osborne. *An Introduction to Game Theory*. Oxford University Press, 2005.

M. J. Osborne and A. Rubinstein. *A Course in Game Theory*. The MIT Press, Cambridge, Massachusetts, 1994.

D. G. Pearce. Rationalizable strategic behavior and the problem of perfection. *Econometrica*, 52(4):1029–1050, 1984.

H. Peters. *Game Theory: A Multi-Leveled Approach*. Springer, Berlin, 2008.

P. Reny. On the existence of pure and mixed strategy nash equilibria in discontinuous games. *Econometrica*, 67(5):1029–1056, 1999.

K. Ritzberger. *Foundations of Non-cooperative Game Theory*. Oxford University Press, Oxford, 2001.

R. T. Rockafellar. *Convex Analysis*. Princeton University Press, Princeton, 1996.

S. L. Roux, P. Lescanne, and R. Vestergaard. Conversion/preference games. *CoRR*, abs/0811.0071, 2008.

Y. Shoham and K. Leyton-Brown. *Essentials of Game Theory: A Concise, Multidisciplinary Introduction*. Morgan and Claypool Publishers, Princeton, 2008.

M. Stegeman. Deleting strictly eliminating dominated strategies. Working Paper 1990/6, Department of Economics, University of North Carolina, 1990.

S. Tijs. *Introduction to Game Theory*. Hindustan Book Agency, Gurgaon, India, 2003.

W. Vickrey. Counterspeculation, auctions, and competitive sealed tenders. *Journal of Finance*, 16:8–27, 1961.

J. von Neumann. Zur theorie der gesellsschaftsspiele. *Mathematische Annalen*, 100: 295–320, 1928.

J. von Neumann and O. Morgenstern. *Theory of Games and Economic Behavior*. Princeton University Press, 1944.

2

Infinite Games and Automata Theory

Christof Löding

RWTH Aachen University

Abstract

This chapter gives an introduction to the connection between automata theory and the theory of two player games of infinite duration. We illustrate how the theory of automata on infinite words can be used to solve games with complex winning conditions, for example specified by logical formulae. Conversely, infinite games are a useful tool to solve problems for automata on infinite trees such as complementation and the emptiness test.

2.1 Introduction

The aim of this chapter is to explain some interesting connections between automata theory and games of infinite duration. The context in which these connections have been established is the problem of automatic circuit synthesis from specifications, as posed by Church [1962]. A circuit can be viewed as a device that transforms input sequences of bit vectors into output sequences of bit vectors. If the circuit acts as a kind of control device, then these sequences are assumed to be infinite because the computation should never halt.

The task in synthesis is to construct such a circuit based on a formal specification describing the desired input/output behaviour. This problem setting can be viewed as a game of infinite duration between two players: The first player provides the bit vectors for the input, and the second player produces the output bit vectors. The winning condition of the game is given by the specification. The goal is to find a strategy for the second player such that all pairs of input/output sequences that can be produced according to the strategy satisfy the specification. Such a strategy can be seen as a realisation of the specification.

This approach using games as a model for the synthesis problem has been taken by Büchi and Landweber [1969], where it is shown that the synthesis problem can be solved by an algorithm for specifications that are written in monadic second-order logic. As a tool they use automata on infinite words: The formula defining the specification is translated into a deterministic automaton over infinite words that accepts precisely those pairs of input/output sequences that satisfy the formula. This reduces the synthesis problem to the computation of a strategy on a finite game graph (composed of the transition structure of the automaton and the choices of the bit vectors by the two players) with a winning condition derived from the acceptance condition of the automaton, usually expressed in terms of the vertices that occur infinitely often during a play on the graph.

Another approach to solve the synthesis problem for monadic second-order logic has been taken by Rabin [1972] using automata on infinite trees. The idea is that the behaviour of a circuit can be represented by an infinite ordered labelled tree of a suitable branching degree: The input sequences are coded by the paths through the tree, where the direction the path takes determines the next input bit vector, and the labels of the nodes along the path determine the outputs produced by the circuit. The key result shows that a monadic second-order specification of admissible input/output sequences can be translated into a finite automaton running on infinite trees such that precisely those trees are accepted that represent circuit behaviours which are admissible w.r.t. the specification. In this way the synthesis problem is reduced to the emptiness problem for automata on infinite trees. It turns out that games are a useful tool to solve these kinds of emptiness problems.

The above descriptions illustrate the interplay between games of infinite duration and different types of automata. The goal of this chapter is to study this relationship in more depth, in particular the following two aspects:

1 How can we use automata to solve problems that arise in the theory of infinite duration games?
2 How can we use games to solve problems that arise in automata theory?

After having introduced the central objects of this chapter, namely games and strategies, in Section 2.2, we consider the first question in Section 2.3: We show how to use automata on infinite words to compute strategies in games with complex winning conditions, e.g., defined in logical formalisms. Section 2.4 is dedicated to the second question: We explain how results on infinite games can help us to obtain results for automata on infinite trees. In

Section 2.5 we give an outlook beyond finite automata, and in Section 2.6 we conclude.

This chapter is written as a gentle introduction to the subject of infinite games and automata theory. Many concepts, techniques, and proofs are explained using examples without being formally rigorous. For the interested reader who wants to learn more about the subject we give some pointers to the literature in the conclusion.

2.2 Basic notations and definitions

For a set X we denote by X^* the set of finite sequences and by X^ω the set of infinite sequences over X. For $\alpha \in X^\omega$ let

$$\mathrm{Inf}(\alpha) = \{x \in X \mid x \text{ occurs infinitely often in } \alpha\}.$$

We can view an infinite sequence $\alpha \in X^\omega$ as a mapping $\alpha : \mathbb{N} \to X$. Consequently, we write $\alpha(i)$ to denote the element at position i in α, i.e.,

$$\alpha = \alpha(0)\alpha(1)\alpha(2)\cdots$$

Infinite sequences are also called infinite words or ω-words.

A *game graph* (also called *arena*) is a tuple $G = (V_{\mathsf{E}}, V_{\mathsf{A}}, E, c)$ with

- V_{E}: vertices of Eva (player 1, circle),
- V_{A}: vertices of Adam (player 2, box),
- $E \subseteq V \times V$: edges with $V = V_{\mathsf{E}} \cup V_{\mathsf{A}}$,
- $c : V \to C$ with a finite set of colours C.

The sets V_{E} and V_{A} are disjoint (each vertex belongs to exactly one of the players). We are interested in plays of infinite duration played on such graphs. Therefore, we assume that each vertex has at least one successor. Most of the time we consider games on finite arenas but in Section 2.4 we also use games on infinite graphs.

Example 2.1 Figure 2.1 shows a simple game graph with $V_{\mathsf{E}} = \{x_1, x_2\}$ and $V_{\mathsf{A}} = \{y_1, y_2\}$. We assume that $C = V$ and that the colouring is the identity function. Whenever we consider game graphs without specifying the colouring, then we implicitly identify the vertices with the colours.

A *play* in G is an infinite sequence $\alpha = v_0 v_1 v_2 \cdots$ of vertices such that $(v_i, v_{i+1}) \in E$ for all $i \geq 0$. By $c(\alpha)$ we denote the corresponding sequence of colours $c(v_0)c(v_1)c(v_2)\cdots$

A *game* is a pair of a game graph and a *winning condition* $\mathcal{G} = (G, \text{Win})$ with $\text{Win} \subseteq C^\omega$. Eva wins a play α if $c(\alpha) \in \text{Win}$. Otherwise Adam wins.

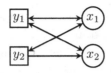

Figure 2.1 A game graph

Example 2.2 We can specify the following winning condition for Eva over the game graph from Figure 2.1, where the colours are identified with the vertices: $y_2 \in \mathrm{Inf}(\alpha) \Leftrightarrow \{x_1, x_2\} \subseteq \mathrm{Inf}(\alpha)$. This means that *Win* contains all those plays

- in which x_1, x_2, and y_2 appear infinitely often, or
- in which y_2 and at least one of x_1 or x_2 appear only finitely often.

Now let us think of a play being built up by the two players by moving a token along the edges of the graph: Eva chooses the next move from vertices in V_{E} and Adam from vertices of V_{A}. Then we are interested in the question of whether Eva has a way to play such that she is sure to win, no matter how Adam plays, i.e., we are interested in the question of whether Eva has a winning strategy. This is formalised in the following definitions.

A **strategy** for Eva is a function $\sigma : V^* V_{\mathsf{E}} \to V$ such that $\sigma(xv) = v'$ implies $(v, v') \in E$. A play $v_0 v_1 v_2 \cdots$ is played according to σ if

$$\forall i : v_i \in V_{\mathsf{E}} \to \sigma(v_0 \cdots v_i) = v_{i+1}.$$

Strategies for Adam are defined similarly with V_{A} instead of V_{E}.

Given an initial vertex v_0 and a strategy σ (for Eva or Adam), the set $Out(\sigma, v_0)$ contains all plays starting in v_0 that are played according to σ (the possible outcomes of σ).

A strategy σ for Eva in a game $\mathcal{G} = (G, \textit{Win})$ is a winning strategy from vertex v_0 if Eva wins all plays α that start in v_0 and are played according to σ, i.e., $c(\alpha) \in \textit{Win}$ for all $\alpha \in Out(\sigma, v_0)$. Similarly, a strategy σ for Adam is winning from v_0 if $c(\alpha) \notin \textit{Win}$ for all $\alpha \in Out(\sigma, v_0)$.

Example 2.3 We continue Example 2.2 and define a winning strategy for Eva. Note that the only choice that Eva can make is in x_1, where she can choose to move to y_1 or to y_2. If she always decides to move to y_2, then Adam could win by never moving to x_2: the resulting play would contain y_2 infinitely often but x_2 only finitely often and thus would be winning for Adam.

If Eva always decides to move to y_1, then Adam could win by alternating between x_1 and x_2. This would result in a game that contains y_2 only finitely often but x_1 and x_2 infinitely often.

From these considerations we see that Eva has to make her choices depending on the behaviour of Adam. A possible way for her to win is to always remember which of the x_i was visited before. When she has to make a choice at x_1, then she moves to y_1 if the previous x_i was also x_1, and she moves to y_2 if the previous x_i was x_2. Playing according to this strategy, Eva can ensure that the infinity sets of the possible plays are $\{y_1, x_1\}$, $\{y_1, x_2\}$, or $\{y_1, y_2, x_1, x_2\}$ and thus winning for her.

Note that this strategy is winning from every vertex, i.e., it does not depend on the initial vertex of the play.

The **winning area** for Eva is the set W_{E} of all vertices from which Eva has a winning strategy:

$$W_{\mathsf{E}} = \{v \in V \mid \text{Eva has a winning strategy from } v\}.$$

The winning area for Adam is denoted W_{A} and is defined in the same way.

A game $\mathcal{G} = (G, Win)$ is **determined** if from each vertex either Eva or Adam has a winning strategy, i.e., if $W_{\mathsf{E}} \cup W_{\mathsf{A}} = V$. The games that we consider in this tutorial are all determined.

The notion of strategy is very general because it allows the players to base their decision of the next move on the whole history of the play. This means that strategies are infinite objects in general. Very often simpler types of strategies are sufficient. The simplest are **positional strategies**, which only depend on the current vertex. For Eva a positional strategy corresponds to a function $\sigma : V_{\mathsf{E}} \to V$ with $(v, \sigma(v)) \in E$ for each $v \in V_{\mathsf{E}}$ (and similarly for Adam). The analysis in Example 2.3 has shown that Eva does not have a positional winning strategy for the considered game.

A generalisation of positional strategies are **finite memory strategies**. These are given by a deterministic finite automaton $(Q, C, q_{in}, \delta, \sigma)$ with input alphabet C, state set Q, initial state q_{in}, transition function δ, and (instead of final states) the strategy function $\sigma : Q \times V_{\mathsf{E}} \to V$ with $(v, \sigma(q, v)) \in E$ for each $v \in V_{\mathsf{E}}$ and $q \in Q$. The idea is that the finite automaton reads the (colour sequence of the) history of the play, and the strategy function chooses the next move depending on the current vertex and the state of the automaton. In this way Eva can use a bounded amount of information on the history of the play.

Example 2.4   The strategy we have defined in Example 2.3 is a finite memory strategy. The corresponding automaton is shown in Figure 2.2. An

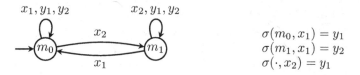

$$\sigma(m_0, x_1) = y_1$$
$$\sigma(m_1, x_1) = y_2$$
$$\sigma(\cdot, x_2) = y_1$$

Figure 2.2 Finite memory strategy

example play together with the sequence of memory states could look as follows, where the moves that are determined by σ are marked:

$$
\begin{array}{cccccccccc}
y_1 & x_1 \xrightarrow{\sigma} y_1 & x_1 \xrightarrow{\sigma} y_1 & x_2 \xrightarrow{\sigma} y_1 & x_1 \xrightarrow{\sigma} y_2 & x_1 \xrightarrow{\sigma} y_1 & \cdots \\
m_0 & m_0' \; m_0 & m_0' \; m_0 & m_0' \; m_1 & m_1' \; m_0 & m_0' \; m_0
\end{array}
$$

We have defined winning conditions to be given by some set $Win \subseteq C^\omega$. Usually, this set Win is defined in terms of the colours that appear infinitely often during a play. Some of the most common winning conditions are listed below:

- A **Büchi condition** is given by a set $F \subseteq C$ of colours. The set Win contains all sequences $\gamma \in C^\omega$ such that $\mathrm{Inf}(\gamma) \cap F \neq \emptyset$, i.e., Eva wins a play α if at least one colour from F occurs infinitely often in α.
- A **Muller condition** is given by a family $\mathcal{F} \subseteq 2^C$ of sets of colours. The set Win contains all sequences $\gamma \in C^\omega$ such that $\mathrm{Inf}(\gamma) \in \mathcal{F}$, i.e., Eva wins if the set of colours that occur infinitely often in α is a set that is listed in $\mathcal{F}$.
- A **parity condition** is specified over a finite set of natural numbers as colours: $C \subseteq \mathbb{N}$. The set Win contains all sequences $\gamma \in C^\omega$ for which the maximal number that occurs infinitely often is even.

Clearly, Büchi conditions and parity conditions are special cases of Muller conditions. For a Büchi condition defined by F the equivalent Muller condition is $\mathcal{F} = \{D \subseteq C \mid D \cap F \neq \emptyset\}$. For a parity condition defined over $C \subseteq \mathbb{N}$ the equivalent Muller condition is $\mathcal{F} = \{D \subseteq C \mid \max(D) \text{ is even}\}$.

The central role of parity conditions in the theory of infinite games on graphs is due to the following result.

Theorem 2.5 (Emerson and Jutla [1988], Mostowski [1991]) *Parity games are determined with positional strategies.*

We make use of this result throughout this chapter. A proof is given in chapter 3, *Algorithms for Solving Parity Games* by Marcin Jurdziński in this

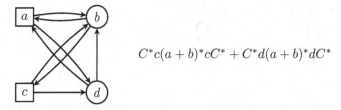

$$C^*c(a+b)^*cC^* + C^*d(a+b)^*dC^*$$

Figure 2.3 Eva wins a play if none of its prefixes matches the regular expression

volume. Other good presentations of can be found in Zielonka [1998] and Thomas [1997].

2.3 Transformation of winning conditions

The goal of this section is to show how to use automata theory to transform complex winning conditions into simpler ones such that solving the simpler game also allows us to solve the original game.

We start with an illustrative example. Consider a game graph with colours $C = \{a, b, c, d\}$. The winning condition is specified by a regular expression r (over the alphabet C): Eva wins a play if none of its prefixes matches the regular expression r. An example for such a game is shown in Figure 2.3. The regular expression in this example defines all words such that there exist two occurrences of c without any occurrence of c or d in between, or two occurrences of d without an occurrence of c or d in between. Eva wins if no prefix of the play satisfies this property. In the depicted game graph she can achieve this goal by the following strategy σ:

- from the d vertex she always moves to b, and
- from the b vertex she moves

  - to c if b was reached from d, and
  - to a if b was reached from a or c.

We now illustrate a general method to compute such strategies. Instead of developing a direct algorithm, we use the fact that regular expressions can be translated into equivalent deterministic finite automata, abbreviated as DFA.[1] Given such an automaton $\mathcal{A}$ we can build the product of the game graph G and $\mathcal{A}$ in such a way that $\mathcal{A}$ reads the play in G. This is illustrated in Figure 2.4, where on the left-hand side the game graph G and the DFA $\mathcal{A}$

---

[1] For background on finite automata we refer the reader to Hopcroft and Ullman [1979].

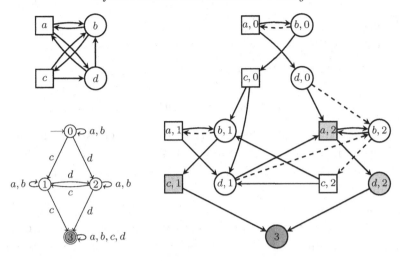

Figure 2.4 Product of the game graph with a DFA yields an equivalent safety game

are shown, and on the right-hand side the product game graph. The meaning of the grey vertices and the dashed edges is explained below. For the moment they can be considered as normal edges and vertices. Formally, the vertices of the product graph are pairs of a vertex of the original graph and a state of $\mathcal{A}$. From a pair (v, q) there is an edge to (v', q') if there is an edge (v, v') in G, and a transition in $\mathcal{A}$ from q to q' with input $c(v)$. So in a play over the product graph the current vertex always encodes the vertex of G and the state that $\mathcal{A}$ would have reached after reading the colour sequence of the current play prefix in G.

Now the goal of Eva is to avoid the final state of $\mathcal{A}$ because this would mean that the play prefix matches the regular expression. In the game graph this event is represented by the bottom vertex labelled 3 (in the full product there would be vertices $(a, 3), \ldots, (d, 3)$ but since Adam wins as soon as one of these vertices is reached they are collapsed into a single vertex).

So the goal of Eva in the new game is to avoid the vertex 3. Such a game is called a safety game because Eva has to remain in the safe area of the game (corresponding to the states $0, 1, 2$ of $\mathcal{A}$). To solve such a game we can simply compute the vertices from which Adam can force to reach the bad vertex. The set of these vertices is called $Attr_A(3)$, the attractor for Adam of the vertex 3. In general, for a set R of vertices, the attractor $Attr_A(R)$ is computed in iterations as follows:

$$
\begin{aligned}
Attr_A^0(R) &= R \\
Attr_A^{i+1}(R) &= Attr_A^i(R) \cup \\
&\quad \{v \in V_A \mid \exists u \in Attr_A^i(R) : (v,u) \in E\} \\
&\quad \{v \in V_E \mid \forall u : (v,u) \in E \rightarrow u \in Attr_A^i(R)\}.
\end{aligned}
$$

The set $Attr_A^i(R)$ contains those vertices from which Adam can ensure to reach a vertex in R after at most i moves. For a finite game graph there exists an index i such that $Attr_A^i(R) = Attr_A^{i+1}(R)$ and we set $Attr_A(R) = Attr_A^i(R)$ for this index i.

From the vertices that are not inside $Attr_A(R)$ Eva has a simple winning strategy to avoid a visit of R: She always moves to a vertex outside of $Attr_A(R)$. The definition of the attractor ensures that such a move is always possible. Furthermore, from outside the attractor Adam does not have the possibility to move inside (again by definition of the attractor).

In the product game graph from the example in Figure 2.4 the attractor for Adam of vertex 3 consists of the grey vertices $(c,1),(d,2)$ (in the first iteration), and $(a,2)$ (in the second iteration). A strategy for Eva to avoid the attractor is given by the dashed arrows.

In the original game, Eva can realise the strategy by running the DFA $\mathcal{A}$ on the play and making her decision based on the current vertex of G, the current state of $\mathcal{A}$, and the strategy from the product game. These are precisely the components required for a strategy automaton as defined in the previous section.

Exercise 2.1   The method illustrated above uses a translation of regular expressions into deterministic finite automata. Analyse the method when using non-deterministic finite automata instead and show that it does not work in general.

For the above example we used a translation from regular expressions to DFAs. For infinitary conditions (something happens infinitely/finitely often) standard DFAs are not enough. To treat such conditions we can use ω-automata.

2.3.1 ω-automata

Automata on infinite words are defined in a similar way to automata on finite words. The main difference is that a run of such an automaton does not have a last state because the input is infinite. For automata on finite words, acceptance of a word by a run is defined in terms of the last state of the run:

it has to be a final state. The definition is replaced by other mechanisms for acceptance, similar to the winning conditions in infinite games.

An ω-**automaton** is of the form $\mathcal{A} = (Q, \Sigma, q_0, \Delta, Acc)$, where Q, Σ, q_0, Δ are as for standard finite automata, i.e., Q is a finite set of states, Σ is the input alphabet, q_0 is the initial state, and $\Delta \subseteq Q \times \Sigma \times Q$ is the transition relation. The component Acc defines the acceptance condition and is explained below.

For an infinite word $\alpha \in \Sigma^\omega$, a **run** of $\mathcal{A}$ on α is an infinite sequence of states $\rho \in Q^\omega$ that starts in the initial state, $\rho(0) = q_0$, and respects the transition relation, $(\rho(i), \alpha(i), \rho(i + 1)) \in \Delta$ for all $i \geq 0$.

It remains to define when such a run is accepting. We are mainly interested in two types of acceptance conditions:

- In a **Büchi automaton** Acc is given as a set $F \subseteq Q$ of states. A run is accepting if it contains infinitely often a state from F.
- In a **parity automaton** Acc is given as a priority mapping $pri : Q \to \mathbb{N}$. A run is accepting if the maximal priority appearing infinitely often is even.

Deterministic automata are defined as usual: there is at most one transition per state and letter.

Figure 2.5 shows a non-deterministic Büchi automaton (on the left-hand side) accepting the language of infinite words over $\Sigma = \{a, b\}$ that contain finitely many b. A simple argument shows that there is no deterministic Büchi automaton for this language (Landweber [1969]):

Exercise 2.2 Show that no deterministic Büchi automaton can accept the language of infinite words over $\Sigma = \{a, b\}$ that contain finitely many b.

Hint: Long sequences of a would always lead such an automaton into an accepting state. Hence, there is some n such that the infinite word $(a^n b)^\omega$ consisting of long a-blocks separated by b would be accepted.

But it is very easy to construct a deterministic parity automaton for this language using the priorities 0 and 1. Such an automaton is shown on the right-hand side of Figure 2.5.

One can show that the two models of non-deterministic Büchi automata and deterministic parity automata are in fact equivalent in expressive power. The difficult direction is the construction of a deterministic parity automaton from a non-deterministic Büchi automaton. The classical subset construction that is used to determinise automata on finite words does not work as illustrated by the following example: Consider the Büchi automaton on the left-hand side of Figure 2.5 and the two inputs $a^\omega = aaaaaa \cdots$, and

Christof Löding

Figure 2.5 A non-deterministic Büchi automaton and a deterministic parity automaton accepting the words containing finitely many b

$(ab)^\omega = ababab\cdots$. Both inputs induce the following sequence of sets of states (the labels above the arrows correspond to the first input, the ones below the arrows to the second one):

$$\{q_0\} \xrightarrow[a]{a} \{q_0, q_1\} \xrightarrow[b]{a} \{q_0, q_1\} \xrightarrow[a]{a} \{q_0, q_1\} \xrightarrow[b]{a} \{q_0, q_1\} \cdots$$

The first input should be accepted, and the second one should be rejected. But since both induce the same sequence of state sets, the subset construction does not carry enough information for determinisation, no matter which acceptance condition we use.

The known determinisation constructions that are of optimal complexity generalise the subset construction by keeping track of several sets that are usually arranged in a tree. The first one was proposed by Safra in 1988. The determinisation theorem itself was already shown by McNaughton in 1966 using a doubly exponential construction.

Theorem 2.6 (McNaughton [1966], Safra [1988]) *For each non-deterministic Büchi automaton with n states there is an equivalent deterministic parity automaton with $2^{O(n \log n)}$ states.*

For some recent work on upper and lower bounds for the determinisation of Büchi automata we refer the reader to Piterman [2006], Kähler and Wilke [2008], Schewe [2009], and Colcombet and Zdanowski [2009].

The other direction of the equivalence between deterministic parity and non-deterministic Büchi automata is left as an exercise.

Exercise 2.3 Show that each deterministic parity automaton can be transformed into an equivalent non-deterministic Büchi automaton.

Hint: The Büchi automaton guesses an even priority at some point and verifies that it occurs infinitely often and that it is the maximal priority from this point onwards.

We call languages that can be accepted by non-deterministic Büchi automata (or equivalently by deterministic parity automata) ω-*regular*.

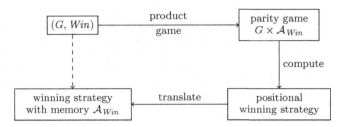

Figure 2.6 Schema for game reductions

2.3.2 Game reductions

The general idea for game reductions is to transform games with a complicated winning condition into games with a simpler winning condition (over a bigger game graph) such that a winning strategy for the simpler but bigger game can be transformed into a winning strategy for the original game (using additional memory).

At the beginning of this section we have already seen how to translate a winning condition that specifies forbidden prefixes by a regular expression into a safety game. The general translation scheme that we apply is as follows (illustrated in Figure 2.6):

- Start from a game $\mathcal{G} = (G, \textit{Win})$ with some ω-regular winning condition $\textit{Win} \subseteq C^\omega$.
- Construct a deterministic ω-automaton $\mathcal{A}_{\textit{Win}}$ for $\textit{Win}$.
- Take the product of G and $\mathcal{A}_{\textit{Win}}$ (the automaton reads the labels of the vertices in G).
- The new winning condition is the acceptance condition of $\mathcal{A}_{\textit{Win}}$ (e.g., a parity condition).
- Winning strategies on the product game are winning strategies on the original game with (additional) memory $\mathcal{A}_{\textit{Win}}$.

We show how to use this technique to reduce Muller games to parity games. For this purpose we construct a deterministic parity automaton that reads sequences α from C^ω and accepts if α satisfies the given Muller condition.

The construction is based on the data structure of 'latest appearance record' (LAR) Büchi [1983], Gurevich and Harrington [1982].[2] The underlying idea is to recall the order in which the colours of the play appeared (starting with an arbitrary order). An LAR is thus a permutation of the colours over which the Muller condition is defined. When reading the next colour of the

---

[2] In Büchi [1983] LARs are called order vectors and they are attributed to McNaughton.

input	d	b	b	d	c	b	a	b	a	c	b	a	b	a	c	
LARs	a	d	b	$\underline{b}$	d	c	b	a	b	a	c	b	a	b	a	c
	b	a	d	d	$\underline{b}$	d	c	b	$\underline{a}$	$\underline{b}$	a	c	b	$\underline{a}$	$\underline{b}$	a
	c	b	$\underline{a}$	a	a	b	$\underline{d}$	c	c	c	$\underline{b}$	$\underline{a}$	$\underline{c}$	c	c	$\underline{b}$
	$\underline{d}$	$\underline{c}$	c	c	c	$\underline{a}$	a	$\underline{d}$	d	d	d	d	d	d	d	d
priorities	7	7	5	1	4	7	5	7	3	3	6	6	6	3	3	6

Figure 2.7 Latest appearance records for a given sequence of colours from $\{a, b, c, d\}$ for the Muller condition $\mathcal{F} = \{\{b, d\}, \{a, b, c\}\}$

sequence, it is moved to the first position in the ordering. To define the parity condition of the automaton we additionally mark the old position of the colour that has been moved. This idea is illustrated in Figure 2.7 for the colour set $C = \{a, b, c, d\}$. The LARs are written vertically, and when reading the next colour it is moved to the top. The numbers below the LARs are the assigned priorities and are explained later.

The marked positions are underlined. We point out that it is not the underlined colour that is marked, but the position. For example, in the fifth LAR in the picture, it is not b that is marked but the second position because this LAR was obtained by moving d from the second position to the front.

Note that in this way the colours that appear only finitely often gather at the end (bottom) of the LAR and that the marker eventually stays in the part of the LAR that keeps changing.

Formally, a **latest appearance record** (LAR) over C is an ordering $d_1 \cdots d_n$ of the elements of C with one marked position h:

$$LAR(C) = \{[d_1 \cdots d_n, h] \mid d_i \in C, d_i \neq d_j \text{ for all } i \neq j, \text{ and } 1 \leq h \leq n\}.$$

The set of LARs serves as the set of states for the parity automaton. The transition function (update of the LARs) is defined as explained above:

$$\delta_{LAR}([d_1 \cdots d_n, h], d) = [d d_1 \cdots d_{i-1} d_{i+1} \cdots d_n, i]$$

for the unique i with $d = d_i$. Note that the LARs and their update do not depend on the Muller condition $\mathcal{F}$.

It remains to assign the priorities to the states, i.e., to the LARs. This is done depending on the size of the part of the LAR that has changed in the last transition. As explained above, the biggest part of the LAR that changes infinitely often represents the set of colours that appear infinitely often and hence the parity automaton should accept if this set belongs to the Muller condition.

If C contains n colours, then we assign the priorities as follows:

$$c_{LAR}([d_1 \cdots d_n, h]) = \begin{cases} 2h - 1 & \{d_1, \ldots, d_h\} \notin \mathcal{F}, \\ 2h & \{d_1, \ldots, d_h\} \in \mathcal{F}. \end{cases}$$

In the example from Figure 2.7 this is shown for the Muller condition $\mathcal{F} = \{\{b, d\}, \{a, b, c\}\}$.

Combining all this we obtain the LAR automaton

$$\mathcal{A}_{LAR} = (LAR(C), C, q_0, \delta_{LAR}, c_{LAR})$$

and the following theorem:[3]

Theorem 2.7 (Büchi [1983], Gurevich and Harrington [1982]) *For a Muller condition $\mathcal{F}$ over C the corresponding deterministic parity automaton $\mathcal{A}_{LAR}$ accepts precisely those $\alpha \in C^\omega$ that satisfy the Muller condition $\mathcal{F}$.*

Now, given a Muller game, we can take the product with the LAR automaton. This results in a parity game for which we can compute the winner and a positional winning strategy. This winning strategy can be implemented over the Muller game using the LAR automaton as memory.

Theorem 2.8 (Büchi [1983], Gurevich and Harrington [1982]) *Muller games are determined with the LAR automaton as memory.*

2.3.3 Logical winning conditions

In this section we show examples for game reductions where the winning conditions of the games are given by logical formulae. We consider two logics: the linear time temporal logic LTL introduced by Pnueli [1981], and monadic second-order logic over infinite words (Büchi [1962]). LTL is widely used in verification, for example the model checker SPIN can verify LTL properties on finite systems (Holzmann [2003]). The interest in monadic second-order logic is more of a theoretical nature. This logic is often used as a yardstick for expressive power because it subsumes many specification logics.

Linear temporal logic

The formulae of LTL are defined over a set $P = \{p_1, \ldots, p_n\}$ of atomic propositions, and are evaluated over infinite sequences of vectors of size n. The ith entry of such a vector codes the truth value of p_i (1 = true, 0 = false).

LTL formulae are built up from

---

[3] The parity condition is not used by Büchi [1983], Gurevich and Harrington [1982] because it has been introduced later but the statement can easily be derived from these papers.

- atomic formulae of the form p_i,
- Boolean combinations, and
- temporal operators:

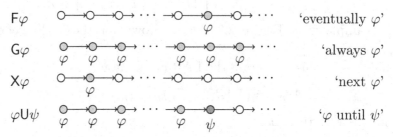

The semantics of the operators is already illustrated in the drawings. We do not give the formal definition here but prefer to explain the semantics using some examples. An atomic formula p_i is true if p_i is true at the beginning of the word, i.e., if the ith entry of the first vector is 1. A formula $X\varphi$ is true if φ is true in the model starting from the second position. For example, $p_1 \wedge X\neg p_2$ is true in

$$\begin{pmatrix}\underline{1}\\1\end{pmatrix}\begin{pmatrix}1\\\underline{0}\end{pmatrix}\begin{pmatrix}0\\1\end{pmatrix}\begin{pmatrix}0\\0\end{pmatrix}\cdots$$

as witnessed by the underlined entries.

A formula $F\varphi$ is true if there exists some position $i \geq 0$ in the word such that φ is true in this position (i.e. in the suffix of the word starting at this position i). A formula $G\varphi$ is true if φ is true at each position of the word. For example, $Gp_2 \wedge Fp_1$ is true in

$$\begin{pmatrix}0\\\underline{1}\end{pmatrix}\begin{pmatrix}0\\\underline{1}\end{pmatrix}\begin{pmatrix}0\\\underline{1}\end{pmatrix}\cdots\begin{pmatrix}0\\\underline{1}\end{pmatrix}\begin{pmatrix}\underline{1}\\\underline{1}\end{pmatrix}\begin{pmatrix}0\\\underline{1}\end{pmatrix}\begin{pmatrix}0\\\underline{1}\end{pmatrix}\begin{pmatrix}1\\\underline{1}\end{pmatrix}\cdots$$

again witnessed by the underlined entries.

A formula $\varphi U\psi$ is true if there is some position where ψ is true, and φ is true in all previous positions. Consider the formula $F(p_3 \wedge X(\neg p_2 U p_1))$. It states that there is some position where p_3 is true such that from the next position p_2 is false until a position is reached where p_1 is true. The words satisfying this formula are of the following shape, where again the underlined entries are those making the formula true:

$$\begin{pmatrix}0\\1\\0\end{pmatrix}\begin{pmatrix}0\\0\\1\end{pmatrix}\cdots\begin{pmatrix}\underline{1}\\0\\1\end{pmatrix}\begin{pmatrix}0\\\underline{0}\\1\end{pmatrix}\begin{pmatrix}0\\\underline{0}\\1\end{pmatrix}\begin{pmatrix}0\\\underline{0}\\0\end{pmatrix}\begin{pmatrix}\underline{1}\\1\\0\end{pmatrix}\cdots$$

We are interested in games with LTL winning conditions, i.e., games of the form (G, φ) for an LTL formula φ. Eva wins the game if the play satisfies φ.

$$\alpha = \left|\begin{pmatrix}1\\0\\1\end{pmatrix}\begin{pmatrix}0\\1\\0\end{pmatrix}\begin{pmatrix}0\\0\\1\end{pmatrix}\begin{pmatrix}0\\0\\1\end{pmatrix}\begin{pmatrix}1\\1\\1\end{pmatrix}\begin{pmatrix}0\\1\\0\end{pmatrix}\cdots\right.$$

$\neg p_2$	1	0	1	1	0	0	$\cdots$
$\neg p_2 \mathsf{U} p_1$	1	0	1	1	1	0	$\cdots$
$\mathsf{X}(\neg p_2 \mathsf{U} p_1)$	0	1	1	1	0	$1^?$	$\cdots$
$p_3 \vee \mathsf{X}(\neg p_2 \mathsf{U} p_1)$	1	1	1	1	1	$1^?$	$\cdots$
$\mathsf{G}(p_3 \vee \mathsf{X}(\neg p_2 \mathsf{U} p_1))$	$1^?$	$1^?$	$1^?$	$1^?$	$1^?$	$1^?$	$\cdots$

Figure 2.8 A Büchi automaton guesses valuations for sub-formulae

To be able to interpret LTL formulae in infinite plays we assume that the set C of colours of the game graph is $\{0, 1\}^n$.

To apply the method of game reduction it suffices to construct an equivalent automaton for a given formula. We explain the underlying idea for transforming an LTL formula into an equivalent (non-deterministic) Büchi automaton. The automaton 'guesses' for each sub-formula of the given formula φ its truth value at the current position and verifies its guesses. Thus, the states of the automaton are mappings that associate to each sub-formula of φ a truth value 0 or 1. Figure 2.8 illustrates how the Büchi automaton works. The question marks in the table indicate that the truth value of the corresponding formulae cannot be verified within the shown prefix of α but depend on the continuation of α.

The verification of guesses works as follows:

- Atomic formulae and Boolean combinations can be verified directly because the truth values of the atomic formulae are coded in the input letter by definition.
- The operators X, G can be verified using the transitions. If the automaton guesses that a formula $\mathsf{X}\psi$ is true at the current position, then ψ has to be true at the next position. If a formula $\mathsf{G}\psi$ is guessed to be true, then ψ also needs to be true, and $\mathsf{G}\psi$ has to be true in the next position.
- The operators F, U are verified using the acceptance condition. We explain the principle for the operator F. This can easily be generalised to U.

  If $\mathsf{F}\psi$ is guessed to be true, then either $\mathsf{F}\psi$ has to be true again in the next position, or ψ itself has to be true in the current position. Using the acceptance condition, the automaton has to ensure that the second option is taken at some point, i.e., that ψ indeed becomes true eventually. For this purpose, we use a slight generalisation of Büchi automata that have several sets $F_1, \ldots, F_k$ of final states. A run is accepting if all sets are visited infinitely often. Now, for each formula $F\psi$ we introduce one set of final states that contains all states in which ψ is true or $F\psi$ is false. This way, once $F\psi$ is guessed to be true, ψ has to become true eventually, because otherwise the set of final states for $F\psi$ will not be visited anymore.

The same principle applies to sub-formulae with the until operator: A formula $\psi_1 U\psi_2$ is true if either ψ_1 is true now and $\psi_1 U\psi_2$ is true again in the next position, or if ψ_2 is true now.

In the first position the automaton has to guess that the whole formula φ is true because it is supposed to accept exactly those words which satisfy the formula.

Exercise 2.4 In the same way as for formulae $F\psi$ we introduce a set of final states for each sub-formula $\psi_1 U\psi_2$. What should the definition of this set of states look like?

Exercise 2.5 The construction from LTL formulae to automata explained above yields a generalised Büchi automaton with several sets of states. Find a construction that transforms a generalised Büchi automaton into an equivalent Büchi automaton with only one set of final states.

Hint: Cycle through the different sets of final states by introducing copies of the Büchi automaton.

Using the idea illustrated above, we obtain the following theorem:

Theorem 2.9 (Vardi and Wolper [1986]) *For each LTL formula φ one can construct an equivalent Büchi automaton $\mathcal{A}_\varphi$ of size exponential in φ.*

Using the determinisation theorem for ω-automata and the method of game reduction, we obtain the following theorem.

Theorem 2.10 *Games (G, φ) with a winning condition given by an LTL formula can be solved in doubly exponential time.*

The theorem has been shown first by Pnueli and Rosner [1989] in a slightly different formulation in the context of synthesising reactive programs. In this setting the goal is to construct a program (such as a controller or circuit) that reads inputs and produces outputs, as already explained in the introduction. A specification is given that relates the input sequences to the output sequences and the task is to synthesise the program automatically from the specification. If this specification is given by an LTL formula, then one can reformulate the problem as a game with LTL winning condition. The program then corresponds to a winning strategy for Eva. In Rosner [1991] it is shown that the doubly exponential complexity is also a lower bound.

In a more general setting the synthesis problem has been posed by Church [1962]. For the case of monadic second-order specifications it has been solved by Büchi and Landweber [1969] as explained in the following.

Monadic second-order logic

We now consider monadic second-order logic over the natural numbers with the successor function. Monadic second-order logic is the extension of first-order logic by the ability to quantify over sets of elements. We do not give the precise definition but only illustrate the syntax with an example. For a more precise treatment of the subject we refer the reader to Thomas [1997].

The underlying structure $(\mathbb{N}, +1)$ consists of the natural numbers as domain and the successor function. The corresponding theory, i.e., the sentences that are true in $(\mathbb{N}, +1)$, is called the 'second-order theory of one successor' (S1S) by Büchi [1962]. We slightly abuse the terminology here and also refer to the logic itself as S1S.

We use small letters $x, y, \ldots$ as first-order variables denoting elements, and capital letters $X, Y, \ldots$ for set variables denoting sets of natural numbers.

Consider the formula

$$\varphi(X) = \exists Y \big(\ 0 \in Y \wedge$$
$$\forall x (x \in Y \leftrightarrow x + 1 \notin Y) \wedge$$
$$\forall x (x \in X \rightarrow x \in Y) \big).$$

It has one free set variable X denoting a set of natural numbers. We can view a set of natural numbers as an ω-word over the alphabet $\{0, 1\}$ by labelling the positions in X by 1, and the other positions by 0.

Using this interpretation, φ defines the set of all ω-words over $\{0, 1\}$ such that 1 can only occur on even positions: The formula states that there is a set Y that contains position 0, and it contains exactly every second position (i.e., Y contains exactly the even positions), and it contains X. Thus, this formula is true for each interpretation of the free variable X by a set containing only even positions.

In general, we consider formulae $\varphi(X_1, \ldots, X_n)$ with n free set variables defining ω-languages over $\{0, 1\}^n$. We have already seen that LTL formulae (which also define languages over the alphabet $\{0, 1\}^n$) can be translated into automata. For S1S formulae we even have a stronger result that the two formalisms are equivalent.

Theorem 2.11 (Büchi [1962]) *A language $L \subseteq (\{0, 1\}^n)^\omega$ is definable by an S1S formula iff it can be accepted by a non-deterministic Büchi automaton.*

Proof A detailed version of this proof can be found in Thomas [1997]. We only give a brief sketch of the ideas.

From formulae to automata one uses an inductive translation, based on the closure properties of automata. To make this approach work, one first introduces a variant of S1S that uses only set variables (and has a predicate saying that a set is a singleton and a predicate for set inclusion). Atomic formulae are easily translated into equivalent automata. For the Boolean combinations one uses the closure properties of automata, and for the existential quantification the projection.

From Büchi automata to formulae one writes a formula that describes the existence of an accepting run. For each state q one uses a set X_q that contains the positions of the run where the automaton is in state q. Then one can easily express that the run starts in the initial state, that infinitely many final states occur, and that the transitions are respected in each step.   □

As for LTL winning conditions, we can now consider games with winning conditions specified by S1S formulae. Using the translation into nondeterministic Büchi automata and the determinisation theorem we can solve such games.

Theorem 2.12 *For games (G, φ) with a winning condition given by an S1S formula φ one can decide the winner and can compute a corresponding winning strategy.*

The complexity of the inductive translation of formulae into automata is rather high because each negation in the formula requires a complementation of the automaton, which is exponential. Thus, the complexity of our algorithm is non-elementary in the size of the formula. From lower bounds on the complexity of deciding S1S presented in Meyer [1975] it follows that we cannot hope for an improvement.

Based on lower bound results for the translation of formulae into automata (see Reinhardt [2002]) one can show that this also applies to the memory required for winning strategies in S1S games. The size of the memory required for a winning strategy in a game with an S1S winning condition cannot be bounded by a function of the form

$$
\left. 2^{2^{2^{\cdot^{\cdot^{\cdot^{2^n}}}}}} \right\} k
$$

for a fixed k.

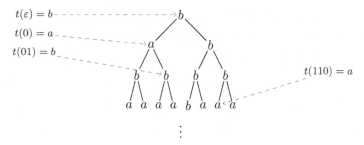

Figure 2.9 The initial part of an infinite tree over the alphabet $\{a, b\}$

2.4 Tree automata

Infinite trees are a useful tool to model the behaviour of discrete systems (circuits, protocols, etc.). These can be described by transition graphs, and the possible behaviours or executions of such a system are captured by an infinite tree: the unravelling of the transition graph. Properties of the system behaviour can thus be specified as properties of infinite trees.

For simplicity we restrict ourselves to complete binary trees. The nodes are labelled by symbols from a finite alphabet Σ. When modelling system executions by infinite trees this alphabet captures properties of the system we are interested in.

Formally, a **tree** is a mapping $t : \{0, 1\}^* \to \Sigma$. The **root** of the tree corresponds to the empty string ε. For some **node** $u \in \{0, 1\}^*$ the **left successor** is $u0$, and the **right successor** is $u1$. This is illustrated in Figure 2.9 showing the initial part of a tree over the alphabet $\{a, b\}$. The name of a node corresponds to the sequence of left (0) and right (1) moves that lead to this node from the root.

We now introduce an automaton model that defines sets (languages) of such infinite trees. This model can be seen as an extension of ω-automata to trees, and it is also an extension of the model of automata on finite trees. As for ω-automata, one can study different models that are distinguished by the form of their acceptance condition. We focus here on parity tree automata, which are defined as follows.

A **parity tree automaton** (PTA) is of the form $\mathcal{A} = (Q, \Sigma, q_{in}, \Delta, pri)$ with a finite set Q of states, a label alphabet Σ, an initial state q_{in}, a transition relation $\Delta \subseteq Q \times \Sigma \times Q \times Q$, and a priority function $pri : Q \to \mathbb{N}$.

A **run** ρ of a PTA on a tree t is a mapping $\rho : \{0, 1\}^* \to Q$ (a Q-labelled tree) that starts in the initial state, $\rho(\varepsilon) = q_{in}$, and that respects

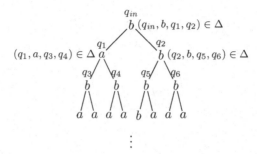

Figure 2.10 A run of a PTA has to respect the transition relation

the transitions, $(\rho(u), t(u), \rho(u0), \rho(u1)) \in \Delta$ for all $u \in \{0,1\}^*$. This is illustrated in Figure 2.10.

The acceptance condition of a PTA is defined via the priority mapping. From games and ω-automata we already know that a sequence of states is accepting if the maximal priority that appears infinitely often is even. We extend this to trees by defining a run to be accepting if the state sequence on each infinite path through the run is accepting, i.e., if on each infinite path the maximal priority that occurs infinitely often is even.

As usual, a tree is accepted if there is an accepting run on this tree. The language of trees accepted by $\mathcal{A}$ is denoted by $T(\mathcal{A})$. We call a language of infinite trees regular if it can be accepted by a parity tree automaton.

Before we come to the properties of PTAs, we make some remarks on other acceptance conditions and give some examples:

- As for games or ω-automata we can define, e.g., tree automata with Muller or Büchi acceptance conditions.
- The expressive power of Muller tree automata and parity tree automata is the same. To transform Muller automata into parity automata one can use the LAR construction presented in the previous section.
- One can show that Büchi tree automata are weaker than parity tree automata. The language of all trees over $\{a, b\}$ such that on each path there are finitely many b cannot be accepted by a Büchi tree automaton but by a PTA. The PTA can easily be obtained by running the parity word automaton from Figure 2.5 on every branch of the tree using the transitions (q_0, a, q_0, q_0), (q_0, b, q_1, q_1), (q_1, a, q_0, q_0), and (q_1, b, q_1, q_1). A proof that a Büchi tree automaton cannot accept this language can be found in Thomas [1997] and in Chapter 8 of Grädel et al. [2002].
- It is rather easy to see that deterministic tree automata are too weak. For example, the set of all trees t over $\{a, b\}$ such that t contains at least one

node labelled b is accepted by a PTA with two states $Q = \{q_b, q\}$, with initial state q_b, priorities $pri(q_b) = 1$, $pri(q) = 2$, and the transitions

$$(q_b, a, q_b, q), \; (q_b, a, q, q_b), \; (q_b, b, q, q), \; (q, a, q, q), \; (q, b, q, q).$$

The state q_b is used to non-deterministically select a path that leads to a node with label b. This is done by the first two transitions. A simple argument shows that this language cannot be accepted by a deterministic parity tree automaton.

We now analyse algorithmic and closure properties of PTAs. Some closure properties are rather easy to obtain.

Proposition 2.13 *The class of regular languages of infinite trees is closed under union, intersection, and projection (relabelling).*

Proof For the closure under union and intersection one can use a classical product construction where the two given automata are executed in parallel. The acceptance condition becomes a Muller condition that expresses that both automata accept for the intersection, or that at least one of the automata accepts for the union. As mentioned above, one can use the LAR construction to turn a Muller automaton into an equivalent parity automaton.

For the projection let $h : \Sigma \to \Gamma$ be a relabelling. It is applied to trees by applying it to each label of the tree. Given a PTA $\mathcal{A}$ for a tree language T we want to construct a PTA for the tree language $h(T) = \{h(t) \mid t \in T\}$. For this purpose we simply replace every transition (q, a, q_0, q_1) in $\mathcal{A}$ by the transition $(q, h(a), q_0, q_1)$. $\qquad \square$

The connection to games is used for the closure under complementation and the emptiness test, as explained in the following.

2.4.1 Complementation

Let us first analyse why the complementation problem for PTAs is a difficult problem. By definition, a tree is accepted if

$$\exists \mathrm{run} \forall \mathrm{path}.(\text{path satisfies acceptance condition}).$$

By negation of this statement we obtain that a tree is not accepted if

$$\forall \mathrm{run} \exists \mathrm{path}.(\text{path does not satisfy acceptance condition}).$$

This exchange of quantifiers makes the problem difficult. But there are two observations to make that lead towards the solution. First of all, statements of the form $\exists \forall \cdots$ are very close to the nature of games and strategies: there exists a move of one player that ensures the win against all moves of the other player. In this case the game has just two rounds: The first player picks a run on the input tree, and the second player picks a path through the run. The first player wins if the path satisfies the acceptance condition. We will modify this game such that the players do not choose these objects in one step but incrementally build them. This allows us to express the acceptance of a tree in the form

$$\exists \text{strategy for Eva } \forall \text{strategies for Adam } (...).$$

Then we use determinacy of these games allowing us to express non-acceptance of a tree as

$$\exists \text{strategy for Adam } \forall \text{strategies for Eva } (...).$$

This statement is in the form of $\exists \forall \cdots$ and we show how to construct an automaton that checks this property.

We start by defining the **membership game** that characterises the membership of a tree t in the language of a given PTA $\mathcal{A} = (Q, \Sigma, q_{in}, \Delta, pri)$. Since one player tries to construct an accepting run and the other player tries to show that the run is not accepting by selecting a path through the run, we call the players CONSTRUCTOR and SPOILER. This game has been proposed by Gurevich and Harrington [1982], where the players are called Automaton and Pathfinder.

The rules of the game are as follows:

- The game starts at the root of the tree in the initial state of $\mathcal{A}$, i.e., in the position (q_{in}, ε).
- The moves of the game from a position (u, q) where $u \in \{0, 1\}^*$ is a node of t, and q is a state of $\mathcal{A}$ are:
  1 CONSTRUCTOR picks a transition (q, a, q_0, q_1) that matches q and the label a of t at u, i.e., $a = t(u)$.
  2 SPOILER chooses a direction and the game moves on to position $(u0, q_0)$ or $(u1, q_1)$.
- A play of this game is an infinite sequence of states and transitions together with the nodes in the tree. For the winning condition only the sequence of states is interesting: CONSTRUCTOR wins if this state sequence satisfies the acceptance condition of $\mathcal{A}$.

The shape of this game is illustrated in Figure 2.11. The dashed lines represent the tree nodes. For each tree node the circles represent states, i.e., the positions of CONSTRUCTOR, and the triangles transitions. The arrows

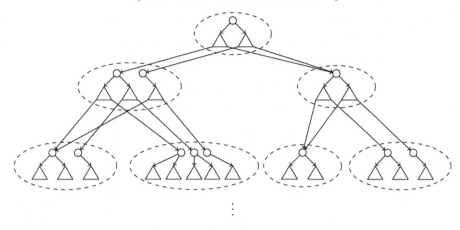

Figure 2.11 Shape of the membership game

from the circles to the triangles indicate that CONSTRUCTOR chooses for a given state a possible transition, and the arrows exiting from the triangles correspond to the choices of SPOILER who moves either to the left or to the right into the corresponding state of the transition.

One should note here that the shape of the game reminds one of a tree but that the game graph itself is not a tree, it is an acyclic graph. For example, in the illustration in Figure 2.11 the leftmost circle in the bottom row can be reached via two different paths. Hence, the existence of positional strategies is not obvious (for game graphs that are trees all strategies are positional because a vertex encodes the full history of the play).

With the picture from Figure 2.11 in mind it is rather easy to see that there is a correspondence between the runs of $\mathcal{A}$ on t and the strategies for CONSTRUCTOR:

- Fixing the transition to be used at the root is the same as defining the first move of CONSTRUCTOR.
- Then SPOILER can only move to the left or to the right. The states at these successors are already fixed by the transition. Defining the strategy for CONSTRUCTOR at these successors is again the same as fixing the transitions for a run, and so on.

By the definition of the winning condition and positional determinacy of parity games we obtain the following lemma.

Lemma 2.14 *A tree t is in $T(\mathcal{A})$ iff there is a positional winning strategy for* CONSTRUCTOR *in the membership game.*

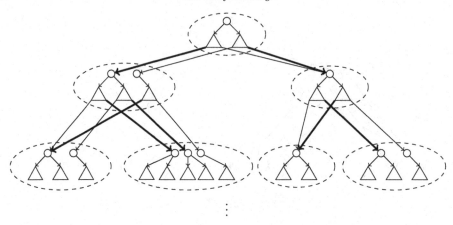

Figure 2.12 Shape of positional strategies for SPOILER in the membership game

Applying the positional determinacy for the negation of the statement, we obtain:

Lemma 2.15   *A tree t is not in $T(\mathcal{A})$ iff there is a positional winning strategy for* SPOILER *in the membership game.*

The next goal is to construct an automaton that checks for a tree t if there is a positional winning strategy for SPOILER in the membership game. By Lemma 2.15 such an automaton suffices to recognise the complement language of $\mathcal{A}$. We start by analysing positional strategies for SPOILER.

A move for SPOILER consists in choosing a direction for a given pair of tree node and transition, as illustrated by the thick edges in Figure 2.12.

Such a positional strategy for SPOILER can be written as a mapping

$$\sigma : \{0,1\}^* \rightarrow (\Delta \rightarrow \{0,1\})$$

that defines for each tree node how the choices of SPOILER for the different transitions are. Let us denote the finite set $\Delta \rightarrow \{0,1\}$ of mappings from transitions to directions $0,1$ by Γ. Then a positional strategy for SPOILER is simply a tree over the alphabet Γ, and hence can be processed by a tree automaton.

Now the next steps in the construction of the complement automaton $\mathcal{C}$ are the following:

- Construct an automaton $\mathcal{A}_{\text{strat}}$ that reads trees of the form $t \times \sigma$, i.e., annotated with a positional strategy for SPOILER such that $\mathcal{A}_{\text{strat}}$ accepts $t \times \sigma$ if σ is winning for SPOILER in the membership game for $\mathcal{A}$ and t.

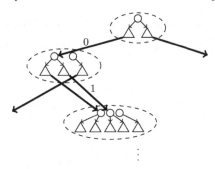

Figure 2.13 A single path through a coding of a positional strategy of
SPOILER

- Obtain $\mathcal{C}$ from $\mathcal{A}_{\text{strat}}$ by omitting the strategy annotation in the labels.
  This operation corresponds to a simple projection that removes the Γ
  component of the labels. This can be seen as $\mathcal{C}$ non-deterministically
  guessing the strategy for SPOILER.

Looking at Figure 2.12, $\mathcal{A}_{\text{strat}}$ has to check that the plays obtained by
following the thick edges (the strategy of SPOILER) do not satisfy the acceptance condition (the strategy is winning for SPOILER). For this task we first
focus on single paths of the tree.

We code these paths by adding to the labels on the path the next direction 0
or 1 taken by the path. In this way we obtain infinite words over $\Sigma \times \Gamma \times \{0, 1\}$.
This is indicated in Figure 2.13, where a single path from the tree shown in
Figure 2.12 is selected.

Now we construct an ω-automaton that checks whether on such paths the
strategy is winning for SPOILER. This ω-automaton has to check whether
all plays that can be obtained by following the thick arrows (the strategy of
SPOILER) *along the given path* do not satisfy the acceptance condition of $\mathcal{A}$.
We obtain this ω-automaton as follows:

- Construct a non-deterministic Büchi automaton that guesses a play along
  the strategy edges of SPOILER and accepts if it does satisfy the acceptance
  condition of $\mathcal{A}$.
- Determinise (see Theorem 2.6) and complement this Büchi automaton, and
  obtain a deterministic parity word automaton $\mathcal{A}_{\text{strat}}^{\text{path}}$ that accepts those
  paths of a tree on which SPOILER's strategy is winning.

Now we can run this deterministic parity word automaton $\mathcal{A}_{\text{strat}}^{\text{path}}$ in parallel
along all paths of the given tree by merging the transitions of $\mathcal{A}_{\text{strat}}^{\text{path}}$ for the

two directions 0 and 1 into a single transition of a tree automaton as follows:

$$\mathcal{A}_{\text{strat}}^{\text{path}} : \quad \delta(q, (a, \gamma, 0)) = q' \qquad \delta(q, (a, \gamma, 1)) = q''$$

$$\mathcal{A}_{\text{strat}} : \qquad\qquad\qquad (q, (a, \gamma), q', q'')$$

for all $q \in Q$, $a \in \Sigma$, and $\gamma \in \Gamma$.

The automaton $\mathcal{C}$ is obtained by omitting the strategy encoding:

$$(q, (a, \gamma), q', q'') \text{ becomes } (q, a, q', q'').$$

From the explanations above it follows that $\mathcal{C}$ indeed accepts the complement language of $\mathcal{A}$, resulting in the following theorem.

Theorem 2.16 (Rabin [1969])   *For a given tree automaton one can construct a tree automaton for the complement language.*

The main steps of the construction described in this section are summarised as follows:

- Characterise acceptance in terms of winning strategies in the membership game.
- Positional determinacy for parity games yields: a tree t is not accepted iff SPOILER has a positional winning strategy in the membership game.
- Construct an automaton that checks if a given strategy of SPOILER is winning. This construction is based on the determinisation of ω-automata.
- Obtain the desired automaton by projection (removing the strategy annotations).

This proof scheme was proposed by Gurevich and Harrington [1982] (see also Thomas [1997]). It is a nice illustration of how determinacy of infinite games can help to solve problems in automata theory. Note that the positional determinacy or winning strategies are not used inside the construction but only to prove the correctness of the construction. The main step in the construction itself is the use of the determinisation theorem for Büchi automata.

In Muller and Schupp [1995] a different proof is presented that only relies on the determinacy of the membership game without making any assumptions on the type of the strategies. From the construction one can derive a finite memory determinacy result for game graphs that have the shape of a membership game.

The size of the complement automaton is determined by the complexity of the determinisation construction for word automata. If $\mathcal{A}$ is a PTA with n states and k priorities, then the Büchi word automaton that has to be determinised is of size $\mathcal{O}(nk)$, and thus the resulting PTA $\mathcal{C}$ is of size $2^{\mathcal{O}(nk\log(nk))}$. The construction presented by Muller and Schupp [1995] slightly improves this to $2^{\mathcal{O}(nk\log(n))}$.

As an application one can now use the closure properties of PTAs to show their equivalence to monadic second-order logic over the infinite tree, i.e., over the structure $(\{0,1\}^*, S_0, S_1)$ consisting of the domain $\{0,1\}^*$ and the two successor relations S_0 and S_1 for moving left or right in the tree. As for S1S the corresponding theory is referred to as S2S (second-order theory of two successors). Again we abuse notation and also refer to the logic as S2S.

In analogy to the results for ω-automata and S1S presented in Section 2.3.3 we obtain the equivalence of S2S and tree automata.

Theorem 2.17 (Rabin [1969])   *A tree language L over the alphabet $\{0,1\}^n$ is definable by an S2S formula iff it can be accepted by a parity tree automaton.*

If we want to check the satisfiability of S2S formulae, we can translate them into tree automata and check these for emptiness. This latter problem is the subject of the next section.

2.4.2 Emptiness

We now want to develop a method that checks for a given PTA $\mathcal{A}$ whether $T(\mathcal{A})$ is empty or not. For the complementation construction we have used the membership game to characterise the acceptance of a tree by the automaton. The idea is that CONSTRUCTOR builds a run and SPOILER chooses a path through this run. The resulting game arena is infinite because the moves available at a certain node depend on the label of the tree at this node. For the emptiness problem we want to know whether there is a tree on which there is a run such that the acceptance condition is satisfied on each path:

$$\exists\text{tree}\exists\text{run}\forall\text{path}.(\text{path satisfies acceptance condition}).$$

Accordingly, we modify the membership game such that CONSTRUCTOR now builds a tree t and a run ρ on t at the same time. This allows us to remove the tree nodes from $\{0,1\}^*$ from the game positions because the moves do not depend on these nodes anymore. This makes the game graph finite.

The *emptiness game* for a PTA $\mathcal{A}$ has the following rules:

- The game positions are $Q \cup \Delta$ (states and transitions of $\mathcal{A}$).
- The initial position is q_{in}.
- From a position q (a state of $\mathcal{A}$) the game proceeds as follows:

  1 CONSTRUCTOR picks a transition (q,a,q_0,q_1),

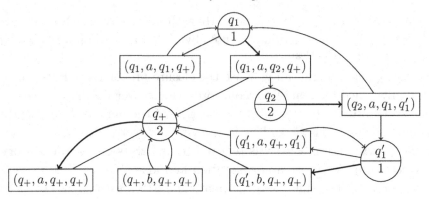

Figure 2.14 The emptiness game for the example PTA. The thick arrows define a winning strategy for CONSTRUCTOR

2 SPOILER chooses a direction and the game moves on to position q_0 or q_1.

- A play of this game is an infinite sequence of states and transitions. For the winning condition only the sequence of states is relevant: The winning condition for CONSTRUCTOR is the acceptance condition of $\mathcal{A}$.

This is a parity game on a finite game graph. In the same way as for the membership game we get the following lemma.

Lemma 2.18 *The language of the PTA $\mathcal{A}$ is not empty iff CONSTRUCTOR has a winning strategy in the emptiness game for $\mathcal{A}$.*

Consider the following example PTA $\mathcal{A}$ over the alphabet $\{a, b\}$ with state set $\{q_1, q_1', q_2, q_+\}$, initial state q_1, and the following transitions and priorities:

$$
\begin{array}{llll}
(q_1, a, q_1, q_+) & (q_1', a, q_+, q_1') & (q_+, a, q_+, q_+) & c(q_1) = c(q_1') = 1 \\
(q_1, a, q_2, q_+) & (q_1', b, q_+, q_+) & (q_+, b, q_+, q_+) & c(q_2) = c(q_+) = 2 \\
(q_2, a, q_1, q_1') & & &
\end{array}
$$

The emptiness game together with a winning strategy for CONSTRUCTOR is shown in Figure 2.14. The nodes of CONSTRUCTOR are labelled with the name of the state and the corresponding priority. The transitions do not have a priority in the game because they are not considered for the winning condition.

Since CONSTRUCTOR has a winning strategy we can deduce that there is a tree that is accepted by $\mathcal{A}$. Furthermore, from a positional winning strategy one can construct a finitely generated tree that is accepted by $\mathcal{A}$. The idea is that the strategy of CONSTRUCTOR associates to each state a

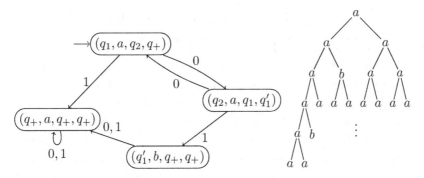

Figure 2.15 A finitely generated (regular) tree corresponding to the winning strategy depicted in Figure 2.14

unique transition to use. At the root we choose the transition associated to the initial state of $\mathcal{A}$. For a given transition SPOILER can choose the left or the right state. At the corresponding next node in the tree we choose the transition associated to this state. A compact representation of the resulting tree is shown on the left-hand side of Figure 2.15. Each transition has two outgoing edges, one labelled 0 for moving to the left successor in the tree, and one labelled 1 for moving to the right successor. The transition associated to the initial state of $\mathcal{A}$ is marked with the small incoming arrow. This graph can be seen as a finite automaton that reads names of tree nodes (words over $\{0, 1\}$) and outputs the transitions to be used in the run on the accepted tree. If we only output the label used in the transition, then we obtain the tree itself, which is shown on the right-hand side of Figure 2.15. It is labelled a everywhere except every second step to the right from the leftmost path.

Trees that are labelled in a regular way in the sense explained above are called **regular trees**.

Theorem 2.19 (Rabin [1969]) *The emptiness problem for parity tree automata is decidable. If the language is not empty, then one can construct a finite representation of a tree in the language.*

Using the translation from S2S to tree automata we obtain the decidability of the theory S2S, or more generally the decidability of the satisfiability for S2S formulae.

Corollary 2.20 (Rabin [1969]) *The satisfiability problem for S2S formulae is decidable.*

2.5 Beyond finite automata

In the previous sections we have considered games with winning conditions that can be described by finite automata. In this section we briefly discuss what happens if we move to non-regular winning conditions. A widely used extension of regular languages are the context-free languages, which can be defined in terms of context-free grammars or pushdown automata (see Hopcroft and Ullman [1979], Sipser [1997]). Even though we are interested in specifications over infinite words, we can use context-free languages of finite words, for example, we can declare a play winning for Eva if it does not contain a prefix that belongs to a given context-free language. Let us refer to this kind of winning condition as a context-free safety condition.

Proposition 2.21 *The problem of finding the winner in a game (G, Win), where Win is a context-free safety condition is undecidable.*

Proof We can give a reduction to the universality problem for context-free languages, i.e., the question of whether a given context-free language contains all words. This problem is known to be undecidable (e.g., Theorem 5.10 of Sipser [1997] or Theorem 8.11 of Hopcroft and Ullman [1979]).

Let L be a context-free language over some alphabet Σ. We aim at constructing a context-free safety game such that Eva has a winning strategy iff $L = \Sigma^*$. The game graph consists only of vertices for Adam, one for each symbol from Σ. The edge relation contains all possible edges. This means that Adam can freely choose a sequence over Σ. If we now consider the context-free safety condition defined by L, then one can easily see that Eva has a winning strategy iff $L = \Sigma^*$. Otherwise Adam can simply play the sequence corresponding to a word not in L. □

At the beginning of Section 2.3 we have considered the same kind of winning condition for regular languages. There we could easily solve the games by constructing a DFA for the given language and then solving a simple safety game on a finite graph. For context-free languages this does not work for two reasons. First of all, context-free languages are accepted by pushdown automata, and therefore taking the product with a finite graph will result in an infinite graph. Furthermore, we have seen that the method does not work if we use non-deterministic automata instead of DFAs (see Exercise 2.1). For the class of context-free languages deterministic pushdown automata are not enough, the non-determinism is required.

What happens if we avoid the second problem by considering winning conditions specified by deterministic pushdown automata? In fact, we can consider deterministic pushdown automata over infinite words by simply equipping a standard pushdown automaton with a parity condition on the state set. Acceptance is defined as before.

Assume *Win* is specified by a deterministic pushdown ω-automaton with parity condition. Taking the product of a game graph G with the pushdown automaton (in the same way as in Section 2.3) results in a parity game on a pushdown graph. These games can be solved and winning strategies can be implemented by pushdown automata.

Theorem 2.22 (Walukiewicz [1996]) *Parity games on pushdown graphs can be solved in exponential time and winning strategies can be implemented by pushdown automata.*

Note that as opposed to Proposition 2.21 the winning condition is specified directly as a parity condition on the pushdown graph. The proof of Theorem 2.22 that is given in Walukiewicz [1996] uses a reduction to games on finite graphs. A construction based on tree automata can be found in Vardi [1998].

As a consequence we obtain that specifications given by deterministic pushdown automata admit an algorithmic solution.

Corollary 2.23 *The problem of deciding the winner in a game (G, Win) for a finite game graph, where Win is defined by a deterministic pushdown ω-automaton (with parity condition), is decidable.*

The result from Theorem 2.22 on pushdown parity games has been extended to the model of higher-order pushdown automata (Cachat [2003]) which use nested stacks, and to the even more expressive model of collapsible higher-order pushdown automata (Hague et al. [2008]), which have a tight relationship to higher-order recursion schemes.

Instead of considering more complex game graphs it is also possible to study more complex winning conditions. This research has been initiated by Cachat et al. [2002], where it was shown that pushdown games with a winning condition of the following form are decidable: 'there exists some configuration (vertex of the game graph) that is visited infinitely often'. This condition has the flavour of a Büchi condition because it asks for some configuration to be visited infinitely often. But since the game graph is infinite and the configuration to be visited infinitely often is quantified existentially, this adds an extra level of complexity. Further results in this direction can be found in Bouquet et al. [2003], Serre [2004], Löding et al. [2004].

2.6 Conclusion

In this chapter we have introduced automata on infinite words and on infinite trees and have illustrated how they are connected to the theory of infinite games. In particular, automata on infinite words are useful for transforming complex winning conditions of infinite games into simpler ones (at the price of increasing the size of the game graph). For automata on infinite trees one can use results from game theory to prove the correctness of the complementation construction, and also to solve algorithmic problems like the emptiness problem. When going beyond finite automata, the problems become more difficult, but we have seen that some decidability results can be retained if the specifications are given by deterministic pushdown automata on infinite words.

The presentation in this chapter is given on a rather informal level. Many constructions are explained using examples without giving precise definitions and proofs. For the interested reader we give some references to other surveys that cover material presented in this chapter: A survey on infinite games and their connection to tree automata is given by Zielonka [1998], containing many algorithms for solving infinite games and problems for tree automata, and a precise analysis of memory requirements for different types of winning conditions. The survey by Thomas [1997] has already been mentioned several times in this chapter. It gives a nice overview of the main constructions in the theory of automata on infinite words and trees, the connections to logic, and also some basics on infinite games. The seminar volume by Grädel et al. [2002] contains many articles on various topics concerning automata on infinite objects, infinite games, and logic. The textbook by Perrin and Pin [2004] covers many aspects of the theory of automata on infinite words. Furthermore, similar to the theory of regular languages of finite words, the book also explains the basics of the algebraic theory of languages of infinite words. Finally, we mention the recent and very detailed survey on automata and logics for infinite words and trees that is given by Vardi and Wilke [2007].

References

A.-J. Bouquet, O. Serre, and I. Walukiewicz. Pushdown games with unboundedness and regular conditions. In *Proceedings of FST TCS 2003: Foundations of Software Technology and Theoretical Computer Science, 23rd Conference*, volume 2914 of *Lecture Notes in Computer Science*, pages 88–99. Springer, 2003.

J. R. Büchi. On a decision method in restricted second order arithmetic. In *International Congress on Logic, Methodology and Philosophy of Science*, pages 1–11. Stanford University Press, 1962.

J. R. Büchi. State-strategies for games in $F_{\sigma\delta} \cap G_{\delta\sigma}$. *The Journal of Symbolic Logic*, 48(4):1171–1198, December 1983.

J. R. Büchi and L. H. Landweber. Solving sequential conditions by finite-state strategies. *Transactions of the American Mathematical Society*, 138:295–311, 1969.

T. Cachat. Higher order pushdown automata, the Caucal hierarchy of graphs and parity games. In *Proceedings of Automata, Languages and Programming, 30th International Colloquium, ICALP 2003*, volume 2719 of *Lecture Notes in Computer Science*, pages 556–569. Springer, 2003.

T. Cachat, J. Duparc, and W. Thomas. Solving pushdown games with a Σ_3 winning condition. In *Proceedings of the Annual Conference of the European Association for Computer Science Logic, CSL 2002*, volume 2471 of *Lecture Notes in Computer Science*, pages 322–336. Springer, 2002.

A. Church. Logic, arithmetic and automata. In *Proceedings of the International Congress of Mathematicians*, pages 23–35, 1962.

T. Colcombet and K. Zdanowski. A tight lower bound for determinization of transition labeled Büchi automata. In *Proceedings of Automata, Languages and Programming, 36th Internatilonal Collogquium, ICALP 2009*, volume 5556 of *Lecture Notes in Computer Science*, pages 151–162. Springer, 2009.

E. A. Emerson and C. S. Jutla. The complexity of tree automata and logics of programs (exteded abstract). In *Proceedings of the 29th Annual Symposium on Foundations of Computer Science, FoCS '88*, pages 328–337, Los Alamitos, California, October 1988. IEEE Computer Society Press.

E. Grädel, W. Thomas, and T. Wilke, editors. *Automata, Logics, and Infinite Games*, volume 2500 of *Lecture Notes in Computer Science*. Springer, 2002.

Y. Gurevich and L. Harrington. Trees, automata and games. In *Proceedings of the 14th Annual ACM Symposium on Theory of Computing, STOC '82*, pages 60–65, 1982.

M. Hague, A. S. Murawski, C.-H. L. Ong, and O. Serre. Collapsible pushdown automata and recursion schemes. In *Proceedings of the Twenty-Third Annual IEEE Symposium on Logic in Computer Science, LICS 2008*, pages 452–461. IEEE Computer Society, 2008.

G. J. Holzmann. *The Spin Model Checker – Primer and Reference Manual*. Addison-Wesley, 2003.

J. E. Hopcroft and J. D. Ullman. *Introduction to Automata Theory, Languages, and Computation*. Addison Wesley, 1979.

D. Kähler and T. Wilke. Complementation, disambiguation, and determinization of Büchi automata unified. In *Proceedings of the 35th International Colloquium on Automata, Languages and Programming, ICALP 2008, Part I*, volume 5125 of *Lecture Notes in Computer Science*, pages 724–735. Springer, 2008.

L. H. Landweber. Decision problems for ω-automata. *Mathematical Systems Theory*, 3:376–384, 1969.

C. Löding, P. Madhusudan, and O. Serre. Visibly pushdown games. In *Proceedings of the 24th Conference on Foundations of Software Technology and Theoretical Computer Science, FST TCS 2004*, volume 3328 of *Lecture Notes in Computer Science*, pages 408–420. Springer, 2004.

R. McNaughton. Testing and generating infinite sequences by a finite automaton. *Information and Control*, 9(5):521–530, 1966.

A. R. Meyer. Weak monadic second order theory of succesor is not elementary-recursive. In *Logic Colloquium*, volume 453 of *Lecture Notes in Mathematics*, pages 132–154. Springer, 1975.

A. W. Mostowski. Games with forbidden positions. Technical Report 78, Uniwersytet Gdański, Instytut Matematyki, 1991.

D. E. Muller and P. E. Schupp. Simulating alternating tree automata by nondeterministic automata: New results and new proofs of the theorems of Rabin, McNaughton and Safra. *Theoretical Computer Science*, 141(1&2):69–107, 1995.

D. Perrin and J.-É. Pin. *Infinite words*, volume 141 of *Pure and Applied Mathematics*. Academic Press, London, 2004.

N. Piterman. From nondeterministic Büchi and Streett automata to deterministic parity automata. In *Proceedings of the 21st IEEE Symposium on Logic in Computer Science (LICS 2006)*, pages 255–264. IEEE Computer Society, 2006.

A. Pnueli. The temporal semantics of concurrent programs. *Theoretical Computer Science*, 13:45–60, 1981.

A. Pnueli and R. Rosner. On the synthesis of a reactive module. In *Proceedings of the Symposium on Principles of Programming Languages, POPL'89*, pages 179–190, 1989.

M. O. Rabin. Decidability of second-order theories and automata on infinite trees. *Transactions of the American Mathematical Society*, 141:1–35, July 1969.

M. O. Rabin. *Automata on Infinite Objects and Church's Problem*. American Mathematical Society, Boston, MA, USA, 1972.

K. Reinhardt. The complexity of translating logic to finite automata. In *Automata, Logics, and Infinite Games*, volume 2500 of *Lecture Notes in Computer Science*, pages 231–238. Springer, 2002.

R. Rosner. *Modular Synthesis of Reactive Systems*. PhD thesis, Weizmann Institute of Science, Rehovot, Israel, 1991.

S. Safra. On the complexity of omega-automata. In *Proceedings of the 29th Annual Symposium on Foundations of Computer Science, FoCS '88*, pages 319–327, Los Alamitos, California, October 1988. IEEE Computer Society Press.

S. Schewe. Tighter bounds for the determinisation of Büchi automata. In *Proceedings of Foundations of Software Science and Computational Structures, 12th International Conference, FOSSACS 2009*, volume 5504 of *Lecture Notes in Computer Science*, pages 167–181. Springer, 2009.

O. Serre. Games with winning conditions of high Borel complexity. In *Proceedings of Automata, Languages and Programming: 31st International Colloquium, ICALP 2004*, volume 3142 of *Lecture Notes in Computer Science*, pages 1150–1162. Springer, 2004.

M. Sipser. *Introduction to the Theory of Computation*. PWS Publishing Company, Boston, 1997.

W. Thomas. Languages, automata, and logic. In G. Rozenberg and A. Salomaa, editors, *Handbook of Formal Language Theory*, volume III, pages 389–455. Springer, 1997.

M. Y. Vardi. Reasoning about the past with two-way automata. In K. G. Larsen, S. Skyum, and G. Winskel, editors, *Proceedings of the 25th International Colloquium on Automata, Languages and Programming, ICALP'98*, volume 1443 of *Lecture Notes in Computer Science*, pages 628–641. Springer, 1998.

M. Y. Vardi and T. Wilke. Automata: from logics to algorithms. In *Logic and Automata – History and Perspectives*, volume 2 of *Texts in Logic and Games*, pages 629–724. Amsterdam University Press, Amsterdam, 2007.

M. Y. Vardi and P. Wolper. An automata-theoretic approach to automatic program verification (preliminary report). In *Proceedings, Symposium on Logic in Computer Science, 16-18 June 1986, Cambridge, Massachusetts, USA*, pages 332–344. IEEE Computer Society, 1986.

I. Walukiewicz. Pushdown processes: Games and model checking. In *Proceedings of the 8th International Conference on Computer Aided Verification, CAV '96*, volume 1102 of *Lecture Notes in Computer Science*, pages 62–74. Springer, 1996.

W. Zielonka. Infinite games on finitely coloured graphs with applications to automata on infinite trees. *Theoretical Computer Science*, 200(1-2):135–183, 1998.

3

Algorithms for Solving Parity Games

Marcin Jurdziński

University of Warwick

Abstract

This is a selective survey of algorithms for solving parity games, which are
infinite games played on finite graphs. Parity games are an important class of
omega-regular games, i.e., games whose payoff functions are computable by a
finite automaton on infinite words. The games considered here are zero-sum,
perfect-information, and non-stochastic. Several state-of-the-art algorithms
for solving parity games are presented, exhibiting disparate algorithmic
techniques, such as divide-and-conquer and value iteration, as well as hybrid
approaches that dovetail the two. While the problem of solving parity games
is in NP and co-NP, and also in PLS and PPAD, and hence unlikely to
be complete for any of the four complexity classes, no polynomial time
algorithms are known for solving it.

3.1 Games on graphs

A *game graph* (V, E, V_0, V_1) consists of a directed graph (V, E), with a set
of vertices V and a set of edges E, and a partition $V_0 \uplus V_1 = V$ of the set
of vertices. For technical convenience, and without loss of generality, we
assume that every vertex has at least one outgoing edge. An infinite game
on the game graph is played by two players, called player 0 and player 1,
player Even and player Odd, or player Min and player Max, etc., depending
on the context. A play of the game is started by placing a token on a starting
vertex $v_0 \in V$, after which infinitely many rounds follow. In every round, if
the token is on a vertex $v \in V_0$ then player 0 chooses an edge $(v, w) \in E$ going
out of vertex v and places the token on w, and if the token is on a vertex

$v \in V_1$ then player 1 moves the token in the same fashion. The outcome of such a play is then an infinite path $\langle v_0, v_1, v_2, \ldots \rangle$ in the game graph.

An infinite game on a graph consists of a game graph and a payoff function $\pi : V^\omega \to \mathbb{R}$. A **payoff function** assigns a payoff $\pi(\overline{v})$ to every infinite sequence of vertices $\overline{v} = \langle v_0, v_1, v_2, \ldots \rangle$ in the game graph. In this chapter we consider only zero-sum games, i.e., if the outcome of a play is the infinite path $\overline{v} \in V^\omega$ then player 0 (player Min) has to pay $\pi(\overline{v})$ to player 1 (player Max). We call a game on a graph a **qualitative game** if the payoff function is Boolean, i.e., if $\pi(V^\omega) \subseteq \{0, 1\}$. In qualitative games, we say that an outcome $\overline{v}$ is winning for player 0 if $\pi(\overline{v}) = 0$, and it is losing for player 0 otherwise; and vice versa for player 1. An alternative, and popular, way of formalising qualitative games is to specify a set $W \subseteq V^\omega$ of outcomes that are winning for player 1, which in our formalisation is $\pi^{-1}(1)$, i.e., the indicator set of the Boolean payoff function π.

A **strategy** for player 0 is a function $\mu : V^+ \to V$, such that if $v \in V^*$ and $w \in V_0$ then $(w, \mu(vw)) \in E$. Strategies for player 1 are defined analogously. Both players follow their strategies μ and χ, respectively, to produce an **outcome** $\mathrm{Outcome}(v_0, \mu, \chi) = \langle v_0, v_1, v_2, \ldots \rangle$ if for all $i \geq 0$, we have that $v_i \in V_1$ implies $v_{i+1} = \mu(v_0 v_1 \cdots v_i)$, and that $v_i \in V_2$ implies $v_{i+1} = \chi(v_0 v_1 \cdots v_i)$. A strategy $\mu : V^\omega \to V$ for player 0 is a **positional strategy** if for all $w, u \in V^*$ and $v \in V_0$, we have $\mu(wv) = \mu(uv)$, i.e., the values of μ are uniquely determined by the last element of its argument. It follows that a function $\mu : V_0 \to V$ uniquely determines a positional strategy for player 0, and we often do not distinguish between the two. Positional strategies for player 1 are defined analogously.

We say that a game, with a game graph (V, E, V_0, V_1) and a payoff function $\pi : V^\omega \to \mathbb{R}$, is determined if:

$$\sup_\chi \inf_\mu \pi(\mathrm{Outcome}(v, \mu, \chi)) = \inf_\mu \sup_\chi \pi(\mathrm{Outcome}(v, \mu, \chi)), \qquad (3.1)$$

for all $v \in V$, where μ and χ range over the sets of strategies for player 0 and player 1, respectively. Note that the inequality

$$\sup_\chi \inf_\mu \pi(\mathrm{Outcome}(v, \mu, \chi)) \leq \inf_\mu \sup_\chi \pi(\mathrm{Outcome}(v, \mu, \chi)) \qquad (3.2)$$

always, and trivially, holds. One interpretation of **determinacy**, i.e., when the converse of inequality (3.2) holds, is that player 0 (player Min) does not undermine her objective of minimising the payoff if she announces her strategy to player 1 (player Max) before the play begins, rather than keeping it secret and acting 'by surprise' in every round. An analogous interpretation holds for player 1.

The following fundamental theorem establishes that determinacy of games on graphs holds for a rich class of payoff functions.

Theorem 3.1 (Martin [1998])   *If the payoff function is bounded and Borel measurable then the game is determined.*

A game is ***positionally determined*** if the equality (3.1) holds for all $v \in V$, where χ on the left hand side of the equality, and μ on the right-hand side of the equality, respectively, are restricted to range over the sets of positional strategies for player 0 and player 1, respectively. In other words, if a game is positionally determined then players can announce their positional strategies with impunity. We say that a class of games enjoys ***positional determinacy*** if all games in this class are positionally determined.

If a game is determined then we define the ***game value*** $\mathrm{Val}(v)$ at vertex $v \in V$ to be the value of either side of equation (3.1). We say that a strategy μ of player 0 is an ***optimal strategy*** if $\sup_\chi \mathrm{Outcome}(v, \mu, \chi) = \mathrm{Val}(v)$ for all $v \in V$. Optimal strategies of player 1 are defined analogously. If the value of a qualitative game at a vertex v is 1 and player 1 has an optimal strategy then we say that the strategy is winning for player 1 from v. Similarly, if the value of a qualitative game at a vertex v is 0 and player 0 has an optimal strategy then we say that the strategy is a ***winning strategy*** for player 0 from v. We define the ***winning sets*** $\mathrm{win}_0(G)$ and $\mathrm{win}_1(G)$ to be the sets of vertices from which players 0 and 1, respectively, have winning strategies.

All games G considered in this chapter are determined, the payoff functions are Boolean, and both players have optimal strategies from every starting vertex. It follows that game values at all vertices are well defined, and from every vertex exactly one of the players has a winning strategy, i.e., $\mathrm{win}_0(G) \uplus \mathrm{win}_1(G) = V$.

The central algorithmic problem studied in this chapter is the computation of the values and optimal strategies for both players in games on graphs. The corresponding decision problem is, given a game graph, a starting vertex v, and a number t, to determine whether $\mathrm{Val}(v) \geq t$. For the special case of qualitative games, the problem of ***deciding the winner*** is, given a starting vertex v, to determine whether $v \in \mathrm{win}_1(G)$.

In order to formalise such algorithmic problems we have to agree on finitary representations of relevant classes of payoff functions. In this chapter we only consider ***Boolean payoff functions*** that can be uniquely specified by their indicator sets, i.e., the sets of outcomes winning for player 1.

Given a set of target vertices $T \subseteq V$, we define the ***reachability payoff*** function by setting its indicator set to:

$$\mathrm{Reach}(T) = \{\langle v_0, v_1, v_2, \ldots \rangle \; : \; v_i \in T \text{ for some } i \geq 0\}.$$

Similarly, for a set of safe vertices $S \subseteq V$, we define the **safety payoff** function by setting its indicator set to:

$$\mathrm{Safe}(S) = \{\langle v_0, v_1, v_2, \ldots \rangle \; : \; v_i \in S \text{ for all } i \geq 0\}.$$

Observe that $\mathrm{Reach}(T) = V^\omega \setminus \mathrm{Safe}(V \setminus T)$. It implies that from a **reachability game** with the target set $T \subseteq V$, by swapping the roles of players 0 and 1 and their payoff functions, we get a **safety game** with the safe set $V \setminus T$, and vice versa.

Given a set of target vertices $T \subseteq V$, we define the **repeated reachability payoff** function, also referred to as **Büchi payoff**, by setting its indicator set to:

$$\mathrm{Büchi}(T) = \{\langle v_0, v_1, v_2, \ldots \rangle \; : \; v_i \in T \text{ for infinitely many } i \geq 0\},$$

and for a set $S \subseteq V$ of safe vertices, we define the **eventual safety payoff** function, also known as **co-Büchi payoff**, function by setting its indicator set to:

$$\mathrm{co\text{-}Büchi}(S) = \{\langle v_0, v_1, v_2, \ldots \rangle \; : \; v_i \in S \text{ for all but finitely many } i \geq 0\}.$$

Again, the repeated reachability and eventual safety payoffs are dual in the sense that from a repeated reachability game with a set of target vertices $T \subseteq V$, by swapping the roles of players 0 and 1 and their payoff functions, we get an eventual safety game with the set of safe vertices $V \setminus T$, and vice versa.

For an infinite sequence $\bar{a} = \langle a_0, a_1, a_2, \ldots \rangle \in A^\omega$, we define its **infinity set** $\mathrm{Inf}(\bar{a})$ by:

$$\mathrm{Inf}(\bar{a}) = \{a \in A \; : \; a_i = a \text{ for infinitely many } i \geq 0\}.$$

Note that the infinity set of every infinite sequence must be non-empty if the set A is finite. For a **priority function** $p : V \to \{1, 2, \ldots, d\}$, we define the **parity payoff** function by setting its indicator set to:

$$\mathrm{Parity}(p) = \{\langle v_0, v_1, v_2, \ldots \rangle \in V^\omega : \max \mathrm{Inf}(\langle p(v_0), p(v_1), p(v_2), \ldots \rangle) \text{ is odd}\}.$$

3.2 Solving repeated reachability and eventual safety games

The main results presented in this section are positional determinacy of repeated reachability games and of eventual safety games, and a simple **divide-and-conquer algorithm** for solving them that runs in time $O(nm)$.

While the algorithm is simple and efficient, its design provides a blueprint
for a divide-and-conquer algorithm for solving parity games discussed in
Section 3.3.

Before we present the algorithm for solving repeated reachability games
we establish positional determinacy of reachability and safety games, and we
describe the structure of the winning sets in reachability and safety games.
For a set $T \subseteq V$ of target vertices, we define the *1-reachability set* by
$reach_1(T) = \bigcup_{i=0}^{\infty} reach_1^i(T)$, where:

$$reach_1^0(T) = T$$
$$reach_1^{i+1}(T) = reach_1^i(T)$$
$$\cup \{v \in V_1 : \text{there is } (v, w) \in E, \text{ such that } w \in reach_1^i(T)\}$$
$$\cup \{v \in V_0 : \text{for all } (v, w) \in E, \text{ we have } w \in reach_1^i(T)\}.$$

A positional strategy for player 1 that maps each of his vertices in a set
$reach_1^{i+1}(T) \setminus reach_1^i(T)$ to its successor in $reach_1^i(T)$ will be referred to as a *T-reachability strategy*. The *0-reachability set* $reach_0(T)$, and positional
T-reachability strategies for player 0, are defined in an analogous way.

Exercise 3.1 Argue that if player 1 follows a T-reachability strategy from
a vertex in $reach_1^i(T)$ then a vertex in T is reached in at most i rounds.
Conclude that if G is a reachability game with a target set $T \subseteq V$, then
$reach_1(T) \subseteq win_1(G)$.   □

A set $U \subseteq V$ is said to be a *1-closed set* if for every vertex $u \in U$,
if u belongs to player 0 then it has a successor in U, and if u belongs to
player 1 then all its successors are in U. A positional strategy for player 0
that maps each of her vertices in a 1-closed set U to a successor in U is called
a *U-trapping strategy*. Sets that are *0-closed*, and positional trapping
strategies for player 1, are defined analogously.

Exercise 3.2 Argue that the set $S = V \setminus reach_1(T)$ is 1-closed, and that
if player 0 follows an S-trapping strategy from a vertex in S then no vertex
in T is ever reached. Conclude that if G is a reachability game with a target
set $T \subseteq V$, then $V \setminus reach_1(T) \subseteq win_0(G)$, and that reachability and safety
games are positionally determined.   □

In the following exercise the reader is asked to provide vital implementation
details of an efficient algorithm for solving reachability and safety games.

Exercise 3.3 Give a detailed description of an algorithm for computing
the set $reach_1(T)$ that runs in time $O(m)$, where $m = |E|$ is the number of
edges in the game graph. Devise an appropriate data structure for directed

graphs, that for every vertex maintains the number of outgoing edges, to achieve this running time bound. □

Theorem 3.2 *Reachability and safety games are positionally determined. The winning sets and positional winning strategies of both players can be computed in time $O(m)$.*

In Figure 3.1 we present a divide-and-conquer algorithm for solving repeated reachability, and hence also for eventual safety, games. The algorithm takes a repeated reachability game G with the target set T as input, and it returns the pair $(win_0(G), win_1(G))$ of the winning sets of both players. The main insight behind the design of this algorithm is that the solution of a repeated reachability game can be obtained from the solution of a subgame that is also a repeated reachability game, and that has fewer vertices.

---

algorithm *Büchi-win*(G)
    if $reach_1(T) = V$
    then $(W_0, W_1) \leftarrow (\emptyset, V)$
    else
        $W_0' \leftarrow V \setminus reach_1(T)$
        $G'' \leftarrow G \setminus reach_0(W_0')$
        $(W_0'', W_1'') \leftarrow$ *Büchi-win*(G'')
        $(W_0, W_1) \leftarrow (V \setminus W_1'', W_1'')$
    endif
    return (W_0, W_1)

Figure 3.1 A divide-and-conquer algorithm for repeated reachability and eventual safety games

In a series of exercises we provide the detailed structure of an inductive correctness proof for the algorithm, and we invite the reader to fill in the details.

Exercise 3.4 Assume that $reach_1(T) = V$. Argue that if player 1 follows a positional T-reachability strategy from an arbitrary starting vertex $v \in V$, then a vertex in T occurs infinitely many times. Conclude that in this case $win_1(G) = V$. □

We say that a set $D \subseteq V$ is a *0-dominion* if it is 1-closed and player 0 has a D-trapping strategy that is winning for her from every starting vertex in D; the latter is called a *0-dominion strategy* on D. The definitions of a *1-dominion* and a *1-dominion strategy* are analogous.

Exercise 3.5   Assume that $reach_1(T) \neq V$, i.e., that $W_0' \neq \emptyset$. Observe that the set W_0' is 1-closed and that if player 0 follows a positional W_0'-trapping strategy μ' from a vertex in W_0' then no vertex in T is ever reached.

Argue that the set $reach_0(W_0')$ is 1-closed, and that a positional strategy $\overline{\mu'}$ that is the union of strategy μ' (on W_0') and a W_0'-reachability strategy (on $reach_0(W_0') \setminus W_0'$) is a $reach_0(W_0')$-trapping strategy. Prove that if player 0 follows strategy $\overline{\mu'}$ from a starting vertex in $reach_0(W_0')$ then vertices in T occur only finitely many times.

Conclude that $reach_0(W_0') \subseteq win_0(G)$, that sets W_0' and $reach_0(W_0')$ are 0-dominions, and that μ' and $\overline{\mu'}$ are 0-dominion strategies.   □

Let $G'' = G \setminus reach_0(W_0')$ be a repeated reachability game that is obtained from game G by removing vertices in the set $reach_0(W_0')$ and edges adjacent to them. Assume that the game G'' is positionally determined, and that there are positional 0-dominion and 1-dominion strategies μ'' and χ'' on the winning sets $W_0'' = win_0(G'')$ and $W_1'' = win_1(G'')$ respectively, in game G''.

Exercise 3.6   Observe that positional determinacy of game G'' implies that $reach_0(W_0') \cup W_0'' = V \setminus W_1''$. Prove that the positional strategy that is the union of $\overline{\mu'}$ and μ'' is a 0-dominion strategy on $V \setminus W_1''$ in game G. Conclude that $V \setminus W_1'' \subseteq win_0(G)$.

Prove that χ'' is a 1-dominion strategy on W_1'' in game G. Conclude that $W_1'' \subseteq win_1(G)$, that repeated reachability and eventual safety games are positionally determined, and that the algorithm *Büchi-win(G)* is correct.   □

Theorem 3.3   *Repeated reachability and eventual safety games are positionally determined.*

Note that the algorithm *Büchi-win(G)* solves two reachability games, and it makes one recursive call on a repeated reachability game $G'' = G \setminus reach_0(W_0')$ whose number of vertices is strictly smaller than that of G. It follows that its worst-case running time can be characterised by the recurrence:

$$T(n) \leq T(n-1) + O(m),$$
$$T(1) = O(1),$$

where $n = |V|$ and $m = |E|$ are the numbers of vertices and edges, respectively, of the game graph, and hence $T(n) = O(nm)$.

Theorem 3.4   *The winning sets and positional winning strategies of both players in repeated reachability and eventual safety games can be computed in time $O(nm)$.*

3.3 Solving parity games

This is the main technical part of this chapter, where we establish positional determinacy of parity games, we discuss the computational complexity of deciding the winner in parity games, and we present several state-of-the-art algorithms for solving them.

In Section 3.3.1 we present a natural generalisation of the divide-and-conquer procedure, presented in Section 3.2 for repeated reachability and eventual safety games, to parity games. While the idea of an inductive argument for construction of winning strategies in omega-regular games can be attributed to McNaughton [1993], here we follow the presentation of McNaughton's algorithm for parity games due to Zielonka [1998]. A by-product of the design and analysis of the algorithm is the fundamental result that parity games are positionally determined (Emerson and Jutla [1991]). We use positional determinacy to infer the result of Emerson et al. [1993] that the problem of deciding the winner in parity games is in NP and in co-NP. We also argue that the running time of the algorithm is $O(m \cdot ((n+d)/d)^d)) = O(n^{d+O(1)})$, where n is the number of vertices in the game graph, m is the number of edges, and $d = \max(p(V))$ is the biggest priority of a vertex in the parity game.

In Section 3.3.2 we present a refinement of the classical divide-and-conquer procedure, due to Jurdziński et al. [2008]. The innovation there is to dovetail the recursive divide-and-conquer procedure with a brute-force search for *dominions*, i.e., sets of vertices inside which a player can trap the opponent forever and win. It turns out that if the size of dominions sought is appropriately chosen then the overall running time of the divide-and-conquer algorithm is $n^{O(\sqrt{n})}$, which is better than $O(n^{d+O(1)})$ if $d = \Omega(n^{(1/2)+\varepsilon})$.

In Section 3.3.3 we present an altogether different algorithm for solving parity games, the progress measure lifting algorithm due to Jurdziński [2000]. The design of the algorithm is based on the concept of a game parity progress measure that witnesses the existence of a winning strategy for one of the players. We establish that relatively small such witnesses exist and that they can be computed in time $O(dm \cdot (n/(d/2))^{d/2}) = O(n^{d/2+O(1)})$, that is better than the divide-and-conquer algorithms of Sections 3.3.1 and 3.3.2 if $d = O(\sqrt{n})$. The procedure for computing progress measures can be viewed as a value iteration procedure that is approximating the least progress measure from below.

Finally, in Section 3.3.4 we present a refinement of the dovetailing divide-and-conquer scheme of Section 3.3.2 due to Schewe [2007]. Schewe's insight is that the dovetailing divide-and-conquer technique can be successfully

combined with an appropriately modified progress measure lifting algorithm
to achieve running time $O(n^{d/3+O(1)})$, which is the best currently known
running time bound for solving parity games with $d = O(\sqrt{n})$.

3.3.1 Divide and conquer

In Figure 3.2 we present a divide-and-conquer algorithm for solving parity
games that generalises the algorithm for solving repeated reachability and
eventual safety games from Section 3.2. The algorithm takes a parity game G
with the priority function $p : V \to \{1, 2, \ldots, d\}$ as input, and it returns the
pair $(win_0(G), win_1(G))$ of the winning sets of both players. Without loss
of generality, we assume that the set $p^{-1}(d)$, of the vertices with highest
priority d, is not empty.

Similarly to the algorithm for solving repeated reachability games, a
solution of the parity game is obtained from solutions of subgames that are
also parity games, and that have strictly smaller size. In contrast to the case of
repeated reachability games, the divide-and-conquer procedure $parity\text{-}win(G)$
may make two recursive calls, one on the subgame $G' = G \setminus reach_j(p^{-1}(d))$
and the other on the subgame $G'' = G \setminus reach_i(W_i')$, where the identity of
player j is determined by the parity of the highest priority d, player i is the
opponent of player j, and W_i' is the winning set of player i in subgame G'.

```
algorithm parity-win(G)
    j ← d mod 2 ; i ← 1 − j
    if reach_j(p^{-1}(d)) = V
    then (W_i, W_j) ← (∅, V)
    else
        G' ← G \ reach_j(p^{-1}(d))
        (W_0', W_1') ← parity-win(G')
        if W_i' = ∅
        then (W_i, W_j) ← (∅, V)
        else
            G'' ← G \ reach_i(W_i')
            (W_0'', W_1'') ← parity-win(G'')
            (W_i, W_j) ← (V \ W_j'', W_j'')
        endif
    endif
    return (W_0, W_1)
```

Figure 3.2 A divide-and-conquer algorithm for parity games

In a series of exercises similar to, and generalising, Exercises 3.4–3.6 we provide the detailed structure of an inductive correctness proof for the algorithm, and we invite the reader to fill in the details.

Exercise 3.7 Assume that $reach_j(p^{-1}(d)) = V$. Argue that if player j follows a positional $p^{-1}(d)$-reachability strategy from an arbitrary starting vertex $v \in V$, then a vertex in $p^{-1}(d)$ occurs infinitely many times. Conclude that in this case $win_j(G) = V$. $\qquad\square$

Assume that the games G' and G'' are positionally determined, and that there are positional i-dominion and j-dominion strategies μ' and χ' on the winning sets $W_i' = win_i(G')$ and $W_j' = win_j(G')$, respectively, in game G', and positional i-dominion and j-dominion strategies μ'' and χ'' on the winning sets $W_i'' = win_i(G'')$ and $W_j'' = win_j(G'')$, respectively, in game G''.

Exercise 3.8 Assume that $W_i' = \emptyset$. Argue that the positional strategy that is the union of χ' and the $p^{-1}(d)$-reachability strategy is a winning strategy for j from every starting vertex in game G. Conclude that in this case $win_j(G) = V$. $\qquad\square$

Exercise 3.9 Assume that $W_i' \neq \emptyset$. Argue that the positional strategy $\overline{\mu'}$ that is the union of μ' and the W_i'-reachability strategy is a positional i-dominion strategy on $reach_i(W_i')$ in game G.

Observe that positional determinacy of game G'' implies that $reach_i(W_i') \cup W_i'' = V \setminus W_j''$. Prove that the positional strategy that is the union of $\overline{\mu'}$ and μ'' is a positional i-dominion strategy on $V \setminus W_j''$ in game G. Conclude that $V \setminus W_j'' \subseteq win_i(G)$.

Prove that χ'' is a j-dominion strategy on W_j'' in game G. Conclude that $W_j'' \subseteq win_j(G)$, that parity games are positionally determined, and that the algorithm *parity-win*(G) is correct. $\qquad\square$

Theorem 3.5 (Emerson and Jutla [1991]) *Parity games are positionally determined.*

Before we carry out a detailed analysis of the worst-case running time of the algorithm *parity-win*(G), we observe that positional determinacy of parity games implies that the problem of deciding the winner in parity games is in NP and in co-NP.

A one-player parity game is a parity game in which either $V_0 = \emptyset$ or $V_1 = \emptyset$, i.e., one of the players owns all vertices in the game graph; in the former case we have a player 1 one-player parity game, and in the latter case we have a player 0 one-player parity game. An alternative, and for all purposes equivalent, definition of a one-player game requires that every

vertex of one of the players has exactly one outgoing edge. A typical example
of a one-player parity game of the latter kind is the strategy subgraph of a
positional strategy: given a positional strategy $\mu : V_0 \to V$ of player 0, its
strategy subgraph is obtained by removing all edges $(v, w) \in V_0 \times V$, such
that $w \neq \mu(v)$; strategy subgraphs of positional strategies of player 1 are
defined analogously. Naturally, a strategy subgraph of a positional strategy
of player 0 is a player 1 one-player game, and a strategy subgraph of a
positional strategy of player 1 is a player 0 one-player game.

Exercise 3.10   Consider a player 1 one-player parity game with a starting
vertex v. We say that a cycle in the game graph of a parity game is odd if the
highest priority of a vertex on that cycle is odd; the cycle is even otherwise.
Argue that player 1 is the winner in the game if and only if an odd cycle is
reachable from v in the game graph.

Design a polynomial time algorithm for deciding the winner in one-player
parity games.   □

It is now easy to establish that deciding the winner in parity games is
in NP: by positional determinacy it suffices to guess a positional strategy χ
for player 1, and that can be done in non-deterministic polynomial time,
and then to run the polynomial time algorithm from Exercise 3.10 on the
strategy subgraph of χ to verify that χ is a winning strategy for player 1. A
co-NP procedure for parity games is analogous: it suffices to swap players 1
and 0 in the above argument, *mutatis mutandis*.

Corollary 3.6 (Emerson et al. [1993])   *The problem of deciding the winner
in parity games is in NP and in co-NP.*

Now we are going to carry out a detailed analysis of the worst-case running
time of the algorithm *parity-win*(G). Note that the algorithm solves two
reachability games by computing sets $reach_j(p^{-1}(d))$ and $reach_i(W_i')$, and
it makes two recursive calls on parity games $G' = G \setminus reach_j(p^{-1}(d))$ and
$G'' = G \setminus reach_i(W_i')$, whose numbers of vertices are strictly smaller than
that of parity game G. It follows that its worst-case running time can be
characterised by the recurrence

$$T(n) \leq 2 \cdot T(n-1) + O(m),$$
$$T(1) = O(1),$$

where $n = |V|$ and $m = |E|$ are the numbers of vertices and edges, respectively,
of the game graph, and hence $T(n) = O(2^n)$.

In the following exercise we ask the reader to carry out a better analysis
of the worst-case running time of the algorithm *parity-win*(G), that takes

into account the maximum priority $d = \max(p(V))$ that occurs in the game graph. Let $n_d = |p^{-1}(d)|$ be the number of vertices with priority d.

Exercise 3.11 Observe that the maximum priority in the parity game $G' = G \setminus reach_j(p^{-1}(d))$ is strictly smaller than d.

Assume that the procedure *parity-win(G)* makes its second recursive call *parity-win(G'')*. Prove that if $reach_i(W_i')$ does not contain a vertex of priority d then $reach_i(W_i') = W_i'$, and that the procedure *parity-win(G'')* does not make any recursive calls (because the condition in the second if-statement obtains).

Argue that the worst-case running time of the procedure *parity-win(G)* can be characterised by the recurrence:

$$
\begin{aligned}
T(n, d, n_d) &\leq T(n, d-1, n_{d-1}) + T(n, d, n_d - 1) + O(m), \\
T(n, d, 1) &\leq 2 \cdot T(n, d-1, n_{d-1}) + O(m), \\
T(n, 1, n_d) &= O(n),
\end{aligned}
$$

and hence also by the recurrence:

$$
\begin{aligned}
T(n, d) &\leq (n_d + 1) \cdot T(n, d-1) + O(n_d m), \\
T(n, 1) &= O(n).
\end{aligned}
$$

Prove that $T(n, d) = O(m \cdot ((n+d)/d)^d) = O(n^{d+O(1)})$. $\qquad\square$

Theorem 3.7 (Emerson and Lei [1986], Emerson and Jutla [1991], Zielonka [1998]) *The winning sets of both players in parity games can be computed in time* $O(m \cdot ((n+d)/d)^d) = O(n^{d+O(1)})$.

3.3.2 Divide and conquer with dominion preprocessing

In this section we present a refinement of the divide-and-conquer algorithm for solving parity games from Section 3.3.1. The purpose of the refinement is to improve the worst-case running time of the algorithm for games with many priorities. More specifically, we present an algorithm for solving parity games that runs in time $n^{O(\sqrt{n})}$, and hence has better worst-case running time than the algorithm from Section 3.3.1 if $d = \Omega(n^{(1/2)+\varepsilon})$, i.e., if the number of priorities in parity games asymptotically exceeds the square root of the number of vertices.

In Figure 3.3 we present an algorithm for solving parity games that dovetails the divide-and-conquer approach of Section 3.3.1 with preprocessing of parity game graphs based on detecting and removing dominions of moderate size.

```
algorithm parity-win-dominion(G)

    n ← |V|; ℓ ← ⌈√(2n)⌉
    (D, i) ← dominion(G, ℓ); j ← 1 − i
    G* ← G \ reach_i(D)
    if D = ∅
    then (W_0, W_1) ← parity-win†(G*)
    else
         (W_0*, W_1*) ← parity-win-dominion(G*)
         (W_i, W_j) ← (V \ W_j*, W_j*)
    endif

    return (W_0, W_1)
```

Figure 3.3 A divide-and-conquer algorithm for parity games with dominion preprocessing

The procedure *parity-win-dominion(G)* takes a parity game G as input, and it returns the pair $(win_0(G), win_1(G))$ of the winning sets of both players.

Assume that the procedure *dominion(G, ℓ)* takes a parity game G and a number ℓ as input, and it returns a pair (D, i) such that D is an i-dominion of size at most ℓ if any such 0-dominion or 1-dominion exists, and it returns $(\emptyset, \perp)$ otherwise. Moreover, the procedure *parity-win†(G)* is a copy of the procedure *parity-win(G)* from Section 3.3.1 in which both recursive calls *parity-win(G')* and *parity-win(G'')* have been replaced by calls *parity-win-dominion(G')* and *parity-win-dominion(G'')*, respectively.

Exercise 3.12 Prove that the algorithm *parity-win-dominion(G)* is correct. Note that the procedures *parity-win-dominion(G)* and *parity-win†(G)* are mutually recursive, and then use an inductive argument similar to that for the algorithm *parity-win(G)* in Section 3.3.1. In particular, in order to justify the **else**-case in procedure *parity-win-dominion(G)*, the arguments similar to those applied to game G'' in Exercise 3.9 may be applied to game $G* = G \setminus reach_i(D)$. □

The rationale for dovetailing the divide-and-conquer approach and preprocessing based on detection and removal of dominions is that, if an appropriate trade-off is chosen between the size of dominions detected and removed, and the cost of detecting them, then the analysis of the worst-case running time of the divide-and-conquer algorithm carried out in Exercise 3.11 can be improved.

Exercise 3.13 Argue that procedure *dominion(G, ℓ)* can be implemented to have worst-case running time $O(n^\ell)$. Note that in order to achieve this running time it is sufficient to consider a naive brute-force search solution that (i) generates all $\binom{n}{\ell}$ sets of vertices of size at most ℓ, and (ii) for each of them verifies if they are 0-closed or 1-closed, and runs the $O(2^\ell)$ divide-and-conquer algorithm to check if they are a 0-dominion or a 1-dominion. □

Exercise 3.14 Assume that a brute-force search $O(n^\ell)$-time implementation of procedure *dominion*(G, ℓ) is used. Argue that the worst-case running time of the algorithm *parity-win-dominion*(G) can be characterised by the recurrence:

$$T(n) \leq T(n-1) + T(n - \ell(n)) + O(n^{\ell(n)}), \qquad (3.3)$$
$$T(1) = O(1).$$

First, argue that the worst case is when the *parity-win*$^\dagger(G)$ call is made in procedure *parity-win-dominion*(G), and then both *parity-win-dominion*(G') and *parity-win-dominion*(G'') calls are made in procedure *parity-win*$^\dagger(G)$. Then, argue that since the set $reach_i(W_i')$ is an i-dominion in game G, and since there is no dominion of size at most ℓ in G, it must be the case that the number of vertices in game $G'' = G \setminus reach_i(W_i')$ is at most $n - \ell(n)$. □

It turns out that if the maximum size $\ell(n)$ of dominions sought is chosen to be $\lceil \sqrt{2n} \rceil$, where $n = |V|$ is the number of vertices, then the size of the tree of recursive calls of algorithm *parity-win-dominion*(G) can be bounded by $n^{O(\sqrt{n})}$. It then follows that $T(n) = n^{O(\sqrt{n})}$.

Exercise 3.15 For every positive integer n, construct a labelled binary tree τ_n in the following way. The root of τ_n is labelled by n. A node labelled by a number $k > 3$ has two children: a left child labelled by $k - 1$ and a right child labelled by $k - \lceil \sqrt{2k} \rceil$. Nodes labelled by numbers 1, 2, and 3 are leaves.

Prove that on every path from the root of τ_n to one of its leaves there are at most $\lfloor \sqrt{2n} \rfloor$ right turns. Use induction and the fact that if $\frac{1}{2}j^2 < n \leq \frac{1}{2}(j+1)^2$ then $n - \lceil \sqrt{2n} \rceil \leq \frac{1}{2}j^2$. Conclude that the number of leaves of τ_n is $n^{O(\sqrt{n})}$, and that if the function $T(n)$ satisfies (3.3) for $\ell(n) = \lceil \sqrt{2n} \rceil$ then $T(n) = n^{O(\sqrt{n})}$. □

Theorem 3.8 (Jurdziński et al. [2008]) *The winning sets and positional winning strategies of both players in parity games can be computed in time* $n^{O(\sqrt{n})}$.

3.3.3 Value iteration: progress measure lifting

The divide-and-conquer algorithm from Section 3.3.1 solves parity games in time $O(m \cdot (n/d)^d) = O(n^{d+O(1)})$, and if $d = \Omega(n^{(1/2)+\varepsilon})$ then the dovetailing algorithm from Section 3.3.2 improves it to $n^{O(\sqrt{n})}$. In this section we present an altogether different algorithm, called the progress measure lifting algorithm, that runs in time $O(dm \cdot (n/(d/2))^{d/2}) = O(n^{d/2+O(1)})$, which is better than either of the other two algorithms if $d = O(\sqrt{n})$.

The design of the progress measure lifting algorithm is based on the concept of a progress measure that is a labelling of vertices in a parity game, which witnesses the existence of a positional dominion strategy in a parity game. Let $p : V \to \{1, 2, \ldots, d\}$ be a priority function, and without loss of generality, assume that d is even. In what follows we identify a function $\xi : V \to \mathbb{N}^{d/2}$ with a sequence of functions $\xi_{d-1}, \ldots, \xi_3, \xi_1 : V \to \mathbb{N}$, and hence $\xi(v) = (\xi_{d-1}(v), \ldots, \xi_3(v), \xi_1(v))$ for every $v \in V$. For a number $q \in \{1, 2, \ldots, d\}$, we write $\xi^{[q]}(v)$ for the tuple $(\xi_{d-1}(v), \ldots, \xi_{q+2}(v), \xi_q(v))$ if q is odd, and for the tuple $(\xi_{d-1}(v), \ldots, \xi_{q+3}(v), \xi_{q+1}(v))$ if q is even. We use the **lexicographic order** for comparisons between tuples of numbers, e.g., $(2, 3, 0) > (2, 2, 4)$ holds, but $(4, 0, 2, 1) \leq (4, 0, 1, 6)$ does not.

We say that a function $\xi : V \to \mathbb{N}^{d/2}$ is a **parity progress measure** if for every edge $(v, w) \in E$, we have that $\xi^{[p(v)]}(v) \geq \xi^{[p(v)]}(w)$, and if $p(v)$ is odd then the inequality is strict. Observe that an equivalent definition of a parity progress measure requires that for every vertex $v \in V$, we have that $\xi^{[p(v)]}(v) \geq \max_{(v,w)\in E} \xi^{[p(v)]}(w)$, and if $p(v)$ is odd then the inequality is strict, where the maxima are taken with respect to the lexicographic order.

Exercise 3.16   Let $\xi : V \to \mathbb{N}^{d/2}$ be a parity progress measure and let $q \in \{1, 3, \ldots, d-1\}$. Argue that on every infinite path, starting from an arbitrary vertex $v \in V$, the number of vertices of the odd priority q that occur before an occurrence of a vertex of priority bigger than q is bounded from above by $\xi_q(v)$. Conclude that for every infinite path, the maximum vertex priority that occurs infinitely many times is even.   □

We say that a function $\xi : V \to \mathbb{N}^{d/2}$ is a **game parity progress measure** if for every vertex $v \in V$, the following conditions hold:

> if $v \in V_0$, then $\xi^{[p(v)]}(v) \geq \min_{(v,w)\in E} \xi^{[p(v)]}(w)$,
> and if $p(v)$ is odd then the inequality is strict;

and

> if $v \in V_1$, then $\xi^{[p(v)]}(v) \geq \max_{(v,w)\in E} \xi^{[p(v)]}(w)$,
> and if $p(v)$ is odd then the inequality is strict.

Exercise 3.17 Let $\xi : V \to \mathbb{N}^{d/2}$ be a game parity progress measure. Consider the positional strategy μ for player 0 that maps every vertex $v \in V_0$ to a successor w that minimises $\xi^{[p(v)]}(w)$.

Use Exercise 3.16 to argue that for every infinite path in the strategy subgraph of μ, the maximum vertex priority that occurs infinitely many times is even. Conclude that the positional strategy μ is winning for player 0 from every starting vertex. □

The above exercise establishes that the existence of a game parity progress measure in a parity game G implies that player 0 has a positional winning strategy from every starting vertex, and hence that $\mathit{win}_0(G) = V$. The following slight refinement of the concept of a game parity progress measure gives us a more flexible tool for witnessing the existence of 0-dominion strategies on arbitrary 0-dominions.

For every positive integer i, consider an extension of the set of i-tuples of numbers by the top element $\top$ that is strictly bigger than every i-tuple. Moreover, let us adopt the notational convention that if $\xi : V \to \mathbb{N}^{d/2} \cup \{\top\}$ then $\xi(v) = \top$ implies that $\xi^{[q]}(v) = \top$ for every q. We say that a function $\xi : V \to \mathbb{N}^{d/2} \cup \{\top\}$ is a (partial) **game parity progress measure** if for every vertex $v \in V$, we have:

$$\text{if } v \in V_0 \text{ and } \xi(v) \neq \top, \text{ then } \xi^{[p(v)]}(v) \geq \min_{(v,w) \in E} \xi^{[p(v)]}(w),$$
$$\text{and if } p(v) \text{ is odd then the inequality is strict;} \tag{3.4}$$

and

$$\text{if } v \in V_1 \text{ and } \xi(v) \neq \top, \text{ then } \xi^{[p(v)]}(v) \geq \max_{(v,w) \in E} \xi^{[p(v)]}(w),$$
$$\text{and if } p(v) \text{ is odd then the inequality is strict.} \tag{3.5}$$

For a game parity progress measure $\xi : V \to \mathbb{N}^{d/2} \cup \{\top\}$, we write $dom(\xi)$ for the **domain** of function ξ, i.e., the set $\xi^{-1}(\mathbb{N}^{d/2})$ of the vertices for which the value of function ζ is not $\top$.

Exercise 3.18 Let $\xi : V \to \mathbb{N}^{d/2} \cup \{\top\}$ be a game parity progress measure. Prove that the set $dom(\xi)$ is a 0-dominion by exhibiting a positional 0-dominion strategy on $dom(\xi)$. Conclude that if $\xi : V \to \mathbb{N}^{d/2} \cup \{\top\}$ is a game parity progress measure on a parity game G then $dom(\xi) \subseteq \mathit{win}_0(G)$. □

Exercise 3.18 implies that the existence of a game parity progress measure with a non-empty domain is a sufficient condition for the existence of a 0-dominion strategy. In the following we establish that this condition is also necessary. Moreover, we argue that the **range** of a game parity progress measure can be bounded by a function of the size of a 0-dominion for which it serves as a witness. The explicit bound obtained plays a key role in the design and analysis of the (game parity) progress measure lifting algorithm.

For a set $D \subseteq V$ and for every odd q, let n_q^D be the number of vertices of priority q in D, and let M_D be the set of tuples $(x_{d-1}, \ldots, x_3, x_1) \in \mathbb{N}^{d/2}$, such that $x_q \in \{0, 1, \ldots, n_q^D\}$. For simplicity, we write n_q for the number n_q^V of vertices of priority q in the whole game graph. Note that the set $M_D \cup \{\top\}$ is totally ordered by the lexicographic order.

Exercise 3.19   Assume that $D \subseteq V$ is a 0-dominion. Prove that there is a game parity progress measure $\xi : V \to M_D \cup \{\top\}$, such that $D \subseteq dom(\xi)$.

One way to approach this task is to first invoke positional determinacy of parity games, and then to formalise the insight that the bounds, considered in Exercise 3.16, for the numbers of occurrences of vertices of an odd priority q before a vertex of priority higher than q occurs, can be 'optimised' not to exceed n_q^D. Another approach is to construct a progress measure $\xi : D \to M_D$ by induction on the size of D, similar to that employed in the design and the proof of correctness of algorithm *parity-win(G)*.   □

We now use the insight from Exercise 3.19, that game parity progress measures with 'small' ranges exist, to devise an efficient algorithm for finding such progress measures, and hence for finding 0-dominions if any exist. In fact, we argue that the ***pointwise-lexicographic least game parity progress measure*** ξ_* exists, and that its domain $dom(\xi_*)$ is the greatest possible, i.e., $dom(\xi_*) = win_0(G)$. Moreover, the algorithm computes this pointwise-lexicographic least progress measure, and it returns the pair $(win_0(G), win_1(G))$ of the winning sets of both players. The algorithm *progress-measure-lifting(G)*, shown in Figure 3.4 can be viewed as a ***value iteration*** procedure that computes the least solution ξ_* of the system of constraints expressed by conditions (3.4) and (3.5).

---

algorithm *progress-measure-lifting(G)*

    for all $v \in V$ do $\xi(v) \leftarrow (0, 0, \ldots, 0) \in \mathbb{N}^{d/2}$

    while $\xi < lift(\xi, v)$ for some $v \in V$

       do $\xi \leftarrow lift(\xi, v)$

    endwhile

    return $(dom(\xi), V \setminus dom(\xi))$

Figure 3.4 The progress measure lifting algorithm for parity games

The algorithm *progress-measure-lifting(G)* uses operators $lift(\cdot, v)$, for all

$v \in V$. In order to define this family of operators we recall the definition of the set M_D, and observe that $M_D \subseteq M_V$ for every $D \subseteq V$. In particular, the latter holds for $D = win_0(G)$ and hence, by Exercise 3.19, there is a game parity progress measure $\xi : V \to M_V \cup \{\top\}$, such that $dom(\xi) = win_0(G)$. For a function $\xi : V \to M_V \cup \{\top\}$ and a vertex $w \in V$, we define $lift(\xi, w) = \xi(w)$ if $w \neq v$, and we set $lift(\xi, v)$ to be the least element of $M_V \cup \{\top\}$ that makes the thus-defined function $lift(\xi, \cdot) : V \to M_V \cup \{\top\}$ satisfy the condition (3.4) or (3.5), respectively, at v.

The condition $\xi < lift(\xi, v)$ of the `while`-loop in the algorithm *progress-measure-lifting*(G) uses the strict inequality symbol $<$ to compare functions. It should be interpreted as the ***pointwise-lexicographic order***, in which for every vertex the lexicographic order on M_V is used, and for the strict pointwise-lexicographic inequality to hold it suffices that the strict lexicographic inequality holds for at least one vertex.

Exercise 3.20 Argue that for all $v \in V$, the operator $lift(\cdot, v)$ is monotone with respect to the pointwise-lexicographic order. Use the Knaster–Tarski theorem for complete lattices to conclude that the least game parity progress measure ξ_* exists in every parity game, and that the `while`-loop in algorithm *progress-measure-lifting*(G) computes it.

Conclude that $win_0(G) = dom(\xi_*)$, and hence that the algorithm *progress-measure-lifting*(G) is correct. □

Finally, we analyse the worst-case running time of algorithm *progress-measure-lifting*(G). The key element of the analysis of the algorithm is an upper bound on the size of the set M_V.

Exercise 3.21 Prove that $|M_V| = \prod_{q \in \{1, 3, \ldots, d-1\}} (n_q + 1) \leq (n/(d/2))^{d/2}$. Provide implementation details of the algorithm *progress-measure-lifting*(G) that make its worst-case running time $O(dm \cdot (n/(d/2))^{d/2})$. In order to establish this worst-case running time bound, use the property that the sum of all vertex out-degrees in a directed graph is $O(m)$, and that lexicographic comparison of $(d/2)$-tuples of numbers can be carried out in time $O(d)$. □

Theorem 3.9 (Browne et al. [1997], Seidl [1996], Jurdziński [2000]) *The winning sets and positional winning strategies of both players in parity games can be computed in time $O(dm \cdot (n/(d/2))^{d/2}) = O(n^{d/2 + O(1)})$.*

3.3.4 Divide and conquer with dominion preprocessing by progress measure lifting

The algorithms in Sections 3.3.2 and 3.3.3 apply very distinct techniques to efficiently solve parity games with a large and small, respectively, number of priorities relative to the number of vertices. In this section we show that the two techniques can be successfully combined to improve the worst-case running time from $O(dm \cdot (n/(d/2))^{d/2}) = O(n^{d/2+O(1)})$ of the latter algorithm to $O(n^{d/3+O(1)})$, which is the best currently known for parity games with $d = O(\sqrt{n})$. The improvement requires a vital modification of the progress measure lifting algorithm from Section 3.3.3.

In Section 3.3.3 we have introduced sets M_D of $(d/2)$-tuples of non-negative integers $(x_{d-1}, \ldots, x_3, x_1)$, where for each odd q the component x_q is bounded by the number n_q^D of vertices of priority q in a set $D \subseteq V$. We argued that this set was sufficiently large to express the values of the pointwise-lexicographic least game parity progress measure, and the algorithm *progress-measure-lifting(G)* computed the least progress measure by iterative application of the $lift(\cdot, v)$ operators.

In this section, for all integers $b > 0$, we consider an alternative set N_b of $(d/2)$-tuples of non-negative integers $(x_{d-1}, \ldots, x_3, x_1)$ that satisfy the condition $\sum_{\text{odd } q} x_q \leq b$. Note that for every $b > 0$, the set $N_b \cup \{\top\}$ is totally ordered by the lexicographic order on $(d/2)$-tuples of numbers, and the $lift(\cdot, v)$ operators can be appropriately modified to select only values in the set $N_b \cup \{\top\}$.

We argue that using sets N_b, for appropriately chosen numbers b, instead of using the set M_V, turns the algorithm *progress-measure-lifting(G)* into an efficient procedure for computing 0-dominions of moderate size, or establishing that no small 0-dominions exist. It is routine and straightforward to adapt the algorithm *progress-measure-lifting(G)* to compute 1-dominions of moderate size, or establishing lack thereof, too.

These combined procedures for computing 0-dominions and 1-dominions of moderate size are then used in a modification of the dovetailing algorithm *parity-win-dominion(G)* from Section 3.3.2, instead of using the brute-force search procedure *dominion(G, ℓ)*. We will refer to this modification of procedure *parity-win-dominion(G)* as procedure *parity-win-dominion†(G)*, the details of which are presented in Figure 3.5. Note that the procedure *parity-win‡(G)*, that is used in procedure *parity-win-dominion†(G)*, is a copy of the procedure *parity-win(G)* from Section 3.3.1 in which both recursive calls *parity-win(G′)* and *parity-win(G″)* have been replaced by calls *parity-win-dominion†(G′)* and *parity-win-dominion†(G″)*, respectively.

```
algorithm parity-win-dominion†(G)

    (D₀, D₁) ← progress-measure-lifting†(G, b)
    D* ← reach₀(D₀) ∪ reach₁(D₁)
    G* ← G \ D*

    if |D*| < b/2
    then (W₀*, W₁*) ← parity-win‡(G*)
    else (W₀*, W₁*) ← parity-win-dominion†(G*)
    endif

    (W₀, W₁) ← (reach₀(D₀) ∪ W₀*, reach₁(D₁) ∪ W₁*)
    return (W₀, W₁)
```

Figure 3.5 A divide-and-conquer algorithm for parity games with dominion preprocessing using modified progress measure lifting

For every integer $b > 0$, we define $\xi_{(b)}$ to be the game parity progress measure computed by the procedure *progress-measure-lifting(G)* that uses the set $N_b \cup \{\top\}$ instead of $M_V \cup \{\top\}$. We also write $\zeta_{(b)}$ for the analogous game parity progress measure for player 1 defined *mutatis mutandis*. In what follows, we write *progress-measure-lifting†(G, b)* for the procedure that combines the above-described modified versions of the progress measure lifting procedures for computing 0-dominions and 1-dominions, respectively, and that returns the pair of sets $(dom(\xi_{(b)}), dom(\zeta_{(b)}))$.

An important property of procedure *dominion(G, ℓ)* used in Section 3.3.2 was that if it failed to produce a dominion of size at most ℓ then there was no dominion of size at most ℓ in game G, and hence it followed that the argument G'' of the call *parity-win-dominion(G'')* in procedure *parity-win†(G)* had at most $n - \ell$ vertices. Unsurprisingly, a similar property holds for the procedure *progress-measure-lifting†(G, b)*: if $dom(\xi_{(b)}) = \emptyset$ then every 0-dominion in game G is of size strictly larger than b. However, in order to achieve the improved $O(n^{d/3+O(1)})$ upper bound for the running time of the algorithm *parity-win-dominion†(G)*, we need a stronger property that allows us to carry out analysis similar to that used in Exercise 3.11. We formulate this stronger property in the following exercise.

Exercise 3.22 Let $b > 0$ be even, and assume that $|dom(\xi_{(b)})| < b/2$. Argue that then $dom(\xi_{(b)}) = dom(\xi_{(b/2)})$, and that $reach_0(dom(\xi_{(b)})) = dom(\xi_{(b)})$.

Prove that there is no 0-dominion of size at most $b/2$ in the game $G \setminus reach_0(dom(\xi_{(b)}))$, using the property that the set of 0-dominions is closed under union. □

In order to achieve the worst-case running time bound $O(n^{d/3+O(1)})$ for the modified divide-and-conquer algorithm *parity-win-dominion*$^\dagger(G)$, we have to make an appropriate choice of the parameter b for the calls to the preprocessing procedure *progress-measure-lifting*$^\dagger(G, b)$. It turns out that a good choice for the analysis of the modified algorithm is $b = 2\lceil n^{2/3}\rceil$, where n is the number of vertices of the parity game in the top-level call of the algorithm *parity-win-dominion*$^\dagger(G)$.

Note that in order to facilitate the running-time analysis of the algorithm, the choice of the parameter b is fixed globally for all recursive calls. This is unlike procedure *parity-win-dominion*(G), in which the parameter ℓ has been always the function of the number of vertices in the actual argument G of each recursive call. It is worth noting that the analysis of the running time of the algorithm *parity-win-dominion*(G) carried out in Section 3.3.2 could have also been done with the parameter ℓ fixed at the top level throughout all recursive calls.

In the following exercise we analyse the worst-case running time of the preprocessing procedure *progress-measure-lifting*$^\dagger(G, b)$.

Exercise 3.23 Argue that $|N_b| = \binom{b+(d/2)}{d/2} = \prod_{i=1}^{d/2} \frac{b+i}{i}$. Prove that for all sufficiently large integers n, if $b = 2\lceil n^{2/3}\rceil$ then we have $\frac{b+1}{1} \cdot \frac{b+2}{2} \cdot \frac{b+3}{3} \cdot \frac{b+4}{4} \leq (n^{2/3})^4$, and $\frac{b+i}{i} \leq n^{2/3}$ for all $i \geq 3$, and hence that $|N_b| \leq n^{d/3}$ for all $d \geq 8$.

Conclude that if $b(n) = 2\lceil n^{2/3}\rceil$ then the worst-case running time of the procedure *progress-measure-lifting*$^\dagger(G, b(n))$ is $O(n^{d/3+O(1)})$. $\qquad\square$

We are now ready to complete the analysis of the worst-case running time of the divide-and-conquer algorithm *parity-win-dominion*$^\dagger(G)$. Observe that if the `else`-case in the algorithm *parity-win-dominion*$^\dagger(G)$ obtains then the argument of the only recursive call *parity-win-dominion*$^\dagger(G^*)$ is clearly a game with no more than $n - \lceil n^{2/3}\rceil$ vertices. On the other hand, if the `then`-case obtains instead, then within the call *parity-win*$^\ddagger(G^*)$ two recursive calls *parity-win-dominion*$^\dagger(G')$ and *parity-win-dominion*$^\dagger(G'')$ are made, the argument G' of the former has at most $d - 1$ priorities if G had d, and the number of vertices of the argument G'' of the latter is, by Exercise 3.22, at most $n - \lceil n^{2/3}\rceil$. In either case, for every $\lceil n^{2/3}\rceil$ decrease in size of game G^* or of G'', at most one recursive call is made to a game with at most $d-1$ priorities. Finally, each recursive call of procedure *parity-win-dominion*$^\dagger(G)$ leads to one call of procedure *progress-measure-lifting*$^\dagger(G, b)$ which, by Exercise 3.23, runs in time $O(n^{d/3+O(1)})$.

Exercise 3.24 Argue that the worst-case running time of the procedure *parity-win-dominion*[†](G) can be characterised by the recurrence:

$$T(n, d) \leq T(n, d-1) + T(n - \lceil n^{2/3} \rceil, d) + O(n^{d/3+O(1)}),$$
$$T(n, 1) = O(n),$$

and hence also by the recurrence:

$$T(n, d) \leq n^{1/3} \cdot T(n, d-1) + O(n^{d/3+O(1)}),$$
$$T(n, 1) = O(n).$$

Prove that $T(n, d) = O(n^{d/3+O(1)})$. □

Theorem 3.10 (Schewe [2007]) *The winning sets and positional winning strategies of both players in parity games can be computed in time* $O(n^{d/3+O(1)})$.

3.4 Related work

This survey of algorithms for solving parity games is not exhaustive. In particular, an important class of **local search algorithms** has not been included here. This class includes **strategy improvement algorithms**, inspired by policy iteration algorithms for **Markov decision processes** (Howard [1960], Puterman [2005]) and **stochastic games** (Filar and Vrieze [1997]), and various **pivoting algorithms** adapted from the theory of the **linear complementarity problem** (Cottle et al. [2009]).

The initial impulse for exploring applications of such local search algorithms to parity games has been the observation by Puri [1995] and Stirling [1995] that there is a polynomial time reduction from parity games to **mean-payoff games** and to **simple stochastic games**. The reduction has also been exploited by Jurdziński [1998] to show that the problems of deciding the winner in parity, mean payoff, discounted, and simple stochastic games are in UP and in co-UP.

Vöge and Jurdziński [2000] have been inspired by the reduction from parity games to discounted games to devise a **discrete strategy improvement** algorithm for parity games. This algorithm has been conjectured to have worst-case polynomial running time, but in a recent breakthrough Friedmann [2009] has dashed those hopes by exhibiting a family of parity games with $O(n)$ vertices on which the algorithm performs $\Omega(2^n)$ iterations. Intriguingly, working with parity games and the discrete strategy improvement algorithm has enabled Friedmann to devise examples of mean-payoff, discounted, and simple stochastic games that make the strategy improvement algorithm take exponentially many steps, a feat which had remained elusive ever since Howard [1960] proposed **policy iteration** algorithms for **Markov decision processes**. Fearnley [2010b] has adapted Friedmann's examples to make Howard's policy iteration take exponentially many iterations also on Markov decision processes, and hence exhibiting a surprising weakness of policy iteration and strategy improvement algorithms, even on (stochastic) one-player games. On the other hand, the proposal of Fearnley [2010a] to consider **non-oblivious strategy improvement** algorithms is a promising new way to explore strategy improvement in the quest for polynomial time algorithms, despite the damage inflicted to this line of research by Friedmann's examples.

Randomised variations of the strategy improvement technique, sometimes referred to as the **Random Facet** algorithms, have been proposed for simple stochastic games by Ludwig [1995] and Björklund and Vorobyov [2007]. They were inspired by a subexponential **randomised simplex algorithm** of Matoušek et al. [1996], and they were the first subexponential (randomised) algorithms for solving parity, mean-payoff, discounted, and simple stochastic games. A recent result of Friedmann et al. [2010] establishes that the Random Facet algorithm requires super-polynomial time on parity games.

An important corollary of the applicability of strategy improvement algorithms to solving games on graphs is that the **search problems** of **computing optimal strategies** in parity, mean-payoff, discounted, and simple stochastic games are in PLS (Johnson et al. [1988]). Moreover, those search problems are also known to be in PPAD (Papadimitriou [1994]) because they can be reduced in polynomial time (Gärtner and Rüst [2005], Jurdziński and Savani [2008]) to the **P-matrix linear complementarity problem** (Cottle et al. [2009]). The latter is in PPAD since it is processed by Lemke's algorithm (Lemke [1965], Papadimitriou [1994], Cottle et al. [2009]). It follows that the problems of computing optimal strategies in games on graphs are unlikely to be complete for either of the two important complexity classes of search problems, unless one of them is included in the other.

The reductions from games on graphs to the P-matrix linear complementarity problem have recently facilitated applications of classical algorithms for the linear complementarity problem to solving games. Fearnley et al. [2010] and Jurdziński and Savani [2008] have considered **Lemke's algorithm**, the **Cottle–Danzig algorithm**, and **Murty's algorithm** for discounted games, and they have shown that each of those pivoting algorithms may require exponential number of iterations on discounted games. Randomised versions of these algorithms require further study.

References

H. Björklund and S. Vorobyov. A combinatorial strongly subexponential strategy improvement algorithm for mean payoff games. *Discrete Applied Mathematics*, 155(2):210–229, 2007.

A. Browne, E. M. Clarke, S. Jha, D. E. Long, and W. R. Marrero. An improved algorithm for the evaluation of fixpoint expressions. *Theor. Comput. Sci.*, 178 (1–2):237–255, 1997.

R. W. Cottle, J.-S. Pang, and R. E. Stone. *The Linear Complementarity Problem*, volume 60 of *Classics in Applied Mathematics*. Society for Industrial & Applied Mathematics, 2009.

E. A. Emerson and C. Jutla. Tree automata, μ-calculus and determinacy. In *Foundations of Computer Science (FOCS)*, pages 368–377. IEEE Computer Society Press, 1991.

E. A. Emerson and C.-L. Lei. Efficient model checking in fragments of the propositional mu-calculus (Extended abstract). In *Logic in Computer Science (LICS)*, pages 267–278. IEEE Computer Society Press, 1986.

E. A. Emerson, C. S. Jutla, and A. P. Sistla. On model-checking for fragments of μ-calculus. In *Computer-Aided Verification (CAV)*, volume 697 of *LNCS*, pages 385–396. Springer, 1993.

J. Fearnley. Non-oblivious strategy improvement. In *Logic for Programming, Artificial Intelligence, and Programming (LPAR)*, 2010a. To appear.

J. Fearnley. Exponential lower bounds for policy iteration. In *International Colloquium on Automata, Languages and Programming (ICALP)*, volume 6199 of *LNCS*, pages 551–562. Springer, 2010b.

J. Fearnley, M. Jurdziński, and R. Savani. Linear complementarity algorithms for infinite games. In *Current Trends in Theory and Practice of Computer Science (SOFSEM)*, volume 5901 of *Lecture Notes in Computer Science*, pages 382–393. Springer, 2010.

J. Filar and K. Vrieze. *Competitive Markov Decision Processes*. Springer, Berlin, 1997.

O. Friedmann. An exponential lower bound for the parity game strategy improvement algorithm as we know it. In *Logic in Computer Science (LICS)*, pages 145–156. IEEE Computer Society Press, 2009.

O. Friedmann, T. D. Hansen, and U. Zwick. A subexponential lower bound for the Random Facet algorithm for parity games. Manuscript, April 2010.

B. Gärtner and L. Rüst. Simple stochastic games and P-matrix generalized linear complementarity problems. In *Fundamentals of Computation Theory (FCT)*, volume 3623 of *Lecture Notes in Computer Science*, pages 209–220. Springer, 2005.

R. A. Howard. *Dynamic Programming and Markov Process*. MIT Press, Cambridge, Massachusetts, 1960.

D. S. Johnson, C. H. Papadimitriou, and M. Yannakakis. How easy is local search? *J. Comput. Syst. Sci.*, 37(1):79–100, 1988.

M. Jurdziński. Small progress measures for solving parity games. In *Symposium on Theoretical Aspects of Computer Science (STACS)*, volume 1770 of *Lecture Notes in Computer Science*, pages 358–369. Springer, 2000.

M. Jurdziński. Deciding the winner in parity games is in UP $\cap$ co-UP. *Inf. Process. Lett.*, 63(3):119–124, 1998.

M. Jurdziński and R. Savani. A simple P-matrix linear complementarity problem for discounted games. In *Computability in Europe (CiE)*, volume 5028 of *LNCS*, pages 283–293. Springer, 2008.

M. Jurdziński, M. Paterson, and U. Zwick. A deterministic subexponential algorithm for solving parity games. *SIAM J. Comput.*, 38(4):1519–1532, 2008.

C. E. Lemke. Bimatrix equilibrium points and mathematical programming. *Management Science*, 11:681–689, 1965.

W. Ludwig. A subexponential randomized algorithm for the simple stochastic game problem. *Inf. Comput.*, 117(1):151–155, 1995.

D. A. Martin. The determinacy of Blackwell games. *J. Symb. Log.*, 63(4):1565–1581, 1998.

J. Matoušek, M. Sharir, and E. Welzl. A subexponential bound for linear programming. *Algorithmica*, 16:498–516, 1996.

R. McNaughton. Infinite games played on finite graphs. *Ann. Pure Appl. Logic*, 65 (2):149–184, 1993.

C. H. Papadimitriou. On the complexity of the parity argument and other inefficient proofs of existence. *J. Comput. Syst. Sci.*, 48:498–532, 1994.

A. Puri. *Theory of Hybrid Systems and Discrete Event Systems*. PhD thesis, University of California, Berkeley, 1995.

M. L. Puterman. *Markov Decision Processes: Discrete Stochastic Dynamic Programming*. Wiley Blackwell, 2005.

S. Schewe. Solving parity games in big steps. In *FSTTCS 2007*, volume 4855 of *Lecture Notes in Computer Science*, pages 449–460. Springer, 2007.

H. Seidl. Fast and simple nested fixpoints. *Inf. Process. Lett.*, 59(6):303–308, 1996.

C. Stirling. Local model checking games (Extended abstract). In *Concurrency Theory (CONCUR)*, volume 962 of *Lecture Notes in Computer Science*, pages 1–11. Springer, 1995.

J. Vöge and M. Jurdziński. A discrete strategy improvement algorithm for solving parity games (Extended abstract). In *Computer Aided Verification (CAV)*, volume 1855 of *Lecture Notes in Computer Science*, pages 202–215. Springer, 2000.

W. Zielonka. Infinite games on finitely coloured graphs with applications to automata on infinite trees. *Theor. Comput. Sci.*, 200(1–2):135–183, 1998.

4

Back and Forth Between Logic and Games

Erich Grädel

RWTH Aachen University

Abstract

In this chapter we discuss relationships between logic and games, focusing on first-order logic and fixed-point logics, and on reachability and parity games. We discuss the general notion of model-checking games. While it is easily seen that the semantics of first-order logic can be captured by reachability games, more effort is required to see that parity games are the appropriate games for evaluating formulae from least fixed-point logic and the modal μ-calculus. The algorithmic consequences of this result are discussed. We also explore the reverse relationship between games and logic, namely the question of how winning regions in games are definable in logic. Finally the connections between logic and games are discussed for more complicated scenarios provided by inflationary fixed-point logic and the quantitative μ-calculus.

4.1 Introduction

The idea that logical reasoning can be seen as a dialectic game, where a proponent attempts to convince an opponent of the truth of a proposition is very old. Indeed, it can be traced back to the studies of Zeno, Socrates, and Aristotle on logic and rhetoric. Modern manifestation of this idea are the presentation of the semantics of logical formulae by means of ***model-checking games*** and the algorithmic evaluation of logical statements via the ***synthesis of winning strategies*** in such games.

model-checking games are two-player games played on an arena which is formed as the product of a structure $\mathfrak{A}$ and a formula ψ where one player, called the Verifier, attempts to prove that ψ is true in $\mathfrak{A}$ while the other player, the Falsifier, attempts to refute this. In contrast to common definitions of the meaning of logical formulae which proceed bottom-up, from atomic formulae through the application of logical operators (such as connectives and quantifiers) to more complicated ones, game-theoretic semantics proceed top-down. Starting with a complicated sentence, Verifier and Falsifier try to justify their claims by moves to supposedly simpler assertions. By playing such an evaluation game the two players thus produce a sequence of formulae that ends when they reach an atomic statement, which cannot be simplified further. The Verifier has succeeded to justify her original claim if the atomic formula reached at the end of the sequence of is true, and Falsifier has won if it is false. We thus assume that the truth of atomic statements can be readily determined, for instance by a look-up in a table.

model-checking games permit us to evaluate logical formulae by solving **algorithmic problems on games** such as the computation of **winning regions** and the construction of **winning strategies**. For the most common logical systems, such as **first-order logic** (FO) or **propositional modal logic** (ML), the construction of the associated model-checking games is straightforward, and the games are simple in several senses. First of all, the goals of the players are the simplest conceivable objectives in such games, namely **reachability objectives**: each player tries to force the play to a terminal position where she has won (like check mate). Secondly, it is the case that in each move, the formula is strictly simplified, so that every play terminates after a number of moves that is bounded by the nesting depth of logical operators in the formula. In particular there are no infinite plays, and this holds no matter whether the structure on which the formula is evaluated is finite or infinite. Finally, in the case of finite game graphs, the winner of such a reachability game can be determined in linear time (with respect to the size of the game graph). Thus, algorithms for solving reachability games can be applied to evaluate first-order formulae, and give us a detailed complexity analysis for the model-checking problem of first-order logic on finite structures.

But life is not always that simple. For expressing properties of finite structures, and for defining combinatorial problems on classes of structures (such as graphs), first-order logic is rather limited. For many tasks arising in computer science there is thus a need of other kinds of logical systems, such as temporal logics, dynamic logics, game logics, transitive closure logics, fixed-point logics and so on, which extend a basic formalism like FO and ML by more powerful operators.

The natural model-checking games for such logics are more complicated than reachability games. In particular, they admit infinite plays. Essential ingredients in the description of such games are the winning conditions for infinite plays. Among the simplest of these are recurrence (or Büchi) conditions, which require that certain good states must occur infinitely often in a play, or eventual safety conditions, which impose that from some point onwards the play must stay outside a bad region. Of special importance for us are *parity games*. These are games of possibly infinite duration where we assign to each position a natural number, and the winner of an infinite play is determined according to whether the least number seen infinitely often in the play is even or odd. The importance of parity games is due to several reasons.

(1) Many classes of games arising in practical applications admit *reductions to parity games* (over larger game graphs). This is the case for games modelling reactive systems, with winning conditions specified in some temporal logic or in monadic second-order logic over infinite paths (S1S), for Muller games, but also for games with partial information appearing in the synthesis of distributed controllers.

(2) Parity games are *positionally determined*. This means that from every position, one of the two players has a winning strategy whose moves depend only on the current position, not on the history of the play. This property is fundamental for the algorithmic synthesis of winning strategies.

(3) Parity games arise as the model-checking games for *fixed-point logics* such as the modal μ-calculus or LFP, the extension of first-order logic by least and greatest fixed-points. Conversely, winning regions of parity games (with a bounded number of priorities) are definable in both LFP and the μ-calculus. Parity games are also of crucial importance in the analysis of structural properties of fixed-point logics.

The last point, the intimate relationship between parity games and fixed-point logic is a central theme of this chapter.

We shall start with an introduction to basic notions on reachability and parity games, explain the notions of winning strategies and winning regions and discuss algorithmic questions related to games. We study connections between logic and games for the special case of reachability games. In particular, we shall present in detail the model-checking games for first-order logic. After that, we introduce logics with least and greatest fixed points, such as LFP and the modal μ-calculus, and explain why parity games are appropriate evaluation games for these logics. We shall also discuss the algorithmic consequences of this result. Then, the reverse relationship between games and logic is explored, namely the question of how winning regions in games are definable in logic. We shall see that for parity games with a bounded number of priorities, winning regions are definable in both LFP and the modal μ-calculus. For parity games with an unbounded number of priorities it is not known whether the winning regions are LFP-definable. We show that this problem is intimately related to the open question of whether parity games are solvable in polynomial time. In the last two sections we shall discuss the relationship between logic and games for more complicated scenarios provided by **inflationary fixed-point logic** and the **quantitative μ-calculus**. In both cases, we can indeed find generalisations of parity games with a balanced two-way relationship to the associated fixed-point logic. On the one hand, we obtain appropriate evaluation games for all formulae in the logic, and on the other hand, the winning regions in the games are definable in the logic

4.2 Reachability games and parity games

We consider turn-based games where two players move a token through a directed graph, tracing out a finite or infinite path. Such a **graph game** is specified by a directed graph $G = (V, E)$, with a partition $V = V_0 \cup V_1$ of the nodes into positions of Player 0 and positions of Player 1. In case $(v, w) \in E$ we call w a successor of v and we denote the set of all successors of v by vE. A **play** in $\mathcal{G}$ is a finite or infinite path $v_0 v_1 \ldots$ formed by the two players starting from a given initial position v_0. Whenever the current position v_i belongs to V_0, then Player 0 chooses a successor $v_{i+1} \in v_i E$, if $v_i \in V_1$, then $v_{i+1} \in v_i E$ is selected by Player 1.

For **reachability games** we define the winning condition either by saying that Player σ loses at positions $v \in V_\sigma$ where no moves are possible, or by explicitly including the sets T_0, T_1 of winning terminal positions for each player into the description of the game. A play that is not won by any of the two players is called a **draw**. In reachability games, infinite plays are draws.

It is often convenient to have games without draws, so that Player 1 wins every play that is not won by Player 0, and vice versa. As the complement of a reachability condition is a **safety** condition this leads to a **reachability-safety game**: the winning condition is given by a set $T \subseteq V$; Player 0 wins a play if it reaches T, and Player 1 wins if it remains inside $V \setminus T$.

There is an extensive theory of games with more general winning conditions for infinite plays that are specified either by logical formulae from some logic on infinite sequences such as temporal logic (LTL), first-order logic (FO), or monadic second-order logic (S1S), or by automata-theoretic conditions such as Muller conditions, Streett–Rabin conditions, or parity conditions (see the contributions by Christof Löding and Marcin Jurdziński to this book). In this chapter, only parity conditions will be used.

A *parity game* is given by a game graph $\mathcal{G} = (V, V_0, V_1, E)$ together with a *priority function* $\Omega : V \rightarrow \omega$ assigning to each position a natural number. An infinite play $\pi = v_0 v_1 \ldots$ is won by Player 0 if the least priority appearing infinitely often in π is even, or no priority appears infinitely often (which may only happen if the range of Ω is infinite).

Winning strategies, winning regions, and determinacy. A (deterministic) *strategy* for Player σ is a partial function $f : V^* V_\sigma \rightarrow V$ that assigns to finite paths through $\mathcal{G}$ ending in a position $v \in V_\sigma$ a successor $w \in vE$. A play $v_0 v_1 \cdots \in V^\omega$ is *consistent* with f if, for each initial segment $v_0 \ldots v_i$ with $v_i \in V_\sigma$, we have that $v_{i+1} = f(v_0 \ldots v_i)$. We say that such a strategy f is *winning* from position v_0 if every play that starts at v_0 and that is consistent with f is won by Player σ. The *winning region* of Player σ, denoted W_σ, is the set of positions from which Player σ has a winning strategy.

A game $\mathcal{G}$, without draws, is called *determined* if $W_0 \cup W_1 = V$, i.e., if from each position one of the two players has a winning strategy. For games with draws, it is appropriate to define determinacy in a slightly different way: we call a game with draws determined if from each position, either one of the two players has a winning strategy, or both players have a strategy to achieve at least a draw. To put it differently, this means that from every position $v \in V \setminus W_\sigma$, Player $1 - \sigma$ has a strategy to guarantee that Player σ does not win. It has been known for almost 100 years that chess is determined in this sense, see Zermelo [1913]. However, we still do not know which of the three possibilities holds for the initial position of chess: whether White has a winning strategy, whether Black has one, or whether both players can guarantee a draw.

There is a large class of games that are known to be determined, including all games for which the winning condition is a Borel set (Martin [1975]). One can show (based on the Boolean Prime Ideal Theorem, which is a weak form of the the Axiom of Choice) that non-determined games exist. However, all games considered in this chapter are determined in a strong sense.

Computing winning regions of reachability games. To solve a game algorithmically means to compute the winning regions for the two players. When considering algorithmic problems of this kind, we always assume that game graphs are finite. For reachability games, the winning regions can easily be computed in polynomial time. Denote by W_σ^n the set of positions from which Player σ has a strategy to win the game in at most n moves. Then $W_\sigma^0 = \{v \in V_{1-\sigma} : vE = \emptyset\}$ is the set of winning terminal positions for Player σ, and we can compute the sets W_σ^n inductively by using

$$W_\sigma^{n+1} := W_\sigma^n \cup \{v \in V_0 : vE \cap W_\sigma^n \neq \emptyset\} \cup \{v \in V_1 : vE \subseteq W_\sigma^n\}$$

until $W_\sigma^{n+1} = W_\sigma^n$.

With a more sophisticated algorithm, which is a clever variant of depth-first search, one can actually compute the winning regions of both players in linear time $O(|V| + |E|)$ (see e.g., Grädel [2007]).

Theorem 4.1 *Winning regions of finite reachability games, and hence also reachability-safety games, can be computed in linear time.*

Further, the problem of computing winning regions of reachability games is complete for PTIME (see Greenlaw et al. [1995]).

Positional determinacy and complexity of parity games. Winning strategies can be very complicated objects since they may depend on the entire history of a play. However, for many important games, including reachability, safety, and parity games, it suffices to consider *positional strategies*, which are strategies that depend only on the current position, not on the history of the play. A game is *positionally determined*, if it is determined, and each player has a positional winning strategy on her winning region.

The positional determinacy of reachability games – and reachability-safety games – is obvious since the winning condition itself is purely positional. For parity games the positional determinacy is a non-trivial and fundamental result. It has been established independently by Emerson and Jutla [1991] and Mostowski [1991] for parity games with a finite game graph. This is generalised by Zielonka [1998] to infinite game graphs with a finite number of priorities. Finally positional determinacy has been extended by Grädel and Walukiewicz [2006] to parity games with $\mathrm{rng}(\Omega) = \omega$.

Theorem 4.2 *Every parity game is positionally determined.*

In a parity game $\mathcal{G} = (V, V_0, V_1, E, \Omega)$, a positional strategy for Player σ, defined on $W \subseteq V$, can be represented by a subgraph $H = (W, S) \subseteq (V, E)$ such that there is precisely one outgoing S-edge from each node $v \in V_\sigma \cap W$ and $vS = vE$ for each node $v \in V_{1-\sigma} \cap W$. On a finite game graph, such a strategy is winning on W if, and only if, the least priority on every cycle in (W, S) has the same parity as σ.

Hence, given a finite parity game $\mathcal{G}$ and a positional strategy (W, S) it can be decided in polynomial time, whether the strategy is winning on W. To decide winning regions we can therefore just guess winning strategies, and verify them in polynomial time.

Corollary 4.3 *Winning regions of parity games (on finite game graphs) can be decided in* NP $\cap$ Co-NP.

In fact, Jurdziński [1998] proved that the problem is in UP $\cap$ Co-UP, where UP denotes the class of NP-problems with unique witnesses. The best known deterministic algorithm has complexity $n^{O(\sqrt{n})}$) (Jurdziński et al. [2006]). For parity games with a number d of priorities the progress measure lifting algorithm by Jurdziński [2000] computes winning regions in time $O(dm \cdot (2n/(d/2))^{d/2}) = O(n^{d/2+O(1)})$, where m is the number of edges, giving a polynomial-time algorithm when d is bounded. The two approaches can be combined to achieve a worst-case running time of $O(n^{n/3+O(1)})$ for solving parity games with d priorities. These, and other, algorithms, are explained in detail in Jurdziński's contribution to this book.

4.3 Reachability games and logic

We now discuss connections between logic and games for the special case of reachability games. We assume that the reader is familiar with first-order logic.

(1) Computing winning regions of reachability games is equivalent, under very simple reductions, to computing minimal models for propositional Horn formulae.
(2) The model-checking games for first-order logic are reachability games.

We will then discuss the definability problem for winning regions of reachability games and see that more powerful formalisms than first-order logic are needed.

4.3.1 Games and Horn formulae

Recall that a **propositional Horn formula** is a conjunction of implication clauses of the form $Z \leftarrow X_1 \wedge \cdots \wedge X_k$ where $X_1, \ldots X_k$ are propositional variables, forming the **body** of the clause, and Z, the **head** of the clause, is either also a propositional variable, or the constant 0. Notice that the body of the clause can also be empty, in which case the clause takes the form

$Z \leftarrow 1$. (Indeed if a Horn formula contains no clause of this form, then it is trivially satisfiable by setting all variables to false.)

It is well known that SAT-HORN, the satisfiability problem for propositional Horn formulae, is PTIME-complete (see Greenlaw et al. [1995]) and solvable in linear time (Dowling and Gallier [1984], Itai and Makowsky [1987]). Hence its computational properties are very similar to those of reachability games. Actually there is a simple way of going back and forth between solving reachability games and finding satisfying assignments for Horn formulae, so that the two problems are solved by essentially the same algorithms.

From reachability games to Horn formulae: Given a finite game graph $\mathcal{G} = (V, V_0, V_1, E)$, we can construct in linear time a propositional Horn formula $\psi_{\mathcal{G}}$ consisting of the clauses $u \leftarrow v$ for all edges $(u, v) \in E$ with $u \in V_0$, and the clauses $u \leftarrow v_1 \wedge \cdots \wedge v_m$ for all nodes $u \in V_1$, where $uE = \{v_1, \ldots, v_m\}$. It is easy to see that the winning region W_0 for Player 0 in $\mathcal{G}$ coincides with the minimal model for $\psi_{\mathcal{G}}$. Hence $v \in W_0$ if the Horn formula $\psi_{\mathcal{G}} \wedge (0 \leftarrow v)$ is unsatisfiable.

From Horn formulae to reachability games: With a Horn formula $\psi = \bigwedge_{i \in I} C_i$ with propositional variables $X_1, \ldots, X_n$ and Horn clauses C_i of the form $Z_i \leftarrow X_{i_1} \wedge \cdots X_{i_m}$ we associate a game $\mathcal{G}_\psi$ as follows. The positions of Player 0 are the initial position 0 and the propositional variables $X_1, \ldots, X_n$, and the positions of Player 1 are the clauses C_i of ψ. Player 0 can move from a position X to any clause C_i with head X, and Player 1 can move from a clause C_i to any variable occurring in the body of C_i. Formally, $\mathcal{G}_\psi = (V, E)$, $V = V_0 \cup V_1$ with $V_0 = \{0\} \cup \{X_1, \ldots, X_n\}$, $V_1 = \{C_i : i \in I\}$, and

$$E = \{(X, C) \in V_0 \times V_1 : X = \text{head}(C)\} \cup$$
$$\{(C, X) \in V_1 \times V_0 : X \in \text{body}(C)\}.$$

Player 0 has a winning strategy for $\mathcal{G}_\psi$ from position X if, and only if, $\psi \models X$. In particular, ψ is unsatisfiable if, and only if, Player 0 wins from position 0.

4.3.2 model-checking games for first-order logic

For a logic L and a domain $\mathcal{D}$ of structures, the **model-checking problem** asks, given a structure $\mathfrak{A} \in \mathcal{D}$ and a formula $\psi \in L$, whether it is the case that $\mathfrak{A} \models \psi$. Model-checking problems can be reformulated in game-theoretic terms using appropriate model-checking games. With a sentence ψ, a structure $\mathfrak{A}$ (of the same vocabulary as ψ), we associate a **model-checking game** $\mathcal{G}(\mathfrak{A}, \psi)$. It is played by two players, **Verifier** and **Falsifier**. Verifier (also called Player 0) tries to prove that $\mathfrak{A} \models \psi$, whereas Falsifier (also called

Player 1) tries to establish that the sentence is false. For first-order logic, the evaluation games are simple, in the sense that (1) all plays are finite (regardless of whether the input structure is finite or infinite) and (2) winning conditions are defined in terms of reachability.

Let us assume that $\mathfrak{A} = (A, R_1, \ldots, R_m)$ is a relational structure and ψ is a first-order sentence in negation normal form, i.e., built up from atoms and negated atoms by means of the propositional connectives $\wedge, \vee$ and the quantifiers $\exists, \forall$. Obviously, any first-order formula can be converted in linear time into an equivalent one in negation normal form. The model-checking game $\mathcal{G}(\mathfrak{A}, \psi)$ has positions $\varphi(\bar{a})$ where $\varphi(\bar{x})$ is a subformula of ψ which is instantiated by a tuple $\bar{a}$ of elements of A. The initial position of the game is the formula ψ.

Verifier (Player 0) moves from positions associated with disjunctions and with formulae starting with an existential quantifier. From a position $\varphi \vee \vartheta$, she moves to either φ or ϑ. From a position $\exists y \varphi(\bar{a}, y)$, Verifier can move to any position $\varphi(\bar{a}, b)$, where $b \in A$. Dually, Falsifier (Player 1) makes corresponding moves for conjunctions and universal quantifications. At atoms or negated atoms, i.e., positions $\varphi(\bar{a})$ of the form $a = a'$, $a \neq a'$, $R\bar{a}$, or $\neg R\bar{a}$, the game is over. Verifier has won the play if $\mathfrak{A} \models \varphi(\bar{a})$; otherwise, Falsifier has won.

Model-checking games are a way of defining the semantics of a logic. The equivalence to the standard definition can be proved by a simple induction.

Theorem 4.4 *Verifier has a winning strategy from position $\varphi(\bar{a})$ in the game $\mathcal{G}(\mathfrak{A}, \psi)$ if, and only if, $\mathfrak{A} \models \varphi(\bar{a})$.*

This suggests a game-based approach to model-checking: given $\mathfrak{A}$ and ψ, construct the game $\mathcal{G}(\mathfrak{A}, \psi)$ and decide whether Verifier has a winning strategy from the initial position.

4.3.3 Complexity of first-order model-checking

A model-checking problem has two inputs: a structure and a formula. We can measure the complexity in terms of both inputs, and this is what is commonly referred to as the **combined complexity** of the model-checking problem (for L and $\mathcal{D}$). However, in many cases, one of the two inputs is fixed, and we measure the complexity only in terms of the other. If we fix the structure $\mathfrak{A}$, then the model-checking problem for L on this structure amounts to deciding $\text{Th}_L(\mathfrak{A}) := \{\psi \in L : \mathfrak{A} \models \psi\}$, the L-**theory** of $\mathfrak{A}$. The complexity of this problem is called the **expression complexity** of the model-checking problem (for L on $\mathfrak{A}$). Especially in finite model theory, one often considers model-checking problems for a fixed formula ψ, which amounts to deciding the **model class** of ψ inside $\mathcal{D}$, $\mathrm{Mod}_{\mathcal{D}}(\psi) := \{\mathfrak{A} \in \mathcal{D} : \mathfrak{A} \models \psi\}$. Its complexity is the **structure complexity** of the model-checking problem (for ψ on $\mathcal{D}$).

Since reachability games can be solved in linear time, the size of the game graph directly gives us an upper bound for the time complexity for first-order model-checking. The size of the model-checking game $\mathcal{G}(\mathfrak{A}, \psi)$ is the number of different instantiations of the subformulae of ψ with elements from $\mathfrak{A}$. It depends on several parameters, including the cardinality of the structure $\mathfrak{A}$, the number of subformulae of ψ (which is of course bounded by the length ψ) and the **width** of ψ which is defined as the maximal number of free variables in subformulae of ψ. Clearly, $|\mathcal{G}(\mathfrak{A}, \psi)| \leq |\psi| \cdot |A|^{\mathrm{width}(\psi)}$, so the crucial parameter is the width of the formula: if we have subformulae with many free variables, then the number of instantiations, and thus the size of the game, becomes very large. In general the combined complexity and the expression complexity of first-order model-checking problem are PSPACE-complete. In turn, the game graphs have polynomial size for any class of first-order formulae with bounded width.

Theorem 4.5 *The model-checking problem for first-order logic is* PSPACE-*complete. For any fixed $k \geq 2$, the model-checking problem for first-order formulae of width at most k is* PTIME-*complete.*

Exercise 4.1 Prove the hardness results. Reduce QBF, the problem of evaluating quantified Boolean formulae, to the model-checking problem for first-order logic on a fixed structure with two elements. Reduce the problem of solving reachability games to the model-checking problem for formulae of width 2.

By applying the game-based analysis of model-checking to the case of a fixed sentence ψ, we see that the structure complexity of first-order logic is much lower than the expression or combined complexity. In particular, the evaluation problem for any fixed first-order sentence can be computed deterministically in logarithmic space.

For a detailed study of the complexity of first-order model-checking, giving precise complexity bounds in terms of deterministic and alternating complexity classes, the reader may consult Grädel [2007].

4.3.4 Definability of winning regions

Let $\mathcal{S}$ be a class of games, represented as structures of some fixed vocabulary. We say that **winning regions on $\mathcal{S}$ are definable in a logic L** if there exist formulae $\psi_0(x)$ and $\psi_1(x)$ of L that define, on each game $\mathcal{G} \in \mathcal{S}$, the winning regions W_0 and W_1 for the two players. This means that, for each game $\mathcal{G} \in \mathcal{S}$, and $\sigma = 0, 1$

$$W_\sigma = \{v \in \mathcal{G} : \mathcal{G} \models \psi_\sigma(v)\}.$$

We can view a logic L and class $\mathcal{S}$ of games as **balanced**, if on the one hand, $\mathcal{S}$ provides model-checking games for L, and on the other hand, the winning regions for games in $\mathcal{S}$ are definable in L.

While reachability games are appropriate model-checking games for first-order logic, the reverse relationship does not hold. Indeed it is well-known that the expressive power of first-order logic, for defining properties of finite or infinite structures, is rather limited. A general result making this precise is **Gaifman's Theorem**, saying that first-order logic can express only **local properties**. For an exact statement and proof of this fundamental result, we refer to Ebbinghaus and Flum [1999]. Perhaps the simplest query that is not local, and hence not first-order definable, is **reachability**: Given a directed graph $G = (V, E)$ and a starting node v, determine the set of all nodes that are reachable from v. This also implies that first-order logic is too weak for reachability games; indeed the reachability problem can be viewed as the problem of computing winning regions in the special case of one-player reachability games.

Theorem 4.6 *Winning regions of reachability games are not first-order definable.*

Thus, already for reachability games, and even more so for parity games, more powerful logics are required to define the winning regions. Appropriate logics for this are fixed-point logics that we are going to study in the next section. In particular, we shall see that LFP and parity games (with a bounded number of priorities) are balanced.

4.4 Logics with least and greatest fixed-points

Consider a formula $\psi(R, \bar{x})$ of vocabulary $\tau \cup \{R\}$ where $\bar{x}$ is a tuple of variables whose length matches the arity of R. Such a formula defines, for every τ-structure $\mathfrak{A}$, an **update operator** $F_\psi : \mathcal{P}(A^k) \to \mathcal{P}(A^k)$ on the class of k-ary relations on A, by

$$F_\psi : R \mapsto \{\bar{a} : (\mathfrak{A}, R) \models \psi(R, \bar{a})\}.$$

A **fixed-point** of F_ψ is a relation R for which $F_\psi(R) = R$. **Fixed-point logics** extend a basic logical formalism (such as first-order logic, conjunctive queries, or propositional modal logic) by formulae defining *fixed-points of relational operators*. Notice that, in general, fixed-points of F_ψ need not exist, or there may exist many of them. We therefore consider special kinds of fixed-points, such as least and greatest, and later inflationary and deflationary fixed-points, and we impose additional conditions on the relational operators to guarantee that these fixed-points exist.

We shall now describe some basic facts of fixed-point theory for powerset lattices $(\mathcal{P}(B), \subseteq)$, where B is an arbitrary (finite or infinite) set. An operator $F : \mathcal{P}(B) \to \mathcal{P}(B)$ is **monotone**, if it preserves inclusion, i.e., $F(X) \subseteq F(Y)$ whenever $X \subseteq Y$. A fixed-point X of F is called the **least fixed-point** of F if $X \subseteq Y$ for all fixed-points Y of F. Similarly, if all fixed-points of F are subsets of a fixed-point X, then X is the **greatest fixed-point** of F.

Theorem 4.7 (Knaster–Tarski) *Every monotone operator $F : \mathcal{P}(B) \to \mathcal{P}(B)$ has a least fixed-point $\mathbf{lfp}(F)$ and a greatest fixed-point $\mathbf{gfp}(F)$. Further, these fixed-points may be written in the form*

$$\mathbf{lfp}(F) = \bigcap \{X : F(X) = X\} = \bigcap \{X : F(X) \subseteq X\}$$
$$\mathbf{gfp}(F) = \bigcup \{X : F(X) = X\} = \bigcup \{X : F(X) \supseteq X\}.$$

A proof can be found in any standard exposition on fixed-point theory or fixed-point logics (see e.g., Grädel [2007]). Least fixed-points can also be constructed inductively. We call an operator $F : \mathcal{P}(B) \to \mathcal{P}(B)$ **inductive** if the sequence of its **stages** X^α (where α ranges over the ordinals), defined by

$$X^0 := \emptyset,$$
$$X^{\alpha+1} := F(X^\alpha), \text{ and}$$
$$X^\lambda := \bigcup_{\alpha < \lambda} X^\alpha \text{ for limit ordinals } \lambda,$$

is increasing, i.e., if $X^\beta \subseteq X^\alpha$ for all $\beta < \alpha$. Obviously, monotone operators are inductive. The sequence of stages of an inductive operator eventually reaches a fixed-point, which we denote by X^∞. The least ordinal β for which $X^\beta = X^{\beta+1} = X^\infty$ is called the **closure ordinal** of F.

Exercise 4.2 Prove that the *cardinality* of the closure ordinal of every inductive operator $F : \mathcal{P}(B) \to \mathcal{P}(B)$ is bounded by the cardinality of B. However, the closure ordinal itself can be larger than $|B|$. Prove this by an example.

Theorem 4.8 *For monotone operators, the inductively constructed fixed-point coincides with the least fixed-point: $X^\infty = \mathbf{lfp}(F)$.*

Proof As X^∞ is a fixed-point, $\mathbf{lfp}(X) \subseteq X^\infty$. For the converse, we show by induction that $X^\alpha \subseteq \mathbf{lfp}(F)$ for all α. As $\mathbf{lfp}(F) = \bigcap\{Z : F(Z) \subseteq Z\}$, it suffices to show that X^α is contained in all Z for which $F(Z) \subseteq Z$.

For $\alpha = 0$, this is trivial. By monotonicity and the induction hypothesis, we have $X^{\alpha+1} = F(X^\alpha) \subseteq F(Z) \subseteq Z$. For limit ordinals λ with $X^\alpha \subseteq Z$ for all $\alpha < \lambda$ we also have $X^\lambda = \bigcup_{\alpha<\lambda} \subseteq Z$. □

The greatest fixed-point can be constructed by a dual induction, starting with $Y^0 = B$, by setting $Y^{\alpha+1} := F(Y^\alpha)$ and $Y^\lambda = \bigcap_{\alpha<\lambda} Y^\alpha$ for limit ordinals. The *decreasing* sequence of these stages then eventually converges to the greatest fixed-point $Y^\infty = \mathbf{gfp}(F)$.

The least and greatest fixed-points are dual to each other. For every monotone operator F, the dual operator $F^d : X \mapsto \overline{F(\overline{X})}$ (where $\overline{X}$ denotes the complement of X) is also monotone, and we have that

$$\mathbf{lfp}(F) = \overline{\mathbf{gfp}(F^d)} \text{ and } \mathbf{gfp}(F) = \overline{\mathbf{lfp}(F^d)}.$$

4.4.1 Least fixed-point logic and reachability games

Least fixed-point logic (LFP) is defined by adding to the syntax of first-order logic the following *least fixed-point formation rule*: If $\psi(R, \overline{x})$ is a formula of vocabulary $\tau \cup \{R\}$ with only positive occurrences of R, if $\overline{x}$ is a tuple of variables, and if $\overline{t}$ is a tuple of terms (such that the lengths of $\overline{x}$ and $\overline{t}$ match the arity of R), then also

$$[\mathbf{lfp}\,R\overline{x} \,.\, \psi](\overline{t}) \text{ and } [\mathbf{gfp}\,R\overline{x} \,.\, \psi](\overline{t})$$

are formulae of vocabulary τ. The free first-order variables of these formulae are those in $(\mathrm{free}(\psi) - \{x : x \text{ in } \overline{x}\}) \cup \mathrm{free}(\overline{t})$.

Semantics. Since R occurs only positive in ψ, the update operator F_ψ, defined by ψ on any τ-structure $\mathfrak{A}$ (providing interpretations for all free variables in the formula) is monotone. We define that $\mathfrak{A} \models [\mathbf{lfp}\,R\overline{x} \,.\, \psi](\overline{t})$ if, and only if, $\overline{t}^{\mathfrak{A}}$ (the tuple of elements of $\mathfrak{A}$ interpreting $\overline{t}$) is contained in $\mathbf{lfp}(F_\psi)$. The definition for greatest fixed-points is analogous.

Obviously, LFP is a fragment of second-order logic. Indeed, by the Tarski–Knaster Theorem,

$$[\mathbf{lfp}\,R\overline{x} \,.\, \psi(R, \overline{x})](\overline{y}) \equiv \forall R((\forall \overline{x}(\psi(R, \overline{x}) \to R\overline{x})) \to R\overline{y})$$
$$[\mathbf{gfp}\,R\overline{x} \,.\, \psi(R, \overline{x})](\overline{y}) \equiv \exists R((\forall \overline{x}(R\overline{x} \to \psi(R, \overline{x})) \wedge R\overline{y}).$$

Perhaps the simplest example of a problem that is expressible in LFP, but not in first-order logic, is **reachability**: Given a graph $G = (V, E)$ and a starting point v, find the set of nodes that are reachable by a path from v. It is definable in LFP, by the formula

$$\psi(x) := [\mathbf{lfp}\, Rx \,.\, x = v \vee \exists z(Rz \wedge Ezx)](x).$$

Indeed, in any graph (G, v), the set $\psi^{G,v} := \{w : G, v \models \psi(w)\}$ is precisely the set of nodes reachable from w.

Exercise 4.3 Prove that the LFP-sentence

$$\psi := \forall y \exists z Fyz \wedge \forall y[\mathbf{lfp}\, Ry \,.\, \forall x(Fxy \to Rx)](y)$$

is an infinity axiom, i.e., it is satisfiable but does not have a finite model.

We have noticed above that winning regions of reachability and safety games are not first-order definable. However it not difficult to generalise the LFP-definition of reachability to **LFP-definitions for the winning regions of reachability (and safety) games**. Consider reachability-safety games $\mathcal{G} = (V, V_0, V_1, E, T)$ where Player 0 wants to reach T and Player 1 tries to stay outside of T. On such games, the winning region W_0 of Player 0 is uniformly definable by the LFP-formula $\psi_0(x) := [\mathbf{lfp}\, Wx \,.\, \varphi](x)$ with

$$\varphi(W, x) := Tx \vee (V_0 x \wedge \exists y(Exy \wedge Wy)) \vee (V_1 \wedge \forall y(Exy \to Wy)).$$

The complement of W_0, which is the winning region for Player 1 for her associated safety condition, is defined by a greatest fixed-point formula $\psi_1(x) := [\mathbf{gfp}\, Wx \,.\, \eta(W, x)](x)$ with

$$\eta(W, x) := \neg Tx \wedge (V_0 x \to \forall y(Exy \to Wy)) \wedge (V_1 \to \exists y(Exy \wedge Wy)).$$

This is just a special case of the **duality between least and greatest fixed-points** which implies that for any formula φ,

$$[\mathbf{gfp}\, R\bar{x} \,.\, \varphi](\bar{t}) \equiv \neg[\mathbf{lfp}\, R\bar{x} \,.\, \neg\varphi[R/\neg R]](\bar{t}),$$

where $\varphi[R/\neg R]$ is the formula obtained from φ by replacing all occurrences of R-atoms by their negations. (As R occurs only positively in φ, the same is true for $\neg\varphi[R/\neg R]$.) Because of this duality, greatest fixed-points are sometimes omitted in the definition of LFP. However, for studying the relationship between LFP and games it is much more convenient to keep the greatest fixed-points, and to use the duality (and De Morgan's laws) to translate LFP-formulae to *negation normal form*, i.e., to push negations all the way to the atoms.

4.4.2 Capturing polynomial time

Let φ be a formula such that, for any given structure $\mathfrak{A}$, the update operator $F_\varphi : \mathcal{P}(A^k) \to \mathcal{P}(A^k)$ is monotone and computable in polynomial time (with respect to $|A|$). Then also the fixed-points $\mathbf{lfp}(F_\varphi)$ and $\mathbf{gfp}(F_\varphi)$ are polynomial-time computable since the inductive constructions of least and greatest fixed points terminate after at most $|A|^k$ iterations of F_φ. Together with the fact that first-order operations are polynomial-time computable we can conclude, by induction, that every LFP-definable property of finite structures is computable in polynomial time.

Theorem 4.9 *Let ψ be a sentence in* LFP. *It is decidable in polynomial time whether a given finite structure $\mathfrak{A}$ is a model of ψ. In short,* LFP $\subseteq$ PTIME.

Further, we have already seen that LFP can define properties that are actually PTIME-complete, such as winning regions in reachability games. This leads to the question of whether LFP can express *all* properties of finite structures that are computable in polynomial time.

This is indeed the case when we consider *ordered finite structures*. We say that a logic L **captures a complexity class** C on a domain $\mathcal{D}$ of finite structures, if (1) for every fixed sentence $\psi \in L$, the complexity of evaluating ψ on structures from $\mathcal{D}$ is a problem in the complexity class C, and (2) every property of structures in $\mathcal{D}$ that can be decided with complexity C is definable in the logic L. For any finite vocabulary τ, we write $\mathrm{Ord}(\tau)$ for the class of all structures $(\mathfrak{A}, <)$, where $\mathfrak{A}$ is a finite τ-structure and $<$ is a linear order on (the universe of) $\mathfrak{A}$. It is one of the most influential results of finite model theory that for every model class $\mathcal{K} \subseteq \mathrm{Ord}(\tau)$ that is decidable in polynomial time, there exists a sentence $\psi \in$ LFP such that $\mathcal{K} = \{\mathfrak{A} \in \mathrm{Ord}(\tau) : \mathfrak{A} \models \psi\}$.

Theorem 4.10 (Immerman and Vardi) *On ordered finite structures, least fixed-point logic captures polynomial time.*

However, in the absence of a linear ordering, LFP fails to express all PTIME-properties. Indeed, there are quite trivial queries on unordered finite structures that are not LFP-definable. A simple example is the question of whether a given finite structure has an even number of elements.

The question of whether there exists a logic that captures PTIME on arbitrary finite structures, originally posed by Chandra and Harel [1982], is the most important open problem of finite model theory. The most promising candidates are suitable extensions of LFP (or other fixed-point logics). However, many people conjecture that no logic whatsoever can capture PTIME on the domain of arbitrary finite structures. Since there exist logics for NP this would imply that P $\neq$ NP.

4.4.3 model-checking games for least fixed-point logic

We now construct evaluation games for LFP-formulae. We make the following assumptions:

(1) Fixed-point formulae do not contain parameters. This means that in a subformula [**fp** $R\overline{x}$. φ] (where **fp** means either **lfp** or **gfp**), the formula $\varphi(R, \overline{x})$ contains no free first-order variables besides those in $\overline{x}$. This is no loss of generality since one can always eliminate parameters, but it may affect the complexity of model-checking algorithms.

(2) Formulae are in negation normal form, i.e., negations apply to atoms only. Due to the standard dualities of first-order operators and the duality of least and greatest fixed points, this is no loss of generality.

(3) Every fixed-point variable is bound only once and the free relation variables are distinct from the fixed-point variables. For every fixed-point variable T occurring in ψ, we write φ_T for the unique subformula in ψ of the form [**fp** $T\overline{x} . \eta(T, \overline{x})$].

(4) Finally, we require that each occurrence of a fixed-point variable T in φ_T is inside the scope of a quantifier. Again, this is no loss of generality.

For two fixed-point variables S, T, we say that S **depends** on T if T occurs free in φ_S. The transitive closure of this dependency relation is called the **dependency order**, denoted by $\sqsubseteq_\psi$. The **alternation level** $al_\psi(T)$ of T in ψ is the maximal number of alternations between least and greatest fixed-point variables on the $\sqsubseteq_\psi$-paths from T. The **alternation depth** $ad(\psi)$ of a fixed-point formula ψ is the maximal alternation level of its fixed-point variables.

For a structure $\mathfrak{A}$ and an LFP-sentence ψ, the arena of the model-checking game $\mathcal{G}(\mathfrak{A}, \psi)$ is defined as for first-order model-checking games, with additional moves for fixed-point formulae. The positions are subformulae of ψ instantiated by elements of $\mathfrak{A}$. The moves are as in the first-order game, except for the positions associated with fixed-point formulae and with fixed-point atoms. At such positions there is a unique move (by Falsifier, say) to the formula defining the fixed-point. For each fixed-point variable T in ψ, there is a unique subformula [**fp** $T\overline{x}$. $\varphi(T, \overline{x})](\overline{y})$ of ψ. From position [**fp** $T\overline{x}$. $\varphi(T, \overline{x})](\overline{b})$, Falsifier moves to $\varphi(T, \overline{b})$, and from any fixed-point atom $T\overline{c}$, she moves to the position $\varphi(T, \overline{c})$.

Notice that if ψ does not contain fixed-points, this game is the model-checking game for first-order logic. However, if we have fixed-points the games may now admit infinite plays. The winning condition for infinite plays will be a parity condition. To motivate the priority assignment let us discuss some special cases:

Consider a formula with just one **lfp**-operator, applied to a first-order formula. The intuition is that from position $[\textbf{lfp } T\overline{x} \, . \, \varphi(T, \overline{x})](\overline{b})$, Verifier tries to establish that $\overline{b}$ enters T at some stage α of the fixed-point induction defined by φ on $\mathfrak{A}$. The game goes to $\varphi(T, \overline{b})$ and from there, as φ is a first-order formula, Verifier can either win the φ-game in a finite number of steps, or force it to a position $T\overline{c}$, where $\overline{c}$ enters the fixed-point at some stage $\beta < \alpha$. The game then resumes at position $\varphi(\overline{c})$. As any descending sequence of ordinals is finite, Verifier will win the game in a finite number of steps. If the formula is not true, then Falsifier can either win in a finite number of steps or force the play to go through infinitely many positions of the form $T\overline{c}$. Hence, these positions should be assigned priority 1 (and all other positions higher priorities) so that such a play will be won by Falsifier. For **gfp**-formulae, the situation is reversed. Verifier wants to force an infinite play, going infinitely often through positions $T\overline{c}$, so **gfp**-atoms are assigned priority 0.

In the general case, we have a formula ψ with nested least and greatest fixed-points, and in an infinite play of $\mathcal{G}(\mathfrak{A}, \psi)$ one may see different fixed-point variables infinitely often. But one of these variables is then the smallest with respect to the dependency order $\sqsubseteq_\psi$. It can be shown that $\mathfrak{A} \models \psi$ if, and only if, this smallest variable is a **gfp**-variable (provided the players play optimally).

Hence, the priority labelling is defined as follows.

(1) Even priorities are assigned to **gfp**-atoms and odd priorities to **lfp**-atoms.
(2) If $S \sqsubseteq_\psi T$ and S, T are fixed-point variables of different kinds, then S-atoms should get a lower priority than T-atoms.
(3) All positions that are not fixed-point atoms, get a maximal (i.e., most irrelevant) priority.

This completes the definition of the game $\mathcal{G}(\mathfrak{A}, \psi)$. Note that the number of priorities in $\mathcal{G}(\mathfrak{A}, \psi)$ is essentially the alternation depth of ψ.

We want to prove that $\mathcal{G}(\mathfrak{A}, \psi)$ is indeed a correct model-checking game for ψ in $\mathfrak{A}$. The proof proceeds by induction on $\mathfrak{A}$. The interesting case concerns fixed-point formulae $\psi(\overline{a}) := [\textbf{gfp}T\overline{x} . \varphi(\overline{x})](\overline{a})$. By the inductive construction of greatest fixed-points, $\mathfrak{A} \models [\textbf{gfp}T\overline{x} . \varphi(\overline{x})](\overline{a})$ if, and only if, $(\mathfrak{A}, T^\alpha) \models \varphi(\overline{a})$ for all stages T^α of the **gfp**-induction of φ on $\mathfrak{A}$. Further, by the induction hypothesis, we know that, for every interpretation T_0 of T, $(\mathfrak{A}, T_0) \models \varphi(\overline{a})$ if, and only if, Player 0 has a winning strategy for the game $\mathcal{G}((\mathfrak{A}, T_0), \varphi(\overline{a}))$.

It suffices therefor to show that Player 0 wins the game $\mathcal{G} := \mathcal{G}(\mathfrak{A}, \psi(\overline{a}))$ if, and only if, she wins all games $\mathcal{G}((\mathfrak{A}, T^\alpha), \varphi(\overline{a})$. But this follows from a general fact on parity game, the so-called **Unfolding Lemma**.

The unfolding of a parity game. Let $\mathcal{G} = (V, V_0, V_1, E, \Omega)$ be a parity game that has at least one node with priority 0 and in which every node v with priority 0 has a unique successor $s(v)$ (i.e., $vE = \{s(v)\}$). This condition holds for the game $Gg(\mathfrak{A}, \psi(\overline{a}))$, since the positions of minimal priority are the fixed-point atoms $T\overline{b}$ which have unique successors $\varphi(\overline{b})$.

Let Z be the set of nodes with priority 0 and let $\mathcal{G}^-$ be the game obtained by deleting from $\mathcal{G}$ all edges $(v, s(v)) \in E \cap (Z \times V)$ so that the nodes in Z become terminal positions. The **unfolding** of $\mathcal{G}$ is a sequence $\mathcal{G}^\alpha$ (where α ranges over the ordinals) which all coincide with $\mathcal{G}^-$ up to the winning conditions for the terminal positions $v \in Z$. For every α, we define a decomposition $Z = Z_0^\alpha \cup Z_1^\alpha$, where Z_σ^α is the set of terminal positions $v \in Z$ at which we declare, for the game $\mathcal{G}^\alpha$, that Player σ has won. Further, for every α, we define W_σ^α to be winning region of Player σ in the game $\mathcal{G}^\alpha$. Note that W_σ^α depends of course on the decomposition $Z = Z_0^\alpha \cup Z_1^\alpha$ (also for positions outside Z). In turn, the decomposition of Z for $\alpha + 1$ depends on the winning sets W_σ^α in $\mathcal{G}^\alpha$. We set

$$Z_0^0 := Z$$
$$Z_0^{\alpha+1} := \{v \in Z : s(v) \in W_0^\alpha\}$$
$$Z_0^\lambda := \bigcap_{\alpha < \lambda} Z_0^\alpha \text{ for limit ordinals } \lambda.$$

By determinacy, $V = W_0^\alpha \cup W_1^\alpha$ for all α, and with increasing α, the winning sets of Player 0 are decreasing and the winning sets of Player 1 are increasing:

$$W_0^0 \supseteq W_0^1 \supseteq \cdots W_0^\alpha \supseteq W_0^{\alpha+1} \supseteq \cdots$$
$$W_1^0 \subseteq W_1^1 \subseteq \cdots W_1^\alpha \subseteq W_1^{\alpha+1} \subseteq \cdots .$$

Hence there exists an ordinal α (whose cardinality is bounded by the cardinality of V) for which $W_0^\alpha = W_0^{\alpha+1} =: W_0^\infty$ and $W_1^\alpha = W_1^{\alpha+1} =: W_1^\infty$. The crucial result on unfoldings of parity games states that these fixed-points coincide with the winning regions W_0 and W_1 of the original game $\mathcal{G}$.

Lemma 4.11 (Unfolding Lemma) $W_0 = W_0^\infty$ *and* $W_1 = W_1^\infty$.

For a proof, see Grädel [2007].

By ordinal induction, one can easily see that the games $\mathcal{G}((\mathfrak{A}, T^\alpha), \varphi(\overline{a}))$ associated with the **gfp**-induction of φ in $\mathfrak{A}$ coincide with the unfolding of the game $\mathcal{G} = \mathcal{G}(\mathfrak{A}, \psi(\overline{a}))$. By the Unfolding Lemma, we conclude that Player 0 wins the game $\mathcal{G}(\mathfrak{A}, \psi(\overline{a}))$ if, and only if, she wins all games $\mathcal{G}((\mathfrak{A}, T^\alpha), \varphi(\overline{a}))$. By the induction hypothesis this holds if, and only if, $(\mathfrak{A}, T^\alpha) \models \varphi(\overline{a})$ for all α, which is equivalent to $\mathfrak{A} \models \psi(\overline{a})$.

For least fixed-point formulae we can dualize the arguments.

Theorem 4.12   *Let ψ be a well-named and parameter-free LFP-formula in negation normal form, and let $\mathfrak{A}$ be a relational structure. Then Player 0 has a winning strategy from position $\psi(\overline{a})$ in the game $\mathcal{G}(\mathfrak{A}, \psi(\overline{a}))$ if, and only if, $\mathfrak{A} \models \psi(\overline{a})$.*

For future reference we note that the model-checking games $\psi(\mathfrak{A}, \psi)$ can not only be easily constructed from $\mathfrak{A}$ and ψ, but are also easily (i.e., first-order) definable inside $\mathfrak{A}$.

Theorem 4.13   *For every structure $\mathfrak{A}$ with at least two elements, and every formula $\varphi(\overline{x}) \in$ LFP the model-checking game $\mathcal{G}(\mathfrak{A}, \varphi)$ is first-order interpretable in $\mathfrak{A}$.*

For finite structures, the size of the game $\mathcal{G}(\mathfrak{A}, \psi(\overline{a}))$ (and the time complexity of its construction) is bounded by $|\psi| \cdot |A|^{\mathrm{width}(\psi)}$. Hence, for LFP-formulae of bounded width, the size of the game is polynomially bounded.

Corollary 4.14   *The model-checking problem for LFP-formulae of bounded width (and without parameters) is in NP ∩ Co-NP, in fact in UP ∩ Co-UP.*

By the complexity results for parity games mentioned at the end of Section 4.2, we obtain complexity bounds for LFP model-checking which are polynomial with respect to the size of the structure, but exponential in the width and the *alternation depth* of the formula.

Corollary 4.15   *The model-checking problem for LFP-formulae of bounded width and bounded alternation depth is solvable in polynomial time.*

We have imposed the condition that the fixed-point formulae do not contain parameters. If parameters are allowed, then, at least with a naive definition of width, Corollary 4.14 is no longer true (unless UP = PSPACE). The intuitive reason is that with parameters one can 'hide' first-order variables in fixed-point variables. Indeed, by Dziembowski [1996] the evaluation problem for quantified Boolean formulae can be reduced to the evaluation of LFP-formulae with two first-order variables (but an unbounded number of monadic fixed-point variables) on a fixed structure with three elements. Hence the expression complexity of evaluating such formulae is PSPACE-complete.

For LFP-formulae of unbounded width, our analysis in terms of model-checking games only gives only exponential time bound. This cannot be improved, even for very simple LFP-formulae (Vardi [1982]).

Theorem 4.16 *The model-checking problem for* LFP-*formulae (of unbounded width) is* EXPTIME-*complete, even for formulae with only one fixed-point operator, and on a fixed structure with only two elements.*

4.4.4 The modal μ-calculus

A fragment of LFP that is of fundamental importance in many areas of computer science (e.g., controller synthesis, hardware verification, and knowledge representation) is the modal μ-calculus L_μ. It is obtained by adding least and greatest fixed-points to propositional modal logic (ML) rather than to FO. In other words L_μ relates to ML in the same way as LFP relates to FO.

Modal logics such as ML and the μ-calculus are evaluated on transition systems (alias Kripke structures, alias coloured graphs) at a particular node. Given a formula ψ and a transition system G, we write $G, v \models \psi$ to denote that G holds at node v of G. Recall that formulae of ML, for reasoning about **transition systems** $G = (V, (E_a)_{a \in A}, (P_b)_{b \in B})$, are built from atomic propositions P_b by means of the usual propositional connectives and the modal operators $\langle a \rangle$ and $[a]$. That is, if ψ is a formula and $a \in A$ is an action, then we can build the formulae $\langle a \rangle \psi$ and $[a] \psi$, with the following semantics:

$$G, v \models \langle a \rangle \psi \text{ iff } G, w \models \psi \text{ for } some \ w \text{ such that } (v, w) \in E_a,$$
$$G, v \models [a] \psi \text{ iff } G, w \models \psi \text{ for } all \ w \text{ such that } (v, w) \in E_a.$$

If there is only one transition relation, i.e., $A = \{a\}$, then we simply write $\square$ and $\lozenge$ for $[a]$ and $\langle a \rangle$, respectively.

ML can be viewed as an extension of propositional logic. However, in our context it is more convenient to view it as a simple fragment of first-order logic. A modal formula ψ defines a query on transition systems, associating with G a set of nodes $\psi^G := \{v : G, v \models \psi\}$, and this set can be defined equivalently by a first-order formula $\psi^*(x)$. This translation maps atomic propositions P_b to atoms $P_b x$, it commutes with the Boolean connectives, and it translates the modal operators by use of quantifiers as follows:

$$(\langle a \rangle \psi)^*(x) := \exists y (E_a xy \wedge \psi^*(y))$$
$$([a]\psi)^*(x) := \forall y (E_a xy \rightarrow \psi^*(y)).$$

Note that the resulting formula has width 2 and can thus be written with only two variables.

Theorem 4.17 *For every formula $\psi \in$ ML, there exists a first-order formula $\psi^*(x)$ of width 2, which is equivalent to ψ in the sense that $G, v \models \psi$ iff $G \models \psi^*(v)$.*

The **modal μ-calculus** L_μ extends ML by the following rule for building fixed-point formulae: If ψ is a formula in L_μ and X is a propositional variable that only occurs positively in ψ, then $\mu X.\psi$ and $\nu X.\psi$ are also L_μ-formulae.

The semantics of these fixed-point formulae is completely analogous to that for LFP. The formula ψ defines on G (with universe V, and with interpretations for other free second-order variables that ψ may have besides X) the monotone operator $F_\psi : \mathcal{P}(V) \rightarrow \mathcal{P}(V)$ assigning to every set $X \subseteq V$ the set $\psi^G(X) := \{v \in V : (G, X), v \models \psi\}$. Now,

$$G, v \models \mu X.\psi \text{ iff } v \in \mathbf{lfp}(F_\psi)$$
$$G, v \models \nu X.\psi \text{ iff } v \in \mathbf{gfp}(F_\psi).$$

Example 4.18 The formula $\mu X.\varphi \vee \langle a \rangle X$ asserts that there exists a path along a-transitions to a node where φ holds. The formula $\nu X.\mu Y.\langle a \rangle ((\varphi \wedge X) \vee Y)$ says that there exists a path from the current node on which φ holds infinitely often.

Exercise 4.4 Prove that the formulae in Example 4.18 do indeed express the stated properties.

The translation from ML into FO extends to a translation from L_μ into LFP.

Theorem 4.19 *Every formula $\psi \in L_\mu$ is equivalent to a formula $\psi^*(x) \in$ LFP of width two.*

Further the argument proving that LFP can be embedded into second-order logic also shows that L_μ is a fragment of **monadic second-order logic** (MSO).

The model-checking games for LFP easily translate into **games for the μ-calculus**. Given a formula $\psi \in L_\mu$ and a transition system $\mathcal{K}$, we obtain a parity game $\mathcal{G}(\mathcal{K}, \psi)$, with positions (φ, v) where φ is a subformula of ψ and

v is a node of $\mathcal{K}$, such that $\mathcal{K}, v \models \varphi$ if, and only if, Player 0 has a winning strategy in $\mathcal{G}(\mathcal{K}, \psi)$ from position (φ, v). As a consequence, an efficient algorithm for solving parity games would also solve the model-checking problem for L_μ.

Since L_μ-formulae can be seen as LFP-formulae of width two, the bounds established in the previous section apply: The model-checking problem for L_μ is in UP $\cap$ Co-UP, and it is a major open problem whether it can be solved in polynomial time. For L_μ-formulae of bounded alternation depths, the associated parity games have a bounded number of priorities and can therefore be solved in polynomial time.

Also the structure complexity can be settled easily. Since L_μ is a fragment of LFP, all properties expressible in L_μ are decidable in polynomial time. Further, there exist $\psi \in L_\mu$ for which the model-checking problem is PTIME-complete. Indeed, winning regions of reachability games are definable not only in LFP, but also in the μ-calculus. In a game $G = (V, V_0, V_1, E)$, Player 0 has a winning strategy from v if, and only if, $G, v \models \mu X.((V_0 \wedge \Diamond X) \vee (V_1 \wedge \Box X))$.

Despite this result, the μ-calculus is far away from a logic that would capture PTIME. Since L_μ is a fragment of MSO, all word languages definable in L_μ are *regular languages*, and of course, not all PTIME-languages are regular.

4.5 Definability of winning regions in parity games

We have seen that the model-checking problem for the LFP and the modal μ-calculus can be reduced to the problem of computing winning regions in parity games. We now discuss the question of whether, and under what conditions, winning regions of parity games are definable in LFP and the μ-calculus.

To study questions of logical definability for parity games (V, V_0, V_1, E, Ω) we need to represent the games as relational structures. We distinguish between two cases.

For fixed d, we consider parity games where the range of the priority function Ω is in $\{0, \ldots, d-1\}$ as structures $\mathcal{G} = (V, V_0, V_1, E, P_0, \ldots, P_{d-1})$ where $P_0, \ldots, P_{d-1}$ are pairwise disjoint unary relations such that P_i is the set of positions v with $\Omega(v) = i$. We denote this class of structures by $\mathcal{PG}_d$.

On the other hand, to consider classes of parity games with an *unbounded number of priorities*, we consider them as structures

$$\mathcal{G} = (V, V_0, V_1, E, \prec, \text{Odd})$$

where $u \prec v$ means that u has a smaller priority than v, and Odd is the set of nodes with an odd priority. We denote this class of structures by $\mathcal{PG}$.

In each case, when we say that winning regions of parity games are definable in a logic L, we mean that there is is a formula ψ_0 and ψ_1 of L such that for any structure $\mathcal{G} \in \mathcal{PG}$ (resp. $\mathcal{PG}_d$), ψ_σ is true in exactly those nodes in $\mathcal{G}$ from which Player σ has a winning strategy.

4.5.1 Parity games with a bounded number of priorities

For any fixed d, the winning regions of parity games in $\mathcal{PG}_d$ are definable by LFP-formulae with d nested fixed-point operators. For Player 0, the formula is

$$\psi_0^d(x) := [\mathbf{gfp}\ R_0 x \,.\, [\mathbf{lfp}\ R_1 x \,.\, \ldots\, [\mathbf{fp}\ R_{d-1} x \,.\, \varphi(x, R_0, \ldots, R_{d-1})](x) \ldots](x),$$

where

$$\varphi(x, R_0, \ldots, R_{d-1}) := \bigvee_{i<d} ((V_0 x \wedge P_i x \wedge \exists y\,(Exy \wedge R_i y)) \vee$$
$$(V_1 x \wedge P_i x \wedge \forall y\,(Exy \rightarrow R_i y))).$$

The fixed-point operators alternate between $\mathbf{gfp}$ and $\mathbf{lfp}$, and hence $\mathbf{fp} = \mathbf{gfp}$ if d is odd, and $\mathbf{fp} = \mathbf{lfp}$ if d is even.

Theorem 4.20 *For every $d \in \mathbb{N}$, the formula ψ_0^d defines the winning region of Player 0 in parity games with priorities $0, \ldots, d-1$.*

Proof In general, LFP-formulae are hard to understand, especially if they have many alternations between least and greatest fixed-points. However, in this case have an elegant argument based on model-checking games to prove that, for every parity game $\mathcal{G} = (V, V_0, V_1, P_0, \ldots, P_{d-1})$ and every position $v \in V$,

$$\mathcal{G} \models \psi_0^d(v) \iff \text{Player 0 has a winning strategy for } \mathcal{G} \text{ from } v.$$

Let $\mathcal{G}^*$ be the model-checking game for the formula $\psi_0^d(v)$ on $\mathcal{G}$ and identify Verifier with Player 0 and Falsifier with Player 1. Hence, Player 0 has a winning strategy for $\mathcal{G}^*$ if, and only if, $\mathcal{G} \models \psi_0^d(v)$.

By the construction of model-checking games, $\mathcal{G}^*$ has positions of the form $\eta(u)$, where $u \in V$ and η is a subformula of ψ_0^d. The priority of a position $R_i u$ is i, and when $\eta(u)$ is not of this form, then its priority is d.

We claim that the game $\mathcal{G}^*$ is essentially, i.e., up to elimination of stupid moves (which would lead to a loss within one or two moves) and up to contraction of several consecutive moves into one, the same as the original game $\mathcal{G}$. To see this, we compare playing $\mathcal{G}$ from a current position $u \in V_0 \cup P_i$ with playing $\mathcal{G}^*$ from any position $\vartheta_k(u)$, where $\vartheta_k(x)$ is the subformula [**gfp** $R_k \ldots$] or [**lfp** $R_k \ldots$] of $\psi_0^d(x)$. In $\mathcal{G}$, Player 0 selects at position u a successor $w \in uE$, and the play proceeds from w. In $\mathcal{G}^*$, the play goes from $\vartheta_k(u)$ through the positions $\vartheta_{k+1}(u), \ldots, \vartheta_{d-1}(u)$ to the inner formula $\varphi(u, R_0, \ldots, R_{d-1})$.

This formula is a disjunction, so Verifier (Player 0) decides how to proceed. But her only reasonable choice at this point is to move to the position $(V_0 u \wedge P_i u \wedge \exists y(Euy \wedge R_i y))$, since with any other choice she would lose one move later. But from there, the only reasonable move of Falsifier (Player 1) is to go to position $\exists y(Euy \wedge R_i y)$, and it is now the turn of Player 0 to select a successor $w \in vE$ and move to $(Euw \wedge R_i w)$. This forces Player 1 to move to $R_i w$ from which the play proceeds to $\vartheta_i(w))$.

Thus one move from u to w in $\mathcal{G}$ corresponds to a sequence of moves in $\mathcal{G}^*$ from $\vartheta_k(u)$ to $\vartheta_i(w)$, but the only genuine choice is the move from $\exists y(Euy \wedge R_i y)$ to $(Euw \wedge R_i w)$, i.e., the choice of a successor $w \in uE$. In $\mathcal{G}$, the position u has priority i, and in $\mathcal{G}^*$ the minimal, and hence relevant, priority that is seen in the sequence of moves from $\vartheta_k(u)$ to $\vartheta_i(w)$ is that of $R_i w$ which is also i. The situation for positions $u \in V_1 \cap P_i$ is the same, except that the play in $\mathcal{G}^*$ now goes through $\forall y(Exy \rightarrow R_i y)$ and it is Player 1 who selects a successor $w \in uE$ and forces the play to $R_i w$.

Hence the (reasonable) choices that have to be made by the players in $\mathcal{G}^*$ and the relevant priorities that are seen are the same as in a corresponding play of $\mathcal{G}$. Thus, Player 0 has a winning strategy for $\mathcal{G}$ from v if, and only if, Player 0 has a winning strategy for $\mathcal{G}^*$ from position $\psi_0^d(v)$. But since $\mathcal{G}^*$ is the model-checking game for $\psi_0^d(v)$ on $\mathcal{G}$ this is the case if, and only if, $\mathcal{G} \models \psi_0^d(v)$. □

The formula ψ_1^d defining the winning region for Player 1 is defined similarly. Notice that the formula ψ_σ^d has width two. An analogous construction can be carried out in the μ-calculus. The corresponding formulae are

$$\mathrm{Win}_d = \nu X_0 \mu X_1 \nu X_2 \ldots \lambda X_{d-1} \bigvee_{j=0}^{d-1} \left((V_0 \wedge P_j \wedge \Diamond X_j) \vee (V_1 \wedge P_j \wedge \Box X_j) \right).$$

Corollary 4.21 *The following three problems are algorithmically equivalent, in the sense that if one of them admits a polynomial-time algorithm, then all of them do.*

(1) Computing winning regions in parity games.

(2) The model-checking problem for LFP-*formulae of width at most* k, *for any* $k \geq 2$.

(3) The model-checking problem for the modal μ-calculus.

4.5.2 Alternation hierarchies

The formulae Win_d also play an important role in the study of the **alternation hierarchy** of the modal μ-calculus. Clearly, Win_d has alternation depth d and it has been shown that this cannot be avoided. As a consequence the alternation hierarchy of the μ-calculus is strict, a result due to Bradfield [1998] and Arnold [1999].

Sometimes, a slightly stronger formulation of this result is needed, for parity games on finite and strongly connected graphs. This easily follows from the general result by the finite model property of the μ-calculus and by a straightforward reduction to strongly connected games.

Theorem 4.22 *Winning regions in parity games in* $\mathcal{PG}_d$ *are not definable by formulae in the* μ-*calculus with alternation depth* $< d$, *even under the assumption that the game graphs are finite and strongly connected.*

For LFP the strictness of the alternation hierarchy also applies, even on certain fixed infinite structures, such as arithmetic $\mathcal{N} = (\mathbb{N}, +, \cdot)$.

However, on **finite structures**, the interleaving of least and greatest fixed points (or of **lfp**-operators and negation) can be completely avoided, at the expense of increasing the arity of fixed-point operators. Indeed, a single application of an **lfp**-operator to a first-order formula suffices to express any LFP-definable property (see Immerman [1986] or Ebbinghaus and Flum [1999]).

Theorem 4.23 *On finite structures, every LFP-formula is equivalent to a formula of the form* $\exists y[\mathbf{lfp} R \overline{x} . \varphi(R, \overline{x})](y, \ldots, y)$.

This result can be strengthened further. Notice that the model-checking game of a formula $\exists y[\mathbf{lfp} R \overline{x} . \varphi(R, \overline{x})](y, \ldots, y)$ is actually a reachability-safety game. The winning region for Player 0 is this definable by an LFP-formula of a particularly simple form, where the **lfp**-operator is applied to a Δ_2-formula.

Theorem 4.24 (Dahlhaus [1987]) *Every LFP-definable property of finite structures can be reduced, by a quantifier-free translation, to the problem of computing winning regions in reachability games.*

Hence even the problem of computing winning regions in reachability games is **complete for LFP** via this logical notion of reduction.

4.5.3 Parity games with an unbounded number of priorities

We now show that winning regions of parity games are not definable in LFP when the game graph may be infinite.

Theorem 4.25 *Winning regions in $\mathcal{PG}$ are not definable in LFP, even under the assumptions that the game graph is countable and the number of priorities is finite.*

Proof Suppose that $\text{Win}(x) \in \text{LFP}$ defines the winning region of Player 0 on $\mathcal{PG}$. We use this formula to solve the model-checking problem for LFP on $\mathfrak{N} = (\omega, +, \cdot)$.

Recall that, for any $\varphi(x) \in \text{LFP}$, we have a parity game $\mathcal{G}(\mathfrak{N}, \varphi)$ such that, for all n

$$\mathfrak{N} \models \varphi(n) \quad \Longleftrightarrow \quad \mathcal{G}(\mathfrak{N}, \varphi) \models \text{Win}(v_n)$$

(where v_n is the initial position associated with $\varphi(n)$)

Further, the model-checking game $\mathcal{G}(\mathfrak{N}, \varphi)$ is first-order interpretable in $\mathfrak{N}$. Hence the formula $\text{Win}(x)$ is mapped, via a first-order translation $\mathfrak{I}_\varphi$, into another LFP-formula $\text{Win}_\varphi(x)$ such that

$$\mathcal{G}(\mathfrak{N}, \varphi) \models \text{Win}(v_n) \quad \Longleftrightarrow \quad \mathfrak{N} \models \text{Win}_\varphi(n).$$

The first-order translation $\text{Win}(x) \mapsto \text{Win}_\varphi(x)$ depends on φ, but does not increase the alternation depth. Hence, on arithmetic, every formula $\varphi(x)$ would be equivalent to one of fixed alternation depth:

$$\mathfrak{N} \models \varphi(n) \quad \Longleftrightarrow \quad \mathfrak{N} \models \text{Win}_\varphi(n).$$

However, it is known that the alternation hierarchy of LFP on arithmetic is strict.   □

Definability on finite graphs. On finite game graphs, the definability issues are different and closely related to complexity. One of the most interesting questions is whether the winning regions are definable in fixed-point logics such as LFP or the μ-calculus.

It is not difficult to see that the μ-calculus is not sufficient (no matter how one would precisely define a μ-calculus on $\mathcal{PG}$). Again, this is a consequence of the strictness of the alternation hierarchy. A μ-calculus formula defining the winning region of Player 0 on $\mathcal{PG}$ could be translated to formulae of the usual μ-calculus on structures $\mathcal{PG}_d$ (for any fixed d) with just a bounded increase of the alternation depth. But this would mean that, for any d, the winning regions of parity games with d priorities can be expressed by a μ-calculus formula with a fixed alternation level, which would contradict the strictness of the alternation hierarchy of L_μ. For details, we refer to Dawar and Grädel [2008]

We now turn to the least fixed-point logic LFP. Clearly, a proof that winning regions of parity games in $\mathcal{PG}$ are LFP-definable would imply that parity games are solvable in polynomial time. Surprisingly, it turns out that also the converse direction holds, despite the fact that LFP is weaker than PTIME.

To prove this, we use a result by Otto [1999] saying that the multi-dimensional μ-calculus, which is a fragment of LFP, captures precisely the *bisimulation-invariant* part of PTIME. See also [Grädel et al., 2007, Section 3.5.3] for an exposition of this result.

Winning positions in parity games are of course invariant under the usual notion of bisimulation (e.g., as structures in $\mathcal{PG}_d$). However, to apply Otto's Theorem for parity games with an unbounded number of priorities, we have to consider bisimulation on structures of the form $\mathcal{G} = (V, V_0, V_1, E, \prec, \mathrm{Odd})$. Let $\tau = \{V_0, V_1, E, \prec, \mathrm{Odd}, v\}$ be the vocabulary of parity games with a starting node, and let $\mathrm{Str}(\tau)$ denote the class of all structures of this vocabulary. If we have two such structures that are indeed parity games, then bisimilarity as τ-structures coincides with the usual notion of bisimilarity in $\mathcal{PG}_d$, for appropriate d. However, not all structures in $\mathrm{Str}(\tau)$ are parity games, and the class of parity games is not closed under bisimulation. An efficient procedure for deciding whether a structure is bisimilar to a parity game is to compute its quotient under bisimulation and checking whether it is a parity game.

For a structure $(\mathcal{G}, v) \in \mathrm{Str}(\tau)$ consider the bisimulation relation $a \sim b$ on elements of $\mathcal{G}$ defined with respect to the binary relations E, $\prec$ and $\prec^{-1}$. That is to say $\sim$ is the largest relation satisfying:

- if $a \sim b$ then a and b agree on the unary relations V_0, V_1 and Odd;
- for every $x \in aE$ there is a $y \in bE$ such that $x \sim y$, and conversely;
- for every x with $a \prec x$ there is a y with $b \prec y$ and $x \sim y$ and conversely; and finally
- for every $x \prec a$ there is a $y \prec b$ such that $x \sim y$, and conversely.

We write $(\mathcal{G}, v)^\sim$ for the *bisimulation quotient* of $(\mathcal{G}, v)$, i.e., the structure whose elements are the equivalence classes in $\mathcal{G}$ with respect to $\sim$ with the relations $V_0, V_1, E, \prec, \text{Odd}$ defined in the natural way and $[v]$ as the starting vertex.

Exercise 4.5 Prove that a structure $(\mathcal{G}, v) \in \text{Str}(\tau)$ is bisimilar to a parity game if, and only if, its bisimulation quotient is a parity game, i.e., $(\mathcal{G}, v)^\sim \in \mathcal{PG}$.

Theorem 4.26 *Let C be any class of parity games on finite game graphs, such that winning positions on its bisimulation quotients are decidable in polynomial time. Then, on C, winning positions are LFP-definable.*

Proof Let $\text{Win}C$ be the class of parity games $(\mathcal{G}, v)$, such that $(\mathcal{G}, v) \in C$, and Player 0 wins from initial position v. It suffices to construct a bisimulation-invariant class X of structures $(\mathcal{H}, u)$ such that

(1) X is decidable in polynomial time,
(2) $X \cap C = \text{Win}C$.

Indeed, by Otto's Theorem X is then definable by an LFP-formula $\psi(x)$, such that, given any parity game $(\mathcal{G}, v) \in C$ we have

$$\mathcal{G}, v \in \text{Win}C \iff \mathcal{G}, v \in X \iff \mathcal{G} \models \psi(v).$$

By assumption, there exists a polynomial time algorithm A which, given a parity game $(\mathcal{G}, v) \in C^\sim$, decides whether Player 0 wins $\mathcal{G}$ from v. It is not important what the algorithm returns for quotients outside $C^\sim$, as long as it is isomorphism-invariant and halts in polynomial time. Finally, let B be the algorithm which, given any finite structure in $\text{Str}(\tau)$, first computes its bisimulation quotient, and then applies algorithm A.

Clearly B is a polynomial time algorithm, since bisimulation quotients are efficiently computable. Further the class X of structures accepted by B is invariant under bisimulation. Indeed, let $\mathcal{H}$ and $\mathcal{H}'$ be two bisimilar structures. Then their bisimulation quotients are isomorphic and are therefore either both accepted or both rejected by A. Finally, $X \cap C = \text{Win}C$. Indeed, given a parity game $\mathcal{G}, v \in C$, then it has the same winner as its bisimulation quotient which is therefore correctly decided by the algorithm B. $\qquad\square$

Corollary 4.27 *On the class $\mathcal{PG}$ of all finite parity games, winning regions are LFP-definable if, and only if, they are computable in polynomial time.*

For further results on the definability of winning regions in parity games, we refer to Dawar and Grädel [2008].

4.6 Inflationary fixed-point logic and backtracking games

LFP and the modal μ-calculus are not the only logics based on fixed-point operators. In the context of finite model theory, a rich variety of fixed-point operators has been studied due to the close connection that the resulting logics have with complexity classes. One of the most prominent fixed-point logics is IFP, the logic of *inflationary fixed points*. In finite model theory the logics IFP and LFP have often been used interchangeably as it has long been known that they have equivalent expressive power on finite structures. More recently, it has been shown by Kreutzer [2004] that the two logics are equally expressive even without the restriction to finite structures. However, it has also been proved by Dawar et al. [2004] that MIC, the extension of propositional modal logic by inflationary fixed-points, is vastly more expressive than the modal μ-calculus L_μ and that LFP and IFP have very different structural properties even when they have the same expressive power. This exploration of the different nature of the fixed-point operators leads naturally to the question of what an appropriate model-checking game for IFP might look like.

Our analysis of why parity games are the appropriate model-checking games for LFP logics relied on the *well-foundedness* of the inductive definition of a least fixed-point. The Verifier who is trying to prove that a certain tuple $\bar{a}$ belongs to a least fixed-point relation R, needs to present a well-founded justification for its inclusion. That is, the inclusion of $\bar{a}$ in R may be based on the inclusion of other elements in R whose inclusion in turn needs to be justified but the entire process must be well-founded. On the other hand, the justification for including an element in a greatest fixed-point may well be circular. This interaction between sequences that are required to be finite and those that are required to be infinite provides the structural correspondence with parity games.

A key difference that arises when we consider inflationary fixed points (and, dually, deflationary fixed-points) is that the stage at which a tuple $\bar{a}$ enters the construction of the fixed-point R may be an important part of the justification for its inclusion. In the case of least and greatest fixed-points, the operators involved are monotone. Thus, if the inclusion of $\bar{a}$ can be justified at some stage, it can be justified at all later stages. In contrast, in constructing an inflationary fixed-point, if $\bar{a}$ is included in the set, it is on the basis of the immediately preceding stage of the iteration. It may be possible to reflect this fact in the game setting by including the iteration stage as an explicit component of the game position. However, this would blow up the game enormously, since we would have to take a separate copy of the arena for each ordinal. Our aim is to leave the notion of the game arena unchanged as the product of the structure and the formula. We wish only to change the rules of the game to capture the nature of the inflationary fixed-point operator.

The change we introduce to parity games is that either player is allowed to *backtrack* to an earlier position in the game, effectively to force a *countback* of the number of stages. That is, when a backtracking move is played, the number of positions of a given priority that are backtracked are counted and this count plays an important role in the succeeding play. The precise definition is given in Section 4.6.2 below. The backtracking games we define are more complex than parity games. Winning strategies are necessarily more complicated, requiring unbounded memory, in contrast to the positional strategies that work for parity games. Furthermore, deciding the winner is PSPACE-hard and remains hard for both NP and Co-NP even when games have only two priorities. In contrast, parity games are known to be decidable in NP ∩ Co-NP and in PTIME when the number of priorities is fixed. We will explain how the model-checking problem for IFP can be represented in the form of backtracking games. The construction allows us to observe that a simpler form of backtracking game suffices which we call *simple* backtracking games, and we will see that the winning regions of simple backtracking games are definable in IFP. Thus, we obtain a tight correspondence between the game and the logic, as exists between LFP and parity games.

4.6.1 Inflationary fixed-point logic

The **inflationary fixed-point** of any operator $F . \mathcal{P}(A^k) \to \mathcal{P}(A^k)$ is defined as the limit of the increasing sequence of sets $(R^\alpha)_{\alpha \in \mathrm{Ord}}$ defined as $R^0 := \emptyset$, $R^{\alpha+1} := R^\alpha \cup F(R^\alpha)$, and $R^\lambda := \bigcup_{\alpha < \lambda} R^\alpha$ for limit ordinals λ. The **deflationary fixed-point** of F is constructed in the dual way starting with A^k as the initial stage and taking intersections at successor and limit ordinals.

Inflationary fixed-point logic (IFP) is obtained from FO by allowing formulae of the form $[\mathbf{ifp} R\overline{x} . \varphi(R, \overline{x})](\overline{x})$ and $[\mathbf{dfp} R\overline{x} . \varphi(R, \overline{x})](\overline{x})$, for arbitrary φ, defining the inflationary and deflationary fixed-point of the operator induced by φ.

To illustrate the power of IFP, we present here a few examples of situations where inflationary and deflationary fixed-points arise.

Bisimulation. Let $\mathcal{K} = (V, E, P_1, \ldots, P_m)$ be a transition system with a binary transition relation E and unary predicates P_i. Bisimilarity on $\mathcal{K}$ is the maximal equivalence relation $\sim$ on V such that any two equivalent nodes satisfy the same unary predicates P_i and have edges into the same equivalence classes. To put it differently, $\sim$ is the greatest fixed-point of the refinement operator $F : \mathcal{P}(V \times V) \to \mathcal{P}(V \times V)$ with

$$F : Z \mapsto \Big\{ (u, v) \in V \times V : \bigwedge_{i \leq m} P_i u \leftrightarrow P_i v$$
$$\wedge \, \forall u'(Euu' \to \exists v'(Evv' \wedge Zu'v'))$$
$$\wedge \, \forall v'(Evv' \to \exists u'(Euu' \wedge Zu'v)) \Big\}.$$

For some applications (one of which will appear in Section 4.6.4) one is interested in having not only the bisimulation relation $\sim$ but also a linear order on the bisimulation quotient $\mathcal{K}/\sim$. That is, we want to define a pre-order $\preceq$ on $\mathcal{K}$ such that $u \sim v$ iff $u \preceq v$ and $v \preceq u$. We can again do this via a fixed-point construction, by defining a sequence $\preceq_\alpha$ of pre-orders (where α ranges over ordinals) such that $\preceq_{\alpha+1}$ refines $\preceq_\alpha$ and $\preceq_\lambda$, for limit ordinals λ, is the intersection of the pre-orders $\preceq_\alpha$ with $\alpha < \lambda$. Let

$$u \preceq_1 v :\Longleftrightarrow \bigwedge_{i \leq m} P_i u \to \Big(P_i v \vee \bigvee_{j < i} (\neg P_j u \wedge P_i v) \Big)$$

(i.e., if the truth values of the P_i at u are lexicographically smaller than or equal to those at v), and for any α, let

$$u \sim_\alpha v :\Longleftrightarrow u \preceq_\alpha v \wedge v \preceq_\alpha u.$$

To define the refinement, we say that the $\sim_\alpha$-class C *separates* two nodes u and v, if precisely one of the two nodes has an edge into C. Now, let $u \preceq_{\alpha+1} v$ if, and only if, $u \preceq_\alpha v$ and there is an edge from v (and hence none from u) into the smallest $\sim_\alpha$-class (w.r.t. $\preceq_\alpha$) that separates u from v (if it exists). Since the sequence of the pre-orders $\preceq_\alpha$ is decreasing, it must indeed reach a fixed-point $\preceq$, and it is not hard to show that the corresponding equivalence relation is precisely the bisimilarity relation $\sim$.

The point that we want to stress here is that $\preceq$ is a deflationary fixed-point of a non-monotone induction. Indeed, the refinement operator on pre-orders is not monotone and does not, in general, have a greatest fixed-point. We remark that is not difficult to give an analogous definition of this order by an inflationary, rather than deflationary induction.

The lazy engineer: iterated relativisation. Let $\varphi(x)$ be a specification that should be satisfied by all states a of a system, which we assume to be described as a relational structure $\mathfrak{A}$. Now, suppose that the engineer notices that the system he designed is faulty, i.e., that there exist elements $a \in \mathfrak{A}$

where φ does not hold. Rather than redesigning the system, he tries to just throw away all bad elements of $\mathfrak{A}$, i.e., he relativises $\mathfrak{A}$ to the substructure $\mathfrak{A}|_\varphi$ induced by $\{a : \mathfrak{A} \models \varphi(a)\}$. Unfortunately, it need not be the case that $\mathfrak{A}|_\varphi \models \forall x \varphi(x)$. Indeed, the removal of some elements may have the effect that others no longer satisfy φ. But the lazy engineer can of course iterate this relativisation procedure and define a (possibly transfinite) sequence of substructures $\mathfrak{A}^\beta$, with $\mathfrak{A}^0 = \mathfrak{A}$, $\mathfrak{A}^{\beta+1} = \mathfrak{A}^\beta|_\varphi$ and $\mathfrak{A}^\lambda = \bigcap_{\beta < \lambda} \mathfrak{A}^\beta$ for limit ordinals λ. This sequence reaches a fixed-point $\mathfrak{A}^\infty$ which satisfies $\forall x \varphi(x)$ – but it may be empty.

This process of iterated relativisation is definable by a fixed-point induction in $\mathfrak{A}$. Let $\varphi|_Z$ be the syntactic relativisation of φ to a new set variable Z, obtained by replacing inductively all subformulae $\exists y \alpha$ by $\exists y(Zy \wedge \alpha)$ and $\forall y \alpha$ by $\forall y(Zy \to \alpha)$. Iterated relativisation means repeated application of the operator

$$F : Z \mapsto \{a : \mathfrak{A}|_Z \models \varphi(a)\} = \{a : \mathfrak{A} \models Za \wedge \varphi|_Z(a)\}$$

starting with $Z = A$ (the universe of $\mathfrak{A}$). Note that F is deflationary but not necessarily monotone.

In logics with inflationary and deflationary fixed points (the universe of) $\mathfrak{A}^\infty$ is uniformly definable in $\mathfrak{A}$ by a formula of the form $[\mathbf{dfp} Zx \,.\, \varphi|_Z](x)$. Since IFP and LFP have the same expressive power, $\mathfrak{A}^\infty$ is also LFP-definable. However, the only known way to provide such a definition is by going through the proof of Kreutzer's Theorem (see Kreutzer [2004]). There seems to be no simple direct definition based on least and greatest fixed-points only.

4.6.2 Parity games with backtracking

Backtracking games are essentially parity games with the addition that, under certain conditions, players can jump back to an earlier position in the play. This kind of move is called backtracking. A backtracking move from position v to an earlier position u is only possible if v belongs to a given set B of backtrack positions, if u and v have the same priority and if no position of smaller priority has occurred between u and v. With such a move, the player who backtracks not only resets the play back to u, she also commits herself to a backtracking distance d, which is the number of positions of priority $\Omega(v)$ that have been seen between u and v. After this move, the play ends when d further positions of priority $\Omega(v)$ have been seen, unless this priority is "released" by a lower priority.

For finite plays we have the winning condition that a player wins if her opponent cannot move. For infinite plays, the winner is determined according to the parity condition, i.e., Player 0 wins a play π if the least priority seen infinitely often in π is even, otherwise Player 1 wins.

Thus the arena $\mathcal{G} := (V, E, V_0, V_1, B, \Omega)$ of a backtracking game is a defined as for parity games, extended by a subset $B \subseteq V$ of backtrack positions. A *play* of $\mathcal{G}$ from initial position v_0 is formed as follows. If, after n steps the play has gone through positions $v_0 v_1 \ldots v_n$ and reached a position $v_n \in V_\sigma$, then Player σ can select a successor $v_{n+1} \in v_n E$; this is called an ordinary move. But if $v_n \in B$ is a backtrack position, of priority $\Omega(v_n) = q$, say, then Player σ may also choose to backtrack; in that case she selects a number $i < n$ subject to the conditions that $\Omega(v_i) = q$ and $\Omega(v_j) \geq q$ for all j with $i < j < n$. The play then proceeds to position $v_{n+1} = v_i$ and we set $d(q) = |\{k : i \leq k < n \wedge \Omega(v_k) = q\}|$. This number $d(q)$ is relevant for the rest of the game, because the play ends when $d(q)$ further positions of priority q have been seen without any occurrence of a priority $< q$. Therefore, a play is not completely described by the sequence $v_0 v_1 \ldots$ of the positions that have been visited. For instance, if a player backtracks from v_n in $v_0 \ldots v_i \ldots v_j \ldots v_n$, it matters whether she backtracks to i or j, even if $v_i = v_j$ because the associated numbers $d(p)$ are different. For a more formal description of how backtracking games are played we refer to Dawar et al. [2006].

It is easy to see that backtracking games are Borel games, so by Martin's Theorem, they are determined. Since parity games are positionally determined the question arises whether this also holds for backtracking games. However, simple examples show that this is not the case and, indeed, no fixed amount of finite memory suffices for winning strategies.

Theorem 4.28 *Backtracking games in general do not admit finite-memory winning strategies.*

Exercise 4.6 Find an example proving this.

Thus, winning strategies for backtracking games are more complex than the strategies needed for parity games. Also the computational complexity of computing winning regions is higher for backtracking games than for parity games. While it is known that winning regions of parity games can be decided in NP $\cap$ Co-NP (and it is conjectured by many that this problem is actually solvable in polynomial time), the corresponding problem for backtracking games is PSPACE-hard. Further, for any fixed number of priorities, parity games can be decided in PTIME, but backtracking games with just two priorities are already NP-hard (see Dawar et al. [2006]).

4.6.3 Games for IFP

We restrict attention to finite structures. The model-checking game for an IFP-formula ψ on a finite structure $\mathfrak{A}$ is a backtracking game $\mathcal{G}(\mathfrak{A}, \psi) = (V, E, V_0, V_1, B, \Omega)$. As in the games for LFP, the positions are subformulae of ψ, instantiated by elements of $\mathfrak{A}$. We only describe the modifications.

We always assume that formulae are in negation normal form, and write $\overline{\vartheta}$ for the negation normal form of $\neg\vartheta$. Consider any **ifp**-formula $\varphi^*(\overline{x}) := [\textbf{ifp}\,T\overline{x}\,.\,\varphi(T, \overline{x})](\overline{x})$ in ψ. In general, φ can have positive or negative occurrences of the fixed-point variable T. We use the notation $\varphi(T, \overline{T})$ to separate positive and negative occurrences of T. To define the set of positions we include also all subformulae of $T\overline{x} \vee \varphi$ and $\overline{T}\overline{x} \wedge \overline{\varphi}$. Note that an **ifp**-subformula in φ is translated into a **dfp**-subformula in $\overline{\varphi}$, and vice versa. To avoid conflicts we have to change the names of the fixed-point variables when doing this, i.e., a subformula $[\textbf{ifp}\,R\overline{y}\,.\,\vartheta(R, \overline{R}, \overline{y})](\overline{y})$ in φ will correspond to a subformula $[\textbf{dfp}\,R'\overline{y}\,.\,\overline{\vartheta}(\overline{R'}, R', \overline{y})](\overline{y})$ of $\overline{\varphi}$ where R' is a new relation variable, distinct from R.

From a position $\varphi^*(\overline{a})$ the play proceeds to $T\overline{a} \vee \varphi(T, \overline{a})$. When a play reaches a position $T\overline{c}$ or $\overline{T}\overline{c}$ the play proceeds back to the formula defining the fixed-point by a regeneration move. More precisely, the regeneration of an **ifp**-atom $T\overline{c}$ is $T\overline{c} \vee \varphi(T, \overline{c})$, the regeneration of $\overline{T}\overline{c}$ is $\overline{T}\overline{c} \wedge \overline{\varphi}(T, \overline{c})$. Verifier can move from $T\overline{c}$ to its regeneration, Falsifier from $\overline{T}\overline{c}$. For **dfp**-subformulae $\vartheta^*(\overline{x}) := [\textbf{dfp}\,R\overline{x}\,.\,\vartheta(R, \overline{x})](\overline{x})$, dual definitions apply. Verifier moves from $\overline{R}\overline{c}$ to its regeneration $\overline{R}\overline{c} \vee \overline{\vartheta}(R, \overline{c})$, and Falsifier can make regeneration moves from $R\overline{c}$ to $R\overline{c} \wedge \vartheta(R, \overline{c})$. The priority assignment associates with each **ifp**-variable T an odd priority $\Omega(T)$ and with each **dfp**-variable R an even priority $\Omega(R)$, such that for any two distinct fixed-point variables S, S', we have $\Omega(S) \neq \Omega(S')$, and whenever S' depends on S, then $\Omega(S) < \Omega(S')$. Positions of the form $S\overline{c}$ and $\overline{S}\overline{c}$ are called S-positions. All S-positions get priority $\Omega(S)$, all other formulae get a higher priority. The set B of backtrack positions is the set of S-positions, where S is any fixed-point variable.

Let us focus on IFP-formulae with a single fixed-point, $\psi := [\textbf{ifp}\,T\overline{x}\,.\,\varphi](\overline{a})$ where $\varphi(T, \overline{x})$ is a first-order formula. When the play reaches a position $T\overline{c}$ Verifier can make a regeneration move to $T\overline{c} \vee \varphi(T, \overline{c})$ or backtrack. Dually, Falsifier can regenerate from positions $\overline{T}\overline{c}$ or backtrack. However, since we have only one fixed-point, all backtrack positions have the same priority and only one backtrack move can occur in a play.

In this simple case, the rules of the backtracking game ensure that infinite plays (which are plays without backtracking moves) are won by Falsifier, since **ifp**-atoms have odd priority. However, if one of the players backtracks after the play has gone through α T-positions, then the play ends when α further T-positions have been visited. Falsifier has won, if the last of these is of form $T\overline{c}$, and Verifier has won if it is of form $\overline{T}\overline{c}$.

The differences between IFP model-checking and LFP model-checking are in fact best illustrated with this simple case. We claim that Verifier has a winning strategy for the game $\mathcal{G}(\mathfrak{A}, \psi)$ if $\mathfrak{A} \models \psi$ and Falsifier has a winning strategy if $\mathfrak{A} \not\models \psi$.

We look at the first-order formulae φ^α defining the stages of the induction. Let $\varphi^0(\overline{a}) = \textit{false}$ and $\varphi^{\alpha+1}(\overline{a}) = \varphi^\alpha(\overline{a}) \vee \varphi[T/\varphi^\alpha, \overline{T}/\overline{\varphi}^\alpha](\overline{x})$. On finite structures $\psi(\overline{a}) \equiv \bigvee_{\alpha<\omega} \varphi^\alpha(\overline{a})$.

The first-order game $\mathcal{G}(\mathfrak{A}, \varphi^\alpha(\overline{a}))$ can be seen as an unfolding of the game $\mathcal{G}(\mathfrak{A}, \psi(\overline{a}))$. Every position in $\mathcal{G}(\mathfrak{A}, \varphi^\alpha(\overline{a}))$ corresponds to a unique position in $\mathcal{G}(\mathfrak{A}, \psi(\overline{a}))$, and conversely, for a pair (p, β) where p is a position of $\mathcal{G}(\mathfrak{A}, \varphi^\alpha(\overline{a}))$ and $\beta \leq \alpha$ is an ordinal, there is a unique associated position p_β of the unfolded game $\mathcal{G}(\mathfrak{A}, \varphi^\alpha(\overline{a}))$. When a play in $\mathcal{G}(\mathfrak{A}, \varphi^\alpha(\overline{a}))$ reaches a position $T\overline{c}$, it is regenerated to either $T\overline{c}$ or $\varphi(T, \overline{c})$ and such a regeneration move decrements the associated ordinal. The corresponding play in $\mathcal{G}(\mathfrak{A}, \varphi^\alpha(\overline{a}))$ proceeds to position $\varphi^\beta(\overline{c})$ or $\varphi[T/\varphi^\beta, \overline{T}/\overline{\varphi}^\beta](\overline{c})$. We can use this correspondence to translate strategies between the two games. Notice that the lifting of a positional strategy f in the unfolded game $\mathcal{G}(\mathfrak{A}, \varphi^\alpha(\overline{a}))$ will produce a non-positional strategy f^* in the original game $\mathcal{G}(\mathfrak{A}, \psi)$: start with $\beta = \alpha$ and, for any position p, let $f^*(p) := f(p_\beta)$; at regeneration moves, the ordinal β is decremented.

Consider now a play in $\mathcal{G}(\mathfrak{A}, \psi)$ after a backtracking move prior to which β T-positions have been visited, and suppose that $\mathfrak{A} \models \varphi^\beta(\overline{a})$. Then Verifier has a winning strategy in the first-order game $\mathcal{G}(\mathfrak{A}, \varphi^\beta(\overline{a}))$ (from position $\varphi^\beta(\overline{a})$) which translates into a (non-positional) strategy for the game $\mathcal{G}(\mathfrak{A}, \psi)$ with the following properties: Any play that is consistent with this strategy will either be winning for Verifier before β T-positions have been seen, or the β-th T-position will be negative.

Similarly, if $\mathfrak{A} \not\models \varphi^\beta(\overline{a})$ then Falsifier has a winning strategy for $\mathcal{G}(\mathfrak{A}, \varphi^\beta(\overline{a}))$, and this strategy translates into a strategy for the game $\mathcal{G}(\mathfrak{A}, \psi)$ by which Falsifier forces the play (after backtracking) from position $\psi(\overline{a})$ to a positive β-th T-position, unless she wins before β T-positions have been seen. We hence have established the following fact.

Lemma 4.29 *Suppose that a play on $\mathcal{G}(\mathfrak{A}, \psi)$ has been backtracked to the initial position $\psi(\overline{a})$ after β T-positions have been visited. Verifier has a winning strategy for the remaining game if, and only if, $\mathfrak{A} \models \varphi^\beta(\overline{a})$.*

From this we obtain the desired result.

Theorem 4.30   *If* $\mathfrak{A} \models \psi(\overline{a})$, *then Verifier wins the game* $\mathcal{G}(\mathfrak{A}, \psi(\overline{a}))$ *from position* $\psi(\overline{a})$. *If* $\mathfrak{A} \not\models \psi(\overline{a})$, *then Falsifier wins the game* $\mathcal{G}(\mathfrak{A}, \psi(\overline{a}))$ *from position* $\psi(\overline{a})$.

Proof   Suppose first that $\mathfrak{A} \models \psi(\overline{a})$. Then there is some ordinal $\alpha < \omega$ such that $\mathfrak{A} \models \varphi^\alpha(\overline{a})$. We construct a winning strategy for Verifier in the game $\mathcal{G}(\mathfrak{A}, \psi(\overline{a}))$ starting at position $\psi(\overline{a})$.

From $\psi(\overline{a})$ the game proceeds to $(T\overline{a} \vee \varphi(\overline{a}))$. At this position, Verifier repeatedly chooses the node $T\overline{a}$ until this node has been visited α-times. After that, she backtracks and moves to $\varphi(\overline{a})$. By Lemma 4.29 and since $\mathfrak{A} \models \varphi^\alpha(\overline{a})$, Verifier has a strategy to win the remaining play.

Now suppose that $\mathfrak{A} \not\models \psi(\overline{a})$. If, after α T-positions, one of the players backtracks, then Falsifier has a winning strategy for the remaining game, since $\mathfrak{A} \not\models \varphi^\alpha(\overline{a})$. Hence, the only possibility for Verifier to win the game in a finite number of moves is to avoid positions $T\overline{b}$ where Falsifier can backtrack. Consider the formulae φ_f^α, with $\varphi_f^0 = false$ and $\varphi_f^{\alpha+1}(\overline{x}) = \varphi[T/\varphi_f^\alpha, \overline{T}/false](\overline{x})$. They define the stages of $[\mathbf{ifp}\, T\overline{x}\,.\,\varphi[T, false](\overline{x})]$, obtained from ψ by replacing negative occurrences of T by $false$. If Verifier could force a finite winning play, with $\alpha - 1$ positions of the form $T\overline{c}$ and without positions $\overline{T}\overline{c}$, then she would in fact have a winning strategy for the model-checking game $\mathcal{G}(\mathfrak{A}, \varphi_f^\alpha(\overline{a}))$. Since ψ_f^α implies φ^α, it would follow that $\mathfrak{A} \models \varphi^\alpha(\overline{a})$. But this is impossible. $\square$

The extension of the proof of Theorem 4.30 to arbitrary IFP-formulae poses no major difficulties. Proceeding by induction on the number of nested fixed-point formulae, one has to combine the argument just given (applied to the outermost fixed-point) with the correctness proof for the LFP-model-checking games. Notice that the essential differences between backtracking games and parity games are in the effects of backtracking moves. Backtracking moves impose a finiteness condition on one priority (unless it is later released by smaller priority) and the effect of such a move remains essentially the same in the general case as in the case of formulae with a single fixed-point. On the other hand, an infinite play in an IFP-model-checking game is a play in which the backtracking moves do not play a decisive role. The winner of such a play is determined by the parity condition and the analysis of such plays closely follows the proof that parity games are the model-checking games for LFP-formulae.

4.6.4 Definability of winning regions in backtracking games

We have seen that backtracking games can be used as model-checking games for IFP. We will now identify a natural subclass of backtracking games, which we call *simple* which is balanced with IFP. This means that for every formula $\varphi \in$ IFP and finite structure $\mathfrak{A}$, the game $\mathcal{G}(\mathfrak{A}, \varphi)$ can trivially be modified to fall within this class and, on the other hand, for every $d \in \mathbb{N}$ there is a formula $\varphi \in$ IFP defining the winning region for Player 0 in any simple backtracking game with at most d priorities. In this sense, simple backtracking games precisely capture IFP model-checking.

Consider the model-checking game $\mathcal{G}(\mathfrak{A}, \varphi)$ and the way backtracking was used there: if Player 0 wanted to backtrack it was always after opening a fixed-point, say $[\mathbf{ifp} R\overline{x} . R\overline{x} \vee \varphi]$. She then looped α times through the $R\overline{x}$ sub-formula and backtracked. By choosing the α she essentially picked a stage of the fixed-point induction on φ and claimed that $\overline{x} \in \varphi^\alpha$. From this observation we can derive two important consequences. As every inflationary fixed-point induction must close after polynomially many steps in the size of the structure $\mathfrak{A}$ and therefore in linearly many steps in terms of the game graph, there is no need for Player 0 to backtrack more than n steps, where n is the size of the game graph. Further, the game can easily be modified such that instead of having the nodes for the disjunction $R\overline{x} \vee \varphi$ and the sub-formula $R\overline{x}$, we simply have a node for φ with a self-loop. In this modified game graph, not only is it sufficient for Player 0 to backtrack no more than n steps, we can, in addition, require that whenever she backtracks from a node v, it must be to v again, i.e., when she decides to backtrack from a node corresponding to the formula φ, she loops α times through φ and then backtracks α steps to φ again. The same is true for Player 1 and her backtracking.

We call a strategy in a backtracking game $\mathcal{G}$ *local* if all backtracking moves from any node v are to a previous occurrence of v. Given a function $f . \mathbb{N} \rightarrow \mathbb{N}$, we call a strategy f-backtracking if all backtracking moves made by the strategy have distance at most $f(|\mathcal{G}|)$. The strategy is called *linear* in case $f(n) = n$ and *polynomial* if f is a polynomial in n.

A backtracking game $\mathcal{G} := (V, E, V_0, V_1, B, \Omega)$ is *simple*, if every node in B has a self-loop and both players have local linear winning strategies on their winning regions.

Theorem 4.31 *For any IFP-formula ψ and every finite structure $\mathfrak{A}$, the model-checking game $\mathcal{G}(\mathfrak{A}, \varphi)$, as defined in Section 4.6.3, is simple.*

We now want to show that the logic IFP is balanced with the class of simple backtracking games, i.e., the winning regions of simple backtracking games are IFP-definable.

Since backtracking games are extensions of parity games we start with the formula defining winning regions in parity games. We take this formula as a starting point for defining an IFP-formula deciding the winner of backtracking games. To define strategies involving backtracking, we first need some preparation. In particular, in order to measure distances we need an ordering on the arenas.

It is easily seen that backtracking games are invariant under bisimulation. Thus, it suffices to consider arenas where no two distinct nodes are bisimilar (we refer to such arenas as *bisimulation minimal*). The next step is to define an ordering on the nodes in an arena. This is done by ordering the bisimulation types realised in it.

Indeed, we have seen above that there is a formula $\varphi_{\mathrm{ord}}(x, y) \in$ IFP defining on every bisimulation minimal arena a linear order. As a result, we can assume that the backtracking games are ordered and that we are given an arithmetical predicate for addition with respect to the order defined above.

Theorem 4.28, saying that there exist backtracking games whose winning strategies require infinite memory, also applies to games with local strategies. In general, the reason for the increased memory consumption is that when the decision to backtrack is made, it is necessary to know which nodes have been seen in the past, i.e., to which node a backtracking move is possible. Furthermore, after a backtracking move occurred, both players have to remember the backtracking distance, as this determines their further moves. However, since here we consider strategies with local backtracking only, it suffices to know the distance of the backtracking moves that are still active, i.e., have not yet been released, whereas the history of the play in terms of nodes visited may safely be forgotten. Thus we can capture all the relevant information about a partial play π ending in position v by the tuple $(v, d_\pi(0), \ldots, d_\pi(k-1))$, where d_π denotes the distance function.

In a backtracking game with priorities $0, \ldots, k-1$, a **configuration** is a pair $(v, \overline{d})$ consisting of a node v and a tuple $\overline{d} \in (\mathbb{N} \cup \{\infty\})^k$. Let π be a (partial) play ending in node v. The configuration of π is defined as the tuple $(v, d_\pi(0), \ldots, d_\pi(k))$.

Recall that in a simple backtracking game the distance of all backtracking moves is at most $n := |\mathcal{G}|$. Furthermore we can assume that we are given a linear order on the nodes of the game graph. Thus the configuration of any (partial) play π in a simple game can be represented by a pair $(v, \overline{d})$ where

$\overline{d} \in \{0, \ldots, n, \infty\}^k$ and we can use nodes in the game graph to represent the values of the d_i.

The structure of the formulae ψ_0^k defining the winning region for Player 0 in backtracking games with priorities $< k$ is similar to the structure of the corresponding LFP-formula for parity games. It has the form

$$\psi_0^k(x) := [\mathbf{gfp} \ R_0 x \overline{d} \,.\, [\mathbf{lfp} \ R_1 x \overline{d} \,.\, \ldots \,.\, [\mathbf{fp} R_{k-1} x \overline{d} \,.\, \varphi(\overline{R}, x, \overline{d})] \ldots](x, \infty, \ldots \infty)$$

with k nested fixed-points, applied to a formula φ which is first-order, up to the IFP-subformula defining the order of the bisimulation types. In its various nested fixed-points the formula builds up sets of configurations $(x, d_0, \ldots, d_{k-1})$ such that if $(x, d_0, \ldots, d_k) \in R_{\Omega(x)}$, then Player 0 can extend any partial play π, ending in node x with $d_\pi(j) = d_j$ for all $j < k$, to a winning play.

We do not give an explicit construction here, but explain the idea. For details, we refer to Dawar et al. [2006].

First of all the formula $\varphi(\overline{R}, x, \overline{d})$ states that for some i, the priority of x is i and the tuple $(d_0, \ldots, d_{k-1})$ has ∞ at all positions greater than i (which corresponds to the fact that a node of priority i releases all backtracking moves on higher priorities). Further, if x is a position of Player 0, then she can win from configuration $(x, \overline{d})$ if she can move to a successor y of x from which she wins the play. Winning from y means that the configuration $(y, \overline{d}')$ reached from $(x, \overline{d})$ by moving to y is in $R_{\Omega(y)}$. Thus the formula must define what it means for $(y, \overline{d}')$ to be the configuration reached from x when moving to y.

This involves a case distinction.

If $d_i = \infty$, Player 0 can either do an ordinary move or, in case $x \in B$, a backtracking move. After an ordinary move to a successor node y of priority j the play will have the configuration $(y, \overline{d}')$ which satisfies $\overline{d}' = (d_0, \ldots, d_j, \infty, \ldots, \infty))$ and which must be in R_j. After a backtracking move, we will have, for some $m \neq \infty$, a configuration $(x, d_0, \ldots, d_{i-1}, m, \infty, \ldots, \infty)$ which must be in R_i

In the case that $d_i = m \leq |\mathcal{G}|$, the formulae must express that Player 0 wins the m-step game on priority i from x. This game is won by Player 0 if there is a successor y of x from which she wins and either the priority j of y is less than i, i.e., all backtracking moves on priorities greater than j are released ($d_l = \infty$ for all $l > j$), or the priority j of y equals i and Player 0 wins the $m - 1$ step game from y (and all d_l with $l < i$ are left unchanged), or the priority j of y is greater than i, in which case the play continues with the configuration $(y, d_0, \ldots, d_i, \infty, \ldots, \infty)$, i.e., all active backtracking moves (whose distances are stored in $d_0, \ldots, d_i$) remain unchanged and the play continues on priority j without any active backtracking moves on priorities greater than i.

It is not difficult to express all this in first-order logic, provided an ordering on priorities is available. For nodes where Player 1 moves the construction is very similar.

Exercise 4.7 Make the construction of the formulae ψ_σ^k explicit, and prove that they indeed define the winning region for Player σ.

Theorem 4.32 *Winning regions of simple backtracking games are definable in IFP.*

4.7 Logic and games in a quantitative setting

Common logical formalisms are two-valued and express qualitative properties. There have been a number of proposals to extend logics such as propositional modal logic ML, the temporal logics LTL and CTL, and the modal μ-calculus L_μ to **quantitative** formalisms where formulae can take, at a given state of a system, not just the values *true* and *false*, but quantitative values, for instance real numbers. There are several scenarios and applications where it is desirable to replace purely qualitative statements by quantitative ones which can be of very different nature: we may be interested in the probability of an event, the value that we assign to an event may depend on to how late it occurs, we can ask for the number of occurrences of an event in a play, and so on. We can consider transition structures, where already the atomic propositions take numeric values, or we can ask about the 'degree of satisfaction' of a property.

While there certainly is ample motivation to extend qualitative specification formalisms to quantitative ones, there are also problems. It has been observed in many areas of mathematics, engineering and computer science where logical formalisms are applied, that quantitative formalisms in general lack the clean and clear mathematical theory of their qualitative counterparts, and that many of the desirable mathematical and algorithmic properties tend to get lost. Also, the definitions of quantitative formalisms are often ad hoc and do not always respect the properties that are relevant for logical methodologies.

Here we discuss to what extent the relationship between the μ-calculus and parity games can be extended to a quantitative μ-calculus and appropriate quantitative model-checking games. The extension is not straightforward and requires that one defines the quantitative μ-calculus in the 'right' way, so as to ensure that it has appropriate closure and duality properties (such as closure under negation, De Morgan equalities, quantifier and fixed-point dualities) to make it amenable to a game-based approach. But once this is done, one can indeed construct a quantitative variant of parity games, and prove that they are the appropriate model-checking games for the quantitative μ-calculus. As in the classical setting the correspondence goes both ways: The value of a formula in a structure coincides with the value of the associated model-checking game, and conversely, the value of quantitative parity games (with a bounded number of priorities) are definable in the quantitative μ-calculus. However, the mathematical properties of quantitative parity games are different from their qualitative counterparts. In particular, they are, in general, not positionally determined, not even up to approximation, and the proof that the quantitative model-checking games correctly describe the value of the formulae is considerably more difficult than for the classical case.

As in the classical case, model-checking games lead to a better understanding of the semantics and expressive power of the quantitative μ-calculus. Further, the game-based approach also sheds light on the consequences of different choices in the design of the quantitative formalism, which are far less obvious than for classical logics.

4.7.1 Quantitative transition systems and quantitative μ-calculus

We write $\mathbb{R}^+$ for the set of non-negative real numbers, and $\mathbb{R}^+_\infty := \mathbb{R}^+ \cup \{\infty\}$. **Quantitative transition systems (QTS)** are directed graphs equipped with quantities at states and with discounts of edges. They have the form $\mathcal{K} = (V, E, \delta, \{P_i\}_{i \in I})$ where (V, E) is a directed graph, with a discount function $\delta : E \to \mathbb{R}^+ \setminus \{0\}$ and functions $P_i : V \to \mathbb{R}^+_\infty$, that assign to each state the values of the predicates at that state. A transition system is **qualitative** if all functions P_i assign only the values 0 or ∞, where 0 stands for *false* and ∞ for *true*, and it is **non-discounted** if $\delta(e) = 1$ for all $e \in E$.

Given predicate functions $\{P_i\}_{i \in I}$, discount factors $d \in \mathbb{R}^+$ and constants $c \in \mathbb{R}^+$, the **quantitative μ-calculus** $Q\mu$ is built in a similar way to the modal μ-calculus, with the following two modifications.

(1) Atomic formulae have the form $|P_i - c|$.
(2) If φ is a $Q\mu$-formula, then so is $d \cdot \varphi$,

Boolean connectives $\wedge$, $\vee$, modal operators $\Diamond$ and $\Box$, and fixed-point operators μ, ν are used as in the syntax of L_μ. The semantics, however, is quite different.

Formulae of $Q\mu$ are interpreted over quantitative transition systems $\mathcal{K} =

$(V, E, \delta, (P_i)_{i \in I})$. The meaning of a formula φ in $\mathcal{K}$ is a function $[\![\varphi]\!]^{\mathcal{K}}$: $V \to \mathbb{R}^+_\infty$. We write $\mathcal{F}$ for the set of functions $f : V \to \mathbb{R}^+_\infty$, with $f_1 \leq f_2$ if $f_1(v) \leq f_2(v)$ for all v. Then $(\mathcal{F}, \leq)$ forms a complete lattice with the constant functions $f = \infty$ as $f = 0$ as top and bottom elements.

The interpretation $[\![\varphi]\!]^{\mathcal{K}} : V \to \mathbb{R}^+_\infty$ is defined as follows:

(1) $[\![|P_i - c|]\!]^{\mathcal{K}}(v) := |P_i(v) - c|$,

(2) $[\![\varphi_1 \wedge \varphi_2]\!]^{\mathcal{K}} := \min\{[\![\varphi_1]\!]^{\mathcal{K}}, [\![\varphi_2]\!]^{\mathcal{K}}\}$ and
$[\![\varphi_1 \vee \varphi_2]\!]^{\mathcal{K}} := \max\{[\![\varphi_1]\!]^{\mathcal{K}}, [\![\varphi_2]\!]^{\mathcal{K}}\}$,

(3) $[\![\Diamond\varphi]\!]^{\mathcal{K}}(v) := \sup_{v' \in vE} \delta(v, v') \cdot [\![\varphi]\!]^{\mathcal{K}}(v')$ and
$[\![\Box\varphi]\!]^{\mathcal{K}}(v) := \inf_{v' \in vE} \frac{1}{\delta(v,v')} [\![\varphi]\!]^{\mathcal{K}}(v')$,

(4) $[\![d \cdot \varphi]\!]^{\mathcal{K}}(v) := d \cdot [\![\varphi]\!]^{\mathcal{K}}(v)$,

(5) $[\![\mu X.\varphi]\!]^{\mathcal{K}} := \inf\{f \in \mathcal{F} : f = [\![\varphi]\!]^{\mathcal{K}[X \leftarrow f]}\}$, and
$[\![\nu X.\varphi]\!]^{\mathcal{K}} = \sup\{f \in \mathcal{F} : f = [\![\varphi]\!]^{\mathcal{K}[X \leftarrow f]}\}$.

When interpreted over qualitative transition systems $Q\mu$ coincides with the classical μ-calculus and we say that $\mathcal{K}, v$ is a model of φ, $\mathcal{K}, v \models \varphi$ if $[\![\varphi]\!]^{\mathcal{K}}(v) = \infty$. For discounted systems we take the natural definition for $\Diamond$ and use the dual one for $\Box$ which motivates the $\frac{1}{\delta}$ factor. It has been proved by Fischer et al. [2009] that this is the only definition for which there is a well-behaved negation operator (with $[\![\neg\varphi]\!]^{\mathcal{K}} = 1/[\![\varphi]\!]^{\mathcal{K}}$) and which gives us the dualities that are needed for natural model-checking games.

Note that all operators in $Q\mu$ are monotone. This guarantees the existence of the least and greatest fixed-points, and their inductive definition according to the Knaster–Tarski Theorem: Given a formula $\mu X.\varphi$ and a quantitative transition system $\mathcal{K}$, we obtain the inductive sequence of functions g_α (for ordinals α) where $g_0 := 0$, $g_{\alpha+1} := [\![\varphi]\!]^{\mathcal{K}[X \leftarrow g_\alpha]}$, and $g_\lambda := \lim_{\alpha < \lambda} [\![\varphi]\!]^{\mathcal{K}[X \leftarrow g_\alpha]}$ for limit ordinals λ. Then $[\![\mu X.\varphi]\!]^{\mathcal{K}} = g_\gamma$ for the minimal ordinal γ with $g_\gamma = g_{\gamma+1}$. For $\nu X.\varphi$ the dual induction applies, starting with $g_0 := \infty$.

4.7.2 Quantitative parity games

Quantitative parity games are modest modifications of classical parity games. Quantitative values are assigned to final positions, where they are interpreted as the payoff for Player 0 at that position, and to moves, where they are interpreted as discounts to the payoff when the play goes through that move.

A ***quantitative parity game*** is a tuple $\mathcal{G} = (V, V_0, V_1, E, \delta, \lambda, \Omega)$ extending a classical parity game by two functions $\delta : E \to \mathbb{R}^+$, assigning to every move a ***discount factor***, and $\lambda : \{v \in V : vE = \emptyset\} \to \mathbb{R}^+_\infty$ assigning to every terminal position a ***payoff value***. The ***outcome*** $p(\pi)$ of a finite play

$\pi = v_0 \ldots v_k$, ending at a terminal position v_k is computed by multiplying all discount factors seen in the play with the payoff value at the final node,

$$p(v_0 v_1 \ldots v_k) = \delta(v_0, v_1) \cdot \delta(v_1, v_2) \cdot \ldots \cdot \delta(v_{k-1}, v_k) \cdot \lambda(v_k).$$

The outcome of an infinite play depends only on the lowest priority seen infinitely often. We assign the value 0 to every infinite play in which the lowest priority seen infinitely often is odd, and ∞ to those in which it is even. Player 0 wants to maximise the outcome whereas Player 1 wants to minimise it.

Determinacy. A quantitative game is ***determined*** if, for each position v, the highest outcome that Player 0 can enforce from v and the lowest outcome Player 1 can assure converge,

$$\sup_{\sigma \in \Gamma_0} \inf_{\rho \in \Gamma_1} p(\pi_{\sigma,\rho}(v)) = \inf_{\rho \in \Gamma_1} \sup_{\sigma \in \Gamma_0} p(\pi_{\sigma,\rho}(v)) =: \mathrm{val}\mathcal{G}(v),$$

where Γ_0, Γ_1 are the sets of all possible strategies for Player 0, Player 1. The outcome defined in this way is the ***value*** of $\mathcal{G}$ at v.

One of the fundamental properties of qualitative parity games is the ***positional determinacy***. Unfortunately, this does not generalise to quantitative parity games. Example 4.33 shows that there are simple quantitative games where no player has a positional winning strategy. In the depicted game there is no optimal strategy for Player 0, and even if one fixes an approximation of the game value, Player 0 needs infinite memory to reach this approximation, because she needs to loop in the second position as long as Player 1 looped in the first one to make up for the discounts. (By convention, we depict positions of Player 0 with a circle and of Player 1 with a square and the number inside is the priority for non-terminal positions and the payoff in terminal ones.)

Example 4.33

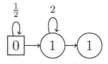

4.7.3 model-checking games for $Q\mu$

Given a quantitative transition system $\mathcal{K} = (S, T, \delta_S, P_i)$ and a $Q\mu$-formula ψ in negation normal form, we define the model-checking game $\mathrm{MC}[\mathcal{K}, \psi] = (V, V_0, V_1, E, \delta, \lambda, \Omega)$, as a quantitative parity game.

Positions and moves. As in games for L_μ, positions are the pairs (φ, s), where φ is a subformula of φ, and $s \in S$ is a state of the $\mathcal{K}$; in addition we have two special positions (0) and (∞). Positions $(|P_i - c|, s), (0)$, and (∞) are terminal positions. Moves are defined as in the games for L_μ, with the following modifications: positions of the form $(\Diamond\psi, s)$ have either a single successor (0), in case s is a terminal state in $\mathcal{K}$, or one successor (ψ, s') for every $s' \in sT$. Analogously, positions of the form $(\Box\psi, s)$ have a single successor (∞), if $sT = \emptyset$, or one successor (ψ, s') for every $s' \in sT$ otherwise. Positions of the form $(d \cdot \psi, s)$ have a unique successor (ψ, s'). Priorities are assigned in the same way as in the model-checking games for L_μ.

Discounts and payoffs. The discount of an edge is d for transitions from positions $(d \cdot \psi, s)$, it is $\delta_S(s, s')$ for transitions from $(\Diamond\psi, s)$ to (ψ, s'), it is $1/\delta_S(s, s')$ for transitions from $(\Box\psi, s)$ to (ψ, s'), and 1 for all outgoing transitions from other positions. The payoff function λ assigns $|[\![P_i]\!](s) - c|$ to all positions $(|P_i - c|, s)$, ∞ to position (∞), and 0 to position (0).

To prove that $\mathrm{MC}(\mathcal{K}, \psi)$ is indeed an appropriate model-checking game it must be shown that the value of the game starting from v coincides with the value of the formula evaluated on $\mathcal{K}$ at v'. In the qualitative case, that means, that ψ holds in $\mathcal{K}, v'$ if Player 0 wins in $\mathcal{G}$ from v.

Theorem 4.34 *For every formula ψ in $Q\mu$, every quantitative transition system $\mathcal{K}$, and $v \in \mathcal{K}$, the game $\mathrm{MC}[\mathcal{K}, \psi]$ is determined and*

$$valMC[\mathcal{K}, \psi](\psi, v) = [\![\psi]\!]^{\mathcal{K}}(v).$$

This is shown by Fischer et al. [2009] using a generalisation of the unfolding method for parity games.

Example 4.35 A model-checking game for $\varphi = \mu X.(P \vee 2 \cdot \Diamond X)$ on the QTS $\mathcal{Q}$ shown in Figure 4.1(a), with $P(1) = 0$, $P(2) = 1$, is depicted in Figure 4.1(b). The nodes are labelled with the corresponding subformulae of φ, and the state of $\mathcal{Q}$. Only the edges with discount factor different from 1 are labelled.

Note that in this game only Player 0 is allowed to make any choices. When we start at the top node, corresponding to an evaluation of φ at 1 in $\mathcal{Q}$, the only choice she has to make is either to keep playing (by looping), or to end the game by moving to a terminal position.

4.7.4 Defining game values in $Q\mu$

As in the case of parity games and LFP (and $L\mu$), also the connection between quantitative parity games and quantitative μ-calculus goes back

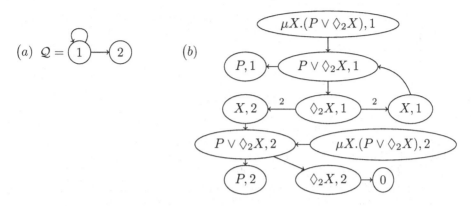

Figure 4.1 Example (a) QTS and (b) model-checking game for $\mu X.(P \vee 2 \cdot \Diamond X)$

and forth. We have seen that quantitative parity games are appropriate model-checking games for the evaluation of $Q\mu$-formulae on quantitative transition systems. For the other direction, we now show that *values* of positions in quantitative parity games (with a bounded number of priorities) are definable in $Q\mu$. It is convenient to describe a quantitative parity game $\mathcal{G} = (V, V_0, V_1, E, \delta_G, \lambda, \Omega_G)$ with priorities in $\{0, \ldots d-1\}$ by a quantitative transition system $\mathcal{Q}_{\mathcal{G}} = (V, E, \delta, V_0, V_1, \Lambda, \Omega)$, where $V_i(v) = \infty$ for positions of Player i, and $V_i(v) = 0$ otherwise, where $\Omega(v) = \Omega_G(v)$ when $vE \neq \emptyset$ and $\Omega(v) = d$ otherwise, with discount function

$$\delta(v, w) = \begin{cases} \delta_G(v, w) & \text{for } v \in V_0, \\ (\delta_G(v, w))^{-1} & \text{for } v \in V_1 \end{cases}$$

and with payoff predicate $\Lambda(v) := \lambda(v)$ in case $vE = \emptyset$ and is $\Lambda(v) = 0$ otherwise.

We then modify the L_μ-formulae Win_d constructed in Section 4.5.1 to quite similar $Q\mu$-formulae

$$\text{QWin}_d = \nu X_0 \mu X_1 \nu X_2 \ldots \lambda X_{d-1} \bigvee_{j=0}^{d-1} ((V_0 \wedge P_j \wedge \Diamond X_j) \vee (V_1 \wedge P_j \wedge \Box X_j)) \vee \Lambda,$$

where $P_i := \neg(\mu X.(2 \cdot X \vee |\Omega - i|))$. Note that $P_i(v) = \infty$ when $\Omega(v) = i$ and $P_i(v) = 0$ otherwise. The formula QWin_d is therefore analogous to the formula Win_d in the qualitative case.

Theorem 4.36 *For every $d \in \mathbb{N}$, the value of any quantitative parity game with priorities in $\{0, \ldots d-1\}$ coincides with the value of $QWin_d$ on the associated transition system.*

Exercise 4.8 Adapt the proof of Theorem 4.20 to get a proof of Theorem 4.36.

References

A. Arnold. The mu-calculus alternation-depth is strict on binary trees. *RAIRO Informatique Théorique et Applications*, 33:329–339, 1999.

J. Bradfield. The modal μ-calculus alternation hierarchy is strict. *Theoretical Computer Science*, 195:133–153, 1998.

A. Chandra and D. Harel. Structure and complexity for relational queries. *Journal of Computer and System Sciences*, 25:99–128, 1982.

E. Dahlhaus. Skolem normal forms concerning the least fixed point. In E. Börger, editor, *Computation Theory and Logic*, number 270 in Lecture Notes in Computer Science, pages 101–106. Springer Verlag, 1987.

A. Dawar and E. Grädel. The descriptive complexity of parity games. In *Proceedings of 22th Annual Conference of the European Association for Computer Science Logic CSL 2008*, pages 354–368, 2008.

A. Dawar, E. Grädel, and S. Kreutzer. Inflationary fixed points in modal logic. *ACM Transactions on Computational Logic*, 5:282 – 315, 2004.

A. Dawar, E. Grädel, and S. Kreutzer. Backtracking games and inflationary fixed points. *Theoretical Computer Science*, 350:174–187, 2006.

W. F. Dowling and J. H. Gallier. Linear-time algorithms for testing the satisfiability of propositional horn formulae. *Journal of Logic Programming*, 1(3):267–284, 1984.

S. Dziembowski. Bounded-variable fixpoint queries are PSPACE-complete. In *10th Annual Conference on Computer Science Logic CSL 96. Selected papers*, Lecture Notes in Computer Science Nr. 1258, pages 89–105. Springer, 1996.

H.-D. Ebbinghaus and J. Flum. *Finite Model Theory*. Springer, 2nd edition, 1999.

A. Emerson and C. Jutla. Tree automata, mu-calculus and determinacy. In *Proc. 32nd IEEE Symp. on Foundations of Computer Science*, pages 368–377, 1991.

D. Fischer, E. Grädel, and L. Kaiser. Model checking games for the quantitative μ-calculus. *Theory of Computing Systems*, 2009.

E. Grädel. Finite Model Theory and Descriptive Complexity. In *Finite Model Theory and Its Applications*. Springer-Verlag, 2007.

E. Grädel and I. Walukiewicz. Positional determinacy of games with infinitely many priorities. *Logical Methods in Computer Science*, 2006.

E. Grädel, P. G. Kolaitis, L. Libkin, M. Marx, J. Spencer, M. Y. Vardi, Y. Venema, and S.Weinstein. *Finite Model Theory and Its Applications*. Springer, Berlin, 2007.

R. Greenlaw, J. Hoover, and W. Ruzzo. *Limits to Parallel Computation. P-Completeness Theory*. Oxford University Press, Oxford, 1995.

N. Immerman. Relational queries computable in polynomial time. *Information and Control*, 68:86–104, 1986.

A. Itai and J. Makowsky. Unification as a complexity measure for logic programming. *Journal of Logic Programming*, 4:105–117, 1987.

M. Jurdziński. Small progress measures for solving parity games. In *Proceedings of 17th Annual Symposium on Theoretical Aspects of Computer Science, STACS*

2000, Lecture Notes in Computer Science Nr. 1770, pages 290–301. Springer, 2000.

M. Jurdziński. Deciding the winner in parity games is in UP ∩ Co-UP. *Information Processing Letters*, 68:119–124, 1998.

M. Jurdziński, M. Paterson, and U. Zwick. A deterministic subexponential algorithm for solving parity games. In *Proceedings of ACM-SIAM Proceedings on Discrete Algorithms, SODA 2006*, pages 117–123, 2006.

S. Kreutzer. Expressive equivalence of least and inflationary fixed point logic. *Annals of Pure and Applied Logic*, 130:61–78, 2004.

D. Martin. Borel determinacy. *Annals of Mathematics*, 102:336–371, 1975.

A. Mostowski. Games with forbidden positions. Technical Report 78, University of Gdańsk, 1991.

M. Otto. Bisimulation-invariant Ptime and higher-dimensional mu-calculus. *Theoretical Computer Science*, 224:237–265, 1999.

M. Vardi. The complexity of relational query languages. In *Proceedings of the 14th ACM Symposium on the Theory of Computing*, pages 137–146, 1982.

E. Zermelo. über eine Anwendung der Mengenlehre auf die Theorie des Schachpiels. In *Proc. 5th Internat. Congr. Mathematicians*, volume 2, pages 501–504, Cambridge, 1913.

W. Zielonka. Infinite games on finitely coloured graphs with applications to automata on infinite trees. *Theoretical Computer Science*, 200:135–183, 1998.

5
Turn-Based Stochastic Games

Antonín Kučera

Masaryk University

Abstract

In this chapter, we give a taxonomy of winning objectives in stochastic turn-based games, discuss their basic properties, and present an overview of the existing results. Special attention is devoted to games with infinitely many vertices.

5.1 Introduction

Turn-based stochastic games are infinitely long sequential games of perfect information played by two 'ordinary' players and a random player. Such games are also known as *simple stochastic games* and are a special type of (simultaneous-choice) *stochastic games* considered by Shapley [1953]. Intuitively, a turn-based stochastic game is a directed graph with a finite or countably infinite set of vertices, where each vertex 'belongs' either to player □, player ◊, or the random player ◯. An example of a turn-based stochastic game with finitely many vertices is given below.

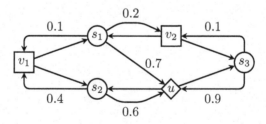

The outgoing transitions of stochastic vertices (drawn as circles) are selected randomly according to fixed probability distributions. In the other vertices (boxes and diamonds), the outgoing transitions are selected by the respective player according to his *strategy*, which may be *randomised* and *history-dependent*. Thus, every pair of strategies for both players determines a *play* of the game, which is a Markov chain obtained by applying the strategies to the original game. The aim of player □ is to maximise the expected *payoff* associated to runs in plays, or to play so that a certain *property* is satisfied. Player ◊ usually (but not necessarily) aims at the opposite.

In computer science, turn-based stochastic games are used as a natural model for discrete systems where the behaviour in each state is either controllable, adversarial, or stochastic. The main question is whether there is a suitable controller (strategy of player □) such that the system satisfies a certain property no matter what the environment and unpredictable users do. For a successful implementation of a controller, it is also important what kind of information about the computational history is required and whether the controller needs to randomise. This is the main source of motivation for considering the abstract problems presented in the next sections.

Since real-world computational systems are usually very large and complex, they can be analysed only indirectly by constructing a simplified *formal model*. A formal model of a given system is an abstract computational device which faithfully reflects the important behavioural aspects of the system. For purposes of formal modeling, the expressive power of *finite-state* devices is often insufficient, and some kind of unbounded data storage (such as counters, channels, stacks, queues, etc.) is needed to obtain a sufficiently precise model. Hence, in the computer science context, the study of turn-based stochastic games is not limited just to finite-state games, but also includes certain classes of *infinite-state* games which correspond to various types of computational devices such as pushdown automata, channel systems, vector addition systems, or process calculi.

5.1.1 Preliminaries

We start by recalling some notation and basic concepts that are necessary for understanding the material presented in subsequent sections.

Words, paths, and runs

In this chapter, the set of all real numbers is denoted by $\mathbb{R}$, and we also use the standard way of writing intervals of real numbers (e.g., $(0, 1]$ abbreviates $\{x \in \mathbb{R} \mid 0 < x \leq 1\}$).

Let M be a finite or countably infinite alphabet. A **word** over M is a finite or infinite sequence of elements of M. The empty word is denoted by ε, and the set of all finite words over M is denoted by M^*. Sometimes we also use M^+ to denote the set $M^* \setminus \{\varepsilon\}$. The length of a given word w is denoted by $len(w)$, where $len(\varepsilon) = 0$ and the length of an infinite word is ∞. The individual letters in w are denoted by $w(0), w(1), \ldots$, and for every infinite word w and every $i \geq 0$ we use w_i to denote the infinite word $w(i), w(i+1), \ldots$

A *transition system* is a pair $\mathcal{T} = (S, \rightarrow)$, where S is a finite or countably infinite set of *states* and $\rightarrow \subseteq S \times S$ a *transition relation* such that for every $s \in S$ there is at least one outgoing transition (i.e., a transition of the form $s \rightarrow t$). We say that $\mathcal{T}$ is *finitely branching* if every $s \in S$ has only finitely many outgoing transitions. A *path* in $\mathcal{T}$ is a finite or infinite word w over S such that $w(i) \rightarrow w(i+1)$ for every $0 \leq i < len(w)$. A *run* is an infinite path. The sets of all finite paths and all runs in $\mathcal{T}$ are denoted by $Fpath(\mathcal{T})$ and $Run(\mathcal{T})$, respectively. Similarly, for a given $w \in Fpath(\mathcal{T})$, we use $Fpath(\mathcal{T}, w)$ and $Run(\mathcal{T}, w)$ to denote the sets of all finite paths and all runs that start with w, respectively. When $\mathcal{T}$ is clear from the context, it is usually omitted (for example, we write just Run instead of $Run(\mathcal{T})$).

Probability spaces

Let A be a finite or countably infinite set. A *probability distribution* on A is a function $\mu : A \rightarrow [0, 1]$ such that $\sum_{a \in A} \mu(a) = 1$. A distribution μ is *rational* if $\mu(a)$ is rational for every $a \in A$, *positive* if $\mu(a) > 0$ for every $a \in A$, and *Dirac* if $\mu(a) = 1$ for some $a \in A$. A Dirac distribution μ where $\mu(a) = 1$ is also denoted by μ_a or just a.

Let Ω be a set of *elementary events*. A *σ-field* over Ω is a set $\mathcal{F} \subseteq 2^\Omega$ that includes Ω and is closed under complement and countable union. A *measurable space* is a pair $(\Omega, \mathcal{F})$ where $\mathcal{F}$ is a σ-field over Ω. An *$\mathcal{F}$-measurable function* over $(\Omega, \mathcal{F})$ is a function $f : \Omega \rightarrow \mathbb{R}$ such that $f^{-1}(I) \in \mathcal{F}$ for every interval I in $\mathbb{R}$.

Example 5.1 Let $\mathcal{T} = (S, \rightarrow)$ be a transition system. Let $\mathcal{B}$ be the least σ-field over Run containing all *basic cylinders* $Run(w)$ where $w \in Fpath$ (i.e., $\mathcal{B}$ is the Borel σ-field generated by open sets in the Cantor topology on Run). Then $(Run, \mathcal{B})$ is a measurable space, and the elements of $\mathcal{B}$ are called *Borel* sets of runs.

The Borel σ-field $\mathcal{B}$ contains many interesting elements. For example, let $s, t \in S$ and let $Reach(s, t)$ be the set of all runs initiated in s which visit t. Obviously, $Reach(s, t)$ is the union of all basic cylinders $Run(w)$ where $w \in Fpath(s)$ and w visits t, and hence $Reach(s, t) \in \mathcal{B}$. Similarly, one can show that the set of all runs initiated in s that visit t infinitely often is Borel.

Actually, most of the 'interesting' sets of runs are Borel, although there exist also subsets of *Run* that are not in $\mathcal{B}$.

Let $A \in \mathcal{B}$, and let $f : Run \rightarrow \{0, 1\}$ be a function which to a given $w \in Run$ assigns either 1 or 0, depending on whether $w \in A$ or not, respectively. Then f is $\mathcal{B}$-measurable, because for every interval I in $\mathbb{R}$ we have that $f^{-1}(I)$ is equal either to *Run*, A, *Run* $\setminus A$, or $\emptyset$, depending on whether $I \cap \{0, 1\}$ is equal to $\{0, 1\}$, $\{1\}$, $\{0\}$, or $\emptyset$, respectively. $\square$

A **probability measure** over a measurable space $(\Omega, \mathcal{F})$ is a function $\mathcal{P} : \mathcal{F} \rightarrow [0, 1]$ such that, for each countable collection $\{A_i\}_{i \in I}$ of pairwise disjoint elements of $\mathcal{F}$, we have that $\mathcal{P}(\bigcup_{i \in I} A_i) = \sum_{i \in I} \mathcal{P}(A_i)$, and moreover $\mathcal{P}(\Omega) = 1$. A **probability space** is a triple $(\Omega, \mathcal{F}, \mathcal{P})$ where $(\Omega, \mathcal{F})$ is a measurable space and $\mathcal{P}$ is a probability measure over $(\Omega, \mathcal{F})$.

A **random variable** over a probability space $(\Omega, \mathcal{F}, \mathcal{P})$ is an $\mathcal{F}$-measurable function $X : \Omega \rightarrow \mathbb{R}$. The **expected value of** X, denoted by $\mathbb{E}(X)$, is defined as the Lebesgue integral $\int_\Omega X \, d\mathcal{P}$. A random variable X is **discrete** if there is a finite or countably infinite subset N of $\mathbb{R}$ such that $\mathcal{P}(X^{-1}(N)) = 1$. The expected value of a discrete random variable X is equal to $\sum_{n \in N} n \cdot \mathcal{P}(X{=}n)$, where $X{=}n$ denotes the set $X^{-1}(\{n\})$.

Markov chains

A **Markov chain** is a tuple $\mathcal{M} = (S, \rightarrow, Prob, \mu)$ where $(S, \rightarrow)$ is a transition system, *Prob* is a function which to each $s \in S$ assigns a positive probability distribution over the outgoing transitions of s, and $\mu : S \rightarrow [0, 1]$ is an *initial* probability distribution. We write $s \xrightarrow{x} t$ to indicate that $s \rightarrow t$ and $Prob(s)((s, t)) = x$.

Consider the measurable space $(Run, \mathcal{B})$ introduced in Example 5.1, i.e., $\mathcal{B}$ is the least σ-field containing all $Run(w)$ such that $w \in Fpath$. By Carathéodory's extension theorem (see, e.g., Billingsley [1995], Kemeny et al. [1976]), there is a unique probability measure $\mathcal{P}_\mu$ over $(Run, \mathcal{B})$ such that for every basic cylinder $Run(w)$ we have that $\mathcal{P}_\mu(Run(w))$ is defined in the 'natural' way, i.e., by multiplying $\mu(w(0))$ with the probabilities of all transitions in w. Thus, we obtain the probability space $(Run, \mathcal{B}, \mathcal{P}_\mu)$.

Example 5.2 Consider the finite-state Markov chain $\mathcal{M}$ of Figure 5.1 with the initial distribution μ_s (recall that μ_s is a Dirac distribution where $\mu_s(s) = 1$). Let $Reach(s, t)$ be the set of all runs initiated in s which visit t. Obviously, $Reach(s, t) = \bigcup_{i=1}^\infty Reach^i(s, t)$, where $Reach^i(s, t)$ consists of all $w \in Reach(s, t)$ that visit t for the first time after exactly i transitions. Further, every $Reach^i(s, t)$ can be partitioned into 2^{i-1} pairwise disjoint basic cylinders according to the first $i - 1$ transitions. Each of these cylinders has

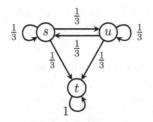

Figure 5.1 A finite-state Markov chain $\mathcal{M}$

the probability $(\frac{1}{3})^i$, hence $\mathcal{P}(Reach^i(s,t)) = (\frac{2}{3})^{i-1} \cdot \frac{1}{3}$. Since $Reach^i(s,t) \cap Reach^j(s,t) = \emptyset$ whenever $i \neq j$, we obtain

$$\mathcal{P}(Reach(s,t)) = \mathcal{P}\left(\bigcup_{i=1}^{\infty} Reach^i(s,t)\right) = \sum_{i=1}^{\infty} \mathcal{P}(Reach^i(s,t)) = \sum_{i=1}^{\infty} \left(\frac{2}{3}\right)^{i-1} \cdot \frac{1}{3} = 1$$

as expected. Also note that $Run(s) \setminus Reach(t)$ is uncountable but its probability is zero. □

Turn-based stochastic games and Markov decision processes

A *(turn-based) stochastic game* is a tuple $G = (V, \mapsto, (V_\square, V_\lozenge, V_\bigcirc), Prob)$ where $(V, \mapsto)$ is a transition system, $(V_\square, V_\lozenge, V_\bigcirc)$ is a partition of V, and *Prob* is a function which to each $v \in V_\bigcirc$ assigns a positive probability distribution on the set of its outgoing transitions. We say that G is *finitely branching* if $(V, \mapsto)$ is finitely branching. A *Markov decision process (MDP)* is a stochastic game where $V_\lozenge = \emptyset$ or $V_\square = \emptyset$. Note that Markov chains can be seen as stochastic games where $V_\square = V_\lozenge = \emptyset$.

A stochastic game is played by two players, $\square$ and $\lozenge$, who select transitions in the vertices of $V_\square$ and $V_\lozenge$, respectively. Let $\odot \in \{\square, \lozenge\}$. A *strategy* for player $\odot$ is a function which to each $wv \in V^*V_\odot$ assigns a probability distribution on the set of outgoing transitions of v. The sets of all strategies for player $\square$ and player $\lozenge$ are denoted by Σ_G and Π_G (or just by Σ and Π if G is understood), respectively. We say that a strategy τ is *memoryless (M)* if $\tau(wv)$ depends just on the last vertex v, and *deterministic (D)* if $\tau(wv)$ is Dirac for all wv. Strategies that are not necessarily memoryless are called *history-dependent (H)*, and strategies that are not necessarily deterministic are called *randomised (R)*. A special type of history-dependent strategies are *finite-memory (F)* strategies. A strategy τ of player $\odot$ is a finite-memory strategy if there is a finite set $C = \{c_1, \ldots, c_n\}$ of *colours*, a *colouring* $\nu : V \to C$, and a deterministic finite-state automaton M over the alphabet C such that for every $wv \in V^*V_\odot$ we have that $\tau(wv)$ depends only on v and the control state entered by M after reading the (unique) word $\nu(wv)$ obtained by replacing each vertex in wv with its associated colour. **Infinite-memory** strategies are strategies which are not finite-memory. To sum up, we consider the following six *types* of strategies: MD, MR, FD, FR, HD, and HR, where $XD \subseteq XR$ for every $X \in \{M, F, H\}$ and $MY \subseteq FY \subseteq HY$ for every $Y \in \{D, R\}$. The sets of all XY strategies of player $\square$ and player $\Diamond$ are denoted by Σ^{XY} and Π^{XY}, respectively (note that $\Sigma = \Sigma^{HR}$ and $\Pi = \Pi^{HR}$).

Every pair of strategies $(\sigma, \pi) \in \Sigma \times \Pi$ and every *initial* probability distribution $\mu : V \to [0, 1]$ determine a unique **play** of the game G, which is a Markov chain $G_\mu^{(\sigma, \pi)}$ where V^+ is the set of states, and $wu \xrightarrow{x} wuu'$ iff $u \mapsto u'$, $x > 0$, and one of the following conditions holds:

- $u \in V_\square$ and $\sigma(wu)$ assigns x to $u \mapsto u'$;
- $u \in V_\Diamond$ and $\pi(wu)$ assigns x to $u \mapsto u'$;
- $u \in V_\bigcirc$ and $u \xrightarrow{x} u'$.

The initial distribution of $G_\mu^{(\sigma, \pi)}$ assigns $\mu(v)$ to all $v \in V$, and zero to the other states. Note that every run w in $G_\mu^{(\sigma, \pi)}$ naturally determines a unique run w_G in G, where $w_G(i)$ is the last vertex of $w(i)$ for every $i \geq 0$.

5.2 Winning objectives in stochastic games

In this section we give a taxonomy of winning objectives in turn-based stochastic games and formulate the main problems of the associated algorithmic analysis. For the rest of this section, we fix a turn-based stochastic game $G = (V, \mapsto, (V_\square, V_\Diamond, V_\bigcirc), Prob)$.

Let $plays(G)$ be the set of all plays of G (i.e., $plays(G)$ consists of all Markov chains of the form $G_\mu^{(\sigma, \pi)}$). For every $\odot \in \{\square, \Diamond\}$, let $yield_\odot : plays(G) \to \mathbb{R}$ be a function which to every play of G assigns the **yield** of player $\odot$.

Remark In the standard terminology of game theory, the yield of a given player under a given strategy profile is usually called a **payoff**. However, in the context of turn-based stochastic games, the word 'payoff' usually refers to a function $f_\odot : Run(G) \to \mathbb{R}$ whose *expected value* is to be maximised by player $\odot$ (see Section 5.2.1 for more details). $\square$

The objective of each player is to maximise his yield. For turn-based stochastic games, most of the studied yield functions are **zero-sum**, i.e., for every play $G_\mu^{(\sigma, \pi)}$ of G we have that

$$yield_\square(G_\mu^{(\sigma, \pi)}) + yield_\Diamond(G_\mu^{(\sigma, \pi)}) = 0.$$

For zero-sum games, it suffices to specify just $yield_\square$, which is denoted simply by *yield*. Then, the objective of player $\square$ and player $\lozenge$ is to maximise and minimise the value of *yield*, respectively.

There are two major classes of zero-sum turn-based stochastic games, which can be characterised as follows:

(1) **Games with Borel measurable payoffs.** Every $\mathcal{B}$-measurable function over $Run(G)$ determines a unique random variable over the runs of a given play of G. The yield assigned to the play is the expected value of this random variable.

(2) **Win–lose games.** A win–lose yield is either 1 or 0 for every play of G, depending of whether the play satisfies a certain property or not, respectively. Typically, the property is encoded as a formula of some probabilistic temporal logic.

These two classes of games are formally introduced and discussed in the next subsections.

Let us note that there are also results about *non-zero-sum* turned-based stochastic games, where the objectives of the (two or more) players are not necessarily conflicting. The main question is the existence and effective computability of Nash equilibria for various classes of players' objectives. The problem has been considered also in the more general setting of simultaneous-choice stochastic games. We refer to Secchi and Sudderth [2001], Chatterjee et al. [2004c, 2006] and Ummels and Wojtczak [2009] for more details.

5.2.1 Games with Borel measurable payoffs

A **payoff** is a bounded[1] $\mathcal{B}$-measurable function $f : Run(G) \to \mathbb{R}$. Observe that for every pair of strategies $(\sigma, \pi) \in \Sigma \times \Pi$ and every initial probability distribution μ on V, the function $f_\mu^{\sigma,\pi} : Run(G_\mu^{(\sigma,\pi)}) \to \mathbb{R}$ defined by $f_\mu^{\sigma,\pi}(w) = f(w_G)$ is a random variable. Thus, every payoff f determines the associated yield defined by

$$yield_f(G_\mu^{(\sigma,\pi)}) = \mathbb{E}(f_\mu^{\sigma,\pi}).$$

As observed by Maitra and Sudderth [1998], the determinacy result for Blackwell games achieved by Martin [1998] implies that for every vertex $v \in V$ we have the following:

$$\sup_{\sigma \in \Sigma} \inf_{\pi \in \Pi} \mathbb{E}(f_v^{\sigma,\pi}) = \inf_{\pi \in \Pi} \sup_{\sigma \in \Sigma} \mathbb{E}(f_v^{\sigma,\pi}). \tag{5.1}$$

---

[1] A real-valued function f is *bounded* if there is $b \in \mathbb{R}$ such that $-b \le f(x) \le b$ for every x in the domain of f.

Hence, every vertex $v \in V$ has its *f-value*, denoted by $val_f(v, G)$ (or just by $val_f(v)$ if G is understood), which is defined by Equality (5.1). Note that this result holds without any additional assumptions about the game G. In particular, G may have infinitely many vertices and some (or all) of them may have infinitely many outgoing transitions.

Remark It is worth noting that the result presented by Maitra and Sudderth [1998] is even more general and holds also for **concurrent** stochastic games (where both players make their choice simultaneously) with an *arbitrary* (not necessarily countable) action and state spaces. The only requirement is that f is a bounded $\mathcal{B}$-measurable function and both players choose their actions at random according to finitely additive probability measures on the power sets of their respective action sets. This can be used, e.g., to show that vertices in various types of *timed* stochastic games have an f-value. $\square$

An important subclass of payoff functions are **qualitative** payoffs which simply classify each run as good or bad according to some criteria. The good runs are assigned 1, and the bad ones are assigned 0. General (not necessarily qualitative) payoffs are also called **quantitative** payoffs.

Note that a qualitative payoff f is just a characteristic function of some Borel set $B_f \subseteq Run(G)$. For every pair of strategies $(\sigma, \pi) \in \Sigma \times \Pi$ and every initial distribution μ we have that

$$\mathbb{E}(f_\mu^{\sigma,\pi}) = \mathcal{P}_\mu(\{w \in Run(G_\mu^{(\sigma,\pi)}) \mid w_G \in B_f\}).$$

Hence, player $\square$ and player $\Diamond$ in fact try to maximise and minimise the *probability* of all runs in B_f, respectively.

Observe that Equality (5.1) does not guarantee the existence of **optimal** strategies for player $\square$ and player $\Diamond$ which would achieve the yield $val_f(v)$ or better against every strategy of the opponent. As we shall see, optimal strategies do *not* exist in general, but they may exist in some restricted cases. On the other hand, Equality (5.1) *does* imply the existence of ε-optimal strategies for an arbitrarily small $\varepsilon > 0$.

Definition 5.3 Let $\varepsilon \geq 0$. A strategy $\hat{\sigma} \in \Sigma$ is an ε-**optimal maximising strategy** in a vertex $v \in V$ if $\inf_{\pi \in \Pi} \mathbb{E}(f_v^{\hat{\sigma},\pi}) \geq val_f(v) - \varepsilon$. Similarly, a strategy $\hat{\pi} \in \Pi$ is an ε-**optimal minimising strategy** in a vertex $v \in V$ if $\sup_{\sigma \in \Sigma} \mathbb{E}(f_v^{\sigma,\hat{\pi}}) \leq val_f(v) + \varepsilon$. Strategies that are 0-optimal are **optimal**.

Qualitative payoffs

Let $C = \{c_1, \ldots, c_n\}$ be a finite set of **colours**, and $\nu : V \to 2^C$ a **valuation**. An important and well-studied class of qualitative payoffs are characteristic functions of ω-*regular* subsets of $Run(G)$. The membership in an ω-regular set of runs is determined by one of the **acceptance conditions** listed below. These conditions correspond to acceptance criteria of finite-state automata over infinite words (see Section 5.2.2 for more details).

- **Reachability and safety.** A run $w \in Run(G)$ satisfies the *reachability* condition determined by a colour $c \in C$ if $c \in \nu(w(i))$ for some $i \geq 0$. The *safety* condition determined by c is dual, i.e., $c \notin \nu(w(i))$ for all $i \geq 0$.

- **Büchi and co-Büchi.** A run $w \in Run(G)$ satisfies the *Büchi* condition determined by a colour $c \in C$ if $c \in \nu(w(i))$ for infinitely many $i \geq 0$. The *co-Büchi* condition is dual, i.e., there are only finitely many $i \geq 0$ such that $c \in \nu(w(i))$.

- **Rabin, Rabin-chain, and Street.** Let $Pairs = \{(c_1, d_1), \ldots, (c_m, d_m)\}$ be a finite set of pairs of colours. A run $w \in Run(G)$ satisfies the *Rabin* condition determined by $Pairs$ if there is $(c, d) \in Pairs$ such that w satisfies the Büchi condition determined by d and the co-Büchi condition determined by c. The *Street* condition determined by $Pairs$ is dual to Rabin, i.e., for every $(c, d) \in Pairs$ we have that w satisfies the co-Büchi condition determined by d or the Büchi condition determined by c.

  For a given colour c, let $V(c)$ be the set of all $v \in V$ such that $c \in \nu(v)$. The *Rabin-chain* (or *parity*) condition is a special case of the Rabin condition where $Pairs$ and ν satisfy $V(c_1) \subset V(d_1) \subset \cdots \subset V(c_m) \subset V(d_m)$.

- **Muller.** Let $M \subseteq 2^C$ be a set of subsets of colours. A run $w \in Run(G)$ satisfies the *Muller* condition determined by M if the set of all $c \in C$ such w satisfies the Büchi condition determined by c is an element of M.

Let us note that ω-regular sets of runs are relatively simple in the sense that they are contained in the first two levels of the Borel hierarchy (the sets of runs satisfying the reachability and safety conditions are in the first level).

Quantitative payoffs

Quantitative payoff functions can capture more complicated properties of runs that are particularly useful in performance and dependability analysis of stochastic systems.

Let $r : V \to \mathbb{R}$ be a bounded function which to every vertex v assigns the *reward* $r(v)$, which can be intuitively interpreted as a price paid by player $\Diamond$ to player $\Box$ when visiting v. The limit properties of rewards that are paid along a given run are captured by the following payoff functions:

- **Limit-average payoff** (also **mean-payoff**) assigns to each $w \in Run(G)$

the average reward per vertex visited along w. For every $n \geq 1$, let $avg^n(w) = \frac{1}{n}\sum_{i=0}^{n-1} r(w(i))$. Since $\lim_{n\to\infty} avg^n(w)$ may not exist for a given run w, the mean-payoff function appears in two flavours, defined as follows:

$$avg\ sup(w) = \limsup_{n\to\infty} avg^n(w) \qquad avg\ inf(w) = \liminf_{n\to\infty} avg^n(w).$$

Let us note that if the players play in a sufficiently 'weird' way, it may happen that $avg\ sup(w) \neq avg\ inf(w)$ for all runs w in a given play, even if the underlying game G has just two vertices.

Mean-payoff functions were introduced by Gillette [1957]. For *finite-state* games, it is sometimes stipulated that the aim of player $\square$ is to maximise the expectation of *avg sup* and the aim of player $\Diamond$ is to minimise the expectation of *avg inf*. For finite-state games, we have that

$$\sup_{\sigma\in\Sigma} \inf_{\pi\in\Pi} \mathbb{E}(avg\ sup_v^{\sigma,\pi}) = \inf_{\pi\in\Pi} \sup_{\sigma\in\Sigma} \mathbb{E}(avg\ inf_v^{\sigma,\pi}) \qquad (5.2)$$

and there are MD strategies $\hat{\sigma} \in \Sigma$ and $\hat{\pi} \in \Pi$ such that $\inf_{\pi\in\Pi} \mathbb{E}(avg\ sup_v^{\hat{\sigma},\pi})$ and $\sup_{\sigma\in\Sigma} \mathbb{E}(avg\ inf_v^{\sigma,\hat{\pi}})$ are equal to the value defined by Equality (5.2) (see Gillette [1957], Liggett and Lippman [1969]).

Note that Equality (5.2) does not follow from Equality (5.1) and is *invalid* for infinite-state games. To see this, consider an arbitrary sequence $(a_i)_{i=0}^{\infty}$ such that $a_i \in \{0, 1\}$ and

$$A_{\text{inf}} = \liminf_{n\to\infty} \frac{1}{n}\sum_{i=0}^{n-1} a_i < \limsup_{n\to\infty} \frac{1}{n}\sum_{i=0}^{n-1} a_i = A_{\text{sup}}.$$

This sequence can be encoded as a game with countably many vertices $v_0, v_1, \ldots$ where $v_i \mapsto v_{i+1}$ and $r(v_i) = a_i$ for all $i \geq 0$. Obviously, for all $(\sigma, \pi) \in \Sigma \times \Pi$ we have that

$$\mathbb{E}(avg\ inf_{v_0}^{\sigma,\pi}) = A_{\text{inf}} < A_{\text{sup}} = \mathbb{E}(avg\ sup_{v_0}^{\sigma,\pi})$$

which means that Equality (5.2) does not hold. Also observe that $val_{avg\ inf}(v_0) \neq val_{avg\ sup}(v_0)$.

- **Discounted payoff** assigns to each $w \in Run(G)$ the sum of discounted rewards

$$\sum_{i=0}^{\infty} d^i \cdot r(w(i))$$

where $0 < d < 1$ is a *discount factor*. Discounting formally captures the natural idea that the far-away future is not as important as the near future.

Observe that the above series converges absolutely which is mathematically convenient.

- **Weighted reachability** payoff assigns to every run w either 0 (if w does not visit a target vertex) or the reward of the first target vertex visited by w. Here, it is usually assumed that r is positive. One can also consider a **discounted reachability** payoff which is a variant of discounted payoff where $r(v)$ is either 1 or 0 depending on whether v is a target vertex or not.

- **lim-max** and **lim-min** payoffs, which assigns to each $w \in Run(G)$ either the maximal or the minimal reward which appears infinitely often along w. More precisely, we assume that r takes only finitely many values, and define $lim\text{-}max(w)$ and $lim\text{-}min(w)$ as the max and min of the set $\{x \in \mathbb{R} \mid r(w(i)) = x \text{ for infinitely many } i \geq 0\}$, respectively.

The presented list of Borel measurable payoffs contains only selected conceptual representatives and it is surely not exhaustive.

The problems of interest

For a given class of turn-based stochastic games G and a given class of payoff functions F, we are interested in answering the following basic questions:

(1) *Do optimal strategies exist for all $G \in G$ and $f \in F$?*

(2) *What is the type of optimal and ε-optimal strategies?*

(3) *Can we compute/approximate $val_f(v)$?*

(4) *Can we compute optimal and ε-optimal strategies?*

If the answer to Question (1) is negative, we also wonder whether the existence of an optimal strategy in a given vertex is decidable and what is the complexity of this problem.

Optimal strategies (if they exist) may require memory and/or randomisation. A full answer to Question (2) should provide an optimal upper bound on the size of the required memory. It can also happen that optimal strategies require memory *or* randomisation, but not necessarily both.

Question (3) can also be reformulated as a decision problem. For a given rational constant ϱ, we ask whether $val_f(v)$ is bounded by ϱ (from above or below). In particular, if f is a qualitative payoff, it is often important to know whether $val_f(v)$ is positive or equal to one, and this special *qualitative* variant of the problem tends to be computationally easier. If G is a class of infinite-state games, $val_f(v)$ can be irrational even if all transition probabilities are rational and f is reachability payoff (a simple example is presented in

Section 5.3). In such cases, all we can hope for is an efficient algorithm which approximates $val_f(v)$ up to an arbitrarily small given precision.

Question (4) also requires special attention in the case of infinite-state games, because then even MD strategies do not necessarily admit a finite description. Since the vertices of infinite-state games typically carry some algebraic structure, optimal strategies may depend just on some finite information gathered by analysing the structure of vertices visited along a run in a play.

The existing results

In this section we give a short summary of the existing results about turn-based stochastic games with Borel measurable payoffs. We start with *finite-state* games.

In general, optimal strategies in finite-state games with the Borel measurable payoff functions introduced in the previous sections exist, do not need to randomise, and are either memoryless or finite-memory. In some cases, memory can be 'traded' for randomness (see Chatterjee et al. [2004a]). The values are rational (assuming that transition probabilities in games are rational) and computable. The main techniques for establishing these results are the following:

- **Strategy improvement.** This technique was originally developed for general stochastic games (see Hoffman and Karp [1966]). An initial strategy for one of the players is successively improved by switching it at positions at which the current choices are not locally optimal.
- **Value iteration.** The tuple of all values is computed/approximated by iterating a suitable functional on some initial vector. For example, the Bellman functional Γ defined in Section 5.3.1 can be used to compute/approximate the values in games with reachability payoffs.
- **Convex optimisations.** These methods are particularly useful for MDPs (see Puterman [1994], Filar and Vrieze [1996]). For example, the tuple of values in MDPs with reachability payoffs is computable in polynomial time by a simple linear program (see below).
- **Graph-theoretic methods.** Typically, these methods are used to design efficient (polynomial-time) algorithms deciding whether the value of a given vertex is equal to one (see, e.g., Chatterjee et al. [1994]).

The individual payoff functions are discussed in greater detail below.

Reachability. Turn-based stochastic games with reachability payoffs were first considered by Condon [1992] where it was shown that the problem of whether $val(v) > \frac{1}{2}$ for a given vertex v is in **NP∩coNP**. It was also observed that both players have optimal MD strategies. The algorithm proposed by Condon [1992] requires transformation of the original game into a ***stopping*** game where ***local optimality equations*** admit a unique solution (i.e., the functional Γ defined in Section 5.3.1 has a unique fixed-point) which is a tuple of rational numbers of linear size. The tuple can then be guessed and verified (which leads to the **NP ∩ coNP** upper bound), or computed by a quadratic program with linear constraints. This algorithm is exponential even if the number of random vertices is fixed. Randomised algorithms with sub-exponential expected running time were proposed by Halman [2007] and Ludwig [1995]. A deterministic algorithm for computing the values and optimal strategies with $\mathcal{O}(|V_O|! \cdot (|V| \cdot |\mapsto| + |p|))$ running time, where $|p|$ is the maximum bit length of a transition probability, was recently proposed by Gimbert and Horn [2008]. This algorithm is *polynomial* for every fixed number of random vertices.

Let us note that the exact complexity of the problem of whether $val(v) > \frac{1}{2}$ remains unsettled, despite substantial effort of the community. Since the problem belongs to **NP∩coNP**, it is not likely to be **NP** or **coNP** complete. At the same time, it is not known to be in **P**. On the other hand, the qualitative variant of the problem (i.e., the question whether $val(v) = 1$) is solvable in polynomial time (this follows, e.g., from a more general result about Büchi objectives achieved by de Alfaro and Henzinger [2000]). For MDPs, the values and optimal strategies are computable in polynomial time (both in the maximising and minimising subcase) by linear programming. Given a MDP $G = (V, \mapsto, (V_\square, V_O), Prob)$ where $V = \{v_1, \ldots, v_n\}$ and v_n is the only target vertex, the tuple of all $val(v_i)$ is computable by the following program (a correctness proof can be found in, e.g., Filar and Vrieze [1996]):

> **minimise** $y_1 + \cdots + y_n$
> subject to
> $\quad y_n = 1$
> $\quad y_i \geq y_j$ $\qquad\qquad$ for all $v_i \mapsto v_j$ where $v_i \in V_\square$ and $i < n$
> $\quad y_i = \sum_{v_i \overset{x}{\mapsto} v_j} x \cdot y_j$ $\quad$ for all $v_i \in V_O$, $i < n$
> $\quad y_i \geq 0$ $\qquad\qquad$ for all $i \leq n$.

An optimal maximising strategy can be constructed in polynomial time even naively (i.e., for each $v \in V_\square$ we successively identify a transition $v \mapsto v'$ such that the tuple of values does not change when the other outgoing transitions of v are removed).

(co-)Büchi. In turn-based stochastic games with Büchi and co-Büchi payoffs, both players have optimal MD strategies, the problem of whether $val(v) \geq \varrho$ for a given rational $\varrho \in [0, 1]$ is in **NP ∩ coNP**, and the problem

of whether $val(v) = 1$ is **P**-complete (see Chatterjee et al. [2004b], de Alfaro and Henzinger [2000]).

Rabin-chain (parity). In turn-based stochastic games with Rabin-chain (parity) payoffs, both players still have optimal MD strategies (see McIver and Morgan [2002], Chatterjee et al. [2004b]). The problem of whether $val(v) \geq \varrho$ for a given rational $\varrho \in [0,1]$ is in **NP ∩ coNP**, and this is currently the best upper bound also for the problem of whether $val(v) = 1$ (see Chatterjee et al. [2004b]).

Rabin and Street. In turn-based stochastic games with Rabin payoffs, player □ has an optimal MD strategy (see Chatterjee et al. [2005]). This does not hold for player ◊, as demonstrated by the following simple example:

Consider the Rabin condition $\{(a, b), (b, a)\}$, where $\nu(u_a) = \{a\}$, $\nu(u_b) = \{b\}$, and $\nu(v) = \emptyset$. Obviously, $val(v) = 0$, but an optimal minimising strategy must ensure that both u_a and u_b are visited infinitely often, which is not achievable by a MD strategy.

Consequently, the problem of whether $val(v) \geq \varrho$ is in **NP** for Rabin payoffs. Since the problem of whether $val(v) = 1$ is **NP**-hard (see Emerson and Jutla [1988]), both problems are **NP**-complete. Since the Street acceptance condition is dual to Rabin, this also implies **coNP**-completeness of the two problems for Street payoffs.

Muller. In turn-based stochastic games with Muller payoffs, both players have optimal FD strategies, and the memory cannot be traded for randomness (i.e., the players do not necessarily have MR optimal strategies). To see this, consider the following game, where $\nu(u_a) = \{a\}$, $\nu(v) = \nu(u) = \emptyset$, $\nu(u_b) = \{b\}$, $\nu(u_c) = \{c\}$, and the Muller condition is $\{\{b\}, \{a, c\}, \{a, b, c\}\}$ (the example is taken from Chatterjee et al. [2004a]):

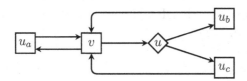

It is easy to check that $val(v) = 1$, and player □ has a FD optimal strategy which in every state wv selects either $v \mapsto u_a$ or $v \mapsto u$, depending on whether the last vertex of w is u_c or not, respectively. It is also easy to see that player □ does not have a MR optimal strategy.

For Muller payoffs, the problem of whether $val(v) \geq \varrho$ is

PSPACE-complete, and the same holds for the problem of whether $val(v) = 1$ (see Chatterjee [2007], Hunter and Dawar [2005]).

Mean-payoff and discounted payoff. In mean-payoff and discounted payoff turn-based stochastic games, both players have optimal MD strategies (see Gillette [1957], Liggett and Lippman [1969]), and the problem of whether $val(v) \geq \varrho$ is in **NP∩coNP**. We refer to Filar and Vrieze [1996], Neyman and Sorin [2003] for more comprehensive expositions of algorithms for mean-payoff and discounted payoff turn-based stochastic games.

Basic properties of the other quantitative payoffs (in particular, *lim-min* and *lim-max* payoffs) are carefully discussed in Chatterjee et al. [2009].

Finally, we give a brief overview of the existing results about *infinite-state* turn-based stochastic games. There are basically three types of such games studied in the literature.

- *Recursive stochastic games*, also known as *stochastic BPA games*. These are games defined over stateless pushdown automata or (equivalently) 1-exit recursive state machines. Roughly speaking, a stochastic BPA game is a finite system of rules of the form $X \hookrightarrow \alpha$, where X is a stack symbol and α is a (possibly empty) sequence of stack symbols. The finitely many stack symbols are split into three disjoint subsets of symbols that 'belong' to player $\square$, player $\Diamond$, or the virtual random player. A *configuration* is a finite sequence of stack symbols. The leftmost symbol of a given configuration is rewritten according to some rule, which is selected by the respective player (for every stochastic stack symbol Y, there is a fixed probability distribution over the rules of the form $Y \hookrightarrow \beta$).

  A *termination* objective is a special type of reachability objective where the only target vertex is ε (i.e., the empty stack). BPA MDPs and stochastic BPA games with termination objectives were studied by Etessami and Yannakakis [2005, 2006]. Some of these results were generalised to *reachability* objectives by Brázdil et al. [2008] and Brázdil et al. [2009a]. BPA MDPs and stochastic BPA games with *positive rewards* were studied by Etessami et al. [2008]. Here, each rule is assigned some fixed reward $r > 0$ which is collected whenever the rule is executed, and the objective of player $\square$ is to maximise the expected total reward (which can be infinite).

- *Stochastic games with lossy channels.* A lossy channel system is a finite-state automaton equipped with a finite number of unbounded but unreliable (lossy) channels. A transition may change a control state and read/write from/to a channel. Since the channels are lossy, an arbitrary number of messages may be lost from the channels before and after each transition. A probabilistic variant of lossy channel systems defines a probabilistic model for message losses. Usually, it is assumed that each individual message is lost independently with probability $\lambda > 0$ in every step. A stochastic game with lossy channels (SGLC) is obtained by splitting the control states into two disjoint subsets that are controlled by player $\square$ and player $\lozenge$, respectively. However, message losses still occur randomly.

In Baier et al. [2006], it was shown that SGLC with qualitative reachability objectives are decidable. MDPs with lossy channels and various ω-regular objectives were examined by Baier et al. [2007]. SGLC with Büchi objectives were studied recently by Abdulla et al. [2008].

- **One-counter stochastic games.** These are stochastic games generated by one-counter machines, i.e., finite-state automata equipped with an unbounded counter which can store non-negative integers. The set of control states is split into three disjoint subsets controlled by player $\square$, player $\lozenge$, or the random player, who are responsible for selecting one of the available transitions. One-counter MDPs with various reachability objectives were recently studied by Brázdil et al. [2010].

5.2.2 Win–lose games

Another important class of zero-sum stochastic turned-based games are *win–lose games* where the objective of player $\square$ is to satisfy some property which is either valid or invalid for every play of G (the associated yield assigns 1 to the plays where the property is valid, and 0 to the other plays). An important subclass of such properties are **temporal objectives** that can be encoded as formulae of suitable temporal logics.

Let φ be a formula which is either valid or invalid in every state of every play of G. We say that a strategy $\sigma \in \Sigma$ is φ**-winning in** v if for every strategy $\pi \in \Pi$ we have that the state v of $G_v^{(\sigma,\pi)}$ satisfies φ. Similarly, a strategy $\pi \in \Pi$ is $\neg\varphi$*-winning in* v if for every $\sigma \in \Sigma$ we have that the state v of $G_v^{(\sigma,\pi)}$ does *not* satisfy φ. We say that G (with φ) is **determined** if for every $v \in V$ either player $\square$ has a φ-winning strategy in v or player $\lozenge$ has a $\neg\varphi$-winning strategy in v.

Temporal logics can be classified as **linear-time** or *branching-time*, depending on whether they 'ignore' the branching structure of transition systems or not, respectively (see, e.g., Emerson [1991]). The syntax of these logics is built upon a countable set $Ap = \{a, b, c, \ldots\}$ of *atomic propositions*. A *valuation* is a function $\nu : V \to 2^{Ap}$ which to every vertex v assigns the set $\nu(v) \subseteq Ap$ of all atomic propositions that are valid in v. Note that ν can be naturally extended to the states of a play of G (for every state $wv \in V^*V$

of a play $G_\mu^{(\sigma,\pi)}$ we put $\nu(wv) = \nu(v))$. For the rest of this section, we fix a valuation ν.

Linear-time logics

Linear-time logics specify properties of runs in transition systems. For a given linear-time formula ψ, the associated temporal property is specified by a constraint on the probability of all runs that satisfy ψ. This constraint is written as a ***probabilistic operator*** $\mathbf{P}^{\succ\varrho}$, where $\succ \in \{>,\geq\}$ and $\varrho \in [0,1]$ is a rational constant. Thus, we obtain a ***linear-time objective*** $\mathbf{P}^{\succ\varrho}\psi$ whose intuitive meaning is 'the probability of all runs satisfying ψ is $\succ$-related to ϱ'. An important subclass of linear-time objectives are ***qualitative linear-time objectives*** where the constant ϱ is either 0 or 1.

An example of a widely used linear-time logic is LTL, introduced in Pnueli [1977]. The syntax of LTL formulae is specified by the following abstract syntax equation:

$$\psi \quad ::= \quad \mathbf{tt} \quad | \quad a \quad | \quad \neg\psi \quad | \quad \psi_1 \wedge \psi_2 \quad | \quad \mathbf{X}\psi \quad | \quad \psi_1 \mathbf{U} \psi_2$$

Here a ranges over Ap. Note that the set $Ap(\psi)$ of all atomic propositions that appear in a given LTL formula ψ is finite. Every LTL formula ψ determines its associated ω-*language* L_ψ consisting of all infinite words u over the alphabet $2^{Ap(\psi)}$ such that $u \models \psi$, where the relation $\models$ is defined inductively as follows (recall that the symbol u_i, where $i \geq 0$, denotes the infinite word $u(i), u(i{+}1), \ldots$):

$u \models \mathbf{tt}$

$u \models a$ iff $a \in u(0)$

$u \models \neg\psi$ iff $u \not\models \psi$

$u \models \psi_1 \wedge \psi_2$ iff $u \models \psi_1$ and $u \models \psi_2$

$u \models \mathbf{X}\psi$ iff $u_1 \models \psi$

$u \models \psi_1 \mathbf{U} \psi_2$ iff $u_j \models \psi_2$ for some $j \geq 0$ and $u_i \models \psi_1$ for all $0 \leq i < j$.

For a given run w of G (or a play of G), we put $w \models^\nu \psi$ iff $\hat{w} \models \psi$, where $\hat{w}$ is the infinite word defined by $\hat{w}(i) = \nu(w(i)) \cap Ap(\psi)$. In the following we also use $\mathbf{F}\psi$ and $\mathbf{G}\psi$ as abbreviations for $\mathbf{tt}\mathbf{U}\psi$ and $\neg\mathbf{F}\neg\psi$, respectively.

Another important formalism for specifying properties of runs in transition systems are finite-state automata over infinite words with various acceptance criteria, such as Büchi, Rabin, Street, Muller, etc. We refer to Thomas [1991] for a more detailed overview of the results about finite-state automata over infinite words. Let M be such an automaton with an input alphabet $2^{Ap(M)}$, where $Ap(M)$ is a finite subset of Ap. Then M can also be understood as a 'formula' interpreted over the runs of G (or a play of G) by stipulating that $w \models^\nu M$ iff $\hat{w}$ is accepted by M, where $\hat{w}$ is the infinite word defined by $\hat{w}(i) = \nu(w(i)) \cap Ap(M)$. Let us note that every LTL formula ψ can be effectively translated into an equivalent finite-state automaton M_ψ which accepts the language L_ψ. If the acceptance condition is Rabin-chain (or more powerful), the automaton M_ψ can be effectively transformed into an equivalent *deterministic* automaton with the same acceptance condition. In general, the cost of translating ψ into M_ψ is at least exponential. On the other hand, there are properties expressible by finite-state automata that cannot be encoded as LTL formulae. We refer to Thomas [1991] for more details.

There is a close connection between linear-time objectives and the ω-regular payoffs introduced in the previous section. Since this connection has several subtle aspects that often lead to confusion, it is worth an explicit discussion. Let $M = (Q, 2^{Ap(M)}, \rightarrow, q_0, Acc)$ be a *deterministic* finite-state automaton, where Q is a finite set of control states, $2^{Ap(M)}$ is the input alphabet, $\rightarrow \subseteq Q \times 2^{Ap(M)} \times Q$ is a total transition function, and Acc some acceptance criterion. Then we can construct a synchronous product of the game G and M, which is a stochastic game $G \times M$ where $V \times Q$ is the set of vertices partitioned into $(V_\Box \times Q, V_\Diamond \times Q, V_\bigcirc \times Q)$ and $(v, q) \mapsto (v', q')$ iff $v \mapsto v'$ and $q \xrightarrow{\mathcal{A}} q'$ where $\mathcal{A} = \nu(q) \cap Ap(M)$. Since M is deterministic and the transition function of M is total, the probability assignment is just inherited from G (i.e., $(v, q) \xmapsto{x} (v', q')$ only if $v \xmapsto{x} v'$). Further, the acceptance criterion of M is translated into the corresponding ω-regular payoff over the runs of $G \times M$ in the natural way. Note that $G \times M$ is constructed so that M just observes the runs of G and the constructed ω-regular payoff just reflects the accepting/rejecting verdict of this observation. Thus, we can reduce the questions about the existence and effective constructibility of a $(\mathbf{P}^{\succ \varrho}M)$-winning strategy for player $\Box$ in a vertex v of G to the questions about the value and effective constructibility of an optimal maximising strategy in the vertex (v, q_0) of $G \times M$. However, this reduction does not always work completely smoothly, particularly for infinite-state games. Some of the reasons are mentioned below.

- For infinite-state games, the product $G \times M$ is not necessarily definable in the same formalism as the original game G. Fortunately, most of the studied formalisms correspond to abstract computational devices equipped with a finite-state control, which can also encode the structure of M. However, this does not necessarily work if the finite-state control is trivial (i.e., it has just one or a fixed number of control states) or if it is required to satisfy some special conditions.

- For infinite-state games, the reduction to ω-regular payoffs described above can be problematic also because optimal maximising/minimising strategies in infinite-state games with ω-regular payoffs (even reachability payoffs) do not necessarily exist. For example, even if we somehow check that the value of (v, q_0) in $G \times M$ is 1, this does yet mean that player $\square$ has a $(\mathbf{P}^{=1}M)$-winning strategy in v.

- For finite-state games, the two problems discussed above usually disappear. However, there are still some issues related to complexity. In particular, the results about the type of optimal strategies in $G \times M$ do not carry over to G. For example, assume that we are given a linear-time objective $\mathbf{P}^{=1}M$ where M is a deterministic Rabin-chain automaton. If G has finitely many states, then $G \times M$ is also finite-state and hence we can rely on the results presented by McIver and Morgan [2002] and Chatterjee et al. [2004b] and conclude that the value of (v, q_0) is computable in time polynomial in the size of $G \times M$ and there is an optimal maximising MD strategy σ computable in polynomial time. From this we can deduce that the existence of a $(\mathbf{P}^{=1}M)$-winning strategy for player $\square$ in v is decidable in polynomial time. However, since the optimal MD strategy σ may depend *both* on the current vertex of G and the current state of M, we cannot conclude that if player $\square$ has some $(\mathbf{P}^{=1}M)$-winning strategy in v, then he also has an MD $(\mathbf{P}^{=1}M)$-winning strategy in v (still, the strategy σ can be translated into a FD $(\mathbf{P}^{=1}M)$-winning strategy which simulates the execution of M on the history of a play).

To sum up, linear-time objectives *are* closely related to ω-regular payoffs, but the associated problems cannot be seen as 'equivalent' in general.

Branching-time logics

Branching-time logics such as CTL, CTL*, or ECTL* (see, e.g., Emerson [1991]) allow explicit existential/universal quantification over runs. Thus, one can express that a given *path formula* holds for some/all runs initiated in a given state.

In the probabilistic setting, the existential/universal path quantifiers are replaced with the *probabilistic operator* $\mathbf{P}^{\succ \varrho}$ introduced in the previous section. In this way, every (non-probabilistic) branching-time logic determines its probabilistic counterpart. The probabilistic variants of CTL, CTL*, and ECTL* are denoted by PCTL, PCTL*, and PECTL*, respectively (see Hansson and Jonsson [1994]).

The syntax of PCTL* *path* and *state* formulae is defined by the following equations:

$$\psi \quad ::= \quad \varphi \quad | \quad \neg\psi \quad | \quad \psi_1 \wedge \psi_2 \quad | \quad \mathbf{X}\psi \quad | \quad \psi_1 \mathbf{U} \psi_2$$

$$\varphi \quad ::= \quad \mathbf{tt} \quad | \quad a \quad | \quad \neg\varphi \quad | \quad \varphi_1 \wedge \varphi_2 \quad | \quad \mathbf{P}^{\succ\varrho}\psi$$

Note that all LTL formulae are PCTL* path formulae. In the case of PCTL, the syntax of path formulae is restricted to $\psi ::= \varphi \mid \mathbf{X}\psi \mid \psi_1\mathbf{U}\psi_2$. Since the expressive power of LTL is strictly smaller than that of finite-state automata over infinite words (see the previous section), the logic CTL* can be further enriched by allowing arbitrary *automata connectives* in path formulae (see Wolper [1981]). The resulting logic is known as *extended CTL* (ECTL*)*, and its probabilistic variant as PECTL*.

Let $G_\mu^{(\sigma,\pi)}$ be a play of G. For every run $w \in Run(G_\mu^{(\sigma,\pi)})$ and every path formula ψ we define the relation $w \models^\nu \psi$ in the same way as in the previous section, where $w \models^\nu \varphi$ iff $w(0) \models^\nu \varphi$ (see below). For every state s of $G_\mu^{(\sigma,\pi)}$ and every state formula φ we define the relation $s \models^\nu \varphi$ inductively as follows:

$$s \models^\nu \mathbf{tt}$$
$$s \models^\nu a \qquad\quad \text{iff} \quad a \in \nu(s)$$
$$s \models^\nu \neg\varphi \qquad\quad \text{iff} \quad s \not\models^\nu \varphi$$
$$s \models^\nu \varphi_1 \wedge \varphi_2 \quad \text{iff} \quad s \models^\nu \varphi_1 \text{ and } s \models^\nu \varphi_2$$
$$s \models^\nu \mathbf{P}^{\succ\varrho}\psi \quad \text{iff} \quad \mathcal{P}_s(\{w \in Run(s) \mid w \models^\nu \psi\}) \succ \varrho$$

A state formula φ is *qualitative* if each occurrence of the probabilistic operator in φ is of the form $\mathbf{P}^{\succ 0}$ or $\mathbf{P}^{\succ 1}$. General (not necessarily qualitative) state formulae are also called *quantitative*.

A **branching-time objective** is a state formula φ of a branching-time probabilistic temporal logic. Important subclasses of branching-time objectives are PCTL, PCTL*, and PECTL* objectives.

Let us note that state formulae of branching-time probabilistic logics are sometimes interpreted directly on vertices of Markov decision processes (see Bianco and de Alfaro [1995]) and stochastic games (see de Alfaro and Majumdar [2004]). Path formulae are interpreted over the runs of G in the same way as above, and all state formulae except for $\mathbf{P}^{\succ\varrho}\psi$ are also interpreted in the natural way. Due to the presence of non-determinism in G, it is not possible to measure the probability of runs in G, and the probabilistic operator $\mathbf{P}^{\succ\varrho}$ has a different meaning defined as follows:

$$v \models^\nu \mathbf{P}^{\succ\varrho}\psi \quad \text{iff} \quad \exists \sigma \in \Sigma \; \forall \pi \in \Pi : \mathcal{P}_v(\{w \in Run(G_v^{(\sigma,\pi)}, v) \mid w \models^\nu \psi\}) \succ \varrho.$$

If G is a Markov decision process, then $v \models^\nu \mathbf{P}^{\succ\varrho}\psi$ iff for every strategy τ

of the only player we have that

$$\mathcal{P}_v(\{w \in Run(G_v^{(\tau)}, v) \mid w \models^\nu \psi\}) \succ \varrho. \tag{5.3}$$

For finite-state MDPs, condition (5.3) is equivalent to

$$\inf_\tau \{\mathcal{P}_v(\{w \in Run(G_v^{(\tau)}, v) \mid w \models^\nu \psi\})\} \succ \varrho \tag{5.4}$$

which is exactly the semantics proposed by Bianco and de Alfaro [1995]. For general (infinite-state) MDPs, conditions (5.3) and (5.4) are not equivalent.

At first glance, one might be tempted to think that $v \models^\nu \psi$ iff player $\square$ has a φ-winning strategy in v. A straightforward induction on the structure of φ reveals that '$\Rightarrow$' holds, but the opposite direction is *invalid*. To see this, consider the formula $\varphi \equiv (\mathbf{P}^{>0}\mathbf{F}a) \vee (\mathbf{P}^{>0}\mathbf{F}b)$ and the vertex v of the following game, where $\nu(u_a) = \{a\}$ and $\nu(u_b) = \{b\}$:

Intuitively, the formula φ says 'a state satisfying a is reachable, or a state satisfying b is reachable'. Note that player $\square$ has a φ-winning strategy in v (in fact, every strategy of player $\square$ is φ-winning). However, $v \not\models^\nu \mathbf{P}^{>0}\mathbf{F}a$, because player $\lozenge$ has a strategy which makes the vertex u_a unreachable. Similarly, $v \not\models^\nu \mathbf{P}^{>0}\mathbf{F}b$, and hence $v \not\models^\nu \varphi$. This means that the *model-checking* problem for stochastic games and formulae of probabilistic branching-time logics (i.e., the question of whether $v \models^\nu \varphi$) is *different* from the problem of deciding the winner in stochastic games with branching-time objectives. As we shall see, this difference is substantial.

The problems of interest

Let $\mathcal{G}$ be a class of turn-based stochastic games and Φ a class of temporal objectives. The most important questions about the games of $\mathcal{G}$ and the objectives of Φ include the following:

(1) *Are all games of $\mathcal{G}$ determined for all objectives of Φ?*
(2) *What is the type of winning strategies if they exist?*
(3) *Who wins in a given vertex?*
(4) *Can we compute winning strategies?*

As we shall see in Section 5.3.2, stochastic games with temporal objectives are *not* necessarily determined (even for linear-time objectives). This means that 'nobody' is an eligible answer to Question (3). Since randomisation and memory can help the players to win, Question (3) can be refined into '*Does player $\square$ (or player $\lozenge$) have a winning strategy of type XY in a given vertex* *v?'* This problem can be decidable even if the existence of *some (i.e., HR)* winning strategy in *v* is undecidable.

The existing results

Finite-state stochastic games with linear-time objectives are rarely studied explicitly because most of the results can be deduced from the corresponding results about stochastic games with ω-regular payoffs (see Section 5.2.1). For infinite-state stochastic games, the relationship between linear-time objectives and ω-regular payoffs is more subtle. For example, even for reachability payoffs, the question of whether $val(v) = 1$ is *not* the same as the question of whether player $\square$ has a $\mathbf{P}^{=1}\mathbf{F}t$-winning strategy in v, where the atomic proposition t is satisfied exactly in the target vertices (the details are given in Section 5.3).

Finite-state turn-based stochastic games with branching-time objectives were first considered by Baier et al. [2004], where it was shown that winning strategies for PCTL objectives may require memory and/or randomisation. Consider the following game, where $\nu(u_a) = \{a\}$, $\nu(u_b) = \{b\}$, and $\nu(v) = \emptyset$.

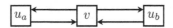

Let

- $\varphi_1 \equiv (\mathbf{P}^{=1}\mathbf{X}a) \wedge (\mathbf{P}^{=1}\mathbf{F}b)$
- $\varphi_2 \equiv (\mathbf{P}^{>0}\mathbf{X}a) \wedge (\mathbf{P}^{>0}\mathbf{X}b)$
- $\varphi_3 \equiv (\mathbf{P}^{>0}\mathbf{X}a) \wedge (\mathbf{P}^{>0}\mathbf{X}b) \wedge (\mathbf{P}^{=1}\mathbf{F}(\mathbf{P}^{=1}\mathbf{G}a))$.

Obviously, player $\square$ has a φ_i-winning strategy for every $i \in \{1, 2, 3\}$, and each such strategy must inevitably use memory for φ_1, randomisation for φ_2, and both memory and randomisation for φ_3.

In Baier et al. [2004], it was also shown that for PCTL objectives, the problem of whether player $\square$ has a MD φ-winning strategy in a given vertex of a given finite-state MDP is **NP**-complete. MR strategies for PCTL objectives were considered by Kučera and Stražovský [2008], where it was shown that the existence of a φ-winning MR strategy in a given vertex is in **EXPTIME** for finite-state turn-based stochastic games, and in **PSPACE** for finite-state MDPs.

In Brázdil et al. [2006], it was noted that turn-based stochastic games with PCTL objectives are *not* determined (for any strategy type). To see this, consider the following game, where $\nu(u_a) = \{a\}$, $\nu(u_b) = \{b\}$, $\nu(u_c) = \{c\}$, $\nu(u_d) = \{d\}$, and $\nu(v) = \nu(v_1) = \nu(v_2) = \emptyset$.

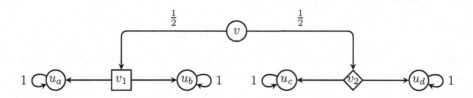

Let

$$\varphi \equiv \left(\mathbf{P}^{=1}\mathbf{F}(a \vee c)\right) \vee \left(\mathbf{P}^{=1}\mathbf{F}(b \vee d)\right) \vee \left((\mathbf{P}^{>0}\mathbf{F}c) \wedge (\mathbf{P}^{>0}\mathbf{F}d)\right).$$

Assume that player $\square$ has a φ-winning strategy σ in v. The strategy σ cannot randomise at v_1, because then both of the subformulae $\mathbf{P}^{=1}\mathbf{F}(a \vee c)$ and $\mathbf{P}^{=1}\mathbf{F}(b \vee d)$ become invalid in v, and player $\Diamond$ can always falsify the subformula $(\mathbf{P}^{>0}\mathbf{F}c) \wedge (\mathbf{P}^{>0}\mathbf{F}d)$. Hence, the strategy σ must choose one of the transitions $v_1 \mapsto u_a$, $v_1 \mapsto u_b$ with probability one. For each of these choices, player $\Diamond$ can falsify the formula φ, which means that σ is not φ-winning. Similarly, one can show that player $\Diamond$ does not have a $\neg\varphi$-winning strategy in v (in particular, note that player $\Diamond$ cannot randomise at v_2, because this would make the subformula $(\mathbf{P}^{>0}\mathbf{F}c) \wedge (\mathbf{P}^{>0}\mathbf{F}d)$ valid).

In Brázdil et al. [2006], it was also shown that for PCTL objectives, the existence of a φ-winning MD strategy for player $\square$ in a given vertex of a finite-state stochastic turn-based game is $\Sigma_2 = \mathbf{NP^{NP}}$-complete, which complements the aforementioned result for MDPs. Further, it was shown that the existence of a φ-winning HR (or HD) strategy in a given vertex of a finite-state MDP is *highly undecidable* (i.e., beyond the arithmetical hierarchy). The proof works even for a fixed *quantitative* PCTL formula ξ. The use of a non-qualitative probability constraint in ξ is in fact *unavoidable* –as it was shown later by Brázdil et al. [2008], the existence of a φ-winning HR (or HD) strategy in finite-state MDPs with *qualitative* PCTL and PECTL* objectives is **EXPTIME**-complete and **2-EXPTIME**-complete, respectively. It is worth noting that these algorithms are actually *polynomial* for every fixed qualitative PCTL or PECTL* formula. A HR (or HD) φ-winning strategy for player $\square$ may require infinite memory, but it can always be implemented by an effectively constructible *one-counter automaton* which reads the history of a play. To get some intuition, consider the following game, where $\nu(u_a) = \{a\}$ and $\nu(y) = \emptyset$ for all vertices y different from u_a.

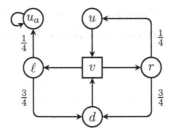

Let $\varphi \equiv \mathbf{P}^{>0}\mathbf{G}(\neg a \wedge (\mathbf{P}^{>0}\mathbf{F}a))$, and let σ be a HD strategy which in every wv selects either $v \mapsto \ell$ or $v \mapsto r$, depending on whether $\#_d(w) - \#_u(w) \leq 0$ or not, respectively. Here $\#_d(w)$ and $\#_u(w)$ denote the number of occurrences of d and u in w, respectively. Obviously, the strategy σ can be implemented by a one-counter automaton. The play $G_v^{(\sigma)}$ initiated in v closely resembles a one-way infinite random walk where the probability of going right is $\frac{3}{4}$ and the probability of going left is $\frac{1}{4}$. More precisely, the play $G_v^{(\sigma)}$ corresponds to the unfolding of the following infinite-state Markov chain (the initial state is grey):

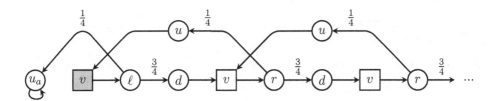

A standard calculation shows that the probability of all $w \in Run(G_v^{(\sigma)})$ initiated in v such that w visits a state satisfying a is equal to $\frac{1}{3}$. Note that for every $w \in Run(G_v^{(\sigma)})$ initiated in v which does *not* visit a state satisfying a we have that $w(i) \models^\nu \neg a \wedge (\mathbf{P}^{>0}\mathbf{F}a)$ for every $i \geq 0$. Since the probability of all such runs is $\frac{2}{3}$, we obtain that the formula φ is valid in the state v of $G_v^{(\sigma)}$. On the other hand, there is no finite-memory φ-winning strategy $\hat{\sigma}$ in v, because then the play $G_v^{(\hat{\sigma})}$ corresponds to an unfolding of a finite-state Markov chain, and the formula φ does not have a finite-state model (see, e.g., Brázdil et al. [2008]).

The memory requirements of φ-winning strategies for various fragments of qualitative branching-time logics were analysed by Brázdil and Forejt [2007] and Forejt [2009]. The decidability/complexity of the existence of HR (or HD) φ-winning strategies in turn-based stochastic games with qualitative branching-time objectives is still open.

5.3 Reachability objectives in games with finitely and infinitely many vertices

As we have already mentioned, the properties of stochastic games with finitely and infinitely many vertices are different in many respects. To illustrate this, we examine the properties of turn-based stochastic games with *reachability* objectives in greater detail. Most of the negative results presented in this section are valid also for the other objectives introduced in Section 5.2.

For the rest of this section, we fix a turn-based stochastic game $G = (V, \mapsto, (V_\square, V_\lozenge, V_\bigcirc), Prob)$ and a set $T \subseteq V$ of **target** vertices. The set of all $w \in Run(G)$ which visit a vertex of T is denoted by $Reach(T)$. Further, for every pair of strategies $(\sigma, \pi) \in \Sigma \times \Pi$ and every initial vertex v, we use $\mathcal{P}_v^{(\sigma,\pi)}(Reach(T))$ to denote the probability $\mathcal{P}_v(\{w \in Run(G_v^{(\sigma,\pi)}) \mid w_G \in Reach(T)\})$.

5.3.1 The existence of a value revisited

Recall that every vertex v of G has a value $val(v)$ defined by Equality 5.1 which now takes the following simple form:

$$\sup_{\sigma \in \Sigma} \inf_{\pi \in \Pi} \mathcal{P}_v^{(\sigma,\pi)}(Reach(T)) = \inf_{\pi \in \Pi} \sup_{\sigma \in \Sigma} \mathcal{P}_v^{(\sigma,\pi)}(Reach(T)). \qquad (5.5)$$

A direct proof of Equality (5.5) is actually simple and instructive. Consider the following (Bellman) functional $\Gamma : [0,1]^{|V|} \to [0,1]^{|V|}$ defined as follows:

$$\Gamma(\alpha)(v) = \begin{cases} 1 & \text{if } v \in T; \\ \sup \{\alpha(v') \mid v \mapsto v'\} & \text{if } v \notin T \text{ and } v \in V_\square; \\ \inf \{\alpha(v') \mid v \mapsto v'\} & \text{if } v \notin T \text{ and } v \in V_\lozenge; \\ \sum_{v \overset{x}{\mapsto} v'} x \cdot \alpha(v') & \text{if } v \notin T \text{ and } v \in V_\bigcirc. \end{cases}$$

Since Γ is a monotonic function over a complete lattice $([0,1]^{|V|}, \sqsubseteq)$, where $\sqsubseteq$ is a component-wise ordering, we can apply the Knaster–Tarski Theorem (see Tarski [1955]) and conclude that Γ has the least fixed-point $\mu\Gamma$. Observe that for every $v \in V$ we have that

$$\mu\Gamma(v) \leq \sup_{\sigma \in \Sigma} \inf_{\pi \in \Pi} \mathcal{P}_v^{(\sigma,\pi)}(Reach(T)) \leq \inf_{\pi \in \Pi} \sup_{\sigma \in \Sigma} \mathcal{P}_v^{(\sigma,\pi)}(Reach(T)).$$

The second inequality follows directly from definitions and it is actually valid for *arbitrary* Borel measurable payoffs. The first inequality is obtained by demonstrating that the tuple of all $\sup_{\sigma \in \Sigma} \inf_{\pi \in \Pi} \mathcal{P}_v^{(\sigma,\pi)}(Reach(T))$ is a fixed-point of Γ, which is also straightforward. So, it remains to show that the inequality

$$\mu\Gamma(v) \le \inf_{\pi\in\Pi} \sup_{\sigma\in\Sigma} \mathcal{P}_v^{(\sigma,\pi)}(\mathit{Reach}(T)) \tag{5.6}$$

cannot be strict.

Let us first assume that every vertex $u \in V_\diamond$ has a **locally optimal** outgoing transition $u \overset{a}{\mapsto} u'$ where $\mu\Gamma(u) = \mu\Gamma(u')$ (in particular, note that if u has finitely many outgoing transitions, some of them must be locally optimal because $\mu\Gamma$ is a fixed-point of Γ). Now consider a MD strategy $\hat{\pi}$ which in every $u \in V_\diamond$ selects some (fixed) locally optimal outgoing transition of u. One can easily show that $\mu\Gamma(v) = \sup_{\sigma\in\Sigma} \mathcal{P}_v^{(\sigma,\hat{\pi})}(\mathit{Reach}(T))$ for every $v \in V$, which implies that Inequality (5.6) is an equality. Further, observe that $\hat{\pi}$ is an optimal minimising strategy in every vertex of G. Thus, we obtain the following:

Proposition 5.4 *If every $u \in V_\diamond$ has a locally optimal outgoing transition, then there is a MD strategy of player $\diamond$ which is optimal minimising in every vertex of G.*

In the general case when the vertices of $V_\diamond$ do not necessarily have locally optimal outgoing transitions (this can of course happen only if G is infinitely branching), Inequality (5.6) is proven as follows. We show that for every $\varepsilon > 0$ and every $v \in V$ there is a HD strategy $\hat{\pi}_\varepsilon \in \Pi$ such that

$$\sup_{\sigma\in\Sigma} \mathcal{P}_v^{(\sigma,\hat{\pi}_\varepsilon)}(\mathit{Reach}(T)) \le \mu\Gamma(v) + \varepsilon.$$

This implies that Inequality (5.6) cannot be strict. Intuitively, in a given state $wu \in V^*V_\diamond$, the strategy $\hat{\pi}_\varepsilon$ selects a transition $u \mapsto u'$ whose **error** $\mu\Gamma(u) - \mu\Gamma(u')$ is 'sufficiently small'. Observe that the error can be made arbitrarily small because $\mu\Gamma$ is a fixed point of Γ. The strategy $\hat{\pi}_\varepsilon$ selects transitions with progressively smaller and smaller error so that the 'total error' $\mathcal{P}_v^{(\sigma,\hat{\pi}_\varepsilon)}(\mathit{Reach}(T)) - \mu\Gamma(v)$ stays bounded by ε no matter what player $\square$ does. A detailed proof can be found in, e.g., Brázdil et al. [2009a].

If G is finitely branching, then Γ is not only monotonic but also **continuous**, i.e., $\Gamma(\bigvee_{i=0}^\infty \vec{y}_i) = \bigvee_{i=0}^\infty \Gamma(\vec{y}_i)$ for every infinite non-decreasing chain $\vec{y}_1 \sqsubseteq \vec{y}_2 \sqsubseteq \vec{y}_3 \sqsubseteq \cdots$ in $([0,1]^{|V|}, \sqsubseteq)$. By the Kleene fixed-point theorem, we have that $\mu\Gamma = \bigvee_{i=0}^\infty \Gamma^i(\vec{0})$, where $\vec{0}$ is the vector of zeros. For every $n \ge 1$, let $\mathit{Reach}^n(G)$ be the set of all $w \in \mathit{Run}(G)$ such that $w(i) \in T$ for some $0 \le i < n$. A straightforward induction on n reveals that

$$\Gamma^n(\vec{0})(v) = \sup_{\sigma\in\Sigma} \inf_{\pi\in\Pi} \mathcal{P}_v^{(\sigma,\pi)}(\mathit{Reach}^n(T)) = \inf_{\pi\in\Pi} \sup_{\sigma\in\Sigma} \mathcal{P}_v^{(\sigma,\pi)}(\mathit{Reach}^n(T)).$$

Further, for every $n \geq 1$ we define HD strategies $\sigma_n \in \Sigma$ and $\pi_n \in \Pi$ as follows:

- The strategies σ_1 and π_1 are defined arbitrarily.
- For all $n \geq 2$ and $wv \in V^*V_\square$ such that $len(wv) < n$, the strategy σ_n selects a transition $v \mapsto v'$ such that $\Gamma^k(\vec{0})(v') = \max\{\Gamma^k(\vec{0})(v'') \mid v \mapsto v''\}$ where $k = n - len(wv)$.
- For all $n \geq 2$ and $wv \in V^*V_\diamond$ such that $len(wv) < n$, the strategy π_n selects a transition $v \mapsto v'$ such that $\Gamma^k(\vec{0})(v') = \min\{\Gamma^k(\vec{0})(v'') \mid v \mapsto v''\}$ where $k = n - len(wv)$.

It is easy to prove that for every $n \geq 1$

$$\Gamma^n(\vec{0})(v) = \inf_{\pi \in \Pi} \mathcal{P}_v^{(\sigma_n, \pi)}(Reach^n(T)) = \sup_{\sigma \in \Sigma} \mathcal{P}_v^{(\sigma, \pi_n)}(Reach^n(T)).$$

A direct corollary to these observations is the following:

Proposition 5.5 *If G is finitely branching, then for all $v \in V$ and $\varepsilon > 0$ there are $n \geq 0$ and a HD strategy $\hat{\sigma} \in \Sigma$ such that $\mathcal{P}_v^{(\hat{\sigma}, \pi)}(Reach^n(T)) \geq val(v) - \varepsilon$ for every $\pi \in \Pi$.*

Finally, let us note that the values in infinite-state games can be irrational, even if all transition probabilities are equal to $\frac{1}{2}$. To see this, consider the following Markov chain $\mathcal{M}$, where t is the only target vertex.

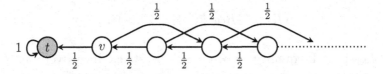

Obviously, $val(v)$ is equal to the probability of all $w \in Run(v)$ which visit t, where μ_v is the initial probability distribution. By inspecting the structure of $\mathcal{M}$, it is easy to see that $val(v)$ has to satisfy the equation $x = \frac{1}{2} + \frac{1}{2}x^3$. Actually, $val(v)$ is the *least* solution of this equation in the interval $[0, 1]$, which is $\frac{\sqrt{5}-1}{2}$ (the 'golden ratio').

5.3.2 Optimal strategies and determinacy

In this section we classify the conditions under which optimal strategies exist, analyse the type of optimal strategies, and resolve the determinacy of games with $\mathbf{P}^{\succ \varrho}\mathbf{F}t$ objectives.

The properties of optimal minimising strategies are summarised in the next proposition.

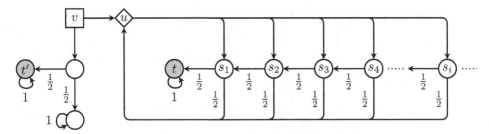

Figure 5.2 An optimal minimising strategy does not necessarily exist.

Proposition 5.6 *Let G be a stochastic game with a reachability objective associated to a set of target vertices T. Let v be a vertex of G. Then*

(a) an optimal minimising strategy in v does not necessarily exist; and if it exists, it may require infinite memory;

(b) an ε-optimal minimising strategy in v may require infinite memory for every fixed $\varepsilon \in (0,1)$;

(c) if G is finitely branching, then there is a MD strategy which is optimal minimising in every vertex of G.

A counterexample for claims (a) and (b) is given in Figure 5.2, where t, t' are the only target vertices. Observe that $val(u) = 0$, but there is no optimal minimising strategy in u. Further, observe that for each fixed $\varepsilon \in (0,1)$, every ε-optimal minimising strategy π in u must employ infinitely many transitions of the form $u \mapsto s_i$ (otherwise, the target vertex t would be inevitably reached with probability 1). Hence, π requires infinite memory. Finally, note that $val(v) = \frac{1}{2}$ and there is an optimal minimising strategy π' in v which requires infinite memory (the strategy π' must ensure that the probability of reaching a target vertex from u is at most $\frac{1}{2}$, because then player $\square$ does not gain anything if she uses the transition $v \mapsto u$; hence, π' requires infinite memory). Claim (c) follows directly from Proposition 5.4.

The properties of optimal maximising strategies are remarkably different from those of optimal minimising strategies. The most notable (and perhaps somewhat surprising) difference is that an optimal maximising strategy may require *infinite memory*, even in finitely branching games.

Proposition 5.7 *Let G be a stochastic game with a reachability objective associated to a set of target vertices T. Let v be a vertex of G. Then*

(a) an optimal maximising strategy in v does not necessarily exist even if G is finitely branching;

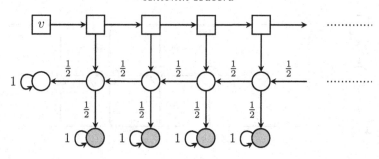

Figure 5.3 An optimal maximising strategy does not necessarily exist

(b) *an optimal maximising strategy in v (if it exists) may require infinite memory even if G is finitely branching;*

(c) *if G has finitely many vertices, then there is a MD strategy which is optimal maximising in every vertex of G.*

A counterexample for claim (a) is given in Figure 5.3 (target vertices are grey). Observe that $val(v) = 1$ but there is no optimal maximising strategy in v. An example demonstrating that an optimal maximising strategy may require infinite memory (originally due to Brožek [2009]) is given in Figure 5.4. The outgoing transitions of the vertex $\hat{v}$ are the same as the outgoing transitions of the vertex v in Figure 5.3 and they are not shown in the picture. Observe that $val(\hat{v}) = 1$ and hence $val(e_i) = 1$ for all $i \geq 1$. Further, we have that $val(s_i) = 1 - (\frac{1}{2})^i$ for all $i \geq 1$, and hence also $val(d_i) = 1 - (\frac{1}{2})^i$ for all $i \geq 1$. From this we get $val(v) = \frac{2}{3}$. Also observe that player $\square$ has a HD optimal maximising strategy σ which simply ensures that player $\lozenge$ cannot gain anything by using transitions $d_i \mapsto e_i$. That is, whenever the vertex $\hat{v}$ is visited, the strategy σ finds a d_i stored in the history of a play, and starts to behave as an ε-optimal maximising strategy in $\hat{v}$, where $\varepsilon < (\frac{1}{2})^i$. Thus, σ achieves the result $\frac{2}{3}$ or better against every strategy of player $\lozenge$. However, for every finite-memory strategy $\hat{\sigma}$ of player $\square$ there is a fixed constant $P^{\hat{\sigma}} < 1$ such that $\mathcal{P}_{\hat{v}}^{(\hat{\sigma},\pi)}(Reach(T)) \leq P^{\hat{\sigma}}$ for every $\pi \in \Pi$. Since $P^{\hat{\sigma}} < 1$, there surely exists $j \geq 1$ such that $P^{\hat{\sigma}} < 1 - (\frac{1}{2})^k$ for all $k > j$. Now let $\hat{\pi}$ be a MD strategy of player $\lozenge$ which in d_i selects either the transition $d_i \mapsto e_i$ or $d_i \mapsto s_i$, depending on whether $i \geq j$ or not, respectively. Now one can easily check that $\mathcal{P}_v^{(\hat{\sigma},\hat{\pi})}(Reach(T)) < \frac{2}{3}$, which means that $\hat{\sigma}$ is not an optimal maximising strategy in v.

Let us note that Claim (b) of Proposition 5.7 does *not* hold for MDPs. By applying Theorem 7.2.11 of Puterman [1994], we can conclude that if there is *some* optimal maximising strategy in a vertex v of a (possibly infinitely

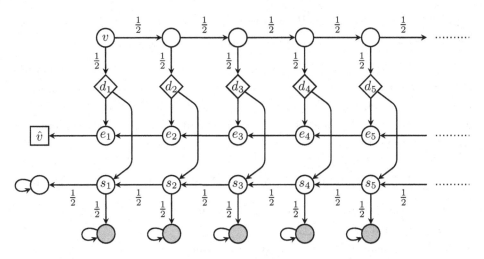

Figure 5.4 An optimal maximising strategy may require infinite memory

branching) MDP G, then there is also an MD optimal maximising strategy in v.

Claim (c) is not as trivial as it might seem. A naive idea of constructing an optimal maximising MD strategy just by selecting *some* value-maximising transition in every vertex does not work. To see this, consider the following MDP, where t is the only target vertex:

Obviously, $val(v) = val(u) = val(t) = 1$, but the MD strategy which selects the transitions $v \mapsto u$ and $u \mapsto v$ in the vertices v and u, respectively, is not optimal maximising. Nevertheless, it is not hard to show that for every vertex of $v \in V_\Box$ there is a transition $v \mapsto v'$ such that the other outgoing transitions of v can be safely removed without influencing the value in any vertex. This result actually holds for all finitely branching stochastic games. Claim (c) then follows immediately because if $V_\Box$ is finite, then we can successively fix such a transition in *every* $v \in V_\Box$.

Proposition 5.8   *Let $G = (V, \mapsto, (V_\Box, V_\Diamond, V_\bigcirc), Prob)$ be a finitely branching stochastic game with a reachability objective associated to a set $T \subseteq V$. For every $v \in V_\Box$ there is a transition $v \mapsto v'$ such that the value of all $u \in V$*

remains unchanged when all outgoing transitions of v except for $v \mapsto v'$ are deleted from G.

Proof Let $v \in V_\square$. If $v \in T$, the transition $v \mapsto v'$ can be chosen arbitrarily. Now assume that $v \notin T$. For every strategy $\tau \in \Sigma \cup \Pi$ we define the (unique) strategy $\tau[v]$ such that $\tau[v](w) = \tau(w')$, where w' is the shortest suffix of w which is either equal to w or starts with v. Intuitively, $\tau[v]$ behaves identically to τ until the vertex v is revisited. Then, $\tau[v]$ 'forgets' the history and behaves as if the play just started in v.

Let us define two auxiliary Borel sets of runs $\neg T \mathbf{U} v$ and $\neg v \mathbf{U} T$ where

- $\neg T \mathbf{U} v$ consists of all $w \in Run(G)$ such that $w(j) = v$ for some $j > 0$ and $w(i) \notin T$ for all $1 \le i < j$;
- $\neg v \mathbf{U} T$ consists of all $w \in Run(G)$ such that $w(j) \in T$ for some $j > 0$ and $w(i) \ne v$ for all $1 \le i < j$.

Observe that for all $(\sigma, \pi) \in \Sigma \times \Pi$ such that $\mathcal{P}_v^{(\sigma,\pi)}(\neg T \mathbf{U} v) < 1$ we have that $\mathcal{P}_v^{(\sigma[v],\pi[v])}(Reach(T))$ is equal to

$$\sum_{i=0}^{\infty} \left(\mathcal{P}_v^{(\sigma,\pi)}(\neg T \mathbf{U} v)\right)^i \cdot \mathcal{P}_v^{(\sigma,\pi)}(\neg v \mathbf{U} T) = \frac{\mathcal{P}_v^{(\sigma,\pi)}(\neg v \mathbf{U} T)}{1 - \mathcal{P}_v^{(\sigma,\pi)}(\neg T \mathbf{U} v)}.$$

For the moment, assume the following equality:

$$\sup_{\sigma \in \Sigma} \inf_{\pi \in \Pi} \mathcal{P}_v^{(\sigma,\pi)}(Reach(T)) = \sup_{\sigma \in \Sigma} \inf_{\pi \in \Pi^{MD}} \mathcal{P}_v^{(\sigma[v],\pi)}(Reach(T)). \tag{5.7}$$

Note that for every $\pi \in \Pi^{MD}$ we have that $\pi = \pi[v]$. For every $\sigma \in \Sigma$ and every transition $v \mapsto v'$, let $\sigma_{v \mapsto v'}$ be the strategy which agrees with σ on all arguments except for v where $\sigma_{v \mapsto v'}(v)$ selects the transition $v \mapsto v'$ with probability 1. It is easy to check that for every $\sigma \in \Sigma$ there must be some σ-*good* transition $v \mapsto v'$ satisfying

$$\inf_{\pi \in \Pi^{MD}} \mathcal{P}_v^{(\sigma[v],\pi)}(Reach(T)) \le \inf_{\pi \in \Pi^{MD}} \mathcal{P}_v^{(\sigma_{v \mapsto v'}[v],\pi)}(Reach(T)).$$

For every $i \ge 1$, let us fix a strategy $\sigma_i \in \Sigma$ such that

$$\inf_{\pi \in \Pi^{MD}} \mathcal{P}_v^{(\sigma_i[v],\pi)}(Reach(T)) \ge val(v) - \frac{1}{2^i}.$$

Since G is finitely branching, there is a transition $v \mapsto v'$ which is σ_i-good for infinitely many i's, and hence the value of v (and therefore also the value of the other vertices of V) does not change if all outgoing transitions of v except for $v \mapsto v'$ are deleted from G.

So, it remains to prove Equality (5.7). We start with the '$\ge$' direction. Let

$\hat{\pi}$ be the MD optimal minimising strategy which exists by Proposition 5.6. Then

$$\sup_{\sigma \in \Sigma} \inf_{\pi \in \Pi} \mathcal{P}_v^{(\sigma,\pi)}(Reach(T)) = \sup_{\sigma \in \Sigma} \mathcal{P}_v^{(\sigma,\hat{\pi})}(Reach(T))$$

$$\geq \sup_{\sigma \in \Sigma} \mathcal{P}_v^{(\sigma[v],\hat{\pi})}(Reach(T))$$

$$\geq \sup_{\sigma \in \Sigma} \inf_{\pi \in \Pi^{MD}} \mathcal{P}_v^{(\sigma[v],\pi)}(Reach(T)).$$

Now assume that the '$\leq$' direction of Equality (5.7) does not hold. Then there is some $\varepsilon > 0$ such that

(1) there is an ε-optimal maximising strategy $\hat{\sigma}$ in v;
(2) for every $\sigma \in \Sigma$ there is $\pi \in \Pi^{MD}$ s.t. $\mathcal{P}_v^{(\sigma[v],\pi)}(Reach(T)) \leq val(v) - 2\varepsilon$.

Note that condition (2) implies that for every $\sigma \in \Sigma$ there is $\pi \in \Pi^{MD}$ such that either $\mathcal{P}_v^{(\sigma,\pi)}(\neg T \mathbf{U} v) = 1$, or $\mathcal{P}_v^{(\sigma,\pi)}(\neg T \mathbf{U} v) < 1$ and

$$\frac{\mathcal{P}_v^{(\sigma,\pi)}(\neg v \mathbf{U} T)}{1 - \mathcal{P}_v^{(\sigma,\pi)}(\neg T \mathbf{U} v)} \leq val(v) - 2\varepsilon.$$

Now consider the strategy $\hat{\sigma}$ of condition (1) and a play initiated in v. Using condition (2) repeatedly, we obtain a strategy $\hat{\pi} \in \Pi$ such that whenever a state of the form wv is visited in the play $G_v^{(\hat{\sigma},\hat{\pi})}$, then either $\mathcal{P}_{wv}^{(\hat{\sigma},\hat{\pi})}(\neg T \mathbf{U} v) = 1$, or $\mathcal{P}_{wv}^{(\hat{\sigma},\hat{\pi})}(\neg T \mathbf{U} v) < 1$ and

$$\frac{\mathcal{P}_{wv}^{(\hat{\sigma},\hat{\pi})}(\neg v \mathbf{U} T)}{1 - \mathcal{P}_{wv}^{(\hat{\sigma},\hat{\pi})}(\neg T \mathbf{U} v)} \leq val(v) - 2\varepsilon.$$

From this we obtain $\mathcal{P}_v^{(\hat{\sigma},\hat{\pi})}(Reach(T)) \leq val(v) - 2\varepsilon$ which is a contradiction.
□

Finally, let us consider a temporal objective $\mathbf{P}^{\geq \varrho}\mathbf{F}t$ where the atomic proposition t is valid exactly in the target vertices of T. The next proposition (taken from Brázdil et al. [2009a]) answers the associated determinacy question. Again, the answer seems somewhat unexpected.

Proposition 5.9 *Let $G = (V, \mapsto, (V_\square, V_\lozenge, V_\bigcirc), Prob)$ be a stochastic game with a temporal objective $\mathbf{P}^{\geq \varrho}\mathbf{F}t$ associated to a subset of target vertices $T \subseteq V$. Then G is not necessarily determined. However, if G is finitely branching, then it is determined.*

Proof A counterexample for the first part of Proposition 5.9 is easy to construct. Let G_u and G_v be the games of Figure 5.2 and Figure 5.3, where

u and v are the initial vertices of G_u and G_v, and T_u and T_v are the sets of target vertices of G_u and G_v, respectively. Consider a game G obtained by taking the disjoint union of G_u and G_v extended with a fresh stochastic vertex s with two outgoing transitions $s \xrightarrow{0.5} u$ and $s \xrightarrow{0.5} v$. The set of target vertices of G is $T_u \cup T_v$, and the initial vertex is s. Since $val(u) = 0$ and $val(v) = 1$, we obtain that $val(s) = \frac{1}{2}$. Now consider the temporal objective $\mathbf{P}^{\geq 0.5}\mathbf{F}t$. First, assume that player $\square$ has a winning strategy $\hat{\sigma}$ in s. Since player $\square$ has no optimal maximising strategy in v, there is a constant $P^{\hat{\sigma}} < \frac{1}{2}$ such that $\mathcal{P}_s^{(\hat{\sigma},\pi)}(Reach(T_v)) \leq P^{\hat{\sigma}}$ for every $\pi \in \Pi$. Since $val(u) = 0$, there is a strategy $\hat{\pi}$ of player $\Diamond$ such that $\mathcal{P}_s^{(\sigma,\hat{\pi})}(Reach(T_u)) < \frac{1}{2} - P^{\hat{\sigma}}$ for every $\sigma \in \Sigma$. Hence, $\mathcal{P}_s^{(\hat{\sigma},\hat{\pi})}(Reach(T_u \cup T_v)) < \frac{1}{2}$ which contradicts the assumption that $\hat{\sigma}$ is a winning strategy for player $\square$. Similarly, one can show that there is no winning strategy for player $\Diamond$ which would achieve the negated objective $\mathbf{P}^{<0.5}\mathbf{F}t$ against every strategy of player $\square$.

Now let us assume that G is finitely branching, and let us fix a vertex v of G. For technical convenience, assume that every target vertex t has only one outgoing transition $t \mapsto t$. The second part of Proposition 5.9 is not completely trivial, because player $\square$ does not necessarily have an optimal maximising strategy in v even if G is finitely branching. Observe that if $\varrho > val(v)$, then player $\square$ has a $(\mathbf{P}^{\succ\varrho}\mathbf{F}t)$-winning strategy in v (he may use, e.g., an ε-optimal maximising strategy where $\varepsilon = (\varrho - val(v))/2$). Similarly, if $\varrho < val(v)$, then player $\Diamond$ has a $(\neg\mathbf{P}^{\succ\varrho}\mathbf{F}t)$-winning strategy in v. Now assume that $\varrho = val(v)$. Obviously, it suffices to show that if player $\Diamond$ does *not* have a $(\neg\mathbf{P}^{\succ\varrho}\mathbf{F}t)$-winning strategy in v, then player $\square$ has a $(\mathbf{P}^{\succ\varrho}\mathbf{F}t)$-winning strategy in v. This means to show that

$$\forall \pi \in \Pi \ \exists \sigma \in \Sigma \ : \ \mathcal{P}_v^{\sigma,\pi}(Reach(T)) \succ \varrho \tag{5.8}$$

implies

$$\exists \sigma \in \Sigma \ \forall \pi \in \Pi \ : \ \mathcal{P}_v^{\sigma,\pi}(Reach(T)) \succ \varrho. \tag{5.9}$$

Observe that if $\succ$ is $>$, then (5.8) does not hold because player $\Diamond$ has an optimal minimising strategy by Proposition 5.6. For the constraint ≥ 0, the statement is trivial. Hence, it suffices to consider the case when $\succ$ is $\geq$ and $\varrho = val(v) > 0$. Assume that (5.8) holds. We say that a vertex $u \in V$ is *good* if

$$\forall \pi \in \Pi \ \exists \sigma \in \Sigma \ : \ \mathcal{P}_u^{\sigma,\pi}(Reach(T)) \geq val(u). \tag{5.10}$$

Further, we say that a transition $u \mapsto u'$ of G is *optimal* if either $u \in V_\bigcirc$, or $u \in V_\square \cup V_\Diamond$ and $val(u) = val(u')$. Observe that for every $u \in V_\square \cup V_\Diamond$ there is at least one optimal transition $u \mapsto u'$, because G is finitely branching.

Further, note that if $u \in V_\square$ is a good vertex, then there is at least one optimal $u \mapsto u'$ where u' is good. Similarly, if $u \in V_\Diamond$ is good then for every optimal transition $u \mapsto u'$ we have that u' is good, and if $u \in V_\bigcirc$ is good and $u \mapsto u'$ then u' is good. Hence, we can define a game $\bar{G}$, where the set of vertices $\bar{V}$ consists of all good vertices of G, and for all $u, u' \in \bar{V}$ we have that (u, u') is a transition of $\bar{G}$ iff $u \mapsto u'$ is an optimal transition of G. The transition probabilities in $\bar{G}$ are the same as in G. Now we prove the following three claims:

(a) For every $u \in \bar{V}$ we have that $val(u, \bar{G}) = val(u, G)$.
(b) $\exists \bar{\sigma} \in \Sigma_{\bar{G}} \; \forall \bar{\pi} \in \Pi_{\bar{G}} : \mathcal{P}_v^{\bar{\sigma}, \bar{\pi}}(Reach(T, \bar{G})) \geq val(v, \bar{G}) = \varrho$.
(c) $\exists \sigma \in \Sigma_G \; \forall \pi \in \Pi_G : \mathcal{P}_v^{\sigma, \pi}(Reach(T, G)) \geq \varrho$.

Note that Claim (c) is exactly (5.9). We start by proving Claim (a). Let $u \in \bar{V}$. Due to Proposition 5.6, there is a MD strategy $\pi \in \Pi_G$ which is optimal minimising in every vertex of G (particularly in u) and selects only the optimal transitions. Hence, the strategy π can also be used in the restricted game $\bar{G}$ and thus we obtain $val(u, \bar{G}) \leq val(u, G)$. Now suppose that $val(u, \bar{G}) < val(u, G)$. By applying Proposition 5.6 to $\bar{G}$, there is an optimal minimising MD strategy $\bar{\pi} \in \Pi_{\bar{G}}$. Further, for every vertex t of G which is not good there is a strategy $\pi_t \in \Pi_G$ such that for every $\sigma \in \Sigma_G$ we have that $\mathcal{P}_t^{\sigma, \pi_t}(Reach(T, G)) < val(u, G)$ (this follows immediately from (5.10)). Now consider a strategy $\pi' \in \Pi_G$ which for every play of G initiated in u behaves in the following way:

- As long as player $\square$ uses only the transitions of G that are preserved in $\bar{G}$, the strategy π' behaves exactly like the strategy $\bar{\pi}$.
- When player $\square$ uses a transition $r \mapsto r'$ which is not a transition in $\bar{G}$ for the first time, then the strategy π' starts to behave either like the optimal minimising strategy π or the strategy $\pi_{r'}$, depending on whether r' is good or not (observe that if r' is good, then $val(r', G) < val(r, G)$ because $r \mapsto r'$ is not a transition of $\bar{G}$).

Now it is easy to check that for every $\sigma \in \Sigma_G$ we have that $\mathcal{P}_u^{\sigma, \pi'}(Reach(T, G)) < val(u, G)$, which contradicts the assumption that u is good.

Now we prove Claim (b). Due to Proposition 5.5, for every $u \in \bar{V}$ we can fix a strategy $\bar{\sigma}_u \in \Sigma_{\bar{G}}$ and $n_u \geq 1$ such that for every $\bar{\pi} \in \Pi_{\bar{G}}$ we have that $\mathcal{P}_u^{\bar{\sigma}_u, \bar{\pi}}(Reach^{n_u}(T, \bar{G})) > val(u, \bar{G})/2$. For every $k \geq 0$, let $B(k)$ be the set of all vertices u reachable from v in $\bar{G}$ via a path of length exactly k which does not visit T. Observe that $B(k)$ is finite because $\bar{G}$ is finitely branching. Further, for every $i \geq 0$ we define a bound m_i inductively as follows: $m_0 = 1$, and $m_{i+1} = m_i + \max\{n_u \mid u \in B(m_i)\}$. Now we define a strategy $\bar{\sigma} \in \Sigma_{\bar{G}}$ which turns out to be $(\mathbf{P}^{\geq \varrho}\mathbf{F}t)$-winning in the vertex v of $\bar{G}$. For every $w \in \bar{V}^*\bar{V}_\square$ such that $m_i \leq |w| < m_{i+1}$ we put $\bar{\sigma}(w) = \bar{\sigma}_u(uw_2)$, where $w = w_1uw_2$, $|w_1| = m_i - 1$ and $u \in \bar{V}$. Now it is easy to check that for every $i \geq 1$ and every strategy $\bar{\pi} \in \Pi_{\bar{G}}$ we have that $\mathcal{P}_v^{\bar{\sigma},\bar{\pi}}(Reach^{m_i}(T,\bar{G})) > (1 - \frac{1}{2^i})\varrho$. This means that the strategy $\bar{\sigma}$ is $(\mathbf{P}^{\geq \varrho}\mathbf{F}t)$-winning in v.

It remains to prove Claim (c). Consider a strategy $\sigma \in \Sigma_G$ which for every play of G initiated in v behaves as follows:

- As long as player $\lozenge$ uses only the optimal transitions, the strategy σ behaves exactly like the strategy $\bar{\sigma}$.
- When player $\lozenge$ uses a non-optimal transition $r \mapsto r'$ for the first time, the strategy σ starts to behave like an ε-optimal maximising strategy in r', where $\varepsilon = (val(r',G) - val(r,G))/2$. Note that since $r \mapsto r'$ is not optimal, we have that $val(r',G) > val(r,G)$.

It is easy to check that σ is $(\mathbf{P}^{\geq \varrho}\mathbf{F}t)$-winning in v. $\qquad\square$

5.4 Some directions of future research

There are many challenging open problems and emerging lines of research in the area of stochastic games. Some of them have already been mentioned in the previous sections. We close by listing a few attractive topics (the presented list is of course far from being complete).

- **Infinite-state games.** The existing results about infinite-state games concern mainly games and MDPs generated by pushdown automata, lossy channel systems, or one-counter automata (see Section 5.2 for a more detailed summary). As indicated in Section 5.3, even in the setting of simple reachability objectives, many questions become subtle and require special attention. There is a plethora of automata-theoretic models with specific advantages, and the corresponding games can have specific objectives relevant to the chosen model. When compared to finite-state games, this field of research appears unexplored and offers many open problems.
- **Games with non-conflicting objectives.** It has been argued that non-zero-sum stochastic games are also relevant for purposes of formal verification of computer systems (see, e.g., Chatterjee et al. [2004c]). In this case, the main problem is the existence and computability of Nash equilibria (see Nash [1950]). Depending on the concrete objectives of the players, a Nash equilibrium may or may not exist, and there can be several

equilibrium points. Some existing literature about non-zero-sum stochastic games is mentioned in Section 5.2. The current knowledge is still limited.

- **Games with time.** The modelling power of continuous-time stochastic models such as continuous-time (semi)Markov chains (see, e.g., Norris [1998], Ross [1996]) or the real-time probabilistic processes of Alur et al. [1991] can be naturally extended by the element of choice. Thus, we obtain various types of continuous-time stochastic games. Stochastic games and MDPs over continuous-time Markov chains were studied by Baier et al. [2005], Neuhäußer et al. [2009], Brázdil et al. [2009b] and Rabe and Schewe [2010]. In this context, it makes sense to consider various types of strategies that measure or ignore the elapsed time, and study specific types of objectives that can be expressed by, e.g., the timed automata of Alur and Dill [1994].

The above discussed concepts are to a large extent orthogonal and can be combined almost arbitrarily. Thus, one can model very complex systems of time, chance, and choice. Many of the fundamental results are still waiting to be discovered.

Acknowledgements: I thank Václav Brožek and Tomáš Brázdil for reading a preliminary draft of this chapter. The work has been supported by the Czech Science Foundation, grant No. P202/10/1469.

References

P. Abdulla, N. Henda, L. de Alfaro, R. Mayr, and S. Sandberg. Stochastic games with lossy channels. In *Proceedings of FoSSaCS 2008*, volume 4962 of *Lecture Notes in Computer Science*, pages 35–49. Springer, 2005.

R. Alur and D. Dill. A theory of timed automata. *Theoretical Computer Science*, 126(2):183–235, 1994. Fundamental Study.

R. Alur, C. Courcoubetis, and D. Dill. Model-checking for probabilistic real-time systems. In *Proceedings of ICALP'91*, volume 510 of *Lecture Notes in Computer Science*, pages 115–136. Springer, 1991.

C. Baier, M. Größer, M. Leucker, B. Bollig, and F. Ciesinski. Controller synthesis for probabilistic systems. In *Proceedings of IFIP TCS'2004*, pages 493–506. Kluwer, 2004.

C. Baier, H. Hermanns, J.-P. Katoen, and B. Haverkort. Efficient computation of time-bounded reachability probabilities in uniform continuous-time Markov decision processes. *Theoretical Computer Science*, 345:2–26, 2005.

C. Baier, N. Bertrand, and P. Schnoebelen. On computing fixpoints in well-structured regular model checking, with applications to lossy channel systems. In *Proceedings of LPAR 2006*, volume 4246 of *Lecture Notes in Computer Science*, pages 347–361. Springer, 2006.

C. Baier, N. Bertrand, and P. Schnoebelen. Verifying nondeterministic probabilistic channel systems against ω-regular linear-time properties. *ACM Transactions on Computational Logic*, 9(1), 2007.

A. Bianco and L. de Alfaro. Model checking of probabilistic and nondeterministic systems. In *Proceedings of FST&TCS'95*, volume 1026 of *Lecture Notes in Computer Science*, pages 499–513. Springer, 1995.

P. Billingsley. *Probability and Measure*. Wiley, Hoboken, New Jersey, 1995.

T. Brázdil and V. Forejt. Strategy synthesis for Markov decision processes and branching-time logics. In *Proceedings of CONCUR 2007*, volume 4703 of *Lecture Notes in Computer Science*, pages 428–444. Springer, 2007.

T. Brázdil, V. Brožek, V. Forejt, and A. Kučera. Stochastic games with branching-time winning objectives. In *Proceedings of LICS 2006*, pages 349–358. IEEE Computer Society Press, 2006.

T. Brázdil, V. Brožek, V. Forejt, and A. Kučera. Reachability in recursive Markov decision processes. *Information and Computation*, 206(5):520–537, 2008.

T. Brázdil, V. Forejt, J. Křetínský, and A. Kučera. The satisfiability problem for probabilistic CTL. In *Proceedings of LICS 2008*, pages 391–402. IEEE Computer Society Press, 2008.

T. Brázdil, V. Forejt, and A. Kučera. Controller synthesis and verification for Markov decision processes with qualitative branching time objectives. In *Proceedings of ICALP 2008, Part II*, volume 5126 of *Lecture Notes in Computer Science*, pages 148–159. Springer, 2008.

T. Brázdil, V. Brožek, A. Kučera, and J. Obdržálek. Qualitative reachability in stochastic BPA games. In *Proceedings of STACS 2009*, volume 3 of *Leibniz International Proceedings in Informatics*, pages 207–218. Schloss Dagstuhl–Leibniz-Zentrum für Informatik, 2009a. A full version is available at arXiv:1003.0118 [cs.GT].

T. Brázdil, V. Forejt, J. Krčál, J. Křetínský, and A. Kučera. Continuous-time stochastic games with time-bounded reachability. In *Proceedings of FST&TCS 2009*, volume 4 of *Leibniz International Proceedings in Informatics*, pages 61–72. Schloss Dagstuhl–Leibniz-Zentrum für Informatik, 2009b.

T. Brázdil, V. Brožek, K. Etessami, A. Kučera, and D. Wojtczak. One-counter Markov decision processes. In *Proceedings of SODA 2010*, pages 863–874. SIAM, 2010.

V. Brožek. *Basic Model Checking Problems for Stochastic Games*. PhD thesis, Masaryk University, Faculty of Informatics, 2009.

K. Chatterjee. *Stochastic ω-regular Games*. PhD thesis, University of California, Berkeley, 2007.

K. Chatterjee, M. Jurdziński, and T. Henzinger. Simple stochastic parity games. In *Proceedings of CSL'93*, volume 832 of *Lecture Notes in Computer Science*, pages 100–113. Springer, 1994.

K. Chatterjee, L. de Alfaro, and T. Henzinger. Trading memory for randomness. In *Proceedings of 2nd Int. Conf. on Quantitative Evaluation of Systems (QEST'04)*, pages 206–217. IEEE Computer Society Press, 2004a.

K. Chatterjee, M. Jurdziński, and T. Henzinger. Quantitative stochastic parity games. In *Proceedings of SODA 2004*, pages 121–130. SIAM, 2004b.

K. Chatterjee, R. Majumdar, and M. Jurdziński. On Nash equilibria in stochastic games. In *Proceedings of CSL 2004*, volume 3210 of *Lecture Notes in Computer Science*, pages 26–40. Springer, 2004c.

K. Chatterjee, L. de Alfaro, and T. Henzinger. The complexity of stochastic Rabin and Streett games. In *Proceedings of ICALP 2005*, volume 3580 of *Lecture Notes in Computer Science*, pages 878–890. Springer, 2005.

K. Chatterjee, T. Henzinger, and M. Jurdziński. Games with secure equilibria. *Theoretical Computer Science*, 365(1–2):67–82, 2006.

K. Chatterjee, L. Doyen, and T. Henzinger. A survey of stochastic games with limsup and liminf objectives. In *Proceedings of ICALP 2009*, volume 5556 of *Lecture Notes in Computer Science*, pages 1–15. Springer, 2009.

A. Condon. The complexity of stochastic games. *Information and Computation*, 96 (2):203–224, 1992.

L. de Alfaro and T. Henzinger. Concurrent omega-regular games. In *Proceedings of LICS 2000*, pages 141–154. IEEE Computer Society Press, 2000.

L. de Alfaro and R. Majumdar. Quantitative solution of omega-regular games. *Journal of Computer and System Sciences*, 68:374–397, 2004.

E. Emerson. Temporal and modal logic. *Handbook of Theoretical Computer Science*, B:995–1072, 1991.

E. Emerson and C. Jutla. The complexity of tree automata and logics of programs. In *Proceedings of FOCS'88*, pages 328–337. IEEE Computer Society Press, 1988.

K. Etessami and M. Yannakakis. Recursive Markov decision processes and recursive stochastic games. In *Proceedings of ICALP 2005*, volume 3580 of *Lecture Notes in Computer Science*, pages 891–903. Springer, 2005.

K. Etessami and M. Yannakakis. Efficient qualitative analysis of classes of recursive Markov decision processes and simple stochastic games. In *Proceedings of STACS 2006*, volume 3884 of *Lecture Notes in Computer Science*, pages 634–645. Springer, 2006.

K. Etessami, D. Wojtczak, and M. Yannakakis. Recursive stochastic games with positive rewards. In *Proceedings of ICALP 2008, Part I*, volume 5125 of *Lecture Notes in Computer Science*, pages 711–723. Springer, 2008.

J. Filar and K. Vrieze. *Competitive Markov Decision Processes*. Springer, Berlin, 1996.

V. Forejt. *Controller Synthesis for Markov Decision Processes with Branching-Time Objectives*. PhD thesis, Masaryk University, Faculty of Informatics, 2009.

G. Gillette. Stochastic games with zero stop probabilities. *Contributions to the Theory of Games, vol III*, pages 179–187, 1957.

H. Gimbert and F. Horn. Simple stochastic games with few random vertices are easy to solve. In *Proceedings of FoSSaCS 2008*, volume 4962 of *Lecture Notes in Computer Science*, pages 5–19. Springer, 2005.

N. Halman. Simple stochastic games, parity games, mean payoff games and discounted payoff games are all LP-type problems. *Algorithmica*, 49(1):37–50, 2007.

H. Hansson and B. Jonsson. A logic for reasoning about time and reliability. *Formal Aspects of Computing*, 6:512–535, 1994.

A. Hoffman and R. Karp. On nonterminating stochastic games. *Management Science*, 12:359–370, 1966.

P. Hunter and A. Dawar. Complexity bounds for regular games. In *Proceedings of MFCS 2005*, volume 3618 of *Lecture Notes in Computer Science*, pages 495–506. Springer, 2005.

J. Kemeny, J. Snell, and A. Knapp. *Denumerable Markov Chains*. Springer, 1976.

A. Kučera and O. Stražovský. On the controller synthesis for finite-state Markov decision processes. *Fundamenta Informaticae*, 82(1–2):141–153, 2008.

T. Liggett and S. Lippman. Stochastic games with perfect information and time average payoff. *SIAM Review*, 11(4):604–607, 1969.

W. Ludwig. A subexponential randomized algorithm for the simple stochastic game problem. *Information and Computation*, 117(1):151–155, 1995.

A. Maitra and W. Sudderth. Finitely additive stochastic games with Borel measurable payoffs. *International Journal of Game Theory*, 27:257–267, 1998.

D. Martin. The determinacy of Blackwell games. *Journal of Symbolic Logic*, 63(4): 1565–1581, 1998.

A. McIver and C. Morgan. Games, probability, and the quantitative μ-calculus. In *Proceedings of LPAR 2002*, volume 2514 of *Lecture Notes in Computer Science*, pages 292–310. Springer, 2002.

J. Nash. Equilibrium points in N-person games. *Proceedings of the National Academy of Sciences*, 36:48–49, 1950.

M. Neuhäußer, M. Stoelinga, and J.-P. Katoen. Delayed nondeterminism in continuous-time Markov decision processes. In *Proceedings of FoSSaCS 2009*, volume 5504 of *Lecture Notes in Computer Science*, pages 364–379. Springer, 2009.

A. Neyman and S. Sorin. *Stochastic Games and Applications*. Kluwer, Dordrecht, 2003.

J. Norris. *Markov Chains*. Cambridge University Press, Cambridge, 1998.

A. Pnueli. The temporal logic of programs. In *Proceedings of 18th Annual Symposium on Foundations of Computer Science*, pages 46–57. IEEE Computer Society Press, 1977.

M. Puterman. *Markov Decision Processes*. Wiley, Hoboken, New Jersey, 1994.

M. Rabe and S. Schewe. Optimal time-abstract schedulers for CTMDPs and Markov games. In *Eighth Workshop on Quantitative Aspects of Programming Languages*, 2010.

S. Ross. *Stochastic Processes*. Wiley, Hoboken, New Jersey, 1996.

P. Secchi and W. Sudderth. Stay-in-a-set games. *International Journal of Game Theory*, 30:479–490, 2001.

L. Shapley. Stochastic games. *Proceedings of the National Academy of Sciences*, 39: 1095–1100, 1953.

A. Tarski. A lattice-theoretical fixpoint theorem and its applications. *Pacific Journal of Mathematics*, 5(2):285–309, 1955.

W. Thomas. Automata on infinite objects. *Handbook of Theoretical Computer Science*, B:135–192, Elsevier, Amsterdam, 1991.

M. Ummels and D. Wojtczak. Decision problems for Nash equilibria in stochastic games. In *Proceedings of CSL 2009*, volume 5771 of *Lecture Notes in Computer Science*, pages 515–529. Springer, 2009.

P. Wolper. Temporal logic can be more expressive. In *Proceedings of 22nd Annual Symposium on Foundations of Computer Science*, pages 340–348. IEEE Computer Society Press, 1981.

6

Games with Imperfect Information: Theory and Algorithms

Laurent Doyen   Jean-François Raskin

CNRS and ENS Cachan   *Université Libre de Bruxelles*

Abstract

We study observation-based strategies for two-player turn-based games played on graphs with parity objectives. An observation-based strategy relies on imperfect information about the history of a play, namely, on the past sequence of observations. Such games occur in the synthesis of a controller that does not see the private state of the plant. Our main results are twofold. First, we give a fixed-point algorithm for computing the set of states from which a player can win with a deterministic observation-based strategy for a parity objective. Second, we give an algorithm for computing the set of states from which a player can win with probability 1 with a randomised observation-based strategy for a reachability objective. This set is of interest because in the absence of perfect information, randomised strategies are more powerful than deterministic ones.

6.1 Introduction

Games are natural models for reactive systems. We consider zero-sum two-player turn-based games of infinite duration played on finite graphs. One player represents a control program, and the second player represents its environment. The graph describes the possible interactions of the system, and the game is of infinite duration because reactive systems are usually not expected to terminate. In the simplest setting, the game is turn-based and with perfect information, meaning that the players have full knowledge of both the game structure and the sequence of moves played by the adversary. The winning condition in a zero-sum graph game is defined by a set of plays that the first player aims to enforce, and that the second player aims to avoid.

Figure 6.5 is taken from the final version of Berwanger et al. [2008] that appeared in Information and Computation 208(10), pp. 1206-1220, ISSN: 0890-5401. It is republished here by permission of Elsevier.

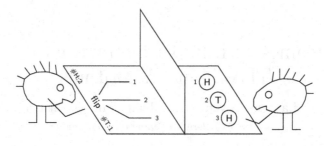

Figure 6.1 The 3-COIN game

We focus on ω-regular sets of plays expressed by the parity condition (see Section 6.2) and we briefly present properties and algorithmic solutions for such games. The theory and algorithms for games with perfect information has been extensively studied by Martin [1975], Emerson and Jutla [1991], Thomas [1995, 2002] and Henzinger [2007].

Turn-based games of perfect information make the strong assumption that the players can observe the state of the game and the previous moves before playing. This is however unrealistic in the design of reactive systems because the components of a system have an internal state that is not visible to the other components, and because their execution is concurrent, each component choosing moves independently of the others. Such situations require us to introduce games with *imperfect information* where the players have partial information about the play. We illustrate the games with imperfect information with the 3-COIN game, shown in Figure 6.1.

> Three coins c_1, c_2, c_3 are arranged on a table, either *head* or *tail* up. Player 1 does not see the coins, but he is informed of the number of heads (H) and tails (T). The coins are manipulated by Player 2. The objective of Player 1 is to have all coins head up (HHH) while avoiding at all cost a configuration where all coins show tail (TTT). The game is played as follows. Initially, Player 2 chooses a configuration of the coins with two heads and one tails. Then, the following rounds are played: Player 1 can choose one coin in the set $\{c_1, c_2, c_3\}$ and ask Player 2 to toggle that coin. Player 2 must execute the choice of Player 1 and he may further decide to exchange the positions of the two other coins. The game stops whenever the three coins are all head up (Player 1 wins) or all tail up (Player 2 wins). Otherwise Player 2 announces the number of heads and tails, and the next round starts.

This is a game with imperfect information for Player 1 as she does not know the exact position of the coins, but only the number of heads and tails. In this game, does Player 1 have a strategy such that for all strategies of Player 2, the game reaches HHH and avoids TTT? We are interested in **observation-based strategies** which rely on the information available to Player 1. In fact, Player 1 has no deterministic observation-based strategy to win the 3-COIN game, because Player 2 can always find a spoiling counter-strategy using his ability to exchange coins after Player 1's move. If we do not allow Player 2 to exchange the coins, then Player 1 has a deterministic observation-based winning strategy consisting in successively trying to toggle every coin. This strategy requires *memory* and it is easy to see that memory is necessary to win this game. On the other hand, if we allow Player 1 to take his decision using a source of randomisation, then she would be able to win the original 3-COIN game with probability 1. This shows that *randomised* strategies are in general more powerful than deterministic strategies.

We study in this chapter mathematical models and algorithms for games with imperfect information. The model that we consider is asymmetric in the sense that Player 1 has imperfect information about the state while Player 2 has perfect knowledge (Reif [1984], Chatterjee et al. [2007], De Wulf et al. [2006]). This model is useful for the design of control programs embedded in an environment that provides observations about its state via shared variables or sensors. We discuss the asymmetry of the definition in Section 6.3.1 and we argue that the existence of deterministic winning strategies for Player 1 does not depend on the ability or not for Player 2 to see the exact position of the game. In the rest of Section 6.3, we present the theory and algorithms to decide the existence of observation-based winning strategies. We use a reduction of games with imperfect information to games with perfect information, and we exploit the structure of this reduction to obtain a tailored data-structure and symbolic algorithms. We focus on *reachability* and *safety* objectives which ask Player 1 to respectively reach and avoid a designated set of target configurations. For parity objectives, we choose to provide a reduction to safety games. We also briefly present algorithms to construct winning strategies.

In Section 6.4, we introduce randomised observation-based strategies and we present an algorithmic solution for reachability and Büchi objectives. The algorithm computes the set of winning positions of the game and constructs a randomised observation-based winning strategy.

6.2 Games with perfect information

Game graphs A *game graph* is a tuple $G = \langle L, l_I, \Sigma, \Delta \rangle$, where L is a finite set of states, $l_I \in L$ is the initial state, Σ is a finite alphabet of actions, and $\Delta \subseteq L \times \Sigma \times L$ is a set of labelled transitions. We require the game graph G to be *total*, i.e., for all $\ell \in L$ and all $\sigma \in \Sigma$, there exists $\ell' \in L$ such that $(\ell, \sigma, \ell') \in \Delta$.

The turn-based game on G is played by two players for infinitely many rounds. The first round starts in the initial location l_I of the game graph. In each round, if the current location is ℓ, Player 1 chooses an action $\sigma \in \Sigma$, and then Player 2 chooses a location ℓ' such that $(\ell, \sigma, \ell') \in \Delta$. The next round starts in ℓ'.

Plays and strategies A *play* in G is an infinite sequence $\pi = \ell_0 \ell_1 \ldots$ such that $\ell_0 = l_I$, and for all $i \geq 0$, there exists $\sigma_i \in \Sigma$ such that $(\ell_i, \sigma_i, \ell_{i+1}) \in \Delta$. We denote by $\mathsf{Inf}(\pi)$ the set of locations that occur infinitely often in π. A *history* is a finite prefix $\pi(i) = \ell_0 \ldots \ell_i$ of a play, and its *length* is $|\pi(i)| = i$. We denote by $\mathsf{Last}(\pi(i)) = \ell_i$ the last location in $\pi(i)$.

A *deterministic strategy* in G for Player 1 is a function $\alpha : L^+ \to \Sigma$ that maps histories to actions, and for Player 2 it is a function $\beta : L^+ \times \Sigma \to L$ such that for all $\pi \in L^+$ and all $\sigma \in \Sigma$, we have $(\mathsf{Last}(\pi), \sigma, \beta(\pi, \sigma)) \in \Delta$. We denote by $\mathcal{A}_G$ and $\mathcal{B}_G$ the set of all Player 1 and Player 2 strategies in G, respectively. A strategy $\alpha \in \mathcal{A}_G$ is *memoryless* if $\mathsf{Last}(\pi) = \mathsf{Last}(\pi')$ implies $\alpha(\pi) = \alpha(\pi')$ for all $\pi, \pi' \in L^+$, that is the strategy only depends on the last location of the history. We define memoryless strategies for Player 2 analogously.

The *outcome* of deterministic strategies α (for Player 1) and β (for Player 2) in G is the play $\pi = \ell_0 \ell_1 \ldots$ such that $\sigma_i = \alpha(\pi(i))$ and $\ell_{i+1} = \beta(\pi(i), \sigma_i)$ for all $i \geq 0$. This play is denoted $\mathsf{outcome}(G, \alpha, \beta)$. A play π is *consistent* with a deterministic strategy α for Player 1 if $\pi = \mathsf{outcome}(G, \alpha, \beta)$ for some deterministic strategy β for Player 2. We denote by $\mathsf{Outcome}_1(G, \alpha)$ the set of plays that are consistent with α. Plays that are consistent with a deterministic strategy for Player 2 and the set $\mathsf{Outcome}_2(G, \beta)$ are defined analogously.

Objectives An *objective* for a game graph $G = \langle L, l_I, \Sigma, \Delta \rangle$ is a set $\varphi \subseteq L^\omega$. We denote by $\overline{\varphi} = L^\omega \setminus \varphi$ the complement of φ. A deterministic strategy α for Player 1 (resp. β for Player 2) is *surely-winning* for an objective φ in G if $\mathsf{Outcome}_1(G, \alpha) \subseteq \varphi$ (resp. if $\mathsf{Outcome}_2(G, \beta) \subseteq \varphi$). We consider the following objectives:

- *Reachability and safety objectives.* Given a set $T \subseteq L$ of target locations, the **reachability objective** $\mathsf{Reach}(T) = \{\ell_0 \ell_1 \ldots \mid \exists k \geq 0 : \ell_k \in T\}$ requires that an observation in T is visited at least once. Dually, the **safety objective** $\mathsf{Safe}(T) = \{\ell_0 \ell_1 \ldots \mid \forall k \geq 0 : \ell_k \in T\}$ requires that only locations in T are visited.

- *Büchi and co-Büchi objectives.* Given a set $T \subseteq L$ of target locations, the **Büchi objective** $\mathsf{Buchi}(T) = \{\pi \mid \mathsf{Inf}(\pi) \cap T \neq \varnothing\}$ requires that at least one location in T is visited infinitely often. Dually, the **co-Büchi objective** $\mathsf{coBuchi}(T) = \{\pi \mid \mathsf{Inf}(\pi) \subseteq T\}$ requires that only locations in T are visited infinitely often.

- *Parity objectives.* For $d \in \mathbb{N}$, let $pr : L \rightarrow \{0, 1, \ldots, d\}$ be a **priority function** that maps each location to a non-negative integer priority. The **parity objective** $\mathsf{Parity}(pr) = \{\pi \mid \min\{pr(\ell) \mid \ell \in \mathsf{Inf}(\pi)\}$ is even$\}$ requires that the minimal priority occurring infinitely often is even.

Given a location $\hat{\ell}$, we also say that Player i ($i = 1, 2$) is surely-winning from $\hat{\ell}$ (or that $\hat{\ell}$ is surely-winning) for an objective φ in G if Player i has a surely-winning strategy in for φ in the game $\hat{G} = \langle L, \hat{\ell}, \Sigma, \Delta \rangle$ where $\hat{\ell}$ is the initial location. A game is **determined** if when player i does not have a surely-winning strategy from a location ℓ for an objective φ, then Player $3 - i$ has a surely-winning strategy from ℓ for the complement objective $\overline{\varphi}$.

Exercise 6.1 Prove the following:

(a) Büchi and co-Büchi objectives are special cases of parity objectives.
(b) The complement of a parity objective is again a parity objective.

The following result shows that (i) parity games are determined and (ii) memoryless strategies are sufficient to win parity games.

Theorem 6.1 (Memoryless determinacy, Emerson and Jutla [1991]) *In all game graphs G with parity objective φ, the following hold:*

- *either Player 1 has a surely-winning strategy in $\langle G, \varphi \rangle$, or Player 2 has a surely-winning strategy in $\langle G, \overline{\varphi} \rangle$;*
- *Player 1 has a surely-winning strategy in $\langle G, \varphi \rangle$ if and only if she has a memoryless surely-winning strategy in $\langle G, \varphi \rangle$;*
- *Player 2 has a surely-winning strategy in $\langle G, \varphi \rangle$ if and only if he has a memoryless surely-winning strategy in $\langle G, \varphi \rangle$.*

Exercise 6.2 Consider a game graph $G = \langle L, l_I, \Sigma, \Delta \rangle$ which is not total, and assume that we modify the rules of the game as follows: if in a round where the current location is ℓ, Player 1 chooses an action $\sigma \in \Sigma$ such that there exists no transition $(\ell, \sigma, \ell') \in \Delta$, then Player 1 is declared losing the game. Given a non-total game graph G and parity objective φ in G, define a generic construction of a total game graph G' along with a parity objective φ' such that Player 1 has a surely-winning strategy in $\langle G, \varphi \rangle$ if and only if he has a surely-winning strategy in $\langle G', \varphi' \rangle$.

Exercise 6.3 Traditionally, a two-player game is a directed graph $\langle V, v_I, E \rangle$ where V is partitioned into V_1, V_2 the sets of vertices of Player 1 and Player 2 respectively, $v_I \in V$ is the initial vertex, and $E \subseteq V \times V$ is a set of edges. We call this model an ***edge-game***. A parity objective is defined by a priority function $pr : V \to \{0, 1, \ldots, d\}$ as above. A (memoryless) strategy for player i $(i = 1, 2)$ is a function $\gamma_i : V_i \to E$ such that $(v, \gamma_i(v)) \in E$ for all $v \in V_i$. The definition of plays and outcomes is adapted accordingly. Show that the edge-games are equivalent to our game graphs by defining a generic transformation (a) from parity edge-games to parity game graphs, and (b) from parity game graphs to parity edge-games, such that player 1 has a surely-winning strategy in one game if and only if he has a surely-winning strategy in the other game.

Hint: for (a), first define an equivalent bipartite graph $\langle V', v_I', E' \rangle$ such that for all edges $(v, v') \in E'$, $v \in V_1'$ if and only if $v' \in V_2'$.

Algorithms We present an algorithmic solution to the problem of deciding, given a game graph G and an objective φ, if Player 1 has a surely-winning strategy for φ in G. The set of locations in which Player 1 has a surely-winning strategy can be computed symbolically as the solution of certain nested fixpoint formulas, based on the ***controllable predecessor operator*** $\mathsf{Cpre} : 2^L \to 2^L$ which, given a set of locations $s \subseteq L$, computes the set of locations $\ell \in L$ from which Player 1 can force the game to be in a location of s in the next round, i.e., she has an action $\sigma \in \Sigma$ such that all transitions from ℓ labelled by σ lead to s. Formally,

$$\mathsf{Cpre}(s) = \{\ell \in L \mid \exists \sigma \in \Sigma \cdot \forall \ell' \in L : \text{ if } (\ell, \sigma, \ell') \in \Delta \text{ then } \ell' \in s\}.$$

Exercise 6.4 (a) Show that Cpre is a monotone operator for the subset ordering i.e., $s \subseteq s'$ implies $\mathsf{Cpre}(s) \subseteq \mathsf{Cpre}(s')$ for all $s, s' \subseteq L$.
(b) Define the controllable predecessor operator for the two-player edge-games of Exercise 6.3.

Consider a game with safety objective $\mathsf{Safe}(T)$. To win such a game, Player 1 has to be able to maintain the game in the set T for infinitely many rounds. For all $i \geq 0$, let $W^i \subseteq L$ be the set of locations from which Player 1 can maintain the game in the set T for at least the next i rounds. Clearly

$W^{i+1} \subseteq W^i \subseteq T$ for all $i \geq 0$, and therefore the sequence of sets $(W^i)_{i \geq 0}$ is decreasing and eventually stabilises. The limit of this sequence is defined as

$$W = \bigcap_{i \geq 0} W^i$$

and this is the set of surely-winning locations for Player 1. This result follows from the facts that for all $i \geq 0$ and from all locations $\ell \in W^{i+1}$, Player 1 can force the game to be in a location of W^i in the next round, and that $W = W^{j+1} = W^j$ for some $j \geq 0$. We can compute the sets W^i as follows:

$$\begin{aligned} W^0 &= T \\ W^{i+1} &= T \cap \mathsf{Cpre}(W^i) \text{ for all } i \geq 0. \end{aligned}$$

Note that the limit W is obtained after at most n iterations where $n = |T|$ is the number of target locations. The set W can also be viewed as the *greatest solution* of the equation $W = T \cap \mathsf{Cpre}(W)$, denoted $\nu W \cdot T \cap \mathsf{Cpre}(W)$. The argument showing that a unique greatest fixpoint exists is not developed in this chapter. We simply mention that it relies on the theory of complete lattices and Kleene's fixpoint theorem.

Theorem 6.2 (Safety games)   *The set of surely-winning positions for Player 1 in safety games with perfect information can be computed in linear time.*

For reachability objectives, the algorithmic solution based on Cpre computes a sequence of sets W^i $(i \geq 0)$ such that from every $\ell \in W^i$, Player 1 can force the game to reach some location $\ell \in T$ within the next i rounds. It can be computed as follows:

$$\begin{aligned} W^0 &= T \\ W^{i+1} &= T \cup \mathsf{Cpre}(W^i) \text{ for all } i \geq 0. \end{aligned}$$

The necessary number of iterations is at most $|L \setminus T|$. In terms of fixpoint, the set W is the *least solution* of the equation $W = T \cup \mathsf{Cpre}(W)$, denoted $\mu W \cdot T \cup \mathsf{Cpre}(W)$.

Theorem 6.3 (Reachability games)   *The set of surely-winning positions for Player 1 in reachability games with perfect information can be computed in linear time.*

For parity objectives, several algorithms have been proposed in the literature (see, e.g., Zielonka [1998], Jurdziński [2000], Schewe [2008], and Friedmann and Lange [2009] for a survey). Using the result of memoryless determinacy (Theorem 6.1), it is easy to show that parity games can be solved in

NP $\cap$ coNP. A major open problem is to know whether parity games with perfect information can be solved in polynomial time.

We present an algorithmic solution for parity games using a reduction to safety games. A variant of this reduction has been presented by Bernet et al. [2002]. In the worst case, it yields safety games of size exponentially larger than the parity game. Such a blow-up is not surprising since safety games can be solved in polynomial time. The reduction gives some insight into the structure of parity games.

Consider a game graph $G = \langle L, l_I, \Sigma, \Delta \rangle$ and a priority function $pr : L \to \{0, 1, \ldots, d\}$ defining the parity objective $\mathsf{Parity}(pr)$ that requires the minimal priority occurring infinitely often to be even. We extend the locations of G with tuples $\langle c_1, c_3, \ldots, c_d \rangle$ of *counters* associated with the odd priorities (we assume that d is odd). The counters are initialised to 0, and each visit to a state with *odd* priority p increments the counter c_p. Intuitively, accumulating visits to an odd priority is potentially bad, except if a smaller even priority is also eventually visited. Therefore, each visit to a state with *even* priority p resets all counters $c_{p'}$ with $p' > p$.

Under these rules, if player 1 has a surely-winning strategy in G for the objective $\mathsf{Parity}(pr)$, then player 1 also has a memoryless surely-winning strategy, and thus can enforce that each counter c_p remains bounded by n_p, the number of locations with priority p. On the other hand, if Player 1 has no strategy that maintains all counter c_p below n_p, then it means that no matter the strategy of Player 1, there exists a strategy of Player 2 such that the outcome of the game visits some location with odd priority p at least twice, without visiting a location of smaller priority. Since we can assume that Player 1 uses a memoryless strategy, this shows that Player 2 can force infinitely many visits to an odd priority without visiting a smaller priority, thus Player 1 cannot win the parity game.

Formally, we define $G' = \langle L', l'_I, \Sigma, \Delta' \rangle$ where

- $L' = L \times [n_1] \times [n_3] \times \ldots \times [n_d]$ where $[n_i]$ denotes the set $\{0, 1, \ldots, n_i\} \cup \{\infty\}$, and n_i is the number of locations with priority i in G;

- $l'_I = (l_I, 0, 0, \ldots, 0)$;

- $\Delta' = \{((\ell_1, c), \sigma, (\ell_2, \mathsf{update}(c, p))) \mid (\ell_1, \sigma, \ell_2) \in \Delta \text{ and } p = pr(q)\}$ where

$$\mathsf{update}(\langle c_1, c_3, \ldots, c_d \rangle, p) = \begin{cases} \langle c_1, \ldots, c_{p-1}, 0, \ldots, 0 \rangle & p \text{ even} \\ \langle c_1, \ldots, c_{p-1}, c_p + 1, c_{p+1}, \ldots, c_d \rangle & p \text{ odd} \end{cases}$$

where we let $c_p + 1 = \infty$ for $c_p \in \{n_p, \infty\}$.

The safety objective for G' is $\mathsf{Safe}(\mathcal{T}_{pr}^G)$ where $\mathcal{T}_{pr}^G = L' \cap (L \times \mathbb{N}^{\lceil \frac{d}{2} \rceil})$ is the set of locations in which no overflow occurred. The following lemma states the correctness of the construction.

Lemma 6.4 *For all game graphs G and priority functions pr, Player 1 is surely-winning in G for the objective* Parity(pr) *if and only if Player 1 is surely-winning in G' for the objective* Safe$(\mathcal{T}_{pr}^{G})$.

Proof First, let α be a winning strategy for Player 1 in G for the parity objective Parity(pr). We construct a strategy α' for Player 1 in the game G' and we show that this strategy is surely-winning for the objective Safe$(\mathcal{T}_{pr}^{G})$. First, without loss of generality we can assume that α is memoryless. We define α' as follows, for all histories π in G', let $(\ell, c) = \mathsf{Last}(\pi)$, and we take $\alpha'(\pi) = \alpha(\ell)$. We show that α' is winning for the objective Safe$(\mathcal{T}_{pr}^{G})$. Towards a contradiction, assume that it is not the case. Then there exists a strategy β' of Player 2 such that outcome$(G', \alpha', \beta') = (\ell_0, c_0)(\ell_1, c_1) \ldots (\ell_n, c_n) \ldots$ leaves $\mathcal{T}_{pr}^{G}$. Let $0 \leq k_1 < k_2$ be such that (ℓ_{k_2}, c_{k_2}) is the first location where a counter (say c_p) reaches the value ∞ (p is the odd priority associated with this counter), and k_1 is the last index where this counter has been reset (k_1 is equal to 0 if the counter has never been reset). As c_p overflows, we know that the subsequence $(\ell_{k_1}, c_{k_1})(\ell_{k_1+1}, c_{k_1+1}) \ldots (\ell_{k_2}, c_{k_2})$ visits $n_p + 1$ locations with priority p. As there are n_p locations with priority p in G, we know that there is at least one location with priority p which is repeating in the subsequence. Let i_1 and i_2 be the two indexes associated with such a repeating location. Between i_1 and i_2, there is no visit to an even priority smaller than p. Because Player 1 is playing a memoryless strategy in G, Player 2 can spoil the strategy of Player 1 by repeating his sequence of choices between i_1 and i_2. This contradicts our hypothesis that α is a winning strategy in G for the parity objective Parity(pr).

Second, let us consider the case where Player 1 is not surely-winning in G for the objective Parity(pr). By determinacy, we know that Player 2 has a surely-winning strategy β for the parity objective $\overline{\mathsf{Parity}(pr)}$. Using a similar argument as above we can construct a strategy β' for Player 2 for surely-winning the reachability objective Reach$(\overline{\mathcal{T}_{pr}^{G}})$. By determinacy, this shows that Player 1 is not surely-winning in G' for the objective Safe$(\mathcal{T}_{pr}^{G})$. $\square$

Note that since Büchi and co-Büchi objectives are parity objectives (see Exercise 6.1), the above reduction to safety games applies and yields a game G' of quadratic size, thus a quadratic-time algorithm for solving Büchi and co-Büchi games.

6.3 Games with imperfect information: surely-winning

In a game with imperfect information, the set of locations is partitioned into information sets called **observations**. Player 1 is not allowed to see what is the current location of the game, but only what is the current observation. Observations provide imperfect information about the current location. For example, if a location encodes the state of a distributed system, the observation may disclose the value of the shared variables, and hide the value of the private variables; or in a physical system, an observation may give a range of possible values for parameters such as temperature, modelling sensor imprecision. Note that the structure of the game itself is known to both players, imperfect information arising only about the current location while playing the game.

6.3.1 Game structure with imperfect information

A **game structure with imperfect information** is a tuple $G = \langle L, l_I, \Sigma, \Delta, \mathcal{O} \rangle$, where $\langle L, l_I, \Sigma, \Delta \rangle$ is a game graph (see Section 6.2) and $\mathcal{O}$ is a set of *observations* that partitions the set L of locations. For each location $\ell \in L$, we denote by $\mathsf{obs}(\ell)$ the unique observation $o \in \mathcal{O}$ such that $\ell \in o$. For each play $\pi = \ell_0 \ell_1 \ldots$, we denote by $\mathsf{obs}(\pi)$ the sequence $\mathsf{obs}(\ell_0)\mathsf{obs}(\ell_1) \ldots$ and we analogously extend $\mathsf{obs}(\cdot)$ to histories, sets of plays, etc.

The game on G is played in the same way as in the perfect information case, but now only the observation of the current location is revealed to Player 1. The effect of the uncertainty about the history of the play is formally captured by the notion of observation-based strategy.

An **observation-based strategy** for Player 1 is a function $\alpha : L^+ \to \Sigma$ such that $\alpha(\pi) = \alpha(\pi')$ for all histories $\pi, \pi' \in L^+$ with $\mathsf{obs}(\pi) = \mathsf{obs}(\pi')$. We often use the notation α^o to emphasise that α is observation-based. Outcome and consistent plays are defined as in games with perfect information.

An objective φ in a game with imperfect information is a set of plays as before, but we require that φ is *observable* by Player 1, i.e., for all $\pi \in \varphi$, for all π' such that $\mathsf{obs}(\pi') = \mathsf{obs}(\pi)$, we have $\pi' \in \varphi$. In the sequel, we often view objectives as sets of infinite sequences of observations, i.e., $\varphi \in \mathcal{O}^\omega$, and we also call them observable objectives. For example, we assume that reachability and safety objectives are specified by a union of target observations, and parity objectives are specified by priority functions of the form $p : \mathcal{O} \to \{0, \ldots, d\}$. The definition of surely-winning strategies is adapted accordingly, namely, a deterministic observation-based strategy α for player 1 is **surely-winning** for an objective $\varphi \in \mathcal{O}^\omega$ in G if $\mathsf{obs}(\mathsf{Outcome}_1(G, \alpha)) \subseteq \varphi$.

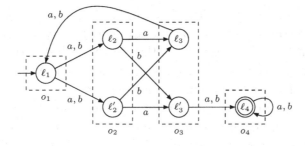

Figure 6.2 A game structure with imperfect information G

Note that games with perfect information can be obtained as the special case where $\mathcal{O} = \{\{\ell\} \mid \ell \in L\}$.

Example Consider the game structure with imperfect information in Figure 6.2. The observations are $o_1 = \{\ell_1\}$, $o_2 = \{\ell_2, \ell'_2\}$, $o_3 = \{\ell_3, \ell'_3\}$, and $o_4 = \{\ell_4\}$. The transitions are shown as labelled edges, and the initial state is ℓ_1. The objective of Player 1 is $\varphi = \mathsf{Reach}(o_4)$, i.e., to reach location ℓ_4. We argue that the game is not surely-winning for Player 1. Let α be an arbitrary deterministic strategy for Player 1. Consider the strategy β for Player 2 as follows: for all $\pi \in L^+$ such that $\mathsf{Last}(\pi) \in o_2$, if $\alpha(\pi) = a$, then in the previous round β chooses the state ℓ_2, and if $\alpha(\pi) = b$, then in the previous round β chooses the state ℓ'_2. Given α and β, the play $\mathsf{outcome}(G, \alpha, \beta)$ never reaches ℓ_4. Similarly, Player 2 has no strategy β to ensure that $\mathsf{obs}(\mathsf{outcome}_2(G, \beta)) \subseteq \bar{\varphi}$ where $\bar{\varphi} = \mathsf{Safe}(\{o_1, o_2, o_3\})$ is the complement of φ. Hence the game is not determined.

We briefly discuss the definition of games with imperfect information. In traditional games with perfect information played on graphs (see Exercise 6.3), locations are partitioned into locations of Player 1 and locations of Player 2, and the players choose edges from the locations they own. It can be shown that for perfect information games, this model is equivalent to our definition (see Exercise 6.3). When extending the classical game model to imperfect information, we need to remember that Player 1 does not see what is the current location, and therefore he could not in general choose an edge from the current location. Instead, one may ask Player 1 to choose in each round one edge per location, thus to be prepared to all situations. This would require an alphabet of actions of the form $L \to \Delta$ which is of exponential size. We prefer a simpler definition where an alphabet Σ of actions is fixed, and each action selects some outgoing edges. In this definition, all locations belong to Player 1 and the choices of Player 2 are modelled by non-determinism.

Another point of interest is the fact that games with imperfect information sound asymmetric, as only Player 1 has a partial view of the play. It should be noted however that for surely-winning, it would be of no help to Player 1 that Player 2 also has imperfect information. Indeed, a surely-winning strategy of Player 1 has to ensure that *all* outcomes are in the objective, and this requirement is somehow independent of the ability or not of Player 2 to see the current location. In terms of strategies, one can show that to spoil a not surely-winning strategy of Player 1, Player 2 does not need to remember the history of the play, but only needs to count the number of rounds that have been played. We say that a deterministic strategy $\beta : L^+ \times \Sigma \to L$ for Player 2 is *counting* if for all $\pi, \pi' \in L^+$ such that $|\pi| = |\pi'|$ and $\mathsf{Last}(\pi) = \mathsf{Last}(\pi')$, and for all $\sigma \in \Sigma$, we have $\beta(\pi, \sigma) = \beta(\pi', \sigma)$.

Theorem 6.5 (Chatterjee et al. [2007]) *Let G be a game structure with imperfect information and φ be an observable objective. There exists an observation-based strategy $\alpha^o \in \mathcal{A}_G$ such that for all $\beta \in \mathcal{B}_G$ we have* $\mathsf{outcome}(G, \alpha^o, \beta) \in \varphi$ *if and only if there exists an observation-based strategy $\alpha^o \in \mathcal{A}_G^O$ such that for all counting strategies $\beta^c \in \mathcal{B}_G$ we have* $\mathsf{outcome}(G, \alpha^o, \beta^c) \in \varphi$.

Exercise 6.5 Prove Theorem 6.5.

The requirement that observations partition the set of locations of the games may seem to be restrictive. For example, in a system using sensors, it would be more natural to allow overlapping observations. For instance, if a control program measures the temperature using sensors, the values that are obtained have finite precision ε. When the sensor returns a value t, the actual temperature lies within the interval $[t - \varepsilon, t + \varepsilon]$. Clearly, for a measure t' such that $|t' - t| < \varepsilon$, we have that $[t - \varepsilon, t + \varepsilon] \cap [t' - \varepsilon, t' + \varepsilon] \neq \varnothing$. As a consequence, the temperature observations overlap and do not form a partition of the space of values.

Exercise 6.6 Show that a game structure with imperfect information in which the observations do not partition the state space can be transformed into an equivalent game structure with imperfect information with partitioning observations in polynomial time.

Consider the game structure with imperfect information in Figure 6.3. The alphabet of actions is $\Sigma = \{a, b\}$ and the objective for Player 1 is to reach location ℓ_4'. The partition induced by the observations is represented

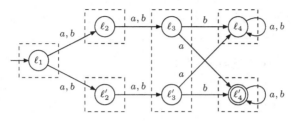

Figure 6.3 Memory is necessary for Player 1 to surely-win the objective Reach(ℓ'_4)

by the dashed sets. We claim that Player 1 has no memoryless observation-based surely-winning strategy in this game. This is because from locations ℓ_3 and ℓ'_3, different actions need to be played to reach ℓ'_4, but since ℓ_3 and ℓ'_3 have the same observation, Player 1 has to play the same action in a memoryless observation-based strategy. However, if Player 1 remembers the previous observation, then he has a surely-winning strategy, namely if $\{\ell_2\}$ was observed in the previous round, then play a, and if $\{\ell'_2\}$ was observed in the previous round, then play b. This shows that memory may be necessary for surely-winning in a game with imperfect information even for a reachability objective. Intuitively, a sequence of past observations provides more precise knowledge about the current location of the game than the current observation only. Therefore, Player 1 should store and update this knowledge along the play to maintain the most precise information possible. Initially, his knowledge is the singleton $\{l_I\}$ (we assume that the structure of the game is known to both players), and if the current knowledge is a set $s \subseteq L$, Player 1 chooses action $\sigma \in \Sigma$, and observation $o \in \mathcal{O}$ is disclosed, then the updated knowledge is $\mathsf{post}^G_\sigma(s) \cap o$ where $\mathsf{post}^G_\sigma(s) = \{\ell' \in L \mid \exists \ell \in s : (\ell, \sigma, \ell') \in \Delta\}$, i.e., the set of all locations reachable from locations in s by playing σ.

6.3.2 Reduction to games with perfect information

Given a **game structure with imperfect information** $G = \langle L, l_I, \Sigma, \Delta, \mathcal{O} \rangle$ with observable parity objective φ, we construct an equivalent game structure (with perfect information) $G^{\mathsf{K}} = \langle S, s_I, \Sigma, \Delta^{\mathsf{K}} \rangle$ with a parity objective φ^{K} which, intuitively, monitors the knowledge that Player 1 has about the current location of the play. The game G^{K} is called **knowledge-based subset construction**. The structure $G^{\mathsf{K}} = \langle S, s_I, \Sigma, \Delta^{\mathsf{K}} \rangle$ is defined as follows.

- The set of locations is $S = \{s \in 2^L \backslash \{\varnothing\} \mid \exists o \in \mathcal{O} \cdot s \subseteq o\}$. In the sequel, we call a set $s \in S$ a *cell*.

- The initial location is $s_I = \{l_I\}$.

- The set of labelled transitions $\Delta^K \subseteq S \times \Sigma \times S$ contains all (s, σ, s') for which there exists $o \in \mathcal{O}$ such that $s' = \mathsf{post}_\sigma^G(s) \cap o$.

Note that since the game graph G is total and the observations form a partition of the locations, the game graph G^K is also total.

To complete the reduction, we show how to translate the objectives. Given a priority function $pr : \mathcal{O} \to \{0, \dots, d\}$ defining the parity objective φ in G, we define the parity objective φ^K in G^K using the priority function pr^K such that $pr^K(s) = pr(o)$ for all $s \in S$ and $o \in \mathcal{O}$ such that $s \subseteq o$.

Theorem 6.6 (Chatterjee et al. [2007]) *Player 1 has an observation-based surely-winning strategy in a game structure G with imperfect information for an observable parity objective φ if and only if Player 1 has a surely-winning strategy in the game structure G^K with perfect information for the parity objective φ^K.*

Exercise 6.7 Write a proof of Theorem 6.6.

Observable safety and reachability objectives are defined by sets $\mathcal{T} \subseteq L$ of target locations that are a union of observations. Hence for all cells $s \in S$, either $s \cap \mathcal{T} = \varnothing$ or $s \subseteq \mathcal{T}$. In the above reduction, such an objective is transformed into an objective of the same type with the set of target cells $\mathcal{T}^K = \{s \in S \mid s \subseteq \mathcal{T}\}$.

Exercise 6.8 Consider a game structure with imperfect information $G = \langle L, l_I, \Sigma, \Delta, \mathcal{O} \rangle$ and a *non-observable* reachability objective defined by $\mathcal{T} \subseteq L$. Construct an equivalent game structure with imperfect information G' with an observable reachability objective $\mathsf{Reach}(\mathcal{T}')$, i.e., such that Player 1 has an observation-based surely-winning strategy in G for $\mathsf{Reach}(\mathcal{T})$ if and only if Player 1 has an observation-based surely-winning strategy in G' for $\mathsf{Reach}(\mathcal{T}')$. Hint: take $G' = \langle L, l_I, \Sigma, \Delta, \mathcal{O}' \rangle$ where $\mathcal{O}' = \{o \cap \mathcal{T} \mid o \in \mathcal{O}\} \cup \{o \cap (L \backslash \mathcal{T}) \mid o \in \mathcal{O}\}$.

Note that non-observable Büchi objectives are more difficult to handle. For such objectives and more generally for non-observable parity objectives, our knowledge-subset construction is not valid and techniques related to Safra's determinisation need to be used (Safra [1988]).

6.3.3 *Symbolic algorithms and antichains*

Theorem 6.6 gives a natural algorithm for solving games with imperfect information with observable objective: apply the algorithms for solving games with perfect information to the knowledge-based subset construction presented above.[1] The symbolic algorithms presented in Section 6.2 are based on the controllable predecessor operator $\mathsf{Cpre} : 2^S \to 2^S$ whose definition can be rewritten for all $q \subseteq S$ as:

$$\mathsf{Cpre}(q) = \{s \in S \mid \exists \sigma \in \Sigma \cdot \forall s' \in S : \text{ if } (s, \sigma, s') \in \Delta^K \text{ then } s' \in q\}$$
$$= \{s \in S \mid \exists \sigma \in \Sigma \cdot \forall o \in \mathcal{O} : \text{ if } s' = \mathsf{post}_\sigma^G(s) \cap o \neq \varnothing \text{ then } s' \in q\}.$$

A crucial property of this operator is that it preserves downward-closedness of sets of cells. Intuitively, Player 1 is in a better situation when her knowledge is more precise, i.e., when her knowledge is a smaller cell according to set inclusion. A set q of cells is **downward-closed** if $s \in q$ implies $s' \in q$ for all $s' \subseteq s$. If Player 1 can force the game G^K to be in a cell of a downward-closed set of cells q in the next round from a cell s, then she is also able to do so from all cells $s' \subseteq s$. Formally, if q is downward-closed, then so is $\mathsf{Cpre}(q)$. It is easy to show that $\cap$ and $\cup$ also preserve downward-closedness, and therefore all sets of cells that are computed for solving games of imperfect information are downward-closed.

As the symbolic algorithms are manipulating downward closed sets, it is valuable to design a data-structure to represent them compactly. We define such a data-structure here. The idea is to represent a set of cells by a set of sets of locations and interpret this set as defining all the cells that are included in one of its element. Clearly, in such a representation having a set of sets with two $\subseteq$-comparable element is not useful, so we can restrict our symbolic representations to be **antichains**, i.e., a set of sets of locations that are $\subseteq$-incomparable.

Antichains for representing downward-closed sets Let us denote by $\mathcal{A}$ the set of $\subseteq$-antichains of sets of locations, that is

$$\mathcal{A} = \{\{s_1, s_2, \ldots, s_n\} \subseteq 2^L \mid \forall 1 \leq i, j \leq n : s_i \subseteq s_j \to i = j\}.$$

Note that an antichain is a set of subsets of locations that are not necessarily cells. We denote by $\mathcal{A}$ the set of antichains. The set $\mathcal{A}$ is partially ordered as follows. For $q, q' \in \mathcal{A}$, let $q \sqsubseteq q'$ iff $\forall s \in q \cdot \exists s' \in q' : s \subseteq s'$. The least upper bound of $q, q' \in \mathcal{A}$ is $q \sqcup q' = \lceil \{s \mid s \in q \text{ or } s \in q'\} \rceil$, and their greatest

---

[1] Note that the symbolic algorithm can be applied without explicitly constructing the knowledge-based construction.

lower bound is $q \sqcap q' = \lceil \{s \cap s' \mid s \in q \text{ and } s' \in q'\} \rceil$. We view antichains as a symbolic representation of $\subseteq$-downward-closed sets of cells. Given an antichain $q \in \mathcal{A}$, let $q{\downarrow} = \{s \in S \mid \exists s' \in q : s \subseteq s'\}$ be the ***downward closure*** of q, i.e., the set of cells that it represents.

Exercise 6.9 Show that $\sqcup$ and $\sqcap$ are indeed the operators of least upper bound and greatest lower bound respectively. By establishing this, you have shown that the set of antichains forms a complete lattice. What are the least and greatest elements of this complete lattice ?

To define a controllable predecessor operator $\mathsf{Cpre}^{\mathcal{A}}$ over antichains, we observe that for all $q \in \mathcal{A}$,

$$\mathsf{Cpre}(q{\downarrow}) = \{s \in S \mid \exists \sigma \in \Sigma \cdot \forall o \in \mathcal{O} \cdot \exists s' \in q : \mathsf{post}_\sigma^G(s) \cap o \subseteq s'\}$$
$$= \{s \in S \mid \exists \sigma \in \Sigma \cdot \forall o \in \mathcal{O} \cdot \exists s' \in q : s \subseteq \widetilde{\mathsf{pre}}_\sigma^G(s' \cup \bar{o})\}$$

where $\bar{o} = L \setminus o$ and $\widetilde{\mathsf{pre}}_\sigma^G(s) = \{\ell \in L \mid \mathsf{post}_\sigma^G(\{\ell\}) \subseteq s\}$. Hence, we define

$$\mathsf{Cpre}^{\mathcal{A}}(q) = \bigsqcup_{\sigma \in \Sigma} \bigsqcap_{o \in \mathcal{O}} \bigsqcup_{s' \in q} \{\widetilde{\mathsf{pre}}_\sigma(s' \cup \bar{o})\}$$

and this operator computes a symbolic representation of the controllable predecessors of the downward-closed set of cells symbolically represented by q.

Lemma 6.7 *For all antichains $q \in \mathcal{A}$, we have $\mathsf{Cpre}^{\mathcal{A}}(q){\downarrow} = \mathsf{Cpre}(q{\downarrow})$.*

Exercise 6.10 Prove Lemma 6.7.

In the definition of $\mathsf{Cpre}^{\mathcal{A}}$, the operations $\widetilde{\mathsf{pre}}$, $\bigsqcup_{\sigma \in \Sigma}$ and $\bigsqcup_{s' \in q}$ can be computed in polynomial time, while $\bigsqcap_{o \in \mathcal{O}}$ can be computed in exponential time by simple application of the definitions. Unfortunately, it turns out that a polynomial-time algorithm is unlikely to exist for computing $\bigsqcap_{o \in \mathcal{O}}$ as the NP-complete problem INDEPENDENTSET can be reduced to it.

Consider a graph $\mathcal{G} = (V, E)$ where V is a set of vertices and $E \subseteq V \times V$ is a set of edges. An ***independent set*** of $\mathcal{G}$ is a set $W \subseteq V$ of vertices such that for all $(v, v') \in E$, either $v \notin W$ or $v' \notin W$, i.e., there is no edge of $\mathcal{G}$ connecting vertices of W. The INDEPENDENTSET problem asks, given a graph $\mathcal{G}$ and size k, to decide if there exists an independent set of $\mathcal{G}$ of size larger than k. This problem is known to be NP-complete. We show that INDEPENDENTSET reduces to computing $\sqcap$.

Let $\mathcal{G} = (V, E)$ be a graph, and for each $e = (v, v') \in E$ let $q_e = \{V \setminus \{v\}, V \setminus \{v'\}\}$. The set $q_e{\downarrow}$ contains all sets of vertices that are independent of the edge e. Therefore, the antichain $q = \lceil \bigsqcap_{e \in E} q_e{\downarrow} \rceil$ contains the maximal

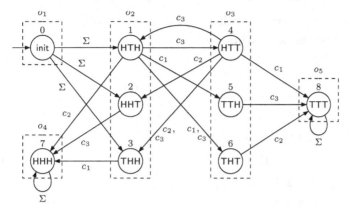

Figure 6.4 The 3-COIN game graph with alphabet $\Sigma = \{c_1, c_2, c_3\}$. The transitions between states 2, 3, 5, and 6 are omitted for the sake of clarity

independent sets of $\mathcal{G}$, and an algorithm to compute q would immediately solve INDEPENDENTSET, showing that such an algorithm running in polynomial time cannot exist unless $P = NP$. The idea of this reduction can be extended to show that $\mathsf{Cpre}^{\mathcal{A}}$ requires exponential time (Berwanger et al. [2008], Filiot et al. [2009]).

Exercise 6.11 Compute the winning cells in the two versions of the 3-COIN game with the symbolic algorithm using the antichain representation. The 3-COIN game graph is given in Figure 6.4. We give here the solutions to this exercise.

- We first consider the version in which Player 2 is allowed to exchange the positions of the coins that are not toggled. To compute the winning cells of the game with imperfect information, we compute the set of all cells that are able to force the cell $\{7\}$. We give here the sequence of antichains computed by our algorithm:

$$X_0 = \{\{7\}\},$$
$$X_1 = X_0 \sqcup \mathsf{Cpre}(X_0) = \{\{1\}, \{2\}, \{3\}, \{7\}\},$$
$$X_2 = X_1 \sqcup \mathsf{Cpre}(X_1) = \{\{1\}, \{2\}, \{3\}, \{4\}, \{5\}, \{6\}, \{7\}\} = X_1$$

and the fixed-point is reached. As $\{0\} \notin X_1{\downarrow}$, this shows that Player 1 does not have a deterministic winning strategy in this game.

- We now consider the version where Player 2 is not allowed to exchange the position of the coins that are not toggled. To compute the winning cells of the game with imperfect information, we compute the set of all cells that are able to force the cell $\{7\}$. We give here the sequence of antichains computed by our algorithm.

$X_0 = \{\{7\}\},$

$X_1 = X_0 \sqcup \mathsf{Cpre}(X_0) = \{\{1\}, \{2\}, \{3\}, \{7\}\},$

$X_2 = X_1 \sqcup \mathsf{Cpre}(X_1) = \{\{1\}, \{2\}, \{3\}, \{4\}, \{5\}, \{6\}, \{7\}\},$

$X_3 = X_2 \sqcup \mathsf{Cpre}(X_2) = \{\{1,2\}, \{2,3\}, \{1,3\}, \{4\}, \{5\}, \{6\}, \{7\}\},$

$X_4 = X_3 \sqcup \mathsf{Cpre}(X_3) = \{\{1,2\}, \{2,3\}, \{1,3\}, \{4,6\}, \{5,6\}, \{4,5\}, \{7\}\},$

$X_5 = X_4 \sqcup \mathsf{Cpre}(X_4) = \{\{1,2,3\}, \{4,6\}, \{5,6\}, \{4,5\}, \{7\}\},$

$X_6 = X_5 \sqcup \mathsf{Cpre}(X_5) = \{\{0,1,2,3\}, \{0,4,6\}, \{0,5,6\}, \{0,4,5\}, \{0,7\}\},$

$X_7 = X_6.$

As $\{0\} \in X_7{\downarrow}$, this shows that Player 1 has a deterministic winning strategy in this version of the 3-coin game.

6.3.4 Strategy construction

The algorithms presented in Section 6.2 for safety and reachability games compute the set of winning positions for Player 1. We can use these algorithms to compute the set of winning cells in a game with imperfect information, using the controllable predecessor operator Cpre^A. This gives a compact representation (an antichain) of the downward-closed set of winning cells. However, it does not construct surely-winning strategies. We show that in general, there is a direct way to construct a surely-winning strategy for safety games, but not for reachability and parity games.

For safety games with perfect information, the fixed-point computation shows that the set of winning positions satisfies the equation $W = \mathcal{T} \cap \mathsf{Cpre}(W)$. Therefore, $W \subseteq \mathsf{Cpre}(W)$, and thus for each $\ell \in W$, there exists an action $\sigma_\ell \in \Sigma$ such that $\mathsf{post}^G_{\sigma_\ell}(\{\ell\}) \subseteq W$. Since, $W \subseteq \mathcal{T}$, it is easy to see that the memoryless strategy playing σ_ℓ in each location $\ell \in W$ is surely-winning.

For safety games with imperfect information, the fixed-point W is represented by an antichain q_{win} such that $W = q_{\mathsf{win}}{\downarrow}$. The strategy construction for safety games with perfect information can be extended as follows. By definition of Cpre^A, for each $s \in q_{\mathsf{win}}$ there exists $\sigma_s \in \Sigma$ such that for all $o \in \mathcal{O}$, we have $\mathsf{post}^G_{\sigma_s}(s) \cap o \subseteq s'$ for some $s' \in q_{\mathsf{win}}$. It is easy to see that the strategy playing σ_s in every cell $s'' \subseteq s$ is surely-winning.

Thus, we can define a surely-winning strategy by the Moore machine $\langle M, m_I, \mathsf{update}, \mu \rangle$ where $M = q_{\mathsf{win}}$, $m_I = s$ such that $s_I \subseteq s$ for some $s \in q_{\mathsf{win}}$, $\mu : M \to \Sigma$ is an output function such that $\mu(s) = \sigma_s$ as defined above for all $s \in M$, and $\mathsf{update} : M \times \mathcal{O} \to M$ is such that if $\mathsf{update}(s, o) = s'$, then $\mathsf{post}_\sigma^G(s) \cap o \subseteq s'$ for $\sigma = \mu(s)$ (note that such an s' exists by the above remark). The automaton A defines the observation-based strategy α such that $\alpha(\pi) = \sigma$ where $\sigma = \mu(s)$ and $s = \mathsf{update}(m_I, \mathsf{obs}(\pi))$ for all $\pi \in L^+$ (where the update function is extended to sequences of observations in the usual way, i.e., $\mathsf{update}(m, o_1 \ldots o_n) = \mathsf{update}(\mathsf{update}(m, o_1), o_2 \ldots o_n))$.

For reachability games, the information contained in the fixpoint of winning positions is not sufficient to extract a surely-winning strategy. Intuitively, a surely-winning strategy needs to stay in the winning set (as in safety games), and moreover should ensure some kind of progress with respect to the target set $\mathcal{T}$ to guarantee that $\mathcal{T}$ is eventually reached. The notion of progress can be formalised by a number $\mathsf{rank}(s)$ associated to each cell s such that Player 1 can enforce to reach the target from cell s within at most $\mathsf{rank}(s)$ rounds.

In a reachability game with perfect information, the rank of a location ℓ in the set of winning positions W is the least i such that $\ell \in W^i$. From a location $\ell \in W$ with rank $r > 0$, a surely-winning strategy can play an action $\sigma_\ell \in \Sigma$ such that $\mathsf{post}_{\sigma_\ell}^G(\{\ell\}) \subseteq W^{r-1}$.

In a game with imperfect information, knowing the rank of the cells in the antichain q_{win} may still not be sufficient to obtain a surely-winning strategy. Consider the game G in Figure 6.5, with reachability objective $\mathsf{Reach}(\{\ell_2\})$ and observations $\{\ell_0, \ell_1\}$ and $\{\ell_2\}$. Since $\mathsf{Cpre}(\{\{\ell_2\}\}) = \{\{\ell_1\}\}$ (by playing action b) and $\mathsf{Cpre}(\{\{\ell_1\}, \{\ell_2\}\}) = \{\{\ell_0, \ell_1\}\}$ (by playing action a), the fixed-point computed by the antichain algorithm is $\{\{\ell_2\}, \{\ell_0, \ell_1\}\}$. However, from $\{\ell_0, \ell_1\}$, after playing a, Player 1 reaches the cell $\{\ell_1\}$ which is not in the fixed-point (however, it is subsumed by the cell $\{\ell_0, \ell_1\}$). Intuitively, the antichain algorithm has forgotten which action is to be played next from $\{\ell_1\}$. Note that playing a again (and thus forever) is not winning.

This example illustrates the fact that the rank of a cell s is not necessarily the same as the rank of a cell $s' \subseteq s$. Therefore, for the purpose of strategy construction, the fixpoint computation needs to store the rank associated with a cell, and refine the rule of eliminating the cells that are subsumed by larger cells to take ranks into account (Berwanger et al. [2009]). In fact, it can be shown that for some family of reachability games with imperfect information, the fixpoint computed in the antichain representation (without rank) is of polynomial size while any finite-memory surely-winning strategy is of exponential size (Berwanger et al. [2008]).

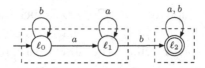

Figure 6.5 A reachability game G

6.4 Games with imperfect information: almost-surely-winning

We revisit the 3-COIN game. In Exercise 6.11, we have seen that Player 1 does not have an observation-based deterministic winning strategy in this game when Player 2 is allowed to exchange the position of the coins that are not toggled. This is because Player 2 can guess the choice that Player 1 will make in the next round. When a deterministic strategy for Player 1 is fixed, this information is formally available to Player 2 but this is not realistic in practice. Player 1 should use a source of randomisation in order to avoid the possibility that Player 2 can guess the choice she will make in the next round. Whenever the game is in a configuration with two heads, Player 1 chooses uniformly at random one of the three coins. Clearly the probability to choose the coin showing tail is $\frac{1}{3}$ no matter if Player 2 has decided to exchange the coins or not at the previous step. Otherwise, she should play the same coin a second time to make sure she comes back to a configuration with two heads. She then repeats the same randomised strategy. Every two rounds, Player 1 has a $\frac{1}{3}$ probability to reach the winning configuration. Note also that she is sure to avoid the losing configuration (all coins on tails). This simple strategy is thus winning the reachability objective with probability one. This illustrates the power of randomised strategies in games with imperfect information.

6.4.1 Playing with randomised strategies

Before going into the formalisation, let us take a look at the example of Figure 6.3. From the initial location ℓ_1, we have seen that Player 1 has no surely-winning strategy for reaching ℓ_4. This is because for all strategies α of Player 1, there exists a play $\pi \in \mathsf{Outcome}_1(G, \alpha)$ that visits ℓ_3 infinitely often, and therefore never visits ℓ_4. However, the strategy β of Player 2 such that $\pi = \mathsf{outcome}(G, \alpha, \beta)$ chooses the successor $\hat{\ell}$ of ℓ_1 in a way that depends on the next move of Player 1, namely $\hat{\ell} = \ell_2$ if α plays action a next, and $\hat{\ell} = \ell_2'$ if α plays action b next. In a concrete implementation of the system, this means that Player 2 needs to predict the behaviour of Player 1 infinitely often in order to win. In practice, since one wrong guess make Player 1 win, this suggests that the probability that Player 2 wins (making infinitely many right guesses) is 0, and thus Player 1 can win with probability 1.

We now formally define a notion of probabilistic winning. First, a *randomised strategy* for Player 1 is a function $\alpha : (L \times \Sigma)^* L \to \mathcal{D}(\Sigma)$ where $\mathcal{D}(\Sigma)$ denotes the set of probability distributions over Σ, i.e., the set of all functions $f : \Sigma \to [0, 1]$ such that $\sum_{\sigma \in \Sigma} f(\sigma) = 1$. Intuitively, if Player 1 uses distribution f, then he plays each action σ with probability $f(\sigma)$. We assume that Player 1 is informed about which actual actions he played. Hence, strategies are mappings from interleaved sequences of states and actions of the form $\rho = \ell_0 \sigma_0 \ell_1 \sigma_1 \ldots \sigma_{n-1} \ell_n$ that we call *labelled histories*. We denote by $L(\rho) = \ell_0 \ell_1 \ldots \ell_n$ the *projection* of ρ onto L^*. A strategy α is *observation-based* if for all pairs of labelled histories ρ, ρ' of the form $\rho = \ell_0 \sigma_0 \ell_1 \sigma_1 \ldots \sigma_{n-1} \ell_n$ and $\rho' = \ell'_0 \sigma_0 \ell'_1 \sigma_1 \ldots \sigma_{n-1} \ell'_n$ such that for all i, $1 \leq i \leq n$, $\mathsf{obs}(\ell_i) = \mathsf{obs}(\ell'_i)$, we have that $\alpha(\rho) = \alpha(\rho')$.

A randomised strategy for Player 2 is a function $\beta : (L \times \Sigma)^+ \to \mathcal{D}(L)$ such that for all labelled histories $\rho = \ell_0 \sigma_0 \ell_1 \sigma_1 \ldots \sigma_{n-1} \ell_n$ and $\sigma \in \Sigma$, for all ℓ such that $\beta(\rho, \sigma)(\ell) > 0$, we have $(\ell_n, \sigma, \ell) \in \Delta$. We extend in the expected way (using projection of labelled histories onto L^* when necessary) the notions of observation-based randomised strategies for Player 2, memoryless strategies, consistent plays, outcome, etc.

Given strategies α and β for Player 1 and Player 2, respectively, and an initial location ℓ_0, the probability of a labelled history $\rho = \ell_0 \sigma_0 \ell_1 \sigma_1 \ldots \sigma_{n-1} \ell_n$ is $\mathbb{P}(\rho) = \prod_{i=0}^{n-1} \alpha(\ell_0 \sigma_0 \ldots \sigma_{i-1} \ell_i)(\sigma_i) \cdot \beta(\ell_0 \sigma_0 \ldots \sigma_{i-1} \ell_i \sigma_i)(\ell_i)$. The probability of a history $\pi = \ell_0 \ell_1 \ldots \ell_n$ is $\mathbb{P}(\pi) = \sum_{\rho \in L^{-1}(\pi)} \mathbb{P}(\rho)$, which uniquely defines the probabilities of measurable sets of (infinite) plays (Vardi [1985]). The safety, reachability, and parity objectives being Borel objectives, they are measurable (Kechris [1995]). We denote by $\mathrm{Pr}_\ell^{\alpha, \beta}(\varphi)$ the probability that an objective φ is satisfied by a play starting in ℓ in the game G played with strategies α and β. A randomised strategy α for Player 1 in G is *almost-surely-winning* for the objective φ if for all randomised strategies β of Player 2, we have $\mathrm{Pr}_{\ell_I}^{\alpha, \beta}(\varphi) = 1$. A location $\hat{\ell} \in L$ is *almost-surely-winning* for φ if Player 1 has an almost-surely-winning randomised strategy α in the game $\hat{G} = \langle L, \hat{\ell}, \Sigma, \Delta \rangle$ where $\hat{\ell}$ is the initial location.

Note that our definition is again asymmetric in the sense that Player 1 has imperfect information about the location of the game while Player 2 has perfect information. While having perfect information does not help Player 2 in the case of surely-winning, it makes Player 2 stronger in the probabilistic case. Recent works (Bertrand et al. [2009], Gripon and Serre [2009]) study a symmetric setting where the two players have imperfect

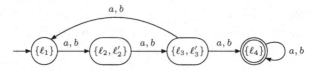

Figure 6.6 The knowledge-based subset construction for the game of Figure 6.3

information. The decision problems are computationally harder to solve (deciding if a location is almost-surely-winning is EXPTIME-complete in our setting, and it becomes 2EXPTIME-complete in the symmetric setting). We choose to present the asymmetric setting for the sake of consistency with the first part of this chapter, because it is a simpler setting, and because the techniques that we present can be adapted to solve the more general case.

6.4.2 An algorithm for reachability objectives

We present an algorithm for computing the locations of a reachability game with imperfect information G from which Player 1 has an almost-surely-winning strategy. The algorithm can be extended to solve Büchi objectives (Chatterjee et al. [2007]). The case of co-Büchi and parity objectives remains open.

Extended subset construction First, note that the reduction to games with perfect information G^K of Section 6.3 does not preserve the notion of almost-surely-winning. The knowledge-based subset construction for the the game of Figure 6.3 is given in Figure 6.6. It is easy to see that for all strategies of Player 1, Player 2 can avoid $\{\ell_4\}$ by always choosing from $\{\ell_3, \ell'_3\}$ the transition back to $\{\ell_1\}$. In the original game, this amounts to allow Player 2 to freely 'switch' between location ℓ_3 and ℓ'_3. However, against Player 1's strategy of playing a and b uniformly at random, Player 2 cannot really decide which location of ℓ_3 or ℓ'_3 is reached, since both have probability $\frac{1}{2}$ to be reached regardless of Player 2's strategy. So, we have to enrich the knowledge-based subset construction to take this phenomenon into account. In the new construction, locations are pairs (s, ℓ) consisting of a cell s and a location $\ell \in s$. To reduce ambiguity, we call such pairs *states*. The cell s encodes the knowledge of Player 1, and the location ℓ keeps track of the choice of Player 2, forcing Player 2 to stick to his choice. Of course, we need to take care that the decisions of Player 1 do not depend on the location ℓ, but only on the cell s.

Given a game structure with imperfect information $G = \langle L, l_I, \Sigma, \Delta, \mathcal{O} \rangle$, we construct the game structure (with perfect information) $H = \mathsf{Knw}(G) = \langle Q, q_I, \Sigma, \Delta_H \rangle$ as follows:

- $Q = \{(s, \ell) \mid \exists o \in \mathcal{O} : s \subseteq o \text{ and } \ell \in s\}$;
- the initial state is $q_I = (\{\, l_I \,\}, l_I)$;
- the transition relation $\Delta_H \subseteq Q \times \Sigma \times Q$ is defined by $((s, \ell), \sigma, (s', \ell')) \in \Delta_H$ iff there is an observation $o \in \mathcal{O}$ such that $s' = \mathsf{post}_\sigma^G(s) \cap o$ and $(\ell, \sigma, \ell') \in \Delta$.

The structure H is called the *extended knowledge-based subset construction* of G. Intuitively, when H is in state (s, ℓ), it corresponds to G being in location ℓ and the knowledge of Player 1 being s. The game $H = \mathsf{Knw}(G)$ is given in Figure 6.7 for the game G of Figure 6.2. Reachability and safety objectives defined by a target set $T \subseteq L$ are transformed into an objective of the same type where the target set of states is $T' = \{(s, \ell) \in Q \mid \ell \in T\}$. A parity objective φ in G defined by a priority function $pr : L \to \mathbb{N}$ is transformed into a parity objective φ^{Knw} in H using the priority function pr^{Knw} such that $pr^{\mathsf{Knw}}(s, \ell) = pr(o)$ for all $(s, \ell) \in Q$ and $o \in \mathcal{O}$ such that $s \subseteq o$.

Equivalence preserving strategies Since we are interested in observation-based strategies for Player 1 in G, we require that the strategies of Player 1 in H only depend on the sequence of knowledge $s_0 \ldots s_i$ in the sequence of previously visited states $(s_0, \ell_0) \ldots (s_i, \ell_i)$. Two states $q = (s, \ell)$ and $q' = (s', \ell')$ of H are *equivalent*, written $q \approx q'$, if $s = s'$, i.e., when the knowledge of Player 1 is the same in the two states. For a state $q \in Q$, we denote by $[q]_\approx = \{q' \in Q \mid q \approx q'\}$ the $\approx$-equivalence class of q. Equivalence and equivalence classes for plays and labelled histories are defined in the expected way. A strategy α for Player 1 in H is *equivalence-preserving* if $\alpha(\rho) = \alpha(\rho')$ for all labelled histories ρ, ρ' of H such that $\rho \approx \rho'$.

Theorem 6.8 (Chatterjee et al. [2007])   *For all game structures G with imperfect information, Player 1 has an observation-based almost-surely-winning strategy in G for a parity objective φ if and only if Player 1 has an equivalence-preserving almost-surely-winning strategy in $H = \mathsf{Knw}(G)$ for the parity objective φ^{Knw}.*

Solving reachability objectives It can be shown that for reachability and Büchi objectives, memoryless strategies are sufficient for Player 1 to almost-surely win the game with perfect information $H = \mathsf{Knw}(G)$. Let

$H = \mathsf{Knw}(G) = \langle Q, q_I, \Sigma, \Delta_H \rangle$, let $\mathsf{Reach}(\mathcal{T})$ with $\mathcal{T} \subseteq Q$ be an observable reachability objective in H, and $\approx$ the equivalence relation between states of H as defined above. Player 1 almost-surely wins from the set of states $W \subseteq Q$ if there exist functions $\mathsf{Allow} : Q \to 2^{\Sigma}$ and $\mathsf{Good} : Q \to \Sigma$ such that for all $q \in W$:

1 for all $q' \approx q$ and for all $\sigma \in \mathsf{Allow}(q)$, $\mathsf{post}_\sigma^H(q') \subseteq W$,
2 in the graph (W, E) with $E = \{(q, q') \in W \times W \mid (q, \mathsf{Good}(q), q') \in \Delta_H\}$, all infinite paths visit a state in $\mathcal{T}$,
3 $\mathsf{Good}(q) \in \mathsf{Allow}(q)$.

Condition 1 ensures that the set W of winning states is never left. This is necessary because if there was a positive probability to leave W, then Player 1 would not win the game with probability 1. Condition 2 ensures that from every state $q \in W$, the target $\mathcal{T}$ is entered with some positive probability (remember that the action $\mathsf{Good}(q)$ is played with some positive probability). Note that if all infinite paths in (W, E) eventually visit $\mathcal{T}$, then all finite paths of length $n = |W|$ do so. Therefore, the probability to reach $\mathcal{T}$ within n rounds can be bounded by a constant $\kappa > 0$, and thus after every n rounds the target set $\mathcal{T}$ is reached with probability at least κ. Since Condition 1 ensures the set W is never left, the probability that the target set has not been visited after $m \cdot n$ rounds is at most $(1 - \kappa)^m$. Since the game is played for infinitely many rounds, the probability to reach $\mathcal{T}$ is $\lim_{m \to \infty} 1 - (1 - \kappa)^m = 1$. By Condition 3, the actions that ensure progress towards the target set can be safely played.

The algorithm to compute the set of states $W \subseteq Q$ from which Player 1 has an equivalence-preserving almost-surely-winning strategy for $\mathsf{Reach}(\mathcal{T})$ is the limit of the following computations:

$$
\begin{aligned}
W^0 &= Q \\
W^{i+1} &= \mathsf{PosReach}(W^i) \text{ for all } i \geq 0
\end{aligned}
$$

where the $\mathsf{PosReach}(W^i)$ operator is the limit of the sequence X^j defined by

$$
\begin{aligned}
X^0 &= \mathcal{T} \\
X^{j+1} &= X^j \cup \mathsf{Apre}(W^i, X^j) \text{ for all } j \geq 0
\end{aligned}
$$

where

$$\mathsf{Apre}(W, X) = \{q \in W \mid \exists \sigma \in \Sigma :$$

$$\mathsf{post}_\sigma^H(q) \subseteq X \text{ and } \forall q' \approx q : \mathsf{post}_\sigma^H(q') \subseteq W\}.$$

The operator $\mathsf{Apre}(W, X)$ computes the set of states q from which Player 1 can ensure that some state of X is visited in the next round with positive

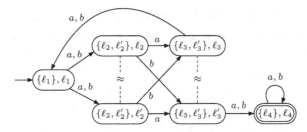

Figure 6.7 Game structure $H = \mathsf{Knw}(G)$ (for G of Figure 6.2)

probability, while ensuring that W is not left, even if the current state is $q' \approx q$ (because if the game is actually in q, then it means that Player 1 cannot be sure that the game is not in q' with some positive probability).

Note that for $W = Q$, the condition $\mathsf{post}_\sigma^H(q') \subseteq W$ is trivial. Hence, for $W^0 = Q$ the set $W^1 = \mathsf{PosReach}(W^0)$ contains all states from which Player 1 can enforce to reach $\mathcal{T}$ with positive probability. Clearly, this set is an over-approximation of the almost-surely-winning states, since from $Q \setminus W^1$ and no matter the strategy of Player 1, the probability that $\mathcal{T}$ is reached is 0. Therefore, we compute in $W^2 = \mathsf{PosReach}(W^1)$ the set of states from which Player 1 can enforce to reach $\mathcal{T}$ with positive probability without leaving W^1, giving a better over-approximation of the set of almost-surely-winning states. The iteration continues until a fixpoint is obtained. Note that $W^0 \supseteq W^1 \supseteq W^2 \supseteq \cdots$ is a decreasing sequence, and $X^0 \subseteq X^1 \subseteq X^2 \subseteq \cdots$ is an increasing sequence for each computation of $\mathsf{PosReach}(W^i)$. This algorithm is thus quadratic in the size of H, and exponential in the size of G.

Theorem 6.9 *The problem of deciding whether Player 1 is almost-surely-winning in a reachability game with imperfect information is EXPTIME-complete.*

It can be shown that the problem is EXPTIME-hard, see Chatterjee et al. [2007], and thus the algorithm developed above is worst-case optimal. For Büchi objectives, an EXPTIME algorithm can be obtained by substituting the first line of the $\mathsf{PosReach}(W^i)$ operator by $X^0 = \mathcal{T} \cap \mathsf{Spre}(W^i)$ where

$$\mathsf{Spre}(W^i) = \mathsf{Apre}(W^i, W^i) = \{q \in W^i \mid \exists \sigma \in \Sigma \cdot \forall q' \approx q : \mathsf{post}_\sigma^H(q') \subseteq W^i\}.$$

Intuitively, we start the iteration in $\mathsf{PosReach}(W^i)$ with those target states from which Player 1 can force to stay in W^i in the next round. This ensures that whenever a target state is reached (which will happen with probability one), Player 1 can continue to play and will again force a visit to the target set with probability one, thus realising the objective $\mathsf{Buchi}(\mathcal{T})$ with probability 1.

Antichains for randomised strategies When computing the set of surely-winning locations of a game with imperfect information, we have shown that antichains of sets of locations are a well-suited data-structure. This idea can be extended for computing the sets of almost-surely-winning locations of a game with imperfect information.

Let $G = \langle L, l_I, \Sigma, \Delta, \mathcal{O} \rangle$ be a game structure with imperfect information, and let H be its extended knowledge based construction, i.e., $H = \mathsf{Knw}(G) = \langle Q, q_I, \Sigma, \Delta_H \rangle$. We define $\preceq \subseteq Q \times Q$ as $(s, \ell) \preceq (s', \ell')$ iff $s \subseteq s'$ and $\ell = \ell'$. This order has the following properties:

- if a state q in H is almost-surely-winning for the observable reachability objective $\mathsf{Reach}(\mathcal{T})$, then for all $q' \preceq q$ in H, q' is almost-surely-winning for the objective $\mathsf{Reach}(\mathcal{T})$;
- given an observable reachability objective $\mathcal{T}$, all the sets $W^0, W^1, \ldots$, and $X^0, X^1, \ldots$ are $\preceq$-downward closed.

Exercise 6.12   Define the operations $\sqcap$, $\sqcup$ for the order $\preceq$. Define the operations $\mathsf{PosReach}$ and Apre so that they operate directly on $\preceq$-antichains.

Exercise 6.13   Apply the fixed-point algorithm above to compute the almost-surely-winning positions in the 3-coin example when Player 2 is allowed to switch coins. Make sure to use antichains during your computations. Extract from the fixed-point an almost-surely-winning observation-based randomised strategy.

We give the solution to the exercise below. To determine the set of cells in our 3-coin game from which Player 1 has a randomised strategy that allows her to win the game with probability one, we execute our fixed-point algorithm. In the computations, we may denote sets of locations by the sequence of their elements, e.g., $\langle 01235 \rangle$ denotes the set $\{0, 1, 2, 3, 5\}$.
$W^0 = \{\langle 012345678 \rangle\} \times \{0, 1, 2, 3, 4, 5, 6, 7, 8\}$. $W^1 = \mathsf{PosReach}(W^0)$ is obtained by the following fixed-point computation. $X^0 = (\langle 7 \rangle, 7)$, $X^1 = X^0 \sqcup \mathsf{Apre}(W^0, X^0) = \{\langle 01234578 \rangle\} \times \{0, 1, 2, 3, 4, 5, 7\} \sqcup \{\langle 01235678 \rangle\} \times \{0, 1, 2, 3, 5, 6, 7\} \sqcup \{\langle 01234678 \rangle\} \times \{0, 1, 2, 3, 4, 6, 7\} = X^2$. $W^2 = W^1$. This fixed-point tells us that Player 1 has a randomised strategy to win the 3-coin game with probability one. The randomised strategy can be extracted from the antichain W^1 and is as follows. In the first round, all choices of Player 1 are equivalent, so she can play c_1. Then she receives the observation o_2 and updates her knowledge to $\{1, 2, 3\}$ which is subsumed by all the elements of the antichain. Then, she plays any action which is associated to those elements with positive probability. The action c_1 is associated with $\{\langle 01235678 \rangle\} \times \{0, 1, 2, 3, 5, 6, 7\}$, action c_2 is associated with $\{\langle 01234578 \rangle\} \times \{0, 1, 2, 3, 4, 5, 7\}$,

and action c_3 is associated with $\{\langle 01234678 \rangle\} \times \{0, 1, 2, 3, 4, 6, 7\}$. Let us consider the different cases:

- If the action c_1 is played then the knowledge of Player 1 becomes $\{5, 6\}$. This knowledge is subsumed by all the elements in $\{\langle 01235678 \rangle\} \times \{0, 1, 2, 3, 5, 6, 7\}$ and the action associated with those element is 1. After playing 1 the knowledge of Player 1 is now $\{1, 2\}$. Again this knowledge is subsumed by all the elements of the fixed-point so Player 1 can play each action in $\{c_1, c_2, c_3\}$ with positive probability. Note that with this knowledge, it is sufficient to choose play with positive probability in the set of actions $\{c_2, c_3\}$, but this optimisation is not necessary if we want to win with probability one, it only reduces the expected time for winning.
- If the action c_2 is played then the knowledge of Player 1 becomes $\{4, 5\}$. This knowledge is subsumed by all the elements in $\{\langle 01234578 \rangle\} \times \{0, 1, 2, 3, 4, 5, 7\}$ and the action associated with those element is c_2. After playing c_2 the knowledge of Player 1 is now $\{2, 3\}$. And we can start again playing all actions in $\{c_1, c_2, c_3\}$ with positive probability.
- The reasoning is similar for action c_3.

So we see that our algorithm proposes at each even round to play an action at random then to replay the same action. With this strategy, if Player 1 plays each action with probability $\frac{1}{3}$ when her knowledge is subsumed by $\{1, 2, 3\}$, she has a probability $\frac{1}{3}$ to reach 7 every two rounds and so she wins with probability 1.

References

J. Bernet, D. Janin, and I. Walukiewicz. Permissive strategies: from parity games to safety games. *Inf. Théorique et Applications*, 36(3):261–275, 2002.

N. Bertrand, B. Genest, and H. Gimbert. Qualitative determinacy and decidability of stochastic games with signals. In *Proc. of LICS: Logic in Computer Science*. IEEE Computer Society Press, 2009. To appear.

D. Berwanger, K. Chatterjee, L. Doyen, T. A. Henzinger, and S. Raje. Strategy construction for parity games with imperfect information. In *Proc. of CONCUR: Concurrency Theory*, Lecture Notes in Computer Science 5201, pages 325–339. Springer-Verlag, 2008.

D. Berwanger, K. Chatterjee, M. De Wulf, L. Doyen, and T. A. Henzinger. Alpaga: A tool for solving parity games with imperfect information. In *Proc. of TACAS: Tools and Algorithms for the Construction and Analysis of Systems*, Lecture Notes in Computer Science 5505, pages 58–61. Springer-Verlag, 2009.

K. Chatterjee, L. Doyen, T. A. Henzinger, and J.-F. Raskin. Algorithms for omega-regular games of incomplete information. *Logical Methods in Computer Science*, 3(3:4), 2007.

M. De Wulf, L. Doyen, and J.-F. Raskin. A lattice theory for solving games of imperfect information. In *Proc. of HSCC 2006: Hybrid Systems—Computation and Control*, Lecture Notes in Computer Science 3927, pages 153–168. Springer-Verlag, 2006.

E. A. Emerson and C. S. Jutla. Tree automata, mu-calculus and determinacy. In *Proc. of FoCS: Foundations of Computer Science*, pages 368–377. IEEE, 1991.

E. Filiot, N. Jin, and J.-F. Raskin. An antichain algorithm for LTL realizability. In *Proc. of CAV: Computer-aided verification*, Lecture Notes in Computer Science 5643, pages 263–277. Springer, 2009.

O. Friedmann and M. Lange. The PGSolver collection of parity game solvers. Technical report, Ludwig-Maximilians-Universität München, 2009.

V. Gripon and O. Serre. Qualitative concurrent games with imperfect information. In *Proc. of ICALP: Automata, Languages and Programming*, 2009. To appear.

T. A. Henzinger. Games, time, and probability: Graph models for system design and analysis. In *Proc. of SOFSEM (1): Theory and Practice of Computer Science*, Lecture Notes in Computer Science 4362, pages 103–110. Springer, 2007.

M. Jurdziński. Small progress measures for solving parity games. In *Proc. of STACS: Theor. Aspects of Comp. Sc.*, LNCS 1770, pages 290–301. Springer, 2000.

A. Kechris. *Classical Descriptive Set Theory*. Springer, Berlin, 1995.

D. Martin. Borel determinacy. *Annals of Mathematics*, 102(2):363–371, 1975.

J. H. Reif. The complexity of two-player games of incomplete information. *Journal of Computer and System Sciences*, 29(2):274–301, 1984.

S. Safra. On the complexity of omega-automata. In *Proc. of FOCS: Foundations of Computer Science*, pages 319–327. IEEE, 1988.

S. Schewe. An optimal strategy improvement algorithm for solving parity and payoff games. In *Proc. of CSL: Computer Science Logic*, Lecture Notes in Computer Science 5213, pages 369–384. Springer, 2008.

W. Thomas. Infinite games and verification. In *Proc. of CAV: Computer Aided Verification*, Lecture Notes in Computer Science 2404, pages 58–64. Springer, 2002.

W. Thomas. On the synthesis of strategies in infinite games. In *Proc. of STACS: Symposium on Theoretical Aspects of Computer Science*, volume 900 of *Lecture Notes in Computer Science*, pages 1–13. Springer, 1995.

M. Vardi. Automatic verification of probabilistic concurrent finite-state systems. In *Proc. of FOCS: Foundations of Computer Science*, pages 327–338. IEEE Computer Society Press, 1985.

W. Zielonka. Infinite games on finitely coloured graphs with applications to automata on infinite trees. *Theoretical Computer Science*, 200:135–183, 1998.

7

Graph Searching Games

Stephan Kreutzer

University of Oxford

Abstract

This chapter provides an introduction to graph searching games, a form of one- or two-player games on graphs that have been studied intensively in algorithmic graph theory. The unifying idea of graph searching games is that a number of searchers wants to find a fugitive on an arena defined by a graph or hypergraph. Depending on the precise definition of moves allowed for the searchers and the fugitive and on the type of graph the game is played on, this yields a huge variety of graph searching games.

The objective of this chapter is to introduce and motivate the main concepts studied in graph searching and to demonstrate some of the central ideas developed in this area.

7.1 Introduction

Graph searching games are a form of two-player games where one player, the *Searcher* or *Cop*, tries to catch a *Fugitive* or *Robber*. The study of graph searching games dates back to the dawn of mankind: running after one another or after an animal has been one of the earliest activities of mankind and surely our hunter-gatherer ancestors thought about ways of optimising their search strategies to maximise their success.

Depending on the type of games under consideration, more recent studies of graph searching games can be traced back to the work of Pierre Bouger, who studied the problem of a pirate ship pursuing a merchant vessel, or more recently to a paper by Parsons [1978] which, according to Fomin and Thilikos [2008], was inspired by a paper by Breisch in the Southwestern Cavers Journal where a problem similar to the following problem was considered: suppose after an accident in a mine some workers are lost in the system of tunnels constituting the mine and a search party is sent into the mine to find them. The problem is to devise a strategy for the searchers which guarantees that the lost workers are found but tries to minimise the number of searchers that need to be sent into the mine. Graph-theoretically, this leads to the following formulation in terms of a game played on a graph which is due to Golovach [1989]. The game is played on a graph which models the system of tunnels, where an edge corresponds to a tunnel and a vertex corresponds to a crossing between two tunnels. The two players are the Fugitive and the Searcher. The Fugitive, modelling the lost worker, hides in an edge of the graph. The Searcher controls a number of searchers which occupy vertices of the graph. The Searcher knows the graph, i.e., the layout of the tunnels, but the current position of the fugitive is unknown to the Searcher. In the course of the game the searchers search edges by moving along an edge from one endpoint to another trying to find the fugitive.

This formulation of the game is known as *edge searching*. More popular in current research on graph searching is a variant of the game called *node searching* which we will describe now in more detail.

Node searching

In node searching, both the fugitive and the searchers occupy vertices of the graph. Initially, the fugitive can reside on any vertex and there are no searchers on the graph. In each round of the play, the Searcher can lift some searchers up or place new searchers on vertices of the graph. This can happen within one move, so in one step the searcher can lift some searchers up and place them somewhere else. However, after the searchers are lifted from the graph but before they are placed again the fugitive can move. He can move to any vertex in the graph reachable from his current position by a path of arbitrary length without going through a vertex occupied by a searcher remaining on the board. In choosing his new position, the fugitive knows where the searchers want to move. This is necessary to prevent 'lucky' moves by the searchers where they accidentally land on a fugitive. The fugitive's goal is to avoid capture by the searchers. In our example above, the fugitive or lost miner would normally not try to avoid capture. But recall that we want the search strategy to succeed independent of how the lost miner moves, and this is modelled by the fugitive trying to escape. If at some point of the game the searchers occupy the same vertex as the fugitive then they have won. Otherwise, i.e., if the fugitive can escape forever, then he wins. The fact that the fugitive tries to avoid capture by a number of searchers has led to these kinds of games being known as *Cops and Robber* games in the literature and we will at various places below resort to this terminology. In particular, we will refer to the game described above as the *Invisible Cops and Robber Game*. The name 'Cops and Robber Game', however, has also been used for a very different type of games. We will describe the differences in Section 7.3.1.

Optimal strategies

Obviously, by using as many searchers as there are vertices we can always guarantee to catch the fugitive. The main challenge with any graph searching game therefore is to devise an optimal search strategy. There are various possible optimisation goals. One is to minimise the number of searchers used in the strategy. Using as few searchers as possible is clearly desirable in many scenarios, as deploying searchers may be risky for them, or it may simply be costly to hire the searchers. Closely related to this is the question of whether with a given bound on the number of searches the graph can be searched at all.

Another very common goal is to minimise the time it takes to search the graph or the number of steps taken in the search. In particular, often one would want to avoid searching parts of the graph multiple times. Think for instance of the application where the task is to clean a system of tunnels of some pollution which is spreading through the tunnels. Hence, every tunnel, once cleaned, must be protected from recontamination which can only be done by sealing off any exit of the tunnel facing a contaminated tunnel. As cleaning is likely to be expensive, we would usually want to avoid having to clean a tunnel twice. Search strategies which avoid having to clean any edge or vertex twice are called *monotone*.

On the other hand, sealing off a tunnel might be problematic or costly and we would therefore aim at minimising the number of tunnels that have to be sealed off simultaneously. In the edge searching game described above, sealing off a tunnel corresponds to putting a searcher on a vertex incident to the edge modelling the tunnel. Hence, minimising this means using as few searchers as possible. Ideally, therefore, we aim at a search strategy that is monotone and at the same time minimises the number of searchers used. This leads to one of the most studied problems with graph searching games, the *monotonicity problem*, the question of whether for a particular type of game the minimal number of searchers needed to catch the fugitive is the same as the minimal number of searchers needed for a monotone winning strategy. Monotonicity of a type of game also has close connections to the complexity of deciding whether k searchers can catch a fugitive on a given graph – monotone strategies are usually of length linear in the size of the graph – and also to decompositions of graphs. As we will see below, for the node searching game considered above this is indeed the case. The first monotonicity proof, for the edge searching variant, was given by LaPaugh [1993] and since then monotonicity has been established for a wide range of graph searching games.

Monotonicity of graph searching games will play an important part of this chapter and we will explore this in detail in Section 7.4.

Applications

The goal of graph searching games is to devise a winning strategy for the searchers that uses as few searchers as possible. The minimal number of searchers needed to guarantee capture of the fugitive on a particular graph thereby yields a complexity measure for the graph, which we call the *search width*. This measure, obviously, depends on the type of game being considered. The search width of a graph measures the connectivity of a graph in some way and it is therefore not surprising that there is a close relationship between width measures defined by graph searching games and other complexity or width measures for graphs studied in the literature, such as the *tree-width* or the *path-width* of a graph. This connection is one of the driving forces behind graph searching games and we will explore it in Section 7.6 below.

Graph searching games have found numerous applications in computer science. One obvious application of graph searching games is to all kinds of search problems and the design of optimal search strategies. In games with an invisible fugitive, searching can also be seen as conquering and an optimal search strategy in this context is a strategy to conquer a country so that at each point of time the number of troops needed to hold the conquered area is minimised.

Furthermore, graph searching games have applications in robotics and the planning of robot movements, as it is explored, for instance, by Guibas et al. [1996]. Another example of this type is the use of graph searching games to network safety as explored by Franklin et al. [2000] where the fugitive models some information and the searchers model intruders, or infected computers, trying to learn this information. The goal here is not to design an optimal search strategy but to improve the network to increase the search number. Graph searching games have also found applications in the study of sequential computation through a translation from pebbling games. We will give more details in Section 7.3.2.

Other forms of graph searching games are closely related to questions in logic. For instance the *entanglement* of a graph is closely related to questions about the variable hierarchy in the modal μ-calculus, as explored by Berwanger and Grädel [2004].

See the annotated bibliography of graph searching by Fomin and Thilikos [2008] for further applications and references.

As different applications require different types of games, it is not surprising that graph searching games come in many different forms. We will give an overview of some of the more commonly used variants of games in the Section 7.3.

Organisation. This chapter is organised as follows. In Section 7.2 we first define graph searching games in an abstract setting and we introduce formally the concept of monotonicity. We also explore the connection between graph searching and reachability games and derive a range of general complexity results about graph searching games. In Section 7.3 we present some of the more commonly used variants of graph searching games. The monotonicity problem and some important tools to show monotonicity are discussed in Section 7.4. Formalisations of winning strategies for the fugitive in terms of *obstructions* are discussed in Section 7.5. We will explore the connections between graph searching and graph decompositions in Section 7.6. Finally, in Section 7.7 we study the complexity of deciding the minimal number of searchers required to search a graph in a given game and we close this chapter by stating open problems in Section 7.8. Throughout the chapter we will use some concepts and notation from graph theory which we recall in the appendix.

7.2 Classifying graph searching games

In the previous section we have described one particular version of graph searching, also known as the *Invisible Cops and Robber* games. Possible variants of this game arise from whether or not the fugitive is invisible, from the type of graph the game is played on, i.e., undirected or directed, a graph or a hypergraph, whether the searchers can move freely to any position or whether they can only move along one edge at a time, whether searchers only dominate the vertex they occupy or whether they dominate other vertices as well, whether the fugitive or the searchers can move in every round or only once in a while, and many other differences. The great variations in graph searching games has made the field somewhat confusing. The fact that the same names are often used for very different games does not help either. In this section we will introduce some of the main variants of the game and attempt a classification of graph searching games.

Most variations do not fundamentally change the nature of the game. The notable exception is between games with a visible fugitive and those where the fugitive is invisible. Essentially, the game with a visible fugitive is a two-player game of perfect information whereas games with an invisible fugitive are more accurately described as one-player games on an (exponentially) enlarged game graph or as two-player games of imperfect information. This difference fundamentally changes the notion of strategies and we therefore introduce the two types of games separately.

7.2.1 Abstract graph searching games

We find it useful to present graph searching games in their most abstract form and then explain how some of the variants studied in the literature can be derived from these abstract games. This will allow us to introduce abstract notions of strategies which then apply to all graph searching games. We will also derive general complexity results for variants of graph searching games. Similar abstract definitions of graph searching games have very recently be given by Amini et al. [2009], Adler [2009] and Lyaudet et al. [2009] for proving very general monotonicity results. Our presentation here only serves the purpose to present the games considered in this paper concisely and in a uniform way and we therefore choose a presentation of abstract graph searching games which is the most convenient for our purpose.

Definition 7.1   An *abstract graph searching game* is a tuple $\mathcal{G} := (V, \mathcal{S}, \mathcal{F}, c)$ where

- V is a set
- $\mathcal{S} \subseteq \mathrm{Pow}(V) \times \mathrm{Pow}(V)$ is the *Searcher admissibility relation*, and
- $\mathcal{F} : \mathrm{Pow}(V)^3 \to \mathrm{Pow}(V)$ is the *Fugitive admissibility function*, and
- $c : \mathrm{Pow}(V) \to \mathbb{N}$ is the *complexity function*.

In the following we will always assume that for every $X \in \mathrm{Pow}(V)$ there is an $X' \in \mathrm{Pow}(V)$ such that $(X, X') \in \mathcal{S}$. This is not essential but will avoid certain notational complications in the definition of strategies below as they otherwise would have to be defined as partial functions.

To give a first example, the Invisible Cops and Robber Game on a graph G introduced in the introduction can be rephrased as an abstract graph searching game $\mathcal{G} := (V, \mathcal{S}, \mathcal{F}, c)$ as follows.

The set V contains the positions the searchers and the fugitive can occupy. In our example, this is the set $V(G)$ of vertices of G.

The Searcher admissibility relation defines the possible moves the searchers can take. As in our example the searchers are free to move from any position to any other position, the Searcher admissibility relation is just $\mathcal{S} := \text{Pow}(V) \times \text{Pow}(V)$.

The fugitive admissibility function models the possible moves of the fugitive: if the searchers currently reside on $X \subseteq V(G)$, the fugitive currently resides somewhere in $R \subseteq V$ and the searchers announce to move to $X' \subseteq V$, then $\mathcal{F}(X, R, X')$ is the set of positions available to the fugitive during the move of the searchers. In the case of the Invisible Cops and Robber Game described above $\mathcal{F}(X, R, X')$ is defined as

$$\{v \in V : \text{there is } u \in R \text{ and a path in } G \setminus (X \cap X') \text{ from } v \text{ to } u \}$$

the set of positions reachable from a vertex in R by a path that does not run through a searcher remaining on the board, i.e., a searcher in $X \cap X'$.

Finally, the complexity function c is defined as $c(X) := |X|$ – the number of vertices in X. The complexity function tells us how many searchers are needed to occupy a position X of the Searcher. On graph searching games played on graphs this is usually the number of vertices in X. However, on games played on hypergraphs searchers sometimes occupy hyper-edges and then the complexity would be the number of edges needed to cover the set X of vertices.

Based on the definition of abstract graph searching games we can now present the rules for invisible and visible games.

7.2.2 Invisible abstract graph searching games

Let $\mathcal{G} := (V, \mathcal{S}, \mathcal{F}, c)$ be an abstract graph searching game. In the variant of graph searching with an invisible fugitive, the searchers occupy vertices in V. The Fugitive, in principle, also occupies a vertex in V but the searchers do not know which one. It is therefore much easier to represent the position of the Fugitive not by the actual position $v \in V$ currently occupied by the fugitive but by the set R of all positions where the fugitive could currently be. This is known as the **fugitive space**, or **robber space**. The goal of the searchers in such a game therefore is to systematically search the set V so that at some point the robber space will be empty.

The rules of the **invisible abstract graph searching game on $\mathcal{G}$** are defined as follows. The initial position of the play is $(X_0 := \varnothing, R_0 := V)$, i.e., initially there are no searchers on the board and the Fugitive can reside on any position in V.

Let $X_i \subseteq V$ be the current position of the searchers and $R_i \subseteq V$ be the current fugitive space. If $R_i = \emptyset$ then the Searcher has won and the game is over. Otherwise, the Searcher chooses $X_{i+1} \subseteq V$ such that $(X_i, X_{i+1}) \in \mathcal{S}$. Afterwards, $R_{i+1} := \mathcal{F}(X_i, R_i, X_{i+1})$ and the play continues at (X_{i+1}, R_{i+1}). If the fugitive can escape forever, then he wins.

Formally, a play in $\mathcal{G} := (V, \mathcal{S}, \mathcal{F}, c)$ is a finite or infinite sequence $\mathcal{P} := (X_0, R_0), \ldots$ such that, for all i, $(X_i, X_{i+1}) \in \mathcal{S}$ and $R_{i+1} := \mathcal{F}(X_i, R_i, X_{i+1})$. Furthermore, if $\mathcal{P}$ is infinite then $R_i \neq \emptyset$, for all $i \geq 0$, and if $\mathcal{P} := (X_0, R_0), \ldots, (X_k, R_k)$ is finite then $R_k = \emptyset$ and $R_i \neq \emptyset$ for all $i < k$. Hence, the Searcher wins all finite plays and the Fugitive wins the infinite plays.

Note that as $R_0 := V$ and $R_{i+1} := \mathcal{F}(X_i, R_i, X_{i+1})$, the entire play is determined by the actions of the Searcher and we can therefore represent any play $\mathcal{P} := (X_0, R_0), \ldots$ by the sequence $X_0, X_1, \ldots$ of searcher positions. Hence, invisible graph searching games are essentially one-player games of perfect information. Alternatively, we could have defined invisible graph searching games as a game between two players where the fugitive also chooses a particular vertex $v_i \in R_i$ at each round but this information is not revealed to the searchers. This would yield a two-player game of partial information. For most applications, however, it is easier to think of these games as one-player games.

We now formally define the concept of strategies and winning strategies. As we are dealing with a one-player game, we will only define strategies for the Searcher.

Definition 7.2 A *strategy* for the Searcher in an invisible abstract graph searching game $\mathcal{G} := (V, \mathcal{S}, \mathcal{F}, c)$ is a function $f : \mathrm{Pow}(V) \times \mathrm{Pow}(V) \to \mathrm{Pow}(V)$ such that $(X, f(X, R)) \in \mathcal{S}$ for all $X, R \subseteq V$.

A finite or infinite play $\mathcal{P} := (X_0, R_0), \ldots$ is *consistent with* f if $X_{i+1} := f(X_i, R_i)$, for all i.

The function f is a *winning strategy* if every play $\mathcal{P}$ which is consistent with f is winning for the Searcher.

If in a play the current position is (X, R), i.e., the searchers are on the vertices in X and the Fugitive space is R, then a strategy for the Searcher tells the Searcher what to do next, i.e., to move the searchers to the new position X'.

Note that implicitly we have defined our strategies to be *positional strategies* in the sense that the action taken by a player depends only on the current position in the play but not on the history. We will see in Section 7.2.6 that

this is without loss of generality as graph searching games are special cases
of reachability games for which such positional strategies suffice.

Example: The Invisible Cops and Robber Game

We have already seen how the Invisible Cops and Robber Game on a graph
G described in the introduction can be formulated as an abstract Invisible
Cops and Robber Game $(V, \mathcal{S}, \mathcal{F}, c)$ where $V := V(G)$ is the set of positions,
$\mathcal{S} := \mathrm{Pow}(V) \times \mathrm{Pow}(V)$ says that the cops can move freely from one position
to another and $\mathcal{F}(X, R, X') := \{v \in V : \text{there is a path in } G \setminus (X \cap X') \text{ from}$
some $u \in R$ to $v \}$. This game was first described as **node searching** by
Kirousis and Papadimitriou [1986]. Here the searchers try to systematically
search the vertices of the graph in a way that the space available to the
fugitive shrinks until it becomes empty.

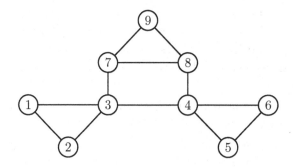

Figure 7.1 Example for an Invisible Cops and Robber Game

To give an example, consider the graph depicted in Figure 7.1. We will
describe a winning strategy for four cops in the Invisible Cops and Robber
Game. The first row contains the cop positions and the second row the
corresponding robber space.

X_i :	$\{1,2,3\}$	$\{3,4\}$	$\{3,4,5,6\}$	$\{3,4,7\}$	$\{4,7,8\}$	$\{7,8,9\}$
R_i :	$\{4,5,6,7,8,9\}$	$\{5,6,7,8,9\}$	$\{7,8,9\}$	$\{8,9\}$	$\{9\}$	$\varnothing$

Note that we have used all four cops only once, at position $\{3, 4, 5, 6\}$. It is
not too difficult to see that we cannot win with three cops. For, consider the
edge $3, 4$ and assume that cops are placed on it. The graph $G \setminus \{3, 4\}$ contains
three components, $\{1, 2\}$, $\{5, 6\}$ and $\{7, 8, 9\}$. Each of these requires at least
three cops for clearing but as soon as one of them is cleared the vertices of
the edge $\{3, 4\}$ adjacent to a vertex in the component must be guarded until
at least a second component of $G \setminus \{3, 4\}$ is cleared. For instance, if we first
clear the triangle $\{1, 2, 3\}$ then the vertex 3 needs to be guarded until 4 and

7 are clear but then there are not enough cops left to clear the rest of the graph.

To formally prove that we cannot search the graph with only three cops we will exhibit structural properties of graphs, called *blockages*, which guarantee the existence of a winning strategy for the robber. This leads to the concept of *obstructions* and corresponding duality theorems which we will study in more detail in Section 7.5.

7.2.3 Visible abstract graph searching games

In this section we describe a variant of graph searching games where the fugitive is visible to the searchers. This fundamentally changes the nature of the game as now the searchers can adapt their strategy to the move of the fugitive. Such graph searching games are now truly two-player games which necessitates some changes to the concepts of strategies.

In particular, it no longer makes sense to represent the position of the fugitive as a fugitive space. Instead we will have to consider individual positions of the fugitive.

Given an abstract game $\mathcal{G} := (V, \mathcal{S}, \mathcal{F}, c)$, the rules of the **visible abstract graph searching game on** $\mathcal{G}$ are defined as follows. Initially, the board is empty.[1] In the first round the Searcher first chooses a set $X_0 \subseteq V$ and then the Fugitive chooses a vertex $v_0 \in V$.

Let $X_i \subseteq V$ and $v_i \in V$ be the current positions of the searchers and the Fugitive respectively. If $v_i \in X_i$ then the Searcher has won and the game is over. Otherwise, the Searcher chooses $X_{i+1} \subseteq V$ such that $(X_i, X_{i+1}) \in \mathcal{S}$. Afterwards, the Fugitive can choose any vertex $v_{i+1} \in \mathcal{F}(X_i, \{v_i\}, X_{i+1})$. If there is none or if $\mathcal{F}(X_i, \{v_i\}, X_{i+1}) \subseteq X_{i+1}$, then again the Searcher wins. Otherwise, the play continues at (X_{i+1}, v_{i+1}). If the Fugitive can escape forever, then he wins.

Formally, a *play* in $\mathcal{G}$ is a finite or infinite sequence $\mathcal{P} := (X_0, v_0), \ldots$ such that $(X_i, X_{i+1}) \in \mathcal{S}$ and $v_{i+1} \in \mathcal{F}(X_i, \{v_i\}, X_{i+1})$, for all $i \geq 0$. Furthermore, if $\mathcal{P}$ is infinite then $v_i \notin X_i$, for all $i \geq 0$, and if $\mathcal{P} := (X_0, v_0), \ldots, (X_k, v_k)$ is finite then $v_k \in X_k$ and $v_i \notin X_i$ for all $i < k$. Hence, the Searcher wins all finite plays and the Fugitive wins the infinite plays.

We now define strategies and winning strategies for the Searcher. In contrast to the invisible case, there is now also a meaningful concept of strategies for the Fugitive. However, here we are primarily interested in

---

[1] There are some variants of games where the robber chooses his position first, but this is not relevant for our presentation.

Searcher strategies but we will come back to formalisations of Fugitive strategies later in Section 7.5.

Definition 7.3 A **strategy** for the Searcher in a visible abstract graph searching game $\mathcal{G} := (V, \mathcal{S}, \mathcal{F}, c)$ is a function $f : \text{Pow}(V) \times V \to \text{Pow}(V)$ such that for all $X \subseteq V$ and $v \in V$, $(X, f(X, v)) \in \mathcal{S}$.

A finite or infinite play $\mathcal{P} := (X_0, v_0), \dots$ is **consistent with** f if $X_{i+1} := f(X_i, v_i)$, for all i.

f is a **winning strategy** if every play $\mathcal{P}$ which is consistent with f is winning for the Searcher.

If in a play the current position is (X, v), i.e., the Searchers are on the vertices in X and the Fugitive is on v, then a strategy for the Searcher tells the Searcher what to do next, i.e., to move the Searchers to the new position X'.

Note that implicitly we have defined our strategies to be *positional strategies* in the sense that the action taken by a player depends only on the current position in the play but not on the history. We will see below that this is without loss of generality as graph searching games are special cases of reachability games for which such positional strategies suffice. Furthermore, the determinacy of reachability games implies that in any visible graph searching game exactly one of the two players has a winning strategy (see Corollary 7.11).

It is worth pointing out the fundamental difference between strategies for the visible and invisible case. In the invisible case, a strategy for the Searcher uniquely defines a play. Therefore, as we have done above, we can represent a strategy for the Searcher in an invisible graph searching game as a sequence $X_0, X_1, \dots$ or Searcher positions.

In the visible case, however, the next searcher position may depend on the choice of the fugitive. Therefore, a Searcher strategy f in the visible case can be described by a rooted directed tree T as follows. The nodes $t \in V(T)$ are labelled by $cops(t) \subseteq V$ and correspond to Searcher positions. The individual edges correspond to the possible robber moves. More formally, the root $r \in V(T)$ of T is labelled by $cops(r) := X_0$ the initial cop position. For every $v \in V \setminus X_0$ there is a successor t_v such that $cops(t_v) := f(cops(t), v)$. The edge (t, t_v) is labelled by v. Now, for every $u \in \mathcal{F}(X_0, v, cops(t_v))$ there is a successor t_u of t_v labelled by $cops(t_u) := f(cops(t_v), u)$. Continuing in this way we can build up a strategy tree which is finite if, and only if, f is a winning strategy. More formally, we define a strategy tree as follows.

Definition 7.4 Let $(V, \mathcal{S}, \mathcal{F}, c)$ be an abstract visible graph searching game.

An **abstract strategy tree** is a rooted directed tree T whose nodes t are labelled by $cops(t) \subseteq V$ and whose edges e are labelled by $search(e) \in V$ as follows.

1 $search(e) \notin cops(s)$ for all edges $e := (s, t) \in E(T)$.
2 If r is the root of T then for all $v \in V \setminus cops(r)$ there is a successor t_v of r in T and $search(r, t_v) := v$.
3 If t is a node with predecessor s and $v := search((s, t))$ then for each $u \in \mathcal{F}(cops(s), v, cops(t))$ there is a successor t_u of t in T so that $search(t, v_u) := u$.

Often this tree can be further simplified. Suppose for instance that there is an edge $(s, t) \in E(T)$ and that there are vertices $u_1, u_2 \in \mathcal{F}(cops(s), v, cops(t)) \setminus cops(t)$ such that $\mathcal{F}(cops(t), u_1, X) = \mathcal{F}(cops(t), u_2, X)$, for all $X \subseteq V(G)$. In this case the two vertices u_1 and u_2 are equivalent in the sense that it makes no sense for the Searcher to play differently depending on whether the fugitive moves to u_1 or u_2 and likewise for the robber. We therefore do not need to have separate sub-trees corresponding to the two different moves.

Example: The Visible Cops and Robber Game

Let us illustrate the definition of abstract graph searching games. In Seymour and Thomas [1993], a graph searching game called the **Cops and Robber Game** is considered, where searchers and the fugitive reside on vertices of a graph $G = (V, E)$. From a position (X, v), where $X \subseteq V$ are the positions of the searchers and $v \in V$ is the current fugitive position, the game proceeds as follows. The searchers can move freely from position $X \subseteq V$ to any other position $X' \subseteq V$. But they have to announce this move publicly and while the searchers move from X to X' the fugitive can choose his new position from all vertices v' such that there is a path in G from v to v' not containing a vertex from $X \cap X'$.

Formulated as an abstract graph searching game, $\mathcal{G} := (V, \mathcal{S}, \mathcal{F}, c)$ we let $V := V(G)$ and $\mathcal{S} := \text{Pow}(V) \times \text{Pow}(V)$, indicating that there is no restriction on the moves of the searchers. The function $\mathcal{F}$ is then defined as

$$\mathcal{F}(X, \{v\}, X') := \{u \in V : \text{there is a path in } G \setminus (X \cap X') \text{ from } v \text{ to } u \}.$$

The complexity function c is defined as $c(X) := |X|$.

To illustrate the game we will show a winning strategy for three cops in the visible Cops and Robber game played on the graph G depicted in Figure 7.1. Initially the cops go on the vertices $\{3, 4\}$. Now the robber has a choice to go in one of the three components of $G \setminus \{3, 4\}$. If he chooses a vertex in $\{1, 2\}$ then the next cop move is to play $\{3, 1, 2\}$. As the cop 3 remains on the board the robber cannot escape and is trapped. Analogously, if the robber chooses a vertex in $\{5, 6\}$ then the cops go to $\{4, 5, 6\}$. Finally, suppose the robber chooses a vertex in $\{7, 8, 9\}$. Now the cops have to be a little more careful. If they were to lift up a cop on the board, say the cop on vertex 3 to place it on 7, then the robber could escape through a path from his current vertex over the vertex 3 to the component $\{1, 2, 3\}$. So the cop on 3 has to remain on the board and the same for 4. To continue with the winning strategy for the cops we place the third cop on the vertex 7. Now the robber can only move to one of 8, 9. We can now lift the cop from 3 and place it on 8, as the cops remaining on 7 and 4 block all exits from the component containing the robber. Putting the cop on 7 leaves only vertex 9 for the robber and in the next move he will be caught by moving the cop from 4 to 9.

Recall that in the invisible graph searching game we needed 4 cops to catch the invisible robber whereas here, knowing the robber position, allows us to save one cop. This example also shows that strategies for the cops are trees rather than just simple sequences of cop positions.

7.2.4 Complexity of strategies

We now define the complexity of a strategy for the Searcher.

Definition 7.5 Let $\mathcal{P} := (X_0, R_0), \ldots$, where $R_i := \{v_i\}$ in case of visible games, be a finite or infinite play in a graph searching game $\mathcal{G} := (V, \mathcal{S}, \mathcal{F}, c)$. The **complexity** of $\mathcal{P}$ is defined as

$$comp(\mathcal{P}) := \max\{c(X_i) : (X_i, R_i) \in \mathcal{P}\}.$$

The **complexity of a winning strategy** f for the Searcher is

$$comp(f) := \max\{comp(\mathcal{P}) : \mathcal{P} \text{ is an } f\text{-consistent play}\}.$$

As outlined in the introduction, the computational problem associated with a graph searching game is to determine a winning strategy for the Searcher that uses as few searchers as possible, i.e., is of lowest complexity.

Definition 7.6 Let $\mathcal{G} := (V, \mathcal{S}, \mathcal{F}, c)$ be an abstract graph searching game. The **search-width** of $\mathcal{G}$ is the minimal complexity of all winning strategies for the Searcher, or ∞ if the Searcher does not have any winning strategies.

A natural computational problem, therefore, is to compute the search-width of a graph searching game. More often we are interested in the corresponding decision problem to decide, given an abstract graph searching game $\mathcal{G} :=$ $(V, \mathcal{S}, \mathcal{F}, c)$ and $k \in \mathbb{N}$, if there is a winning strategy in $\mathcal{G}$ for the Searcher of complexity at most k. We will usually restrict this problem to certain classes of graph searching games, such as Visible Cops and Robber Games. In these cases we will simply say 'the Visible Cops and Robber Game has complexity C'. Furthermore, often this problem is further restricted to games with a fixed number of Searchers.

Definition 7.7 Let $k \in \mathbb{N}$. The *k-searcher game* on $\mathcal{G} := (V, \mathcal{S}, \mathcal{F}, c)$ is defined as the graph searching game $\mathcal{G}' := (V, \mathcal{S}', \mathcal{F}, c)$ on the restriction of $\mathcal{G}$ to $\mathcal{S}' := \{(X, X') : (X, X') \in \mathcal{S} \text{ and } c(X), c(X') \leq k\}$.

7.2.5 Monotonicity

In this section we formally define the concept of monotone strategies. Let $\mathcal{G} := (V, \mathcal{S}, \mathcal{F}, c)$ be an abstract graph searching game.

Definition 7.8 A play $\mathcal{P} := (X_0, R_0), \ldots$, where $R_i := \{v_i\}$ in case of visible graph searching games, is **cop-monotone** if for all $v \in V$ and $i \leq l \leq j$: if $v \in X_i$ and $v \in X_j$ then $v \in X_l$.

$\mathcal{P}$ is **robber-monotone** if $\mathcal{F}(X_i, R_i, X_{i+1}) \supseteq \mathcal{F}(X_{i+1}, R_{i+1}, X_{i+2})$, for all $i \leq 0$.

A strategy is cop- or robber-monotone if any play consistent with the strategy is cop- or robber-monotone.

As outlined above, monotone winning strategies have the advantage of being efficient in the sense that no part of the graph is searched more than once. In most games, this also means that the strategies are short, in the sense that they take at most a linear number of steps.

Lemma 7.9 *Let $\mathcal{G} := (V, \mathcal{S}, \mathcal{F}, c)$ be an abstract graph searching game with the property that the robber space does not decrease if the cops do not move. Then every play consistent with a cop-monotone winning strategy f will end after at most $|V|$ steps.*

Proof Note that by definition of Searcher strategies the move of the searchers only depends on the current searcher position and the fugitive space or position. Hence, from the assumption that no part of the graph is cleared if the searchers do not move, we can conclude that if at some point the searchers do not move and the fugitive stands still, the play would be infinite and hence losing for the searchers.

Therefore, the cops have to move at every step of the game and as they can never move back to a position they left previously, they can only take a linear number of steps. □

Almost all games considered in this chapter have the property that no player is forced to move and therefore, if the searchers do not move, the fugitive space does not decrease. An exception is the game of entanglement studied by Berwanger and Grädel [2004] where the fugitive has to move at every step and therefore it can be beneficial for the searchers not to move.

A similar lemma as before can often be shown for robber monotone strategies as the robber space is non-increasing. However, this would require the game to be such that there is a bound on the number of steps the cops have to make to ensure that the robber space actually becomes smaller. In almost all games such a bound can easily be found, but formalising this in an abstract setting does not lead to any new insights.

7.2.6 Connection to reachability games

In this section we rephrase graph searching games as reachability games and derive some consequences of this. A *reachability game* is a game played on an arena $\mathfrak{G} := (A, V_0, E, v_0)$ where (A, E) is a directed graph, $V_0 \subseteq A$ and $v_0 \in A$. We define $V_1 := A \setminus V_0$. The game is played by two players, Player 0 and Player 1, who push a token along edges of the digraph. Initially the token is on the vertex v_0. In each round of the game, if the token is on a vertex $v_i \in V_0$ then Player 0 can choose a successor v_{i+1} of v_i, i.e., $(v_i, v_{i+1}) \in E$, and push the token along the edge to v_{i+1} where the play continues. If the token is on a vertex in V_1 then Player 1 can choose the successor. The winning condition is given by a set $X \subseteq A$. Player 0 wins if at some point the token is on a vertex in X or if the token is on a vertex in V_1 which has no successors. If the token never reaches a vertex in X or if at some point Player 0 cannot move anymore, then Player 1 wins. See [Grädel et al., 2002, Chapter 2] for details of reachability games.

A positional strategy for Player i in a reachability game can be described as a function $f_i : V_i \to A$ assigning to each vertex v where the player moves a successor $f(v)$ such that $(v, f(v)) \in E$. f_i is a winning strategy if the player wins every play consistent with this strategy. For our purposes we need two results on reachability games, *positional determinacy* and the fact that the winning region for a player in a reachability game can be computed in linear time.

Lemma 7.10

1 *Reachability games are positionally determined, i.e., in every reachability game exactly one of the players has a winning strategy and this can be chosen to be positional.*

2 *There is a linear time algorithm which, given a reachability game (A, V_0, E, v_0) and a winning condition $X \subseteq A$, decides whether Player 0 has a winning strategy in the game.*

Let $\mathcal{G} := (V, \mathcal{S}, \mathcal{F}, c)$ be a visible graph searching game. We associate with $\mathcal{G}$ a game arena $\mathfrak{G} := (A, V_0, E, v_0)$ where

$$A := \text{Pow}(V) \times V \cup$$
$$\{(X, v, X') \in \text{Pow}(V) \times \text{Pow}(V) \times V : (X, X') \in \mathcal{S}\}.$$

Nodes $(X, v) \in \text{Pow}(V) \times V$ correspond to positions in the graph searching games. A node $(X, v, X') \in \text{Pow}(V) \times V \times \text{Pow}(V)$ will correspond to the intermediate position where the searchers have announced that they move from X to X' and the fugitive can choose his new position $v' \in \mathcal{F}(X, \{v\}, X')$. There is an edge from (X, v) to (X, v, X') for all X' such that $(X, X') \in \mathcal{S}$. Furthermore, there is an edge from (X, v, X') to (X', v') for all $v' \in \mathcal{F}(X, \{v\}, X')$.

All nodes of the form (X, v) belong to Player 0 and nodes (X, v, X') belong to Player 1. Finally, the winning condition contains all nodes (X, v) for which $v \in X$.

Now, it is easily seen that from any position (X, v) in the graph searching game, the Searcher has a winning strategy if, and only if, Player 0 has a winning strategy in $\mathfrak{G}$ from the node (X, v). Lemma 7.10 implies the following corollary.

Corollary 7.11 *For every fixed k, in every visible graph searching game exactly one of the two players has a winning strategy in the k-searcher game.*

Similarly, for the invisible graph searching game, we define a game arena $\mathfrak{G}$ as follows. The vertices are pairs (X, R) where $X, R \subseteq V$ and there is an edge between (X, R) and (X', R') if $(X, X') \in \mathcal{S}$ and $R' := \mathcal{F}(X, R, X')$. All nodes belong to Player 0. Again it is easily seen that Player 0 has a winning strategy from node (X, R) in $\mathfrak{G}$ if, and only if, the Searcher has a winning strategy in the invisible graph searching game starting from (X, R).

7.3 Variants of graph searching games

In this section we present some of the main variants of games studied in the literature.

7.3.1 A different Cops and Robber game

Nowakowski and Winkler [1983] study a graph searching game, also called a *Cops and Robber game*, where the two players take turns and both players are restricted to move along an edge. More formally, starting from a position (X, r), first the Searcher moves and can choose a new position X' obtained from X by moving some searchers to neighbours of their current position. Once the searchers have moved the fugitive can then choose a neighbour of his current position, provided he has not already been caught. See Alspach [2006] for a survey of this type of game.

In our framework of graph searching games, this game, played on a graph G, can be formalised as $\mathcal{G} := (V, \mathcal{S}, \mathcal{F}, c)$ where

- $V := V(G)$.
- A pair (X, X') is in $\mathcal{S}$ if there is a subset $Y \subseteq X$ (these are the searchers that move) and a set Y' which contains for each $v \in Y$ a successor v' of v, i.e., a vertex with $(v, v') \in E(G)$, and $X' \subseteq Y' \cup X \setminus Y$.
- For a triple (X, v, X') we define $\mathcal{F}(X, v, X')$ to be empty if $v \in X'$ and otherwise the set of vertices u s.t. $u \notin X'$ and $(v, u) \in E(G)$.
- Finally, $c(X) := |X|$ for all $X \subseteq V$.

We will refer to this type of game as *turn-based*. Goldstein and Reingold [1995] study turn-based Cops and Robber games on directed graphs and establish a range of complexity results for variations of this game ranging from LOGSPACE-completeness to EXPTIME-completeness. Among other results they show the following theorem.

Theorem 7.12 (Goldstein and Reingold [1995]) *The turn-based Cops and Robber game on a strongly connected digraph is* EXPTIME-*complete.*

The study of this type of game forms a rich and somewhat independent branch of graph searching games. To keep the presentation concise, we will mostly be focusing on games where the two players (essentially) move simultaneously and are not restricted to moves of distance one. See Alspach [2006] and Fomin and Thilikos [2008] and references therein for a guide to the rich literature on turn-based games.

7.3.2 Node and edge searching with an invisible fugitive

We have already formally described the rules of the (non turn-based) Invisible
Cops and Robber Game in Section 7.2.2. This game has been introduced as
node-searching by Kirousis and Papadimitriou [1986] who showed that it is
essentially equivalent to pebbling games used to analyse the complexity of
sequential computation.

Pebble games are played on an acyclic directed graph. In each step of
a play we can remove a pebble from a vertex or place a new pebble on a
vertex provided that all its predecessors carry pebbles. The motivation for
pebble games comes from the analysis of register allocation for sequential
computation, for instance for computing arithmetical expressions. The vertices of a directed acyclic graph corresponds to sub-terms that have to be
computed. Hence, to compute the value of a term represented by a node t
we first need to compute the value of its immediate sub-terms represented by
the predecessors of t. A pebble on a node means that the value of this node
is currently contained in a register of the processor. To compute a value of
a term in a register the values of its sub-terms must also be contained in
registers and this motivates the rule that a pebble can only be placed if its
predecessors have been pebbled.

Initially the graph is pebble free and the play stops once all vertices have
been pebbled at least once. The minimal number of pebbles needed for a
directed graph representing an expression t is the minimal number of registers
that have to be used for computing t. Kirousis and Papadimitriou [1986]
show that pebble games can be reformulated as graph searching games with
an invisible fugitive and therefore register analysis as described above can be
done within the framework of graph searching games.

In the same paper they show that *edge searching* and *node searching* are
closely related. Recall from the introduction that the edge searching game
is a game where the robber resides on edges of the graph. The searchers
occupy vertices. In each move, the searchers can clear an edge by sliding
along it, i.e., if a searcher occupies an endpoint of an edge then he can move
to the other endpoint and thereby clears the edge. As shown by Kirousis and
Papadimitriou [1986], if G is a graph and G' is the graph obtained from G by
sub-dividing each edge twice, then the minimal number of cops required to
catch the fugitive in the node searching game on G, called the **node search
number** of G, is one more than the minimal number of searchers required
in the edge searching game on G', called the **edge search number** of G'.
Conversely, if G is a graph and G' is obtained from G by replacing each edge

by three parallel edges, then the edge search number of G' is one more than the node search number of G.

LaPaugh [1993] proved that the edge searching game is monotone thereby giving the first monotonicity proof for a graph searching game. Using the correspondence between edge searching and node searching, Kirousis and Papadimitriou [1986] establish monotonicity for the node searching game. Bienstock and Seymour [1991] consider a version of invisible graph searching, called *mixed searching*, where the searcher can both slide along an edge or move to other nodes clearing an edge as soon as both endpoints are occupied. They give a simpler monotonicity proof for this type of game which implies the previous two results.

A very general monotonicity proof for games with an invisible robber based on the concept of sub-modularity was given by Fomin and Thilikos [2003]. We will present an even more general result using sub-modularity in Section 7.4 below.

Using a reduction from the MIN-CUT INTO EQUAL-SIZED SUBSETS problem, Megiddo et al. [1988] showed that edge searching is NP-complete. Using the correspondence between edge and node searching outlined above, this translates into NP-completeness of the node searching variant, i.e., the Invisible Cops and Robber Game defined above.

7.3.3 Visible Robber games

We have already introduced the visible cops and robber game above. This game was studied by Seymour and Thomas [1993] in relation to tree-width, a connection which we will present in more depth in Section 7.6. In this paper they introduce a formalisation of the robber strategies in terms of *screens*, nowadays more commonly referred to as *brambles*, and use this to prove monotonicity of the visible cops and robber game. A monotonicity proof unifying this result and the results obtained for invisible robber games has been given by Mazoit and Nisse [2008]. We will review this proof method in Section 7.4 below.

Arnborg et al. [1987] proved by a reduction from the MINIMUM CUT LINEAR ARRANGEMENT problem that determining for a given graph the minimal k such that G can be represented as a *partial k-tree* is NP-complete. This number is equal to the tree-width of G and therefore deciding the tree-width of a graph is NP-complete. We will see in Section 7.6 that the minimal number of searchers, called the **visible search width** of G, required to catch a visible fugitive in the visible Cops and Robber game on a graph G

is equal to the tree-width of G plus one. Hence, deciding the visible search width of a graph is NP-complete.

7.3.4 Lazy or inert fugitives

In the games studied so far the fugitive was allowed to move at every step of the game. The **inert** variant of visible and invisible graph searching is obtained by restricting the fugitive so that he can only move if a searcher is about to land on his position. More formally, the inert graph searching game $\mathcal{G} := (V, \mathcal{S}, \mathcal{F}, c)$ is defined as an abstract graph searching game where for all $X, X' \subseteq V$ and $v \in V$, $\mathcal{F}(X, v, X') = v$ if $v \notin X'$.

Inert fugitive games can be defined for visible and invisible fugitives. However, as often in life, being lazy and visible is usually not a good idea wherefore the invisible game has received much more attention. Dendris et al. [1997] study the invisible inert fugitive game and show it to be equivalent to the visible cops and robber game. Richerby and Thilikos [2008] study the inert case for a visible fugitive.

7.3.5 Games played on directed graphs

The games studied so far have been played on undirected graphs but many have natural counterparts on directed graphs. Let us first consider the visible Cops and Robber game played on an undirected graph. Suppose that the current position for the searchers is X and the robber is on a vertex v. If the searchers announce their intention to move to their new position X' then the robber can move to any vertex u reachable in $G \setminus (X \cap X')$ from his current position v. Obviously this formulation of the game is equivalent to the formulation where the robber can move freely in the connected component of $G \setminus (X \cap X')$ containing v. While the two presentations are equivalent on undirected graphs they yield two very different games when translated to directed graphs.

Definition 7.13 Let G be a directed graph and let $V := V(G)$, $c(X) := |X|$ for all $X \subseteq V(G)$ and $(X, X') \in \mathcal{S}$ for all $X, X' \subseteq V(G)$.

1 The **reachability game** on G is defined as the abstract graph searching game $\mathcal{G} := (V, \mathcal{S}, \mathcal{F}, c)$, where the Fugitive admissibility function $\mathcal{F}$ is defined as $\mathcal{F}(X, R, X') := \{v \in V : \text{there is an } u \in R \text{ and a directed path in } G \setminus (X \cap X') \text{ from } v \text{ to } u\}$.

2 The **strongly connected component (SCC) game** on G is defined as the abstract graph searching game $\mathcal{G} := (V, \mathcal{S}, \mathcal{F}, c)$, where the Fugitive

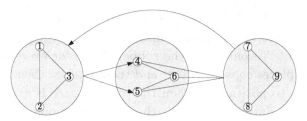

Figure 7.2 A visible directed reachability game

admissibility function $\mathcal{F}$ is defined as $\mathcal{F}(X, R, X') := \{v \in V : \text{there is an } u \in R \text{ such that } u \text{ and } v \text{ are in the same strongly connected component of } G \setminus (X \cap X')\}$.

To demonstrate the games and the fundamental difference between games on undirected and directed graphs, we give an example of a directed visible reachability game.

Consider the directed graph depicted in Figure 7.3.5. An undirected edge indicates a directed edge in both directions. The graph consists of two cliques of three vertices each which we will call $C_L := \{1, 2, 3\}$ and $C_R := \{7, 8, 9\}$. An edge connecting a clique to a specific vertex means that every vertex of the clique is connected to this vertex. That is, every vertex of C_l has a directed edge to 4 and 5 and every vertex of C_R has a directed edge to every vertex in C_L and also an undirected edge (two directed edges in either direction) to the vertices $4, 5, 6$ in the middle.

On this graph, five cops have a winning strategies against the robber as follows. As every vertex in C_R has an edge to every other vertex, the cops must first occupy all vertices in C_R, which takes three cops. In addition they put two cops on 4 and 5. Now the robber has a choice to either move to 6 or to a vertex in the clique C_L. If he goes to C_L we lift all cops from C_R and place them on C_L capturing the robber, as the only escape route from C_L is through the vertices 4 and 5 which are both blocked.

If on the other hand the robber decides to move to 6 then we lift the two cops from 4 and 5 and place one of them on 6. Now the robber can move to one of 4 or 5 but whatever he does we can then place the space cop on the chosen vertex capturing the robber.

Note that this strategy is non-monotone as the robber can reach the vertices 4 and 5 after they have already been occupied by a cop. Kreutzer and Ordyniak [2008] show that there is no monotone strategy with five cops on this graph, showing that the directed reachability game is non-monotone.

This example also demonstrates the crucial difference between games played on undirected and directed graphs. For, let G be an undirected graph with some cops being on position X and let R be the robber space, i.e., the component of $G \setminus X$ containing the robber. Now, for every $Y \subseteq V(G)$, if the Cop player places cops on $X \cup Y$ and then removes them from Y again, i.e., moves back to position X, then the robber space is exactly the same space R as before. Intuitively, this is the reason why non-monotone moves are never necessary in the undirected cops and robber game. For a game played on directed graphs, this is not the case as the example above shows. If $X := \{6, 7\}$ and $Y := C_R$ then once the cops go on $X \cup Y$ and the robber has moved to C_L, the cops can be lifted from C_R without the robber being able to regain control of the lost vertices.

To see that the two variants of directed graph searching games presented above are very different consider the class of *trees with backedges* as studied, e.g., by Berwanger et al. [2006]. The idea is to take a tree and add an edge from every node to any of its (direct or indirect) predecessors up to the root. Then it is easily seen that two searchers suffice to catch a visible fugitive in the SCC game on these trees but to catch the fugitive in the reachability game we need at least as many cops as the height of tree. (It might be a good exercise to prove both statements.) Hence, the difference between the two game variants can be arbitrarily large. On the other hand, we never need more searchers to catch the fugitive in the SCC game than in the reachability game as every move allowed to the fugitive in the latter is also a valid move in the former.

The visible SCC game has been introduced in connection with **directed tree-width** by Johnson et al. [2001]. Barát [2006] studies the invisible reachability game and established its connection to *directed path-width*. Finally, the visible reachability game was explored by Berwanger et al. [2006] and its inert variant by Hunter and Kreutzer [2008]. See also Hunter [2007].

As we have seen above, the visible, invisible and inert invisible graph searching games as well as their edge and mixed search variants are all monotone on undirected graphs. For directed graphs the situation is rather different. Whereas Barát [2006] proved that the invisible reachability game is monotone, all other game variants for directed graphs mentioned here have been shown to be non-monotone. For the SCC game this was shown by Johnson et al. [2001] for the case of searcher monotonicity and by Adler [2007] for fugitive monotonicity. However, Johnson et al. [2001] proved that the visible SCC game is at least *approximately monotone*. We will review the proof of this result in Section 7.4 below.

The visible reachability game as well as the inert reachability game were shown to be non-monotone by Kreutzer and Ordyniak [2008].

7.3.6 Games played on hypergraphs

Graph searching games have also found applications on hypergraphs. Gottlob et al. [2003] study a game called the **Robber and Marshal game** on hypergraphs. In the game, the fugitive, here called the robber, occupies vertices of the hypergraph whereas the searchers, here called marshals, occupy hyper-edges. The game is somewhat different from the games discussed above as a marshal moving from a hyper-edge e to a hyper-edge h still blocks the vertices in $e \cap h$. In particular, one marshal is enough to search an acyclic graph, viewed as a hypergraph in the obvious way, whereas we always need at least two cops for any graph containing at least one edge in the visible cops and robber game.

Formally, given a hypergraph $H := (V(H), E(H))$ the Robber and Marshal game on H is defined as $\mathcal{G}_H := (V, \mathcal{S}, \mathcal{F}, c)$ where

- $V := V(H) \dot\cup E(H)$
- $(X, X') \in \mathcal{S}$ if $X, X' \subseteq E(H)$
- $\mathcal{F}(X, R, X') := \varnothing$ if $R \not\subseteq V(H)$ or $R \subseteq \{v \in V(H) : \exists e \in X, v \in e\}$ and otherwise $\mathcal{F}(X, R, X') := \{v \in V(H) : \text{there is a path in } H \text{ from a vertex } u \in R \text{ to } v \text{ not going through any vertex in } \bigcup X \cap \bigcup X'\}$
- $c(X) := |X|$.

Robber and Marshal games have been studied in particular in connection to hypergraph decompositions such as hypertree-width and generalised hypertree-width and approximate duality theorems similar to the one we will establish in Sections 7.4.2 and 7.6 have been proved by Adler et al. [2005].

7.3.7 Further variants

Finally, we briefly comment on further variants of graph searching. Here we concentrate on games played on undirected graphs, but some of the variants translate easily to other types of graphs such as digraphs or hypergraphs.

An additional requirement sometimes imposed on the searchers is that at every step in a play the set of vertices occupied by searchers needs to be **connected**. This is, for instance, desirable if the searchers need to stay within communication range. See, e.g., Fomin and Thilikos [2008] for references on connected search.

Another variation is obtained by giving the searchers a greater radius of visibility. For instance, we can consider the case where a searcher not only dominates his own vertex but also all vertices adjacent to it. That is, to catch the robber it is only necessary to trap the robber in the neighbourhood of a searcher. In particular in the invisible fugitive case, such games model the fact that often searchers can see further than just their current position, for instance using torch lights, but they still cannot see the whole system of tunnels they are asked to search. Such games, called **domination games**, were introduced by Fomin et al. [2003]. Kreutzer and Ordyniak [2009] study complexity and monotonicity of these games and show domination games are not only algorithmically much harder compared to classical cops and robber games, they are also highly non-monotone (see Section 7.4.3 below).

Besides graph searching games inspired by applications related to graph searching, there are also games which fall under the category of graph searching games but were inspired by applications in logic. In particular, Berwanger and Grädel [2004] introduce the game of **entanglement** and its relation to the variable hierarchy of the modal μ-calculus.

7.4 Monotonicity of graph searching

As mentioned before, monotonicity features highly in research on graph searching games for a variety of reasons. In this section we present some of the most important techniques that have been employed for proving monotonicity results in the literature.

In Section 7.4.1, we first introduce the concept of *sub-modularity*, which has been used (at least implicitly) in numerous monotonicity results, and demonstrate this technique by establishing monotonicity of the visible cops and robber game discussed above.

Many graph searching games on undirected graphs have been shown to be monotone. Other games, for instance many games on directed graphs, are not monotone and examples showing that searchers can be saved by playing non-monotonic have been given. In some cases, however, at least *approximate monotonicity* can be retained in the sense that there is a function $f : \mathbb{N} \rightarrow \mathbb{N}$ such that if k searchers can win by a non-monotone strategy then no more then $f(k)$ searchers are needed to win by a monotone strategy. Often f is just a small constant. Many proofs of approximate monotonicity use the concept of *obstructions*. We will demonstrate this technique in Section 7.4.2 for the case of directed graph searching.

7.4.1 Monotonicity by sub-modularity

The aim of this section is to show that the visible cops and robber game on undirected graphs is monotone. The proof presented here essentially follows

Mazoit and Nisse [2008]. We will demonstrate the various constructions in this part by the following example.

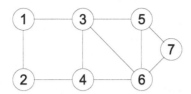

Figure 7.3 Example graph G for monotonicity proofs

Recall the representation of winning strategies for the Cop player in terms of strategy trees in Definition 7.4. In this tree, a node t corresponds to a cop position $cops(t)$ and an out-going edge $e := (t, s)$ corresponds to a robber move to a vertex $search(e) := v$. Clearly, if the cops are on vertices $X := cops(t)$ and u, v are in the same component of $G \setminus X$, then it makes no difference for the game whether the robber moves to u or v, because whatever the cops do next, the robber can move to exactly the same positions. We therefore do not need to have two separate sub-trees for u and v and can combine vertices in the same component. Thus, we can rephrase strategy trees for the visible cops and robber game as follows. To distinguish from search trees defined below we deviate from the notation of Definition 7.4 and use $robber(e)$ instead of $search(e)$.

Definition 7.14 Let G be an undirected graph. A ***strategy tree*** is a rooted directed tree T whose nodes t are labelled by $cops(t) \subseteq V(G)$ and whose edges $e \in E(T)$ are labelled by $robber(e) \subseteq V(G)$ as follows.

1 If r is the root of T then for all components C of $G \setminus cops(r)$ there is a successor t_C of r in T and $robber(r, t_C) := V(C)$.
2 If t is a node with predecessor s and $C' := robber((s, t))$ then for each component C of $G \setminus cops(t)$ contained in the same component of $G \setminus (cops(s) \cap cops(t))$ as C' there is an edge $e_C := (t, t_C) \in E(T)$ that $robber(e_C) := V(C)$.

A strategy tree is ***monotone*** if for all $(s, t), (t, t') \in E(T)$ $robber(s, t) \supseteq robber(t, t')$.

Towards proving monotonicity of the game it turns out to be simpler to think of the cops and the robber as controlling edges of the graph rather than vertices. We therefore further reformulate strategy trees into what we will call *search trees*. Here, a component housing a robber, or a robber space in general, will be represented by the set of edges contained in the component

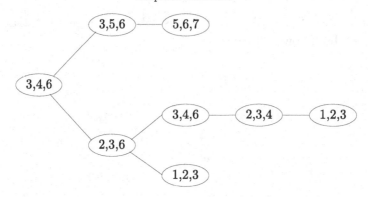

Figure 7.4 Non-monotone strategy tree for the graph in Figure 7.3

plus the edges joining this component to the cop positions guarding the robber space. We will next define the notion of a border for a set of edges.

Definition 7.15   Let E be a set. We denote the set of partitions $\mathcal{P} := (X_1, \ldots, X_k)$ of E by $\mathcal{P}(E)$, where we do allow degenerate partitions, i.e., $X_i = \varnothing$ for some i.

Definition 7.16   Let G be a graph and let $F \subseteq E(G)$. By $\delta(F)$ we denote the *border* of F, i.e., the set of vertices incident to an edge in F and also to an edge in $E(G) \setminus F$.

We extend the definition to partitions $P := \{X_1, \ldots, X_r\} \in \mathcal{P}(E(G))$ by setting

$$\delta(P) := \left\{ v \in V(G) : \begin{array}{l} \text{there are edges } e \in X_i \text{ and } f \in X_j, \\ \text{for some } 1 \leq i < j \leq r, \text{ s.t. } v \in e \text{ and } v \in f \end{array} \right\}.$$

The intuition behind a border is that if the robber controls the edges in F and the cops want to prevent the robber from escaping then they need to guard the vertices in $\delta(F)$. For a partition P of the edge set, this means that if the cops want to split the graph into the sub-graphs defined by the individual sets of edges, they have to put cops on $\delta(P)$. For example, in the graph in Figure 7.3 we get $\delta(\{12, 13\}, \{24, 34, 46\}, \{35, 36, 56, 57, 67\}) = \{2, 3, 6\}$.

Definition 7.17   Let G be a graph. A *search-tree* of G is a tuple

$$(T, \textit{new}, \textit{search}, \textit{clear})$$

where

- T is finite a directed tree
- *clear*, *new* $: V(T) \to \mathrm{Pow}(E(G))$

- $search : E(T) \rightarrow \mathrm{Pow}(E(G))$

such that

1 if $t \in V(T)$ and $e_1, \ldots, e_r$ are the out-going edges of t then

$$\{new(t), clear(t), search(e_1), \ldots, search(e_r)\}$$

form a (possibly degenerated) partition of $E(G)$ and
2 $search(e) \cap clear(t) = \varnothing$ for every edge $e := (s, t) \in E(T)$.

Let $t \in V(T)$ be a node with out-going edges $e_1, \ldots, e_r$. We define

$$guard(t) := V[new(t)] \cup \delta\big(search(e_1), \ldots, search(e_r), clear(t)\big)$$

and the width $w(t)$ of a node t as $w(t) := |guard(t)|$. The width of a search tree is $\max\{w(t) : t \in V(T)\}$.

An edge $e := (s, t) \in V(T)$ is called *monotone* if $search(e) \cup clear(t) = E(G)$. Otherwise it is called *non-monotone*. We call T **monotone** if all edges are monotone.

It is not too difficult to see that any strategy tree $(T, cops, robber)$ corresponds to a search tree $(T, new, search, clear)$ over the same underlying directed tree T, where

$$new(t) := \{e = \{u, v\} \in E(G) : u, v \in cops(t)\}$$
$$search(s, t) := \{e = \{u, v\} \in E(G) : u \in robber(e) \text{ or } v \in robber(e)\}$$
$$clear(t) := E(G) \setminus \big(new(t) \cup \bigcup_{(t,t') \in E(T)} search(t, t')\big).$$

Figure 7.5 shows the search tree corresponding to the strategy tree in Figure 7.4. Here, the node labels correspond to $new(t)$, e.g., the label '34,36,46' of the root corresponds to the edges $(3, 4), (3, 6)$ and $(4, 6)$ cleared by initially putting the cops on the vertices $3, 4, 6$. The edge label in brackets, e.g., (35,36,X) corresponds to the *clear* label of their endpoint. Here, X is meant to be the set 56, 57, 67 of edges and is used to simplify presentation. Finally, the edge labels with a grey background denote the *search* label of an edge.

Note that for each node $t \in V(T)$ the cop position $cops(t)$ in the strategy tree is implicitly defined by $guard(t)$ in the search tree. While every strategy tree corresponds to a search tree, not every search tree has a corresponding strategy tree. For instance, if there is an edge $e := (s, t) \in V(T)$ in the search tree such that $search(e) \cap clear(t) \neq E(G)$ then this means that initially the cops are $guard(s)$ with the robber being somewhere in $search(e)$ and from there the cops move to $guard(t)$. By doing so the cops decide to give up some part of what they have already searched and just consider $clear(t)$ to be

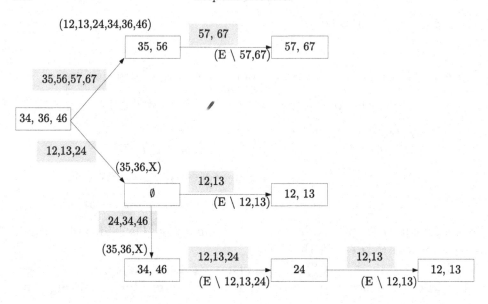

Figure 7.5 Search tree for the strategy tree in Figure 7.4

free of the robber. Everything else is handed over to the robber and will be searched later. However, the corresponding move from $guard(s)$ to $guard(t)$ may not be possible in the cops and robber game in the sense that if the cops were to make this move the robber might have the chance to run to vertices inside $clear(t)$. Intuitively, the move from $guard(s)$ to $guard(t)$ corresponds to a *retreat move*, where we allow the cops to retreat from a current position to a new position inside their cleared area without allowing the robber to change position during this move. See Ordyniak [2009] for a description of search trees as strategy trees for the *cops and robber game with retreat*. However, such a retreat move is not possible in the Cops and Robber game and therefore not every search tree corresponds to a strategy tree. However, if the search tree is monotone then it does not contain any retreat moves and therefore monotone search trees have corresponding strategy trees.

The following lemma now follows immediately.

Lemma 7.18 *If there is a strategy tree for k cops on a graph G then there is a search tree of width k on G. Conversely, if there is a monotone search tree on a graph G then there exists a monotone strategy tree of the same width.*

Essentially, our monotonicity proof for the cops and robber game now consists of showing that whenever there is a search tree of width k in a graph G then there is a monotone search tree of the same width.

Sub-modularity

We begin by introducing the concept of sub-modularity and an extension thereof.

Definition 7.19 Let E be a set and $\phi : \mathrm{Pow}(E) \to \mathbb{N}$ be a function.

1 ϕ is **symmetric** if $\phi(X) = \phi(E \setminus X)$ for all $X \subseteq E$.
2 ϕ is **sub-modular** if $\phi(X) + \phi(Y) \geq \phi(X \cap Y) + \phi(X \cup Y)$ for all $X, Y \subseteq E$.

A symmetric and sub-modular function is called a **connectivity function**.

For our proof here we will work with an extension of sub-modularity to partitions of a set E.

Definition 7.20 If $P := \{X_1, \dots, X_k\} \in \mathcal{P}(E)$ is a partition of a set E and $F \subseteq E$ then we define $P_{X_i \uparrow F}$ as

$$P_{X_i \uparrow F} := \{X_1 \cap F, \ \dots, X_{i-1} \cap F, \ X_i \cup F^c, \ X_{i+1} \cap F, \dots, X_k \cap F\},$$

where $F^c := E \setminus F$.

Definition 7.21 Let E be a set. A **partition function** is a function $\phi : \mathcal{P}(E) \to \mathbb{N}$. ϕ is **sub-modular** if for all $P := \{X_1, \dots, X_k\} \in \mathcal{P}(E), Q := \{Y_1, \dots, Y_s\} \in \mathcal{P}(E)$ and all i, j

$$\phi(P) + \phi(Q) \geq \phi(P_{X_i \uparrow Y_j}) + \phi(Q_{Y_j \uparrow X_i}).$$

It is worth pointing out that the definition of sub-modularity of partition functions indeed extends the usual definition of sub-modularity as defined above. For, if $P := \{X, X^c\}$ and $Q := \{Y, Y^c\}$ are bipartitions of a set E then

$$\begin{aligned}
\phi(P) + \phi(Q) &\geq \phi(P_{X \uparrow Y^c}) + \phi(Q_{Y^c \uparrow X}) \\
&= \phi(X \cup (Y^c)^c, X^c \cap Y^c) + \phi(Y \cap X, Y^c \cup X^c) \\
&= \phi(X \cup Y, X^c \cap Y^c) + \phi(Y \cap X, Y^c \cup X^c) \\
&= \phi(X \cup Y, (X \cup Y)^c) + \phi(Y \cap X, (Y \cap X)^c).
\end{aligned}$$

Hence, if we set $\Phi(X) := \phi(X, X^c)$ then this corresponds to the usual notion of sub-modularity of Φ as defined above.

We show next that the border function in Definition 7.16 is sub-modular.

Lemma 7.22 *Let G be a graph and $\phi(P) := |\delta(P)|$ for all partitions $P \in \mathcal{P}(E(G))$. Then ϕ is sub-modular.*

Proof Let $P := \{X_1, \ldots, X_r\}$ and $Q := \{Y_1, \ldots, Y_s\}$ be partitions of $E :=$ $E(G)$. Let $1 \leq i \leq r$ and $q \leq j \leq s$. By rearranging the sets P and Q we can assume w.l.o.g. that $i = j = 1$. We want to show that

$$\phi(P) + \phi(Q) \geq \phi(P_{X_1 \uparrow Y_1}) + \phi(Q_{Y_1 \uparrow X_1})$$
$$= |\delta(X_1 \cup Y_1^c, X_2 \cap Y_1, \ldots, X_r \cap Y_1\}| +$$
$$|\delta(Y_1 \cup X_1^c, Y_2 \cap X_1, \ldots, Y_s \cap X_1\}|.$$

We will prove the inequality by showing that if a vertex $v \in V(G)$ is contained in one of the sets $\delta(P_{X_1 \uparrow Y_1}), \delta(Q_{Y_1 \uparrow X_1})$ occurring on the right-hand side, i.e., is contributing to a term on the right, then the vertex is also contributing to a term on the left. And if this vertex contributes to both terms on the right then it also contributes to both on the left.

Towards this aim, let $v \in V(G)$ be a vertex. Suppose first that v is contained in exactly one of $\delta(P_{X_1 \uparrow Y_1})$ or $\delta(Q_{Y_1 \uparrow X_1})$, i.e., contributes only to one term on the right-hand side. W.l.o.g. we assume $v \in \delta(P_{X_1 \uparrow Y_1})$. If there is $1 \leq i < j < r$ such that v is contained in an edge $e_1 \in X_i$ and $e_2 \in X_j$, then $v \in \delta(P)$. Otherwise, v must be incident to an edge $e \in Y_1^c$ and also to an edge $f \in X_j \cap Y_1$, for some $j > 1$. But then $v \in \delta(Q)$ as the edge f occurs in Y_1 and the edge e must be contained in one of the Y_l, $l > 1$.

Now, suppose $v \in \delta(P_{X_1 \uparrow Y_1})$ and $v \in \delta(Q_{Y_1 \uparrow X_1})$. But then, v is incident to an edge in $e \in X_i \cap Y_1$, for some $i > 1$, and also to an edge $f \in Y_j \cap X_1$, for some $j > 1$. Hence, $f \in X_1$ and $e \in X_i$ and therefore $v \in \delta(P)$ and, analogously, $e \in Y_1$ and $f \in Y_j$ and therefore $v \in \delta(Q)$. Hence, v contributes 2 to the left-hand side. This concludes the proof. $\qquad\square$

We will primarily use the sub-modularity of ϕ in the following form.

Lemma 7.23 *Let G be a graph and $P := \{X_1, \ldots, X_k\} \in \mathcal{P}(E(G))$ be a partition of $E(G)$. Let $F \subseteq E(G)$ such that $F \cap X_1 = \varnothing$.*

$$\text{If } |\delta(F)| \leq |\delta(X_1)| \text{ then } |\delta(P_{X_1 \uparrow F})| \leq |\delta(P)|$$
$$\text{If } |\delta(F)| < |\delta(E_1)| \text{ then } |\delta(P_{X_1 \uparrow F})| < |\delta(P)|.$$

Proof By sub-modularity of $\phi(P) := |\delta(P)|$ we know that

$$|\delta(P)| + |\delta(\{F, F^c\})| \geq |\delta(P_{X_1 \uparrow F})| + |\delta(\{F \cup X_1^c, F^c \cap X_1\})|.$$

But, as $F \cap X_1 = \varnothing$ we have $F \cup X_1^c = X_1^c$ and $F^c \cap X_1 = X_1$. Hence, we have

$$|\delta(P)| + |\delta(\{F, F^c\})| \geq |\delta(P_{X_1 \uparrow F})| + |\delta(\{X_1, X_1^c\})|$$

and therefore

$$|\delta(P)| \geq |\delta(P_{X_1 \uparrow F})| + (|\delta(\{X_1, X_1^c\})| - |\delta(\{F, F^c\})|)$$

from which the claim follows. ◻

Monotonicity of the visible Cops and Robber Game

We are now ready to prove the main result of this section.

Theorem 7.24 *The visible cops and robber game on undirected graphs is monotone.*

As discussed above, the theorem follows immediately from the following lemma.

Lemma 7.25 *Let G be a graph and T be a search tree of G of width k. Then there is a monotone search tree of G of width k.*

Proof Let $m := |E(T)|$. We define the *weight* of a search tree $\mathcal{T} := (T, new, search, clear)$ as

$$weight(\mathcal{T}) := \sum_{t \in V(T)} |w(t)|$$

and its *badness* as

$$bn := \sum_{\substack{e \in E(T) \\ e \text{ non-monotone}}} m^{-dist(e)}$$

where the distance $dist(e)$ of an edge $e := (s, t)$ is defined as the distance of t from the root of T.

Given two search trees $\mathcal{T}_1, \mathcal{T}_2$ we say that $\mathcal{T}_1$ is *tighter* than $\mathcal{T}_2$ if $w(\mathcal{T}_1) < w(\mathcal{T}_2)$ or $w(\mathcal{T}_1) = w(\mathcal{T}_2)$ and $bn(\mathcal{T}_1) < bn(\mathcal{T}_2)$. Clearly, the tighter relation is a well-ordering.

Hence, to prove the lemma, we will show that if $\mathcal{T} := (T, new, search, clear)$ is a non-monotone search tree of G then there is tighter search tree of G of the same width as $\mathcal{T}$.

Towards this aim, let $e := (s, t) \in E(T)$ be a non-monotone edge in $\mathcal{T}$. *Case 1.* Assume first that $|\delta(search(e))| \leq |\delta(clear(e))|$ and let $e_1, \ldots, e_r$ be the out-going edges of t. We define a new search tree $\mathcal{T}' := (T, new', search', clear')$ where $new'(v) := new(v), clear'(v) := clear(v)$ for all $v \neq t$ and $search'(f) = search(f)$ for all $f \neq e$ and

$$clear'(t) := E(G) \setminus search(e)$$
$$new'(t) := new(t) \cap search(e)$$
$$search'(e_i) := search(e_i) \cap search(e).$$

By construction, $\{clear'(t), new'(t), search'(e_1), \ldots, search'(e_r)\}$ form a partition of $E(G)$. Furthermore, for all $f := (u, v) \in E(T)$ we still have

$clear(v) \cap search(f) = \varnothing$ and therefore T' is a search tree. We have to show that it is tighter than T. Clearly, the weight of all nodes $v \neq t$ remains unchanged. Furthermore, we get

$$|guard(t)| = |\delta\big(clear(t), search(e_1), \ldots, search(e_r)\big) \cup V[new(t)]| \quad (7.1)$$
$$= |\delta(new(t), clear(t), search(e_1), \ldots, search(e_r)) \cup$$
$$\big(V[new(t)] \setminus \delta(new(t))\big)| \quad (7.2)$$
$$= |\delta(new(t), clear(t), search(e_1), \ldots, search(e_r))| \;+$$
$$|\big(V[new(t)] \setminus \delta(new(t))\big)| \quad (7.3)$$
$$\geq |new'(t), \delta(clear'(t), search'(e_1), \ldots, search'(e_r))| \;+$$
$$|\big(V[new(t)] \cap search(e) \setminus \delta(new(t)) \cap search(e)\big)| \quad (7.4)$$
$$= |\delta(clear'(t), search'(e_1), \ldots, search'(e_r)) \cup$$
$$\big(V[new'(t)] \cap search(e)\big)|$$
$$= |guard'(t)|.$$

The equality between (7.1) and (7.2) follows from the fact that $V[new(t)] \cap \delta(new(t), clear(t), search(e_1), \ldots, search(e_r)) = \delta(new(t))$. The equality of (7.2) and (7.3) then follows as the two sets are disjoint by construction. The inequality in (7.4) follows from Lemma 7.23 above.

If $|\delta(search(e))| > |\delta(clear(e))|$ then the inequality in (7.4) is strict and therefore in this case we get $w_{T'}(t) < w_T(t)$ and therefore $weight(T') < weight(T)$.

Otherwise, if $|\delta(search(e))| = |\delta(clear(e))|$ then the inequality in (7.4) may not be strict and we therefore only get that $w_{T'}(t) \leq w_T(t)$ and therefore $weight(T') \leq weight(T)$. However, in this case the edge e is now monotone, by construction, and the only edges which may now have become non-monotone are $e_1, \ldots, e_r$ whose distance from the root is larger than the distance of e from the root. Therefore, the badness of T' is less than the badness of T. This concludes the first case where $|\delta(search(e))| \leq |\delta(clear(e))|$.

Case 2. Now assume $|\delta(search(e))| > |\delta(clear(e))|$ and let $e_1, \ldots, e_r$ be the out-going edges of s other than e. We define a new search tree $T' := (T, new', search')$ where $new'(v) := new(v)$, $clear'(v) := clear(v)$ for all $v \neq t$ and $search'(f) = search(f)$ for all $f \neq e$ and

$$search'(e) := E(G) \setminus clear(t)$$
$$new'(s) := new(s) \cap clear(t)$$
$$search'(e_i) := search(e_i) \cap clear(t) \qquad \text{for all } 1 \leq i \leq r$$
$$clear'(s) := clear(s) \cap clear(t).$$

Arguing as in the previous case, we see that the weight of T' is less than the weight of T. This concludes the proof. □

We demonstrate the construction in the proof by the search tree in Figure 7.5. Let s be the root of that tree, with $new(s) := \{34, 36, 46\}$ and t be the successor of s with $new(t) := \emptyset$. Let $e := (s, t)$. Thus, $search(e) := \{12, 13, 24\}$ and $clear(t) := \{35, 36, X\}$, where $X := \{56, 57, 67\}$.

Clearly, the edge e is non-monotone as

$$search(e) \cup clear(t) := \{12, 13, 24, 35, 36, 56, 57, 67\} \subsetneq E(G).$$

For instance the edge $34 \notin search(e) \cup clear(t)$.

Now, $\delta(search(e)) := \{3, 4\} \subseteq V(G)$ and $\delta(clear(t)) := \{3, 6\}$ and therefore we are in Case 1 of the proof above. Let e_1 be the edge from t to the node labelled $\{34, 46\}$ and let e_2 be the other out-going edge from t.

We construct the new search tree which is exactly as the old one except that now

$$clear'(t) := E(G) \setminus search(e) = \{34, 35, 36, 46, 56, 57, 67\}$$
$$new'(t) := new(t) \cap search(e) := \emptyset$$
$$search'(e_1) := search(e_1) \cap search(e) := \{24\}$$
$$search'(e_2) := search(e_2) \cap search(e) := \{12, 13\}.$$

The new search tree is shown in Figure 7.6. Note that $guard'(t)$ is now

$$guard'(t) := V[new'(t)] \cup \delta(clear'(e)) \cup \delta(search'(e_1)) \cup \delta(search'(e_2))$$
$$= \emptyset \cup \{3, 4\} \cup \{2, 4\} \cup \{2, 3\}$$
$$= \{2, 3, 4\}.$$

That is, in the new search tree the cops start on the vertices $3, 4, 6$ as before but now, if the robber moves into the component $\{1, 2\}$, then they go to $\{2, 3, 4\}$ as might be expected. Continuing in this way we would gradually turn the search tree into a monotone search tree corresponding to a monotone strategy.

Further applications of sub-modularity

Sub-modularity has been used in numerous results establishing monotonicity of graph searching games. A very general application of this technique has been given by Fomin and Thilikos [2003] where it was shown that all invisible graph searching games defined by a sub-modular border function are monotone. The proof presented above has been given by Mazoit and

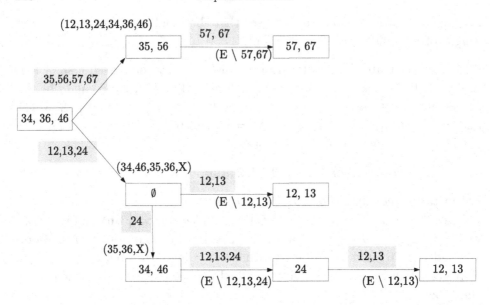

Figure 7.6 Search tree for the strategy tree in Figure 7.4

Nisse [2008]. More recently, Amini et al. [2009], Lyaudet et al. [2009] and Adler [2009] gave very abstract monotonicity proofs for games defined by sub-modular borders which apply to a wide range of games played on graphs, hypergraphs, matroids, etc. unifying many previous results.

7.4.2 Approximate monotonicity

In the previous section we have seen an important tool to establish monotonicity for certain types of games whose border function is sub-modular. However, not all games have sub-modular border functions and not all games are monotone. In some cases where games are not monotone they are at least *approximately monotone* in the following sense.

Definition 7.26   A class $\mathcal{C}$ of graph searching games is ***approximately monotone*** if there is a function $f : \mathbb{N} \to \mathbb{N}$ such that for all games $\mathcal{G} \in \mathcal{C}$ and all $k \in \mathbb{N}$, if k searchers have a winning strategy on $\mathcal{G}$ then at most $f(k)$ searchers have a monotone winning strategy on $\mathcal{G}$.

An important tool for establishing approximate monotonicity is to use *obstructions*. In this section we demonstrate this idea by showing the following theorem whose proof is derived from Johnson et al. [2001]. We will say more about obstructions in Section 7.5

Theorem 7.27 *The visible SCC Cops and Robber game on directed graphs is approximately monotone. More formally, if G is a directed graph, then for all k, if k cops can catch the robber on G then $3k + 2$ cops can catch the robber with a monotone strategy.*

The proof of this theorem relies on the concept of a *haven*, which is a representation of a winning strategy for the robber. Essentially, the proof idea is to iteratively construct a monotone winning strategy for $3k + 2$ cops, starting from some initial position. If at some point of the construction we cannot extend the monotone winning strategy then this will give us enough information for constructing a haven of order k showing that the robber can win against k cops even in the non-monotone game.

Definition 7.28 Let G be a directed graph. A *haven of order k* in G is a function $h : [V(G)]^{\leq k} \to \mathrm{Pow}(V)$ such that for all $X \in [V(G)]^{\leq k}$

1 $h(X)$ is a (non-empty) strongly connected component of $G - X$ and
2 if $Y \subseteq X$ then $h(Y) \supseteq h(X)$.

Let G be a directed graph. W.l.o.g. we assume that G is strongly connected. Otherwise, we can search the components of G one by one.

Obviously, if G has a haven of order k then the robber wins against k cops in the visible SCC game by always staying in the component $h(X)$ whenever the cops are on X. To prove the theorem it therefore suffices to show that if there is no haven of order k then at most $3k + 2$ cops have a monotone winning strategy.

We are going to describe a monotone winning strategy for $3k + 2$ cops. Throughout the proof, W will always denote the current robber space. Initially, therefore, we set $W := V(G)$.

In their first move, the cops arbitrarily choose a set Y of $2k + 1$ vertices on which they place the searchers. If for every set Z' of $\leq k$ vertices there is a strong component $C(Z)$ of $G \setminus Z$ such that $|Y \cap V(C)| \geq k + 1$, then the function h mapping any set Z' with $|Z'| \leq k$ to $C(Z')$ is a haven of order k. For, any two $C(Z')$ and $C(Z'')$ contain more than $\frac{1}{2}$ of the vertices in Y and therefore must share a vertex.

Hence, if there is no such haven, then there must be a Z' of $\leq k$ vertices such that no component C' of $G \setminus Z'$ contains more than k vertices of Y. To define the next step of the monotone winning strategy for the cops we choose a vertex $w \in W$ arbitrarily and place additional cops on $Z := Z' \cup \{w\}$. At this stage, no more than $3k + 2$ cops are on the board. Now let the robber choose his next position, that is a strong component C of $G \setminus (Y \cup Z)$ contained in W. Let C' be the strong component of $G \setminus Z$ containing C. Clearly, C is also a strong component of $G \setminus (Z \cup (V(C') \cap Y))$. So we can safely remove all cops from the board except for those on $(Z \cup (V(C') \cap Y))$. But by construction of Z, $|V(C') \cap Y| \leq k$ and therefore there are at most $k + 1 + k = 2k + 1$ cops on the board. Furthermore, $V(C) \subsetneq W$ as $Z \cap W \neq \emptyset$. Hence, the robber space has become strictly smaller. We can therefore continue in this way to define a monotone winning strategy for the cops unless at some point we have found a haven of order k. This concludes the proof of Theorem 7.27 as the existence of a haven of order k means that the robber wins against k cops.

Further examples

Similar methods as in this example can be employed in a variety of cases. For instance, for the Robber and Marshal Game on hypergraphs presented in Section 7.3.6, Adler [2004] gave examples showing that these games are non-monotone. But again, using a very similar technique as in the previous proof, Adler et al. [2005] showed that if k Marshals have a winning strategy on a hypergraph then $3k + 1$ Marshals have a monotone winning strategy.

Open problems

We close this section by stating an open problem. Consider the visible directed reachability game on a directed graph G as defined in Section 7.3.5. The question of whether this game is monotone has been open for a long time. Kreutzer and Ordyniak [2008] have exhibited examples of games where $3k - 1$ cops have a wining strategy but at least $4k - 2$ cops are needed for a monotone strategy, for all values of k. We have seen an example for the special case of $k = 2$ in Section 7.3.5 above.

Similarly, they give examples for the invisible inert directed reachability game where $6k$ cops have a winning strategy but no fewer than $7k$ cops have a monotone winning strategy, again for all values of k.

However, the problem of whether these games are at least approximately monotone has so far been left unanswered.

Open Problem 7.29 *Are the directed visible reachability and the inert invisible directed reachability game approximately monotone?*

7.4.3 Games which are strongly non-monotone

We close this section by giving an example for a class of games which is not even approximately monotone. Recall the definition of *domination games* given in Section 7.3.7. Domination games are played on undirected graphs.

The searchers and the fugitive occupy vertices but a searcher not only controls the vertex it occupies but also all of its neighbours. Again we can study the visible and the invisible variant of the game.

Kreutzer and Ordyniak [2009] showed that there is a class $\mathcal{C}$ of graphs such that for all $G \in \mathcal{C}$ 2 searchers have a winning strategy on G but for every $k \in \mathbb{N}$ there is a graph $G_k \in \mathcal{C}$ such that no fewer than k searchers are needed for a monotone winning strategy. A similar result has also been shown for the visible case.

7.5 Obstructions

So far we have mostly studied strategies for the Searcher. However, if we want to show that k searchers have no winning strategy in a graph searching game $\mathcal{G}$, then we have to exhibit a winning strategy for the fugitive. The existence of a winning strategy for the fugitive on a graph searching game played on an undirected graph G gives a certificate that the graph is structurally fairly complex. Ideally, we would like to represent winning strategies for the fugitive in a simple way so that these strategies can be characterised by the existence of certain structures in the graph. Such structures have been studied intensively in the area of graph decompositions and have come to be known as *obstructions*.

In this section we will look at two very common types of obstructions, called *havens* and *brambles*, which have been defined for numerous games. We will present these structures for the case of the visible cops and robber game played on an undirected graph.

We have already seen havens for the directed SCC game but here we will define them for the undirected case.

Definition 7.30 Let G be a graph. A **haven of order** k in G is a function $h : [V(G)]^{\leq k} \to \mathrm{Pow}(V)$ such that for all $X \in [V(G)]^{\leq k}$ $f(X)$ is a component of $G - X$ and if $Y \subseteq X$ then $h(Y) \supseteq h(X)$.

It is easily seen that if there is a haven of order k in G then the robber wins against k cops on G.

Lemma 7.31 *If h is a haven bramble of order k in a graph G then the robber wins against k cops on G and conversely if the robber has a winning strategy against k cops then there is a haven of order k in G.*

An alternative way of formalising a robber winning strategy is to define the strategy as a set of connected sub-graphs. This form of winning strategies is known as a **bramble**.

Definition 7.32 Let G be a graph and $B, B' \subseteq V(G)$. B and B' **touch** if $B \cap B' \neq \emptyset$ or there is an edge $\{u, v\} \in E(G)$ with $u \in B$ and $v \in B'$.

A **bramble** in a graph G is a set $\mathcal{B} := \{B_1, \dots, B_l\}$ of sets $B_i \subseteq V(G)$ such that

1 each B_i induces a connected sub-graph $G[B_i]$ and
2 for all i, j, B_i and B_j touch.

The **order** of $\mathcal{B}$ is

$$\min\{|X| : X \subseteq V(G) \text{ s.t. } X \cap B \neq \emptyset \text{ for all } B \in \mathcal{B}\}.$$

The **bramble width** $\operatorname{bw}(G)$ of G is the maximal order of a bramble of G.

We illustrate the definition by giving a bramble of order 3 for the graph depicted in Figure 7.1. In this graph, the set

$$\mathcal{B} := \{\{1, 2, 3\}, \quad \{7, 8, 9\}, \quad \{4, 5, 6\}\}$$

forms a bramble of order 3.

It is easily seen that the existence of a bramble of order k yields a winning strategy for the robber against k cops.

To give a more interesting example, consider the class of *grids*. A grid is a graph as indicated in Figure 7.7 depicting a 4×5-grid.

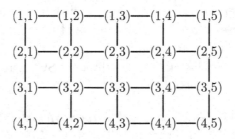

Figure 7.7 4×5-grid

More generally, an $n \times m$-grid is a graph with vertex set $\{(i, j) : 1 \leq i \leq n, 1 \leq j \leq m\}$ and edge set

$$\{(i, j), (i', j')) : |i - i'| + |j - j'| = 1\}.$$

If G is an $n \times m$-grid then its i-th row is defined as the vertices $\{(i, j) : 1 \leq j \leq m\}$ and its j-th column as $\{(i, j) : 1 \leq i \leq n\}$. A *cross* in a grid is the union of one row and one column. For any $n \times n$-grid we can define a bramble

B_n consisting of all crosses $\{(s, j) : 1 \leq j < n\} \cup \{(i, t) : 1 \leq i < n\}$, where $1 \leq s, t < n$, of the sub-grid induced by the vertices $\{(i, j) : 1 \leq i, j \leq n - 1\}$ together with the sets $B := \{(n, j) : 1 \leq j \leq n\}$ and $R := \{(i, n) : 1 \leq i < n\}$ containing the bottom-most row and the right-most column except the last vertex of that column.

It is readily verified that this is a bramble. Clearly any pair of crosses shares a vertex and therefore touches. On the other hand, every cross touches the bottom row B and also the rightmost column R. Finally, B and L touch also.

The order of B_n is $n + 1$. For, to cover every element of B_n we need two vertices to cover B and R, and they are disjoint and also disjoint from the other elements in B_n. But to cover the crosses we need at least $n - 1$ vertices as otherwise there would be a row and a column in the sub-grid of G_n without the bottom-row and right-most column from which no vertex would have been chosen. But then the corresponding cross would not be covered.

Grids therefore provide examples of graphs with very high bramble width. We will show now that this also implies that the number of cops needed to search the graph is very high. The following is the easy direction of the theorem below.

Lemma 7.33 *If B is a bramble of order $k + 1$ in a graph G then the robber wins against k cops on G.*

Proof We describe a winning strategy for the robber against k cops. Let X be the initial position of the cops. As the order of B is $k + 1$, there is at least one set $B \in B$ not containing any cops and the robber can choose any vertex from this set. Now, suppose that after some steps, the cops are on X and the robber is on a vertex in a set $B \in B$ not containing any cop. Now suppose the cops go from X to X'. If X' does not contain a vertex from B then the robber does not move. Otherwise, there is a $B' \in B$ not containing any vertex from X' and while the cops move from X to X', the robber can go from his current position in B to a new position in B' as B and B' are connected and touch. This defines a winning strategy for the robber. □

The converse of the previous result is also true but much more complicated to show.

Theorem 7.34 (Seymour and Thomas [1993]) *Let G be a graph and $k \geq 0$ be an integer. G contains a bramble of order $\geq k$ if, and only if, no fewer than k cops have a winning strategy in the visible Cops and Robber game on G if, and only if, no fewer than k cops have a monotone winning strategy in the visible Cops and Robber game on G.*

We refrain from giving the proof here and refer to Seymour and Thomas [1993] (where brambles were called screens) or the excellent survey by Reed [1997].

The previous result was stated in terms of tree-width rather than winning strategies for the cops and is often referred to as the **tree-width duality theorem**. A very general way of establishing duality theorems of this form was studied by Amini et al. [2009], Adler [2009] and Lyaudet et al. [2009] and by Fomin and Thilikos [2003] for the case of an invisible robber.

7.6 An application to graph-decompositions

As outlined in the introduction, graph searching games have found various applications in a number of areas in computer science. Among those, their application in structural graph theory has been a particularly driving force behind developments in graph searching. We demonstrate this by deriving a close connection between undirected cops and robber games and a graph structural concept called *tree-width*.

The concept of *tree-width* was developed by Robertson and Seymour [1982 –] as part of their celebrated graph minor project, even though concepts such as *partial k-trees*, which subsequently have been shown to be equivalent to tree-width, were known before.

Definition 7.35 Let G be a graph. A **tree-decomposition** of G is a pair $\mathcal{T} := (T, (B_t)_{t \in V(T)})$ where T is a tree and $B_t \subseteq V(G)$ for all $t \in V(T)$ such that

1 for all $v \in V(G)$ the set $\{t : v \in B_t\}$ induces a non-empty sub-tree of T and
2 for every edge $e := \{u, v\} \in E(G)$ there is a $t \in V(T)$ such that $\{u, v\} \subseteq B_t$.

The **width** $w(\mathcal{T})$ of $\mathcal{T}$ is

$$w(\mathcal{T}) := \max\{|B_t| : t \in V(T)\} - 1.$$

The **tree-width** of G is the minimal width of a tree-decomposition of G.

We will frequently use the following notation: if $S \subseteq T$ is a sub-tree of T then $B(S) := \{v : v \in B_l \text{ for some } l \in V(S)\}$.

From a graph structural point of view, the tree-width of a graph measures the similarity of a graph to being a tree. However, the concept also has immense algorithmic applications as from an algorithmic point of view a tree-decomposition yields a recursive decomposition of a graph into small sub-graphs and this allows us to use the same dynamic programming approaches to solve problems on graphs of small tree-width that can be employed on trees. Determining the tree-width of a graph is NP-complete as shown by Arnborg et al. [1987], but there is an algorithm, due to Bodlaender [1996], which, given a graph G computes an optimal tree-decomposition in time $\mathcal{O}(2^{p(\mathrm{tw}(G))} \cdot |G|)$, for some polynomial p. Combining this with dynamic programming yields a powerful tool to solve NP-hard problems on graph classes of small tree-width. See Bodlaender [1997, 1998, 2005] for surveys including a wide range of algorithmic examples.

To help gain some intuition about tree-decompositions we establish some simple properties and a normal form for tree-decompositions. We first agree on the following notation. From now on we will consider the tree T of a tree-decomposition to be a rooted tree, where the root can be chosen arbitrarily. If T is a rooted tree and $t \in V(T)$ then T_t is the sub-tree *rooted at t*, i.e., the sub-tree containing all vertices s such that t lies on the path from the root of T to s.

Lemma 7.36 *If G has a tree-decomposition of width k then it has a tree-decomposition $(T, (B_t)_{t \in V(T)})$ of width k so that if $\{s, t\} \in E(T)$ then $B_s \not\subseteq B_t$ and $B_t \not\subseteq B_s$.*

Proof Let $\mathcal{T} := (T, (B_t)_{t \in V(T)})$ be a tree-decomposition such that $B_s \subseteq B_t$ for some edge $\{s, t\} \in E(T)$. Then we can remove s from T and make all neighbours of s other than t neighbours of t. Repeating in this way we generate a tree-decomposition of the same width with the desired property. $\qquad \Box$

Definition 7.37 Let G be a graph. A **separation** of G is a triple (A, S, B) of non-empty sets such that $A \cup S \cup B = V(G)$ and there is no path in $G \setminus S$ from a vertex in A to a vertex in B.

Lemma 7.38 *Let $\mathcal{T} := (T, (B_t)_{t \in V(T)})$ be a tree-decomposition of a graph G and let $e := \{s, t\} \in E(T)$. Let T_s be the sub-tree of $T - e$ containing s and let T_t be the sub-tree of $T - e$ containing t. Finally, let $S := B_s \cap B_t$. Then $(B(T_t) \setminus S, S, B(T_s) \setminus S)$ is a separation in G.*

Exercise. Prove this lemma.

Definition 7.39 A tree-decomposition $\mathcal{T} := (T, (B_t)_{t \in V(T)})$ of a graph G is in *normal form* if whenever $t \in V(T)$ is a node and C is a component of $G \setminus B_t$ then there is exactly one successor t_C of t in T such that $V(C) = \bigcup_{s \in V(T_t)} B_s$.

Lemma 7.40 *If G has a tree-decomposition of width k then it also has a tree-decomposition of width k in normal form.*

Proof Let $\mathcal{T} := (T, (B_t)_{t \in V(T)})$ be a tree-decomposition of G. Let $t \in V(T)$. By Lemma 7.38, for every component C of $G \setminus B_t$ there is exactly one neighbour s of t such that $V(C) \subseteq B(T_s)$, where T_s is the component of $T - t$ containing s. So suppose that there are two components C, C' such that $C \cup C' \subseteq B(T_s)$ for some neighbour s of t. Let $\mathcal{T}'$ be the tree-decomposition obtained from $\mathcal{T}$ as follows. Take an isomorphic copy of T_s rooted at a vertex s' and add this as an additional neighbour of t. In the next step we replace every $B(l)$ by $B(l) \cap V(C)$ if $l \in V(T_s)$ and by $B(l) \setminus V(C)$ if $l \in V(T_{s'})$. We proceed in this way till we reach a tree-decomposition in normal form of the same width. $\qquad\square$

The presence of a tree-decomposition of small width in a graph G is a witness that the graph has a rather simple structure and that its tree-width is small. But what would a certificate for large tree-width look like? If the tree-width of a graph is very large than there should be some structure in it that causes this high tree-width. Such structural reasons for width parameters to be high are usually referred to as *obstructions*. It turns out that using a graph searching game connection of tree-width, such obstructions can easily be identified as we can use the formalisations of winning strategies for the robber given in Section 7.5 above.

We aim next at establishing a game characterisation of tree-width in terms of the visible Cops and Robber game. It is not difficult to see that strategy trees for monotone winning strategies correspond to tree-decompositions.

Lemma 7.41 *Let G be an undirected graph of tree-width at most $k + 1$. Then k cops have a monotone winning strategy on G in the visible cops and robber game. Conversely, if $k + 1$ cops have a monotone winning strategy in the visible cops and robber game on G then the tree-width of G is at most k.*

Proof Assume first that $k + 1$ cops have a monotone winning strategy on G and let $\mathcal{T} := (T, cops, robber)$ be a strategy tree witnessing this as defined in Definition 7.14. As $\mathcal{T}$ represents a monotone strategy, we can w.l.o.g. assume that for each node $t \in V(T)$, $cops(t)$ only contains vertices that can be reached by the robber. Formally, if $t \in V(T)$ and $t_1, \ldots, t_r$ are its out-neighbours, then if $v \in cops(t)$ there must exist an edge $\{v, u\} \in E(G)$ with $u \in robber((t, t_i))$ for at least one i. Clearly, it is never necessary to put a cop on a vertex that has no neighbour in the robber space as these cops cannot be reached by the robber. It is a simple exercise to show that under this assumption $(T, (cops(t))_{t \in V(T)})$ is a tree-decomposition of G.

Towards the converse, let $\mathcal{T} := (T, (B_t)_{t \in V(T)})$ be a tree-decomposition of G of width at most k. By Lemma 7.40, we can assume that $\mathcal{T}$ is in normal form. But then it is easily seen that $(T, cops, robber)$ with $cops(t) := B_t$ and $robber((t, s)) := B(T_s) \setminus B_t$ is a monotone strategy tree, where T_s is the component of $T - (t, s)$ containing s. $\qquad \square$

The previous lemma together with the monotonicity of the visible Cops and Robber game proved in Theorems 7.24 and 7.34 imply the following corollary. Note that it is the monotonicity of the game that brings the different concepts – winning strategies, tree-decompositions, obstructions – together to form a uniform characterisation of tree-width and search numbers. This is one of the reasons why monotonicity has been studied so intensively especially in structural graph theory.

Corollary 7.42 *For all graphs G: $\mathrm{tw}(G) = \mathrm{bw}(G) = \mathrm{cw}(G) - 1$, where $\mathrm{bw}(G)$ denotes the bramble width and $\mathrm{cw}(G)$ the minimal number of cops required to win the visible cops and robber game.*

A similar characterisation can be given for the invisible Cops and Robber Game. A **path-decomposition** of a graph G is a tree-decomposition $(T, (B_t)_{t \in V(T)})$ of G where T is a simple path. The **path-width** of a graph is the minimal width of a path-decomposition of G. Similarly as above we can show that the path-width $\mathrm{pw}(G)$ of a graph is just one less than the minimal number of cops required to catch an invisible robber (with a monotone strategy) on G. The obstructions for path-width corresponding to brambles are called **blockages**. See Bienstock et al. [1991] for details.

7.7 Complexity of graph searching

In this section we study the complexity of computing the least number of searchers required to win a given graph searching game. As usual we will view this as a decision problem asking for a given game and a number k whether k searchers can catch a fugitive or whether they can even do so with a monotone strategy.

We have already stated a number of complexity results in Section 7.3. The aim of this section is to establish much more general results valid for almost all graph searching games within our framework.

Note that all variations of graph searching games described in this chapter – as games played on undirected, directed or hypergraphs, inert variants, etc. – can all be described by suitably defining the relation $\mathcal{S}$ and the function $\mathcal{F}$ in a graph searching game $(V, \mathcal{S}, \mathcal{F}, c)$. The only exception is the distinction between visible and invisible fugitives, which cannot be defined in the description of the game. We can therefore speak about the class $\mathcal{C}$ of the Cops and Robber games played on undirected graphs but have to say explicitly whether we mean the visible or invisible variant.

We will study the complexity questions both within classical complexity as well as parameterised complexity. But before that, we need to agree on the size of a graph searching game. For this we need to following restriction on games.

Definition 7.43 A class $\mathcal{C}$ of graph searching games is *concise* if

1 there is a polynomial $p(n)$ such that for every $\mathcal{G} := (V, \mathcal{S}, \mathcal{F}, c) \in \mathcal{C}$ and all $X \in \text{Pow}(V)$, $c(X) \leq p(|X|)$ and

2 given $X, X' \subseteq V$ the relation $\mathcal{S}(X, X')$ can be decided in polynomial time and

3 given $X, X', R \subseteq V$ and $v \in V$ we can decide in polynomial time whether $v \in \mathcal{F}(X, R, X')$.

This condition rules out degenerate cases where, e.g., all Searcher positions have complexity 1. But it also disallows games where deciding whether a move is possible for any of the players is already computationally very complex. All graph searching games studied in this chapter are concise.

Definition 7.44 The *size* $|\mathcal{G}|$ of a graph searching game $\mathcal{G} := (V, \mathcal{S}, \mathcal{F}, c)$ is defined as $|V|$.

This definition is in line with the intuitive definition of size for, e.g., the visible cops and robber game where the input would only be the graph, and therefore the size would be the order or the size of the graph, whereas the rules of the game are given implicitly.

7.7.1 Classical complexity bounds for graph searching games

In this section we present some general complexity bounds for graph searching games in the framework of classical complexity.

Definition 7.45 Let $\mathcal{C}$ be a concise class of graph searching games. The problem VIS-SEARCH WIDTH($\mathcal{C}$) is defined as

VIS SEARCH WIDTH($\mathcal{C}$)	
Input:	$\mathcal{G} \in \mathcal{C}$ and $k \in \mathbb{N}$
Problem:	Is there a winning strategy for k searchers on $\mathcal{G}$ against a visible fugitive?

We define MON VIS SEARCH WIDTH($\mathcal{C}$) as the problem to decide whether k searchers have a monotone winning strategy on $\mathcal{G}$.

The corresponding problems INVIS SEARCH WIDTH($\mathcal{C}$) and MON INVIS SEARCH WIDTH($\mathcal{C}$) for the invisible variant are defined analogously.

To simplify presentation we will refer to this problem simply as 'the visible graph searching game on $\mathcal{C}$' and likewise for the invisible variant.

Games with a visible fugitive

We first consider the case of arbitrary, non-monotone strategies.

Lemma 7.46 *Let $\mathcal{C}$ be a class of graph searching games.*

1 The visible graph searching game on $\mathcal{C}$ can be solved in exponential time.
2 The k-searcher visible graph searching game on $\mathcal{C}$ can be solved in polynomial time.
3 There are examples of visible graph searching games which are EXPTIME-complete.

Proof Given $\mathcal{G} \in \mathcal{C}$ construct the game graph $\mathfrak{G}$ of the corresponding reachability game as defined in Section 7.2.6 above. As $\mathcal{C}$ is concise, this graph is of exponential size and can be constructed in exponential time. We can then use Lemma 7.10 to decide whether or not the Searcher has a winning strategy.

If the complexity is restricted to some fixed k, then the game graph is of polynomial size and therefore the game can be decided in polynomial time.

An example of a visible graph searching game which is complete for EXPTIME has been given by Goldstein and Reingold [1995], see Theorem 7.12. □

If we are only interested in the existence of monotone strategies, then we can prove slightly better complexity bounds.

Lemma 7.47 *Let $\mathcal{C}$ be a concise class of graph searching games.*

1 The Searcher-monotone visible graph searching game on $\mathcal{C}$ can be solved in polynomial space.
2 The Searcher-monotone k-searcher visible graph searching game on $\mathcal{C}$ can be solved in polynomial time.

Proof In a Searcher-monotone strategy the Searcher can only make at most polynomially many steps as he is never allowed to return to a vertex once vacated. As $\mathcal{C}$ is concise, this means that a complete play can be kept in polynomial space which immediately implies the result.

If, in addition, the number of searchers is restricted to a fixed k, we can use a straightforward alternating logarithmic space algorithm for it.   □

For Fugitive-monotone strategies we can obtain a similar result if the searchers can move freely. In any Fugitive-monotone game the Fugitive space can only decrease a linear number of times. However, a priori we have no guarantee that in between two positions where the Fugitive space does decrease, the searchers only need to make a linear number of steps. In particular, in game variants where the cops can only move along an edge or where their movement is restricted similar to the entanglement game, there might be variants where they need a large number of steps before the robber space shrinks again.

Games with an invisible fugitive

Lemma 7.48   *Let $\mathcal{C}$ be a concise class of graph searching games.*

1. *The invisible graph searching game on $\mathcal{C}$ can be solved in polynomial space.*
2. *The k-searcher invisible graph searching game on $\mathcal{C}$ can be solved in polynomial space.*
3. *There are examples of games which are PSPACE-hard even in the case where k is fixed.*

Proof   Recall that a winning strategy for the Searcher in an invisible graph searching game can be described by the sequence $X_0, \ldots, X_k$ of searcher positions. As $\mathcal{C}$ is concise, any such position only consumes polynomial space. We can therefore guess the individual moves of the searcher reusing space as soon as a move has been made. In this way we only need to store at most two Searcher positions and the fugitive space, which can all be done in polynomial space.

Clearly, Part 1 implies Part 2. Kreutzer and Ordyniak [2009] show that the invisible domination game is PSPACE-complete even for two cops, which shows Part 3.   □

Finally, we show that the complexity drops if we only consider monotone strategies in invisible graph searching games.

Lemma 7.49   *Let $\mathcal{C}$ be a concise class of graph searching games.*

1. *The Searcher-monotone invisible graph searching game on $\mathcal{C}$ can be solved in NP.*
2. *The Searcher-monotone k-searcher visible graph searching game on $\mathcal{C}$ can be solved in NP.*

3 There are examples of invisible graph searching games which are NP-complete.

Proof In a Searcher-monotone strategy the cop-player can only make at most polynomially many steps as he is never allowed to return to a vertex once vacated. As $\mathcal{C}$ is concise, this means that a complete strategy for the Searcher can be kept in polynomial space and therefore we can simply guess a strategy and then check that it is a winning strategy by playing it. This, clearly, can be done in polynomial time.

Megiddo et al. [1988] show that the invisible graph searching game is NP-complete and as this game is monotone Part 3 follows. □

The following table summarises the general results we can obtain.

variant		*visible*	*invisible*
k free	non-monotone	EXPTIME	PSPACE
	monotone	PSPACE	NP
k-Searcher	non-monotone	PTIME	PSPACE
	monotone	PTIME	NP

7.7.2 Parametrised complexity of graph searching

Due to their close connection to graph decompositions, graph searching games have been studied intensively with respect to parametrised complexity. We refer to Downey and Fellows [1998] and Flum and Grohe [2006] for an introduction to parameterised complexity.

Definition 7.50 Let $\mathcal{C}$ be a concise class of graph searching games. The problem p-VIS SEARCH WIDTH($\mathcal{C}$) is defined as

p-VIS SEARCH WIDTH($\mathcal{C}$)
Input: $\mathcal{G} \in \mathcal{C}$ and $k \in \mathbb{N}$
Parameter: k
Problem: Is there a winning strategy for k searchers on $\mathcal{G}$ in the visible fugitive game?

p-VIS SEARCH WIDTH($\mathcal{C}$) is *fixed-parameter tractable* (fpt) if there is a computable function $f : \mathbb{N} \to \mathbb{N}$, a polynomial $p(n)$ and an algorithm deciding the problem in time $f(k) \cdot p(|\mathcal{G}|)$.

The problem is in the complexity class **XP** if there is a computable function $f : \mathbb{N} \to \mathbb{N}$ and an algorithm deciding the problem in time $|\mathcal{G}|^{f(k)}$.

Analogously we define p-MON VIS SEARCH WIDTH($\mathcal{C}$) as the problem to decide whether k searchers have a monotone winning strategy on $\mathcal{G}$ and the corresponding invisible fugitive variants.

The correspondence between visible graph searching games and reachability games immediately implies the following theorem.

Theorem 7.51 *Let $\mathcal{C}$ be a concise class of abstract graph searching games. Then the visible graph searching game on $\mathcal{C}$ is in XP.*

This, however, fails for the case of invisible graph searching games. For instance, Kreutzer and Ordyniak [2009] show that deciding whether two searchers have a winning strategy in the invisible domination game is PSPACE-complete and therefore the problem cannot be in XP unless PSPACE = PTIME.

Much better results can be obtained for the visible and invisible Cops and Robber game on undirected graphs. Bodlaender [1996] presented a linear-time parametrised algorithm for deciding the tree-width and the path-width of a graph. As we have seen above, these parameters correspond to the visible and invisible Cops and Robber Game on undirected graphs showing that the corresponding decision problems are fixed-parameter tractable.

The corresponding complexity questions for directed reachability games, on the other hand, are wide open.

7.8 Conclusion

The main objective of this chapter was to provide an introduction to the area of graph searching games and the main techniques used in this context. Graph searching has developed into a huge and very diverse area with many problems still left to be solved. Besides specific open problems such as the approximate monotonicity of directed reachability games in the visible and invisible inert variant, there is the general problem of finding unifying proofs for the various monotonicity and complexity results developed in the literature. Another active trend in graph searching is to extend the framework beyond graphs or hypergraphs to more general or abstract structures such as matroids.

Acknowledgement: I would like to thank Isolde Adler for carefully proof reading the manuscript.

References

I. Adler. Marshals, monotone marshals, and hypertree-width. *Journal of Graph Theory*, 47(4):275–296, 2004.

I. Adler. Directed tree-width examples. *J. Comb. Theory, Ser. B*, 97(5):718–725, 2007.

I. Adler. Games for width parameters and monotonicity. *available from arXiv.org as*, abs/0906.3857, 2009.

I. Adler, G. Gottlob, and M. Grohe. Hypertree-width and related hypergraph invariants. In *Proceedings of the 3rd European Conference on Combinatorics, Graph Theory and Applications (EUROCOMB'05)*, DMTCS Proceedings Series, pages 5–10, 2005.

B. Alspach. Searching and sweeping graphs: a brief survey. *Matematiche (Catania)*, 59:5–37, 2006.

O. Amini, F. Mazoit, N. Nisse, and S. Thomassé. Submodular partition functions. *Discrete Mathematics*, 309(20):6000–6008, 2009.

S. Arnborg, D. Corneil, and A. Proskurowski. Complexity of finding embeddings in a *k*-tree. *SIAM Journal on Algebraic Discrete Methods*, 8:277–284, 1987.

J. Barát. Directed path-width and monotonicity in digraph searching. *Graphs and Combinatorics*, 22(2):161–172, 2006.

D. Berwanger and E. Grädel. Entanglement – a measure for the complexity of directed graphs with applications to logic and games. In *LPAR*, pages 209–223, 2004.

D. Berwanger, A. Dawar, P. Hunter, and S. Kreutzer. Dag-width and parity games. In *Symp. on Theoretical Aspects of Computer Science (STACS)*, 2006.

D. Bienstock and P. Seymour. Monotonicity in graph searching. *Journal of Algorithms*, 12(2):239–245, 1991.

D. Bienstock, N. Robertson, P. D. Seymour, and R. Thomas. Quickly excluding a forest. *J. Comb. Theory, Ser. B*, 52(2):274–283, 1991.

H. Bodlaender. A linear-time algorithm for finding tree-decompositions of small tree-width. *SIAM Journal on Computing*, 25:1305–1317, 1996.

H. Bodlaender. A partial k-aboretum of graphs with bounded tree-width. *Theoretical Computer Science*, 209:1–45, 1998.

H. L. Bodlaender. Discovering treewidth. In *SOFSEM*, pages 1–16, 2005.

H. L. Bodlaender. Treewidth: Algorithmic techniques and results. In *Proc. of Mathematical Foundations of Computer Science (MFCS)*, volume 1295 of *Lecture Notes in Computer Science*, pages 19–36, 1997.

N. Dendris, L. Kirousis, and D. Thilikos. Fugitive search games on graphs and related parameters. *Theoretical Computer Science*, 172(1–2):233–254, 1997.

R. Diestel. *Graph Theory*. Springer-Verlag, 3rd edition, 2005.

R. Downey and M. Fellows. *Parameterized Complexity*. Springer, Berlin, 1998.

J. Flum and M. Grohe. *Parameterized Complexity Theory*. Springer, Berlin, 2006.

F. Fomin and D. Thilikos. On the monotonicity of games generated by symmetric submodular functions. *Discrete Applied Mathematics*, 131(2):323–335, 2003.

F. Fomin, D. Kratsch, and H. Müller. On the domination search number. *Discrete Applied Mathematics*, 127(3):565–580, 2003.

F. V. Fomin and D. M. Thilikos. An annotated bibliography on guaranteed graph searching. *Theoretical Computer Science*, 399(3):236–245, 2008.

M. K. Franklin, Z. Galil, and M. Yung. Eavesdropping games: a graph-theoretic approach to privacy in distributed systems. *J. ACM*, 47(2):225–243, 2000.

A. S. Goldstein and E. M. Reingold. The complexity of pursuit on a graph. *Theor. Comput. Sci.*, 143(1):93–112, 1995.

P. Golovach. Equivalence of two formalizations of a search problem on a graph. *Vestnik Leningrad Univ. Math.*, 22(1):13–19, 1989.

G. Gottlob, N. Leone, and F. Scarcello. Robbers, marshals, and guards: game theoretic and logical characterizations of hypertree width. *Journal of Computer and Systems Science*, 66(4):775–808, 2003.

E. Grädel, W. Thomas, and T. Wilke, editors. *Automata, Logics, and Infinite Games*, volume 2500 of *Lecture Notes in Computer Science*. Springer, 2002.

L. J. Guibas, J.-C. Latombe, S. M. Lavalle, D. Lin, and R. Motwani. A visibility-based pursuit-evasion problem. *International Journal of Computational Geometry and Applications*, 9:471–494, 1996.

P. Hunter. *Complexity and Infinite Games on Finite Graphs*. PhD thesis, Computer Laboratory, University of Cambridge, 2007.

P. Hunter and S. Kreutzer. Digraph measures: Kelly decompositions, games, and ordering. *Theoretical Computer Science (TCS)*, 399(3), 2008.

T. Johnson, N. Robertson, P. D. Seymour, and R. Thomas. Directed tree-width. *J. Comb. Theory, Ser. B*, 82(1):138–154, 2001.

L. M. Kirousis and C. H. Papadimitriou. Searching and pebbling. *Theoretical Computer Science*, 47(3):205–218, 1986.

S. Kreutzer and S. Ordyniak. Digraph decompositions and monotonocity in digraph searching). In *34th International Workshop on Graph-Theoretic Concepts in Computer Science (WG)*, 2008.

S. Kreutzer and S. Ordyniak. Distance-d-domination games. In *34th International Workshop on Graph-Theoretic Concepts in Computer Science (WG)*, 2009.

A. S. LaPaugh. Recontamination does not help to search a graph. *Journal of the ACM*, 40:224–245, 1993.

L. Lyaudet, F. Mazoit, and S. Thomassé. Partitions versus sets : a case of duality. *available at arXiv.org*, abs/0903.2100, 2009.

F. Mazoit and N. Nisse. Monotonicity of non-deterministic graph searching. *Theor. Comput. Sci.*, 399(3):169–178, 2008.

N. Megiddo, S. L. Hakimi, M. R. Garey, D. S. Johnson, and C. H. Papadimitriou. The complexity of searching a graph. *J. ACM*, 35(1):18–44, 1988.

R. Nowakowski and P. Winkler. Vertex-to-vertex pursuit in a graph. *Discrete Mathematics*, 43:235–239, 1983.

S. Ordyniak. *Complexity and Monotonicity in Graph Searching*. PhD thesis, Oxford University Computing Laboratory, 2009.

T. Parsons. Pursuit-evasion in a graph. *Theory and Applications of Graphs, Lecture Notes in Mathematics*, 642:426–441, 1978.

B. Reed. Tree width and tangles: A new connectivity measure and some applications. In R. Bailey, editor, *Surveys in Combinatorics*, pages 87–162. Cambridge University Press, 1997.

D. Richerby and D. M. Thilikos. Searching for a visible, lazy fugitive. In *Workshop on Graph-Theoretical Methods in Computer Science*, pages 348–359, 2008.

N. Robertson and P. Seymour. Graph minors I – XXIII, 1982 –. Appearing in Journal of Combinatorial Theory, Series B since 1982.

P. D. Seymour and R. Thomas. Graph searching and a min-max theorem for tree-width. *Journal of Combinatorial Theory, Series B*, 58(1):22–33, 1993.

Appendix Notation

Our notation for graphs follows Diestel [2005] and we refer to this book for more information about graphs. This book also contains an excellent introduction to structural graph theory and the theory of tree-width or graph decompositions in general.

If V is a set and $k \in \mathbb{N}$ we denote by $[V]^{\leq k}$ the set of all subsets of V of cardinality at most k. We write $\mathrm{Pow}(V)$ for the set of all subsets of V.

All structures and graphs in this section are finite. If G is a graph we denote its vertex set by $V(G)$ and its edge set by $E(G)$. The **size** of a graph is the number of edges in G and its **order** is the number of vertices.

If $e := \{u, v\} \in E(G)$ then we call u and v **adjacent** and u and e **incident**.

H is a **sub-graph** of G, denoted $H \subseteq G$, if $V(H) \subseteq V(G)$ and $E(H) \subseteq E(G)$. If G is a graph and $X \subseteq V(G)$ we write $G[X]$ for the sub-graph of G **induced** by X, i.e., the graph (X, E') where $E' := \{\{u, v\} \in E(G) : u, v \in X\}$. We write $G \setminus X$ for the graph $G[V(G) \setminus X]$. If $e \in E(G)$ is a single edge we write $G - e$ for the graph obtained from G by deleting the edge e and analogously we write $G - v$, for some $v \in V(G)$, for the graph obtained from G by deleting v and all incident edges.

The **neighbourhood** $N_G(v)$ of a vertex $v \in V(G)$ in an undirected graph G is defined as $N_G(v) := \{u \in V(G) : \{u, v\} \in E(G)\}$.

A graph G is **connected** if G is non-empty and between any two $u, v \in V(G)$ there exists a path in G linking u and v. A **connected component** of a graph G is a maximal connected sub-graph of G.

A directed graph G is **strongly connected** if it is non-empty and between any two $u, v \in V(G)$ there is a directed path from u to v. A **strongly connected component**, or just a **component**, of G is a maximal strongly connected sub-graph of G.

A **clique** is an undirected graph G such that $\{u, v\} \in E(G)$ for all $u, v \in V(G)$, $u \neq v$.

A **tree** is a connected acyclic undirected graph. A **directed tree** is a tree T such that there is one vertex $r \in V(T)$, the **root** of T, and every edge of T is oriented away from r.

Finally, a **hypergraph** is a pair $H := (V, E)$ where $E \subseteq \mathrm{Pow}(V)$ is a set of **hyperedges**, where each hyperedge is a set of vertices. We write $V(H)$ and $E(H)$ for the set of vertices and hyperedges of H.

8

Beyond Nash Equilibrium: Solution Concepts for the 21st Century

Joseph Y. Halpern

Cornell University, Ithaca, NY

Abstract

Nash equilibrium is the most commonly-used notion of equilibrium in game theory. However, it suffers from numerous problems. Some are well known in the game theory community; for example, the Nash equilibrium of the repeated prisoner's dilemma is neither normatively nor descriptively reasonable. However, new problems arise when considering Nash equilibrium from a computer science perspective: for example, Nash equilibrium is not robust (it does not tolerate 'faulty' or 'unexpected' behaviour), it does not deal with coalitions, it does not take computation cost into account, and it does not deal with cases where players are not aware of all aspects of the game. Solution concepts that try to address these shortcomings of Nash equilibrium are discussed.

8.1 Introduction

Nash equilibrium is the most commonly-used notion of equilibrium in game theory. Intuitively, a Nash equilibrium is a ***strategy profile*** (a collection of strategies, one for each player in the game) such that no player can do better by deviating. The intuition behind Nash equilibrium is that it represents a possible steady state of play. It is a fixed-point where each player holds correct beliefs about what other players are doing, and plays a best response to those beliefs. Part of what makes Nash equilibrium so attractive is that in games where each player has only finitely many possible deterministic strategies, and we allow mixed (i.e., randomised) strategies, there is guaranteed to be a Nash equilibrium [Nash, 1950a] (this was, in fact, the key result of Nash's thesis).

For quite a few games, thinking in terms of Nash equilibrium gives insight into what people do (there is a reason that game theory is taught in business schools!). However, as is well known, Nash equilibrium suffers from numerous problems. For example, the Nash equilibrium in games such as the repeated prisoner's dilemma is to always defect (see Section 8.3 for more discussion of the repeated prisoner's dilemma). It is hard to make a case that rational players 'should' play the Nash equilibrium in this game when 'irrational' players who cooperate for a while do much better! Moreover, in a game that is only played once, why should a Nash equilibrium arise when there are multiple Nash equilibria? Players have no way of knowing which one will be played. And even in games where there is a unique Nash equilibrium (like the repeated prisoner's dilemma), how do players obtain correct beliefs about what other players are doing if the game is played only once? (See [Kreps, 1990] for a discussion of some of these problems.)

Not surprisingly, there has been a great deal of work in the economics community on developing alternative solution concepts. Various alternatives to and refinements of Nash equilibrium have been introduced, including, among many others, *rationalizability, sequential equilibrium, (trembling hand) perfect equilibrium, proper equilibrium,* and *iterated deletion of weakly dominated strategies.* (These notions are discussed in standard game theory texts, such as [Fudenberg and Tirole, 1991] and [Osborne and Rubinstein, 1994].) Despite some successes, none of these alternative solution concepts address the following three problems with Nash equilibrium, all inspired by computer science concerns.

- Although both computer science and distributed computing are concerned with multiple agents interacting, the focus in the game theory literature has been on the strategic concerns of agents – rational players choosing strategies that are best responses to strategies chosen by the other player; the focus in distributed computing has been on problems such as fault tolerance and asynchrony, leading to, for example work on Byzantine agreement [Fischer et al., 1985, Pease et al., 1980]. Nash equilibrium does not deal with 'faulty' or 'unexpected' behaviour, nor does it deal with colluding agents. In large games, we should expect both.

- Nash equilibrium does not take computational concerns into account. We need solution concepts that can deal with resource-bounded players, concerns that are at the heart of cryptography.

- Nash equilibrium presumes that players have common knowledge of the structure of the game, including all the possible moves that can be made in every situation and all the players in the game. This is not always reasonable in, for example, the large auctions played over the internet.

• Nash equilibrium presumes that players know what other players are doing (and are making a best response to it). But how do they gain this knowledge in a one-shot game, particularly if there are multiple equilibria?

In the following sections, I discuss each of these issues in more detail, and sketch solution concepts that can deal with them, with pointers to the relevant literature.

8.2 Robust and resilient equilibrium

Nash equilibrium tolerates deviations by one player. It is perfectly consistent with Nash equilibrium that two players could do much better by deviating in a coordinated way. For example, consider a game with $n > 1$ players where players must play either 0 or 1. If everyone plays 0, everyone gets a payoff of 1; if exactly two players play 1 and the rest play 0, then the two who play 1 get a payoff of 2, and the rest get 0; otherwise, everyone gets 0. Clearly everyone playing 0 is a Nash equilibrium, but any pair of players can do better by deviating and playing 1.

Say that a Nash equilibrium is *k-resilient* if it tolerates deviations by coalitions of up to k players. The notion of resilience is an old one in the game theory literature, going back to Aumann [1959]. Various extensions of Nash equilibrium have been proposed in the game theory literature to deal with coalitions [Bernheim et al., 1989, Moreno and Wooders, 1996]. However, these notions do not deal with players who act in unexpected ways.

There can be many reasons that players act in unexpected ways. One, of course, is that they are indeed irrational. However, often seemingly irrational behaviour can be explained by players having unexpected utilities. For example, in a peer-to-peer network like Kazaa or Gnutella, it would seem that no rational agent should share files. Whether or not you can get a file depends only on whether other people share files. Moreover, there are disincentives for sharing (the possibility of lawsuits, use of bandwidth, etc.). Nevertheless, people do share files. However, studies of the Gnutella network have shown that almost 70 percent of users share no files and nearly 50 percent of responses are from the top 1 percent of sharing hosts [Adar and Huberman, 2000]. Is the behaviour of the sharing hosts irrational? It is if we assume appropriate utilities. But perhaps sharing hosts get a big kick out of being the ones that provide everyone else with the music they play. Is that so irrational? In other cases, seemingly irrational behaviour can be explained by faulty computers or a faulty network (this, of course, is the concern that work on Byzantine agreement is trying to address), or a lack of understanding of the game.

To give just one example of a stylised game where this issue might be relevant, consider a group of n bargaining agents. If they all stay and bargain, then all get 2. However, if any agent leaves the bargaining table, those who leave get 1, while those who stay get 0. Clearly everyone staying at the bargaining table is a k-resilient Nash equilibrium for all $k \geq 0$, and it is Pareto optimal (everyone in fact gets the highest possible payoff). But, especially if n is large, this equilibrium is rather 'fragile'; all it takes is one person to leave the bargaining table for those who stay to get 0.

Whatever the reason, as pointed out by Abraham et al. [2006], it seems important to design strategies that tolerate such unanticipated behaviour, so that the payoffs of the users with 'standard' utilities do not get affected by the non-standard players using different strategies. This can be viewed as a way of adding fault tolerance to equilibrium notions. To capture this intuition, Abraham et al. [2006] define a strategy profile to be *t-immune* if a player who does *not* deviate is no worse off if up to t players do deviate. Note the difference between resilience and immunity. A strategy profile is resilient if deviators do not gain by deviating; a profile is immune if non-deviators do not get hurt by deviators. In the example above, although everyone bargaining is a k-resilient Nash equilibrium for all $k \geq 0$, it is not 1-immune.

Of course, we may want to combine resilience and immunity; a strategy profile is (k, t)-*robust* if it is both k-resilient and t-immune. (All the informal definitions here are completely formalised in [Abraham et al., 2006, 2008].) A Nash equilibrium is just a $(1,0)$-robust equilibrium. Unfortunately, for $(k, t) \neq (1, 0)$, a (k, t)-robust equilibrium does not exist in general, even if we allow mixed strategies (i.e., even if players can randomise). Nevertheless, there are a number of games of interest where they do exist; in particular, they can exist if players can take advantage of a *mediator*, or trusted third party. To take just one example, consider Byzantine agreement [Pease et al., 1980]. Recall that in Byzantine agreement there are n soldiers, up to t of which may be faulty (the t stands for *traitor*), one of which is the general. The general has an initial preference to attack or retreat. We want a protocol that guarantees that (1) all *non-faulty* soldiers reach the same decision, and (2) if the general is non-faulty, then the decision is the general's preference. It is trivial to solve Byzantine agreement with a mediator: the general simply sends the mediator his preference, and the mediator sends it to all the soldiers.

The obvious question of interest is whether we can *implement* the mediator. That is, can the players in the system, just talking among themselves (using what economists call 'cheap talk'), simulate the effects of the mediator. This is a question that has been of interest to both the computer science community and the game theory community. In game theory, the focus has been on whether a Nash equilibrium in a game with a mediator can be implemented using cheap talk (cf. [Barany, 1992, Ben-Porath, 2003, Forges, 1990, Gerardi, 2004, Heller, 2005, Urbano and Vila, 2002, 2004]). In cryptography, the focus has been on **secure multiparty computation** [Goldreich et al., 1987, Shamir et al., 1981, Yao, 1982]. Here it is assumed that each agent i has some private information x_i (such private information, like the general's preference, is typically called the player's **type** in game theory).

Fix a function f. The goal is to have agent i learn $f(x_1, \ldots, x_n)$ without learning anything about x_j for $j \neq i$ beyond what is revealed by the value of $f(x_1, \ldots, x_n)$. With a trusted mediator, this is trivial: each agent i just gives the mediator its private value x_i; the mediator then sends each agent i the value $f(x_1, \ldots, x_n)$. Work on multiparty computation provides general conditions under which this can be done (see [Goldreich, 2004] for an overview). Somewhat surprisingly, despite there being over 20 years of work on this problem in both computer science and game theory, until recently, there has been no interaction between the communities on this topic.

Abraham et al. [2006, 2008] essentially characterise when mediators can be implemented. To understand the results, three games need to be considered: an **underlying game** Γ, an extension Γ_d of Γ with a mediator, and a cheap-talk extension Γ_{CT} of Γ. Γ is assumed to be a **(normal-form) Bayesian game**: each player has a type from some type space with a known distribution over types, and must choose an action (where the choice can depend on his type). The utilities of the players depend on the types and actions taken. For example, in Byzantine agreement, the possible types of the general are 0 and 1, his possible initial preferences (the types of the other players are irrelevant). The players' actions are to attack or retreat. The assumption that there is a distribution over the general's preferences is standard in game theory, although not so much in distributed computing. Nonetheless, in many applications of Byzantine agreement, it seems reasonable to assume such a distribution. A cheap talk game **implements** a Nash equilibrium $\vec{\sigma}$ of a game with a mediator if the cheap talk game has a Nash equilibrium $\vec{\sigma}'$ such that $\vec{\sigma}$ and $\vec{\sigma}'$ induce the same distribution over actions in the underlying game, for each type vector of the players. With this background, I can summarise the results of Abraham et al.

- If $n > 3k+3t$, a (k, t)-robust strategy $\vec{\sigma}$ with a mediator can be implemented using cheap talk (that is, there is a (k, t)-robust strategy $\vec{\sigma}'$ in the cheap talk game such that $\vec{\sigma}$ and $\vec{\sigma}'$ induce the same distribution over actions in the underlying game). Moreover, the implementation requires no knowledge of other agents' utilities, and the cheap talk protocol has bounded running time that does not depend on the utilities.

- If $n \leq 3k + 3t$ then, in general, mediators cannot be implemented using cheap talk without knowledge of other agents' utilities. Moreover, even if other agents' utilities are known, mediators cannot, in general, be implemented without having a $(k + t)$-punishment strategy (that is, a strategy that, if used by all but at most $k+t$ players, guarantees that every player gets a worse outcome than they do with the equilibrium strategy) nor with bounded running time.
- If $n > 2k + 3t$, then mediators can be implemented using cheap talk if there is a punishment strategy (and utilities are known) in finite expected running time that does not depend on the utilities.
- If $n \leq 2k + 3t$ then mediators cannot, in general, be implemented, even if there is a punishment strategy and utilities are known.
- If $n > 2k + 2t$ and there are broadcast channels then, for all ϵ, mediators can be ϵ-implemented (intuitively, there is an implementation where players get utility within ϵ of what they could get by deviating) using cheap talk, with bounded expected running time that does not depend on the utilities.
- If $n \leq 2k + 2t$ then mediators cannot, in general, be ϵ-implemented, even with broadcast channels. Moreover, even assuming cryptography and polynomially-bounded players, the expected running time of an implementation depends on the utility functions of the players and ϵ.
- If $n > k + 3t$ then, assuming cryptography and polynomially-bounded players, mediators can be ϵ-implemented using cheap talk, but if $n \leq 2k+2t$, then the running time depends on the utilities in the game and ϵ.
- If $n \leq k + 3t$, then even assuming cryptography, polynomially-bounded players, and a $(k + t)$-punishment strategy, mediators cannot, in general, be ϵ-implemented using cheap talk.
- If $n > k + t$ then, assuming cryptography, polynomially-bounded players, and a public-key infrastructure (PKI), we can ϵ-implement a mediator.

All the possibility results showing that mediators can be implemented use techniques from secure multiparty computation. The results showing that if $n \leq 3k + 3t$, then we cannot implement a mediator without knowing utilities and that, even if utilities are known, a punishment strategy is required, use the fact that Byzantine agreement cannot be reached if $t < n/3$; the impossibility result for $n \leq 2k+3t$ also uses a variant of Byzantine agreement.

These results provide an excellent illustration of how the interaction between computer science and game theory can lead to fruitful insights. Related work on implementing mediators can be found in [Gordon and Katz, 2006, Halpern and Teadgue, 2004, Izmalkov et al., 2005, Kol and Naor, 2008, Lepinski et al., 2004, Lysyanskaya and Triandopoulos, 2006].

8.3 Taking computation into account

Nash equilibrium does not take computation into account. To see why this might be a problem, consider the following example, taken from [Halpern and Pass, 2010].

Example 8.1   You are given an n-bit number x. You can guess whether it is prime, or play safe and say nothing. If you guess right, you get $10; if you guess wrong, you lose $10; if you play safe, you get $1. There is only one Nash equilibrium in this one-player game: giving the right answer. But if n is large, this is almost certainly not what people will do. Even though primality testing can be done in polynomial time, the costs for doing so (buying a larger computer, for example, or writing an appropriate program), will probably not be worth it for most people. The point here is that Nash equilibrium is not taking the cost of computing whether x is prime into account.   □

There have been attempts in the game theory community to define solution concepts that take computation into account, going back to the work of Rubinstein [1986]. (See [Kalai, 1990] for an overview of the work in this area in the 1980s, and [Ben-Sasson et al., 2007] for more recent work.) Rubinstein assumed that players choose a finite automaton to play the game rather than choosing a strategy directly; a player's utility depends both on the move made by the automaton and the complexity of the automaton (identified with the number of states of the automaton). Intuitively, automata that use more states are seen as representing more complicated procedures. Rafael Pass and I [2010] provide a general game-theoretic framework that takes computation into account. (All the discussion in this section is taken from [Halpern and Pass, 2010].) Like Rubinstein, we view all players as choosing a machine, but we use Turing machines, rather than finite automata. We associate a complexity, not just with a machine, but with the machine and its input. This is important in Example 8.1, where the complexity of computing whether x is prime depends, in general, on the length of x.

The complexity could represent the running time of or space used by the machine on that input. The complexity can also be used to capture the complexity of the machine itself (e.g., the number of states, as in Rubinstein's case) or to model the cost of searching for a new strategy to replace one that the player has been given. (This makes sense if the game comes along with a recommended strategy, as is typically the case in mechanism design. One of the reasons that players follow a recommended strategy is that there may be too much effort involved in trying to find a new one.)

We again consider Bayesian games, where each player has a type. In a standard Bayesian game, an agent's utility depends on the type profile and the action profile (that is, every player's type, and the action chosen by each player). In a ***computational Bayesian game***, each player i chooses a Turing machine. Player i's type t_i is taken to be the input to player i's Turing machine M_i. The output of M_i on input t_i is taken to be player i's action. There is also a complexity associated with the pair (M_i, t_i). Player i's utility again depends on the type profile and the action profile, and also on the complexity profile. The reason we consider the whole complexity profile in determining player i's utility, as opposed to just i's complexity, is that, for example, i might be happy as long as his machine takes fewer steps than j's. Given these definitions, we can define Nash equilibrium as usual. With this definition, by defining the complexity appropriately, it will be the case that playing safe for sufficiently large inputs will be an equilibrium.

Computational Nash equilibrium also gives a plausible explanation of observed behaviour in finitely-repeated prisoner's dilemma.

Example 8.2   Recall that in the prisoner's dilemma, there are two prisoners, who can choose to either cooperate or defect. As described in the table below, if they both cooperate, they both get 3; if they both defect, then both get 1; if one defects and the other cooperates, the defector gets 5 and the cooperator gets -5. (Intuitively, the cooperator stays silent, while the defector 'rats out' his partner. If they both rat each other out, they both go to jail.)

	C	D
C	$3, 3$	$-5, 5$
D	$5, -5$	$-3, -3$

It is easy to see that defecting dominates cooperating: no matter what the other player does, a player is better off defecting than cooperating. Thus, 'rational' players should defect. And, indeed, (D, D) is the only Nash equilibrium of this game. Although (C, C) gives both players a better payoff than (D, D), this is not an equilibrium.

Now consider the finitely repeated prisoner's dilemma (FRPD), where the prisoner's dilemma is played for some fixed number N of rounds. The only Nash equilibrium is to always defect; this can be seen by a backwards induction argument. (The last round is like the one-shot game, so both players should defect; given that they are both defecting at the last round, they should both defect at the second-last round; and so on.) This seems quite unreasonable. And, indeed, in experiments, people do not always defect. In fact, quite often they cooperate throughout the game. Are they irrational? It is hard to call this irrational behaviour, given that the 'irrational' players do much better than supposedly rational players who always defect. There have been many attempts to explain cooperation in FRPD in the literature (see, for example, [Kreps et al., 1982]). Indeed, there have even been well-known attempts that take computation into account; it can be shown that if players are restricted to using a finite automaton with bounded complexity, then there exist equilibria that allow for cooperation [Neyman, 1985, Papadimitriou and Yannakakis, 1994]. However, the strategies used in those equilibria are quite complex, and require the use of large automata; as a consequence this approach does not seem to provide a satisfactory explanation of why people choose to cooperate.

Using the framework described above leads to a straightforward explanation. Consider the ***tit for tat*** strategy, which proceeds as follows: a player cooperates at the first round, and then at round $m + 1$, does whatever his opponent did at round m. Thus, if the opponent cooperated at the previous round, then you reward him by continuing to cooperate; if he defected at the previous round, you punish him by defecting. If both players play tit for tat, then they cooperate throughout the game. Interestingly, tit for tat does exceedingly well in FRPD tournaments, where computer programs play each other [Axelrod, 1984].

Tit for tat is a simple program, which needs very little memory. Suppose that we charge even a modest amount for memory usage, and that there is a discount factor δ, with $0.5 < \delta < 1$, so that if the player gets a reward of r_m in round m, his total reward over the whole N-round game (not including the cost of memory usage) is taken to be $\sum_{m=1}^{N} \delta^m r_m$. In this case, it is easy to see that, no matter what the cost of memory is, as long as it is positive, for a sufficiently long game, it will be a Nash equilibrium for both players to play tit for tat. For the best response to tit for tat is to play tit for tat up to the last round, and then to defect. But following this strategy requires the player to keep track of the round number, which requires the use of extra memory. The extra gain of \$2 achieved by defecting at the last round, if sufficiently discounted, will not be worth the cost of keeping track of the round number. (A similar argument works without assuming a discount factor (or, equivalently, taking $\delta = 1$) if we assume that the cost of memory increases unboundedly with N.)

Note that even if only one player is charged for memory, and memory is free for the other player, then there is a Nash equilibrium where the bounded player plays tit for tat, while the other player plays the best response of cooperating up to (but not including) the last round of the game, and then defecting in the last round.   □

Although with standard games there is always a Nash equilibrium, this is not the case when we take computation into account, as the following example shows.

Example 8.3 Consider roshambo (rock-paper-scissors). We model playing rock, paper, and scissors as playing 0, 1, and 2, respectively. The payoff to player 1 of the outcome (i, j) is 1 if $i = j \oplus 1$ (where $\oplus$ denotes addition mod 3), -1 if $j = i \oplus 1$, and 0 if $i = j$. Player 2's playoffs are the negative of those of player 1; the game is a zero-sum game. As is well known, the unique Nash equilibrium of this game has the players randomising uniformly between 0, 1, and 2.

Now consider a computational version of roshambo. Suppose that we take the complexity of a deterministic strategy to be 1, and the complexity of a strategy that uses randomisation to be 2, and take player i's utility to be his payoff in the underlying game minus the complexity of his strategy. Intuitively, programs involving randomisation are more complicated than those that do not randomise. With this utility function, it is easy to see that there is no Nash equilibrium. For suppose that (M_1, M_2) is an equilibrium. If M_1 uses randomisation, then 1 can do better by playing the deterministic strategy $j \oplus 1$, where j is the action that gets the highest probability according to M_2 (or one of them in the case of ties). Similarly, M_2 cannot use randomisation. But, as mentioned above, there is no equilibrium for roshambo with deterministic strategies.

In practice, people do not play the (unique) Nash equilibrium (which randomises uniformly among rock, paper, and scissors). It is well known that people have difficulty simulating randomisation; we can think of the cost for randomising as capturing this difficulty. Interestingly, there are roshambo tournaments (indeed, even a Rock Paper Scissors World Championship – see http://www.worldrps.com), and books written on roshambo strategies [Walker and Walker, 2004]. Championship players are clearly not randomising uniformly (they could not hope to get a higher payoff than an opponent by randomising). The computational framework provides a psychologically plausible account of this lack of randomisation.   □

Is the lack of Nash equilibrium a problem? Perhaps not. For one thing, it can be shown that if, in a precise sense, randomisation is free, then there is always a Nash equilibrium (see [Halpern and Pass, 2010]; note that this does not follow from Nash's theorem [1950a] showing that every finite standard game has a Nash equilibrium since it says, among other things, that the Nash equilibrium is computable – it can be played by Turing machines). Moreover, taking computation into account should cause us to rethink things. In particular, we may want to consider other solution concepts. But, as the examples above show, Nash equilibrium does seem to make reasonable predictions in a number of games of interest. Perhaps of even more interest, using computational Nash equilibrium lets us provide a game-theoretic account of security.

The standard framework for multiparty security does not take into account whether players have an incentive to execute the protocol. That is, if there were a trusted mediator, would player i actually use the recommended protocol even if i would be happy to use the services of the mediator to compute the function f? Nor does it take into account whether the adversary has an incentive to undermine the protocol.

Roughly speaking, the game-theoretic definition says that Π is a ***game-theoretically secure*** (cheap-talk) protocol for computing f if, for all choices of the utility function, if it is a Nash equilibrium to play with the mediator to compute f, then it is also a Nash equilibrium to use Π to compute f. Note that this definition does not mention privacy. It does not need to; this is taken care of by choosing the utilities appropriately. Pass and I [2010] show that, under minimal assumptions, this definition is essentially equivalent to a variant of ***zero knowledge*** [Goldwasser et al., 1989] called ***precise zero knowledge*** [Micali and Pass, 2006]. Thus, the two approaches used for dealing with 'deviating' players in two game theory and cryptography – *Nash equilibrium* and *zero-knowledge 'simulation'* – are intimately connected; indeed, they are essentially equivalent once we take computation into account appropriately.

8.4 Taking (lack of) awareness into account

Standard game theory models implicitly assume that all significant aspects of the game (payoffs, moves available, etc.) are common knowledge among the players. However, this is not always a reasonable assumption. For example, sleazy companies assume that consumers are not aware that they can lodge complaints if there are problems; in a war setting, having technology that an enemy is unaware of (and thus being able to make moves that the enemy is unaware of) can be critical; in financial markets, some investors may not be aware of certain investment strategies (complicated hedging strategies, for example, or tax-avoidance strategies).

To understand the impact of adding the possibility of unawareness to the analysis of games, consider the game shown in Figure 8.1 (this example, and all the discussion in this section, is taken from [Halpern and Rêgo, 2006]). One Nash equilibrium of this game has A playing across$_A$ and B playing down$_B$. However, suppose that A is not aware that B can play down$_B$. In that case, if A is rational, A will play down$_A$. Although A would play across$_A$ if A knew that B were going to play down$_B$, A cannot even contemplate this possibility, let alone know it. Therefore, Nash equilibrium does not seem to be the appropriate solution concept here.

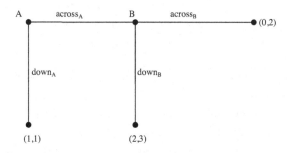

Figure 8.1 A simple game

To find an appropriate analogue of Nash equilibrium in games where players may be unaware of some possible moves, we must first find an appropriate representation for such games. The first step in doing so is to explicitly represent what players are aware of at each node. We do this by using what we call an ***augmented game***.

Recall that an ***extensive game*** is described by a game tree. Each node in the tree describes a partial history of the game – the sequence of moves that led to that node. Associated with each node is the player that moves at that node. Some nodes where a player i moves are grouped together into an ***information set for player*** i. Intuitively, if player i is at some node in an information set I, then i does not know which node of I describes the true situation; thus, at all nodes in I, i must make the same move. An augmented game is an extensive game with one more feature: associated with each node in the game tree where player i moves is the ***level of awareness*** of player i – the set of histories that player i is aware of. (The formal definition of an augmented game can be found in [Halpern and Rêgo, 2006].)

We use the player's awareness level as a way of keeping track of how the player's awareness changes over time. For example, perhaps A playing across$_A$ will result in B becoming aware of the possibility of playing down$_B$. In financial settings, one effect of players using certain investment strategies is that other players become aware of the possibility of using that strategy. Strategic thinking in such games must take this possibility into account. We would model this possibility by having some probability of B's awareness level changing.

For example, suppose that in the game shown in Figure 8.1

- players A and B are aware of all histories of the game;
- player A is uncertain as to whether player B is aware of run $\langle$across$_A$, down$_B\rangle$ and believes that B is unaware of it with probability p; and
- the type of player B that is aware of the run $\langle$across$_A$, down$_B\rangle$ is aware that player A is aware of all histories, and B knows that A is uncertain about his (B's) awareness level and knows the probability p.

Because A and B are actually aware of all histories of the underlying game, from the point of view of the modeller, the augmented game is essentially identical to the game described in Figure 8.1, with the awareness level of both players A and B consisting of all histories of the underlying game. However, when A moves at the node labelled A in the modeller's game, she believes that the actual augmented game is Γ^A, as described in Figure 8.2. In Γ^A, nature's initial move captures A's uncertainty about B's awareness level. At the information set labelled $A.1$, A is aware of all the runs of the underlying game. Moreover, at this information set, A believes that the true game is Γ^A.

At the node labelled $B.1$, B is aware of all the runs of the underlying game and believes that the true game is the modeller's game; but at the node labelled $B.2$, B is not aware that he can play down$_B$, and so believes that the true game is the augmented game Γ^B described in Figure 8.3. At the nodes labelled $A.3$ and $B.3$ in the game Γ^B, neither A nor B is aware of the move down$_B$. Moreover, both players think the true game is Γ^B.

As this example should make clear, to model a game with possibly unaware players, we need to consider, not just one augmented game, but a collection of them. Moreover, we need to describe, at each history in an augmented game, which augmented game the player playing at that history believes is the actual augmented game being played.

To capture these intuitions, starting with an underlying extensive-form game Γ, we define a ***game with awareness based on*** Γ to be a tuple $\Gamma^* = (\mathcal{G}, \Gamma^m, \mathcal{F})$, where

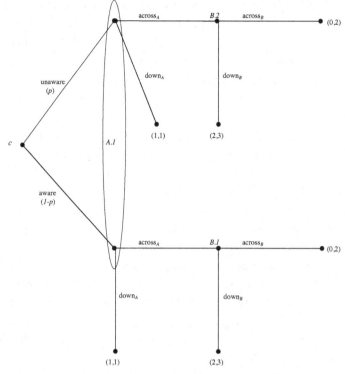

Figure 8.2 The augmented game Γ^A

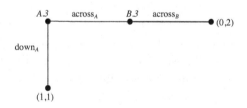

Figure 8.3 The augmented game Γ^B

- $\mathcal{G}$ is a countable set of augmented games based on Γ, of which one is Γ^m;
- $\mathcal{F}$ maps an augmented game $\Gamma^+ \in \mathcal{G}$ and a history h in Γ^+ such that $P^+(h) = i$ to a pair (Γ^h, I), where $\Gamma^h \in \mathcal{G}$ and I is an information set for player i in game Γ^h.

Intuitively, Γ^m is the game from the point of view of an omniscient modeller. If player i moves at h in game $\Gamma^+ \in \mathcal{G}$ and $\mathcal{F}(\Gamma^+, h) = (\Gamma^h, I)$, then Γ^h is the game that i believes to be the true game when the history is h, and I consists of the set of histories in Γ^h he currently considers possible. For example, in the examples described in Figures 8.2 and 8.3, taking Γ^m to be the augmented game in Figure 8.1, we have $\mathcal{F}(\Gamma^m, \langle\rangle) = (\Gamma^A, I)$, where I is the information set labelled $A.1$ in Figure 8.2, and $\mathcal{F}(\Gamma^A, \langle\text{unaware,across}_A\rangle) = (\Gamma^B, \{\langle\text{across}_A\rangle\})$. There are a number of consistency conditions that have to be satisfied by the function $\mathcal{F}$; the details can be found in [Halpern and Rêgo, 2006].

The standard notion of Nash equilibrium consists of a profile of strategies, one for each player. Our generalisation consists of a profile of strategies, one for each pair (i, Γ'), where Γ' is a game that agent i considers to be the true game in some situation. Intuitively, the strategy for a player i at Γ' is the strategy i would play in situations where i believes that the true game is Γ'. To understand why we may need to consider different strategies consider, for example, the game of Figure 8.1. B would play differently depending on whether or not he was aware of down$_B$. Roughly speaking, a profile $\vec{\sigma}$ of strategies, one for each pair (i, Γ'), is a ***generalised Nash equilibrium*** if $\sigma_{i,\Gamma'}$ is a best response for player i if the true game is Γ', given the strategies $\sigma_{j,\Gamma'}$ being used by the other players in Γ'. As shown by [Halpern and Rêgo, 2006], every game with awareness has a generalised Nash equilibrium.

A standard extensive-form game Γ can be viewed as a special case of a game with awareness, by taking $\Gamma^m = \Gamma$, $\mathcal{G} = \{\Gamma^m\}$, and $\mathcal{F}(\Gamma^m, h) = (\Gamma^m, I)$, where I is the information set that contains h. Intuitively, Γ corresponds to the game of awareness where it is common knowledge that Γ is being played. We call this the ***canonical representation*** of Γ as a game with awareness. It is not hard to show that a strategy profile $\vec{\sigma}$ is a Nash equilibrium of Γ iff it is a generalised Nash equilibrium of the canonical representation of Γ as a game with awareness. Thus, generalised Nash equilibrium can be viewed as a generalisation of standard Nash equilibrium.

Up to now, I have considered only games where players are not aware of their lack of awareness. But in some games, a player might be aware that there are moves that another player (or even she herself) might be able to make, although she is not aware of what they are. Such awareness of unawareness can be quite relevant in practice. For example, in a war setting, even if one side cannot conceive of a new technology available to the enemy, they might believe that there is some move available to the enemy without understanding what that particular move is. This, in turn, may encourage peace overtures. To take another example, an agent might delay making a decision because she considers it possible that she might learn about more possible moves, even if she is not aware of what these moves are.

Although, economists usually interpret awareness as 'being able to conceive about an event or a proposition', there are other possible meanings for this concept. For example, awareness may also be interpreted as 'understanding the primitive concepts in an event or proposition', or as 'being able to determine if an event occurred or not', or as 'being able to compute the consequences of some fact' [Fagin and Halpern, 1988]. If we interpret 'lack of awareness' as 'unable to compute' (note that this interpretation is closely related to the discussion of the previous section!), then awareness of unawareness becomes even more significant. Consider a chess game. Although all players understand in principle all the moves that can be made, they are certainly not aware of all consequences of all moves. A more accurate representation of chess would model this computational unawareness explicitly. We provide such a representation.

Roughly speaking, we capture the fact that player i is aware that, at a node h in the game tree, there is a move that j can make she (i) is not aware by having i's subjective representation of the game include a 'virtual' move for j at node h. Since i might have only an incomplete understanding of what can happen after this move, i simply describes what she believes will be the game after the virtual move, to the extent that she can. In particular, if she has no idea what will happen after the virtual move, then she can describe her beliefs regarding the payoffs of the game. Thus, our representation can be viewed as a generalisation of how chess programs analyse chess games. They explore the game tree up to a certain point, and then evaluate the board position at that point. We can think of the payoffs following a virtual move by j in i's subjective representation of a chess game as describing the evaluation of the board from i's point of view. This seems like a much more reasonable representation of the game than the standard complete game tree!

All the definitions of games with awareness can be generalised to accommodate awareness of unawareness. In particular, we can define a generalised Nash equilibrium as before, and once again show that every game with awareness (now including awareness of unawareness) has a generalised Nash equilibrium [Halpern and Rêgo, 2006].

There has been a great deal of work recently on modelling unawareness in games. The first papers on the topic were by Feinberg [2004, 2005]. My work with Rêgo [2006] was the first to consider awareness in extensive games, modelling how awareness changed over time. There has been a recent flurry on the topic in the economics literature; see, for example, [Heifetz et al., 2006b, Li, 2006a,b, Ozbay, 2007]. Closely related is work on logics that include awareness. This work started in the computer science literature [Fagin and Halpern, 1988], but more recently, the bulk of the work has appeared in the economics literature (see, for example, [Dekel et al., 1998, Halpern, 2001, Halpern and Rêgo, 2008, Heifetz et al., 2006a, Modica and Rustichini, 1994, 1999]).

8.5 Iterated regret minimisation

Consider the well-known *traveller's dilemma* [Basu, 1994, 2007]. Suppose that two travellers have identical luggage, for which they both paid the same price. Their luggage is damaged (in an identical way) by an airline. The airline offers to recompense them for their luggage. They may ask for any dollar amount between $2 and $100. There is only one catch. If they ask for the same amount, then that is what they will both receive. However, if they ask for different amounts – say one asks for m and the other for m', with $m < m'$ – then whoever asks for m (the lower amount) will get $(m + p)$, while the other traveller will get $(m - p)$, where p can be viewed as a reward for the person who asked for the lower amount, and a penalty for the person who asked for the higher amount.

It seems at first blush that both travellers should ask for $100, the maximum amount, for then they will both get that. However, as long as $p > 1$, one of them might then realise that he is actually better off asking for $99 if the other traveller asks for $100, since he then gets $(99+p)$. In fact, $99 *weakly dominates* $100, in that no matter what Traveller 1 asks for, Traveller 2 is always at least as well off asking for $99 than $100, and in one case (if Traveller 2 asks for $100) Traveller 1 is strictly better off asking for $99. Thus, it seems we can eliminate 100 as an amount to ask for. However, once we eliminate 100, a similar argument shows that 98 weakly dominates 99. And once we eliminate 99, then 97 weakly dominates 98. Continuing this argument, both travellers end up asking for $2! In fact, it is easy to see that (2,2) is the only Nash equilibrium. Indeed, with any other pair of requests, at least one of the travellers would want to change his request if he knew what the other traveller was asking. Since (2,2) is the only Nash equilibrium, it is also the only sequential and perfect equilibrium. Moreover, it is the only rationalizable strategy profile; and, once we allow mixed strategies, (2,2) is the only strategy that survives iterated deletion of strongly dominated strategies. (It is not necessary to understand these solution concepts in detail; the only point that I am trying make here is that all standard solution concepts lead to (2,2).)

This seems like a strange result. It seems that no reasonable person – even a game theorist! – would ever play 2. Indeed, when the traveller's dilemma was empirically tested among game theorists (with $p = 2$) they typically did not play anywhere close to 2. Becker, Carter, and Naeve [2005] asked members of the Game Theory Society (presumably, all experts in game theory) to submit a strategy for the game. Fifty-one of them did so. Of the 45 that submitted pure strategies, 33 submitted a strategy of 95 or higher, and 38 submitted a strategy of 90 or higher; only three submitted the 'recommended' strategy of 2. The strategy that performed best (in pairwise matchups against all submitted strategies) was 97, which had an average payoff of \$85.09. The worst average payoff went to those who played 2; it was only \$3.92.

Another sequence of experiments by Capra et al. [1999] showed, among other things, that this result was quite sensitive to the choice of p. For low values of p, people tended to play high values, and keep playing them when the game was repeated. By way of contrast, for high values of p, people started much lower, and converged to playing 2 after a few rounds of repeated play. The standard solution concepts (Nash equilibrium, rationalizability, etc.) are all insensitive to the choice of p; for example, (2,2) is the only Nash equilibrium for all choices of $p > 1$.

Arguably, part of the problem here is that Nash equilibrium presumes that players know what other players are doing. I now consider a solution concept that Rafael Pass and I [2009] recently introduced, *iterated regret minimisation*, that attempts to deal with this problem, and exhibits the same qualitative behaviour as that observed in experiments in many games of interest. (The discussion in the rest of this section is taken almost verbatim from [Halpern and Pass, 2009].)

The idea of minimising regret was introduced (independently) in decision theory by Niehans [1948] and Savage [1951]. To explain how we use it in a game-theoretic context, I first review how it works in a single-agent decision problem. Suppose that an agent chooses an act from a set A of acts. The agent is uncertain as to the true state of the world; there is a set S of possible states. Associated with each state $s \in S$ and act $a \in A$ is the utility $u(a, s)$ of performing act a if s is the true state of the world. For simplicity, we take S and A to be finite here. The idea behind the *minimax regret* rule is to hedge the agent's bets, by doing reasonably well no matter what the actual state is.

Formally, for each state s, let $u^*(s)$ be the best outcome in state s; that is, $u^*(s) = \max_{a \in A} u(a, s)$. The *regret* of a in state s, denoted $regret_u(a, s)$, is $u^*(s) - u(a, s)$; that is, the regret of a in s is the difference between the utility of the best possible outcome in s and the utility of performing act a in s. Let $regret_u(a) = \max_{s \in S} regret_u(a, s)$. For example, if $regret_u(a) = 2$, then in each state s, the utility of performing a in s is guaranteed to be within 2 of the utility of any act the agent could choose, even if she knew that the actual state was s. The minimax-regret decision rule orders acts by their regret; the 'best' act is the one that minimises regret. Intuitively, this rule is trying to minimise the regret that an agent would feel if she discovered what the situation actually was: the 'I wish I had chosen a' instead of a' feeling.

Despite having been used in decision making for over 50 years, up until recently, there was little work on applying regret minimisation in the context of game theory. Rather than giving formal definitions here, I explain how regret can be applied in the context of the traveller's dilemma. For ease of exposition, I restrict attention to pure strategies.

The acts for each player are that player's pure strategy choices; the states are the other player's pure strategy choices. Each act-state pair is then just a strategy profile; the utility of the act-state pair for player i is just the payoff to player i of the strategy profile. Intuitively, each agent is uncertain about what the other agent will do, and tries to choose an act that minimises his regret, given that uncertainty.

It is easy to see that, if the penalty/reward p is such that $2 \leq p \leq 49$, then the acts that minimise regret are the ones in the interval $[100 - 2p, 100]$; the regret for all these acts is $2p - 1$. For if player 1 asks for an amount $m \in [100 - 2p, 100]$ and player 2 asks for an amount $m' \leq m$, then the payoff to player 1 is at least $m' - p$, compared to the payoff of $m' + p - 1$ (or just m' if $m' = 2$) that is achieved with the best response; thus, the regret is at most $2p - 1$ in this case. If, instead, player 2 asks for $m' > m$, then player 1 gets a payoff of $m + p$, and the best possible payoff in the game is $99 + p$, so his regret is at most $99 - m \leq 2p - 1$. On the other hand, if player 1 chooses $m < 100 - 2p$, then his regret will be $99 - m > 2p - 1$ if player 2 plays 100. This proves the claim. If $p \geq 50$, then the unique act that minimises regret is asking for \$2.

Suppose that $2 \leq p \leq 49$. Applying regret minimisation once suggests using a strategy in the interval $[100 - 2p, 100]$. But we can iterate this process. If we assume that both players use a strategy in this interval, then the strategy that minimises regret is that of asking for $\$(100 - 2p + 1)$. A straightforward check shows that this has regret $2p - 2$; all other strategies have regret $2p - 1$. If $p = 2$, this approach singles out the strategy of asking for \$97, which was found to be the best strategy by Becker, Carter, and Naeve [2005]. As p increases, the act that survives this iterated deletion process goes down, reaching 2 if $p \geq 50$. This matches (qualitatively) the findings of Capra et al. [1999]. (Capra et al. actually considered a slightly different game where the minimum bid was p (rather than 2). If we instead consider their version of the game, we get an even closer qualitative match to their experimental observations.) As we show in [Halpern and Pass, 2009], iterated regret minimisation captures experimental behaviour in a number of other game as well, including the Centipede Game [Rosenthal, 1982], Nash bargaining [Nash, 1950b], and Bertrand competition [Dufwenberg and Gneezy, 2000].

I conclude this discussion by making precise the sense in which iterated regret minimisation does not require knowledge of the other players' strategies (or the fact that they are rational). Traditional solution concepts typically assume common knowledge of rationality, or at least a high degree of mutual knowledge of rationality. For example, it is well known that rationalizability can be characterised in terms of common knowledge of rationality [Tan and Werlang, 1988], where a player is rational if he has some beliefs according to which what he does is a best response in terms of maximizing expected utility; Aumann and Brandenburger [1995] show that Nash equilibrium requires (among other things) mutual knowledge of rationality (where, again, rationality means playing a utility-maximizing best response); and Brandenburger, Friedenberg, and Keisler [2008] show that iterated deletion of weakly dominated strategies requires sufficiently high mutual assumption of rationality, where 'assumption' is a variant of 'knowledge', and 'rationality' means 'does not play a weakly dominated strategy'. This knowledge of rationality essentially also implies knowledge of the strategy used by other players.

But if we make this assumption (and identify rationality with minimising regret), we seem to run into a serious problem with iterated regret minimisation, which is well illustrated by the traveller's dilemma. As we observed earlier, the strategy profile $(97, 97)$ is the only one that survives iterated regret minimisation when $p = 2$. However, if agent 1 knows that player 2 is playing 97, then he should play 96, not 97! That is, among all strategies, 97 is certainly not the strategy that minimises regret with respect to $\{97\}$.

Some of these difficulties also arise when dealing with iterated deletion of weakly dominated strategies. The justification for deleting a weakly dominated strategy is the existence of other strategies. But this justification may disappear in later deletions. As Mas-Colell, Whinston, and Green [1995, p. 240] put in their textbook when discussing iterated deletion of weakly dominated strategies:

[T]he argument for deletion of a weakly dominated strategy for player i is that he contemplates the possibility that every strategy combination of his rivals occurs with positive probability. However, this hypothesis clashes with the logic of iterated deletion, which assumes, precisely, that eliminated strategies are not expected to occur.

Brandenburger, Friedenburg, and Kiesler [2008] resolve this paradox in the context of iterated deletion of weakly dominated strategies by assuming that strategies were not really eliminated. Rather, they assumed that strategies that are weakly dominated occur with infinitesimal (but non-zero) probability. Unfortunately, this approach does not seem to help in the context of iterated regret minimisation. Assigning deleted strategies infinitesimal probability will not make 97 a best response to a set of strategies where 97 is given very high probability. Pass and I deal with this problem by essentially reversing the approach taken by Brandenburger, Friedenberg, and Keisler. Rather than assuming common knowledge of rationality, we assign successively lower probability to higher orders of rationality. The idea is that now, with overwhelming probability, no assumptions are made about the other players; with probability ϵ, they are assumed to be rational, with probability ϵ^2, the other players are assumed to be rational and to believe that they are playing rational players, and so on. (Of course, 'rationality' is interpreted here as minimising expected regret.) Thus, players proceed lexicographically. Their first priority is to minimise regret with respect to all strategies; their next priority is to minimise regret with respect to strategies that a rational player would use; and so on. For example, in the traveller's dilemma, all the choices between 96 and 100 minimise regret with respect to all strategies. To choose among them, we consider the second priority: minimising regret with respect to strategies that a rational player would use. Since a rational player (who is minimising regret) would choose a strategy between 96 and 100, and 97 minimises regret with respect to these strategies, 97 is preferred to the other strategies between 96 and 100. In [Halpern and Pass, 2009], this intuition is formalised, and a formal epistemic characterisation is provided for iterated regret minimisation. This characterisation emphasises the fact that this approach makes minimal assumptions about the strategies used by the other agent.

Of course, an agent may have some beliefs about the strategies used by other agents. These beliefs can be accommodated by allowing the agent to start the deletion process with a smaller set of strategies (the ones that he considers the other players might actually use). The changes required to deal with this generalisation are straightforward.

Example 8.4 The role of prior beliefs is particularly well illustrated in the finitely repeated prisoner's dilemma. Recall that always defecting is the only Nash equilibrium of FRPD; it is also the only strategy that is rationalizable, and the only one that survives iterated deletion of weakly dominated strategies. Nevertheless, in practice, we see quite a bit of cooperation. We have already seen, in Example 8.2, one approach to explaining cooperation, in terms of memory costs. Here is another in terms of regret.

Suppose that prisoner's dilemma is played for N rounds. There are 2^{2^N-1} pure strategies for each player in N-round FRPD; computing the regret of each one can be rather complicated. Thus, when using regret, it is reasonable for the players to focus on a much more limited set of strategies. Suppose that each player believes that the other player is using a strategy where he plays tit for tat for some number k of rounds, and then defects from then on. Call this strategy s_k. (So, in particular, s_0 is the strategy of always defecting and s_N is tit for tat.) A straightforward argument shows that if a player believes that the other player is playing a strategy of the form s_k for some k with $0 \le k \le N$, then the strategy that minimises player 1's regret is either s_{N-1}, s_1, or s_0; see [Halpern and Pass, 2009] for details. Moreover, for sufficiently large N (it turns out that $N > ((u_3 + u_2 - u_1)/(u_2 - u_1)) + 1$ suffices), the strategy that minimises regret is s_{N-1}. Thus, if each player believes that the other player is playing a strategy of the form s_k – a reasonable set of strategies to consider – then we get a strategy that looks much more like what people do in practice.   □

8.6 Conclusions

As I mentioned earlier, economists have considered quite a few alternatives to Nash equilibrium, including ϵ-Nash equilibrium, subgame perfect equilibrium, sequential equilibrium, rationalizability, and many other notions [Osborne and Rubinstein, 1994]. But none of these directly addresses the concerns that I have addressed here: fault tolerance, computation, lack of awareness, and lack of knowledge of other players' strategies. The results and approaches of this chapter are are clearly only first steps. Here are some directions for further research (some of which I am currently engaged in with my collaborators):

- While (k, t)-robust equilibrium does seem to be a reasonable way of capturing some aspects of robustness, for some applications, it does not go far enough. I said earlier that in economics, all players were assumed to be strategic, or 'rational'; in distributed computing, all players were either 'good' (and followed the recommended protocol) or 'bad' (in which case they could be arbitrarily malicious). Immunity takes into account the bad players. The definition of immunity requires that the rational players are not hurt no matter what the 'bad' players do. But this may be too strong. As Ayer et al. [2005] point out, it is reasonable to expect a certain fraction of players in a system to be 'good' and follow the recommended protocol, even if it is not a best reply. In general, it may be hard to figure out what the best reply is, so if following the recommended protocol is not unreasonable, they will do that. (Note that this can be captured in a computational model of equilibrium, by charging for switching from the recommended strategy.)

There may be other standard ways that players act irrationally. For example, Kash, Friedman, and I [2007] consider **scrip systems**, where players perform work in exchange for scrip. There is a Nash equilibrium where everyone uses a **threshold strategy**, performing work only when they have less scrip than some threshold amount. Two standard ways of acting 'irrationally' in such a system are to (a) hoard scrip and (b) provide service for free (this is the analogue of posting music on Kazaa). A robust solution should take into account these more standard types of irrational behaviour, without perhaps worrying as much about arbitrary irrational behaviour.

- The definitions of computational Nash equilibrium considered only Bayesian games. What would appropriate solution concepts be for extensive-form games? Some ideas from the work on awareness seem relevant here, especially if we think of 'lack of awareness' as 'unable to compute'.

- Where do the beliefs come from in an equilibrium with awareness? That is, if I suddenly become aware that you can make a certain move, what probability should I assign to you making that move? Ozbay [2007] proposes a solution concept where the beliefs are part of the solution concept. He considers only a simple setting, where one player is aware of everything (so that revealing information is purely strategic). Can his ideas be extended to a more general setting?

- Agents playing a game can be viewed participating in a concurrent, distributed protocol. Game theory does not take the asynchrony into account, but it can make a big difference. For example, all the results from [Abraham et al., 2006, 2008] mentioned in Section 8.2 depend on the system being synchronous. Things are more complicated in asynchronous settings. Getting solution concepts that deal well with asynchrony is clearly important.

- Another issue that plays a major role in computer science but has thus far not been viewed as significant in game theory, but will, I believe, turn out to be important to the problem of defining appropriate solution concepts, is the analogue of specifying and verifying programs. Games are typically designed to solve certain problems. Thus, for example, economists want to design a spectrum auction so that the equilibrium has certain features. As I pointed out in an earlier overview [Halpern, 2003], game theory has typically focused on 'small' games: games that are easy to describe, such as the prisoner's dilemma. The focus has been on subtleties regarding basic issues such as rationality and coordination. To the extent that game theory is used to tackle larger, more practical problems, and especially to the extent that it is computers, or software agents, playing games, rather than people, it will be important to specify carefully exactly what a solution to the game must accomplish. For example, in the context of a spectrum auction, a specification will have to address what should happen if a computer crashes while an agent is in the middle of transmitting a bid, how to deal with agents bidding on slow lines, dealing with agents who win but then go bankrupt, and so on.

Finding logics to reason about solutions, especially doing so in a way that takes into account robustness and asynchrony, seems to me a difficult and worthwhile challenge. Indeed, one desideratum for a good solution concept is that it should be easy to reason about. Pursuing this theme, computer scientists have learned that one good way of designing correct programs is to do so in a modular way. Can a similar idea be applied in game theory? That is, can games designed for solving smaller problems be combined in a seamless way to solve a larger problem? If so, results about *composability of solutions* will be needed; we might want solution concepts that allow for such composability.

Acknowledgements: Work supported in part by NSF under under grants ITR-0325453 and IIS-0534064, and by AFOSR under grant FA9550-05-1-0055. Thanks to Krzysztof Apt for useful comments.

References

I. Abraham, D. Dolev, R. Gonen, and J. Y. Halpern. Distributed computing meets game theory: robust mechanisms for rational secret sharing and multiparty computation. In *Proc. 25th ACM Symposium on Principles of Distributed Computing*, pages 53–62, 2006.

I. Abraham, D. Dolev, and J. Y. Halpern. Lower bounds on implementing robust and resilient mediators. In *Fifth Theory of Cryptography Conference*, pages 302–319, 2008.

E. Adar and B. Huberman. Free riding on Gnutella. *First Monday*, 5(10), 2000.

R. J. Aumann. Acceptable points in general cooperative *n*-person games. In A. W. Tucker and R. D. Luce, editors, *Contributions to the Theory of Games IV,*

Annals of Mathematical Studies 40, pages 287–324. Princeton University Press, Princeton, N. J., 1959.

R. J. Aumann and A. Brandenburger. Epistemic conditions for Nash equilibrium. *Econometrica*, 63(5):1161–1180, 1995.

R. Axelrod. *The Evolution of Cooperation*. Basic Books, New York, 1984.

A. S. Ayer, L. Alvisi, A. Clement, M. Dahlin, J. P. Martin, and C. Porth. BAR fault tolerance for cooperative services. In *Proc. 20th ACM Symposium on Operating Systems Principles (SOSP 2005)*, pages 45–58, 2005.

I. Barany. Fair distribution protocols or how the players replace fortune. *Mathematics of Operations Research*, 17:327–340, 1992.

K. Basu. The traveler's dilemma. *Scientific American*, June:90–95, 2007.

K. Basu. The traveler's dilemma: paradoxes of rationality in game theory. *American Economic Review*, 84(2):391–395, 1994.

T. Becker, M. Carter, and J. Naeve. Experts playing the Traveler's Dilemma. Discussion paper 252/2005, Universität Hohenheim, 2005.

E. Ben-Porath. Cheap talk in games with incomplete information. *Journal of Economic Theory*, 108(1):45–71, 2003.

E. Ben-Sasson, A. Kalai, and E. Kalai. An approach to bounded rationality. In *Advances in Neural Information Processing Systems 19 (Proc. of NIPS 2006)*, pages 145–152. 2007.

B. D. Bernheim, B. Peleg, and M. Whinston. Coalition proof Nash equilibrium: concepts. *Journal of Economic Theory*, 42(1):1–12, 1989.

A. Brandenburger, A. Friedenberg, and J. Keisler. Admissibility in games. *Econometrica*, 76(2):307–352, 2008.

M. Capra, J. K. Goeree, R. Gomez, and C. A. Holt. Anamolous behavior in a traveler's dilemma. *American Economic Review*, 89(3):678–690, 1999.

E. Dekel, B. Lipman, and A. Rustichini. Standard state-space models preclude unawareness. *Econometrica*, 66:159–173, 1998.

M. Dufwenberg and U. Gneezy. Price competition and market concentration: an experimental study. *International Journal of Industrial Organization*, 18:7–22, 2000.

R. Fagin and J. Y. Halpern. Belief, awareness, and limited reasoning. *Artificial Intelligence*, 34:39–76, 1988.

Y. Feinberg. Subjective reasoning—games with unawareness. Technical Report Research Paper Series #1875, Stanford Graduate School of Business, 2004.

Y. Feinberg. Games with incomplete awareness. Technical Report Resarch Paper Series #1894, Stanford Graduate School of Business, 2005.

M. J. Fischer, N. A. Lynch, and M. S. Paterson. Impossibility of distributed consensus with one faulty processor. *Journal of the ACM*, 32(2):374–382, 1985.

F. Forges. Universal mechanisms. *Econometrica*, 58(6):1341–64, 1990.

D. Fudenberg and J. Tirole. *Game Theory*. MIT Press, Cambridge, Mass., 1991.

D. Gerardi. Unmediated communication in games with complete and incomplete information. *Journal of Economic Theory*, 114:104–131, 2004.

O. Goldreich. *Foundations of Cryptography, Vol. 2*. Cambridge University Press, 2004.

O. Goldreich, S. Micali, and A. Wigderson. How to play any mental game. In *Proc. 19th ACM Symposium on Theory of Computing*, pages 218–229, 1987.

S. Goldwasser, S. Micali, and C. Rackoff. The knowledge complexity of interactive proof systems. *SIAM Journal on Computing*, 18(1):186–208, 1989.

D. Gordon and J. Katz. Rational secret sharing, revisited. In *SCN (Security in Communication Networks) 2006*, pages 229–241, 2006.

J. Y. Halpern. Alternative semantics for unawareness. *Games and Economic Behavior*, 37:321–339, 2001.

J. Y. Halpern. A computer scientist looks at game theory. *Games and Economic Behavior*, 45(1):114–132, 2003.

J. Y. Halpern and R. Pass. Iterated regret minimization: a new solution concept. In *Proc. Twenty-First International Joint Conference on Artificial Intelligence (IJCAI '09)*, pages 153–158, 2009.

J. Y. Halpern and R. Pass. Game theory with costly computation. In *Proc. First Symposium on Innovations in Computer Science*, 2010.

J. Y. Halpern and L. C. Rêgo. Interactive unawareness revisited. *Games and Economic Behavior*, 62(1):232–262, 2008.

J. Y. Halpern and L. C. Rêgo. Extensive games with possibly unaware players. In *Proc. Fifth International Joint Conference on Autonomous Agents and Multiagent Systems*, pages 744–751, 2006. Full version available at arxiv.org/abs/0704.2014.

J. Y. Halpern and V. Teadgue. Rational secret sharing and multiparty computation: extended abstract. In *Proc. 36th ACM Symposium on Theory of Computing*, pages 623–632, 2004.

A. Heifetz, M. Meier, and B. Schipper. Interactive unawareness. *Journal of Economic Theory*, 130:78–94, 2006a.

A. Heifetz, M. Meier, and B. Schipper. Unawareness, beliefs and games. Unpublished manuscript, available at www.econ.ucdavis.edu/faculty/schipper/unawprob.pdf, 2006b.

Y. Heller. A minority-proof cheap-talk protocol. Unpublished manuscript, 2005.

S. Izmalkov, S. Micali, and M. Lepinski. Rational secure computation and ideal mechanism design. In *Proc. 46th IEEE Symposium on Foundations of Computer Science*, pages 585–595, 2005.

E. Kalai. Bounded rationality and strategic complexity in repeated games. In *Game Theory and Applications*, pages 131–157. Academic Press, San Diego, 1990.

I. Kash, E. J. Friedman, and J. Y. Halpern. Optimizing scrip systems: efficiency, crashes, hoarders, and altruists. In *Proc. Eighth ACM Conference on Electronic Commerce*, pages 305–315, 2007.

G. Kol and M. Naor. Cryptography and game theory: Designing protocols for exchanging information. In *Theory of Cryptography Conference*, pages 320–339, 2008.

D. Kreps, P. Milgrom, J. Roberts, and R. Wilson. Rational cooperation in finitely repeated prisoners' dilemma. *Journal of Economic Theory*, 27(2):245–252, 1982.

D. M. Kreps. *Game Theory and Economic Modeling*. Oxford University Press, Oxford, UK, 1990.

M. Lepinski, S. Micali, C. Peikert, and A. Shelat. Completely fair SFE and coalition-safe cheap talk. In *Proc. 23rd ACM Symposium on Principles of Distributed Computing*, pages 1–10, 2004.

J. Li. Information structures with unawareness. Unpublished manuscript, 2006a.

J. Li. Modeling unawareness without impossible states. Unpublished manuscript, 2006b.

A. Lysyanskaya and N. Triandopoulos. Rationality and adveresarial behavior in multi-party comptuation. In *CRYPTO 2006*, pages 180–197, 2006.

A. Mas-Colell, M. Whinston, and J. Green. *Microeconomic Theory.* Oxford University Press, Oxford, U.K., 1995.

S. Micali and R. Pass. Local zero knowledge. In *Proc. 38th ACM Symposium on Theory of Computing*, pages 306–315, 2006.

S. Modica and A. Rustichini. Awareness and partitional information structures. *Theory and Decision*, 37:107–124, 1994.

S. Modica and A. Rustichini. Unawareness and partitional information structures. *Games and Economic Behavior*, 27(2):265–298, 1999.

D. Moreno and J. Wooders. Coalition-proof equilibrium. *Games and Economic Behavior*, 17(1):80–112, 1996.

J. Nash. Equilibrium points in n-person games. *Proc. National Academy of Sciences*, 36:48–49, 1950a.

J. Nash. The barganing problem. *Econometrica*, 18:155–162, 1950b.

A. Neyman. Bounded complexity justifies cooperation in finitely repated prisoner's dilemma. *Economic Letters*, 19:227–229, 1985.

J. Niehans. Zur preisbildung bei ungewissen erwartungen. *Scbweizerische Zietschrift für Volkswirtschaft und Statistik*, 84(5):433–456, 1948.

M. J. Osborne and A. Rubinstein. *A Course in Game Theory.* MIT Press, Cambridge, Mass., 1994.

E. Ozbay. Unawareness and strategic announcements in games with uncertainty. In *Theoretical Aspects of Rationality and Knowledge: Proc. Eleventh Conference (TARK 2007)*, pages 231–238, 2007.

C. H. Papadimitriou and M. Yannakakis. On complexity as bounded rationality. In *Proc. 26th ACM Symposium on Theory of Computing*, pages 726–733, 1994.

M. Pease, R. Shostak, and L. Lamport. Reaching agreement in the presence of faults. *Journal of the ACM*, 27(2):228–234, 1980.

R. W. Rosenthal. Games of perfect information, predatory pricing, and the chain store paradox. *Journal of Economic Theory*, 25:92–100, 1982.

A. Rubinstein. Finite automata play the repeated prisoner's dilemma. *Journal of Economic Theory*, 39:83–96, 1986.

L. J. Savage. The theory of statistical decision. *Journal of the American Statistical Association*, 46:55–67, 1951.

A. Shamir, R. L. Rivest, and L. Adelman. Mental poker. In D. A. Klarner, editor, *The Mathematical Gardner*, pages 37–43. Prindle, Weber, and Schmidt, Boston, Mass., 1981.

T. Tan and S. Werlang. The Bayesian foundation of solution concepts of games. *Journal of Economic Theory*, 45(45):370–391, 1988.

A. Urbano and J. E. Vila. Computational complexity and communication: coordination in two-player games. *Econometrica*, 70(5):1893–1927, 2002.

A. Urbano and J. E. Vila. Computationally restricted unmediated talk under incomplete information. *Economic Theory*, 23(2):283–320, 2004.

G. Walker and D. Walker. *The Official Rock Paper Scissors Strategy Guide.* Simon & Schuster, New York, 2004.

A. Yao. Protocols for secure computation (extended abstract). In *Proc. 23rd IEEE Symposium on Foundations of Computer Science*, pages 160–164, 1982.

Index

Printed in the United States
by Baker & Taylor Publisher Services